This book is dedicated to

Dr. Jeffrey Mishlove

Who thought aloud with the most brilliant minds at the end of history

And whose Socratic dialogues allowed their thinking to nurture

The souls of the coming guardians, who will learn to hurl lightning-bolts.

May we all be as ethical and good-humored as this gadfly.

"I'm playing into your hand, and with your own cards… I'm exploiting the impossible. Or, more accurately, it's a question of making the impossible possible… something that would bring about the one real revolution in this world of ours, if people would only take it in."

— ALBERT CAMUS, *Caligula*

PROMETHEUS
AND ATLAS

JASON REZA JORJANI

PROMETHEUS
AND ATLAS

LONDON
ARKTOS
2016

Printed in the United Kingdom.

ISBN 978-1-910524-67-1

BIC-CLASSIFICATION
Unexplained phenomena / the paranormal (VXQ)
Western philosophy: c. 1600 to c. 1900 (HPCD)
Religion and beliefs (HR)

EDITOR
John B. Morgan

COVER DESIGN
Andreas Nilsson

LAYOUT
Tor Westman

ARKTOS MEDIA LTD.
www.arktos.com

CONTENTS

"Jason Jorjani's *Prometheus & Atlas* is what profound philosophical writing used to be but has long refused to be: visionary in its method and content, sweeping in its scope, literally mythical, and, above all, positive. That is a gross understatement, though. His notions of the paranormal as normal, of a coming spectral revolution, of a future spectral technology, and of a still unrealized but very real superhuman potential come together to form a coherent but still emerging worldview that is neither modern nor postmodern but something other and more."

— JEFFREY J. KRIPAL, Professor of Philosophy and Religious Thought and former Chair of the Department of Religious Studies at Rice University, author of *Authors of the Impossible: The Paranormal and the Sacred*

"*Prometheus & Atlas* is the most brilliant treatise relating to parapsychological material that I have ever encountered... it is also a very serious exploration of depth psychology and mythology. Jorjani's emphasis on what he terms 'the spectral' affords us an opportunity to expand some of our existing models concerning psi. ...Jorjani has written the definitive book regarding the proper place of psi phenomena in the history of philosophical ideas... However, *Prometheus & Atlas* takes the argument much further and demonstrates that parapsychology and psi phenomena can be viewed, not only within the history of philosophy, but in the larger context of cultural history itself. Jorjani examines the mechanistic worldview [that] dominates science and has led to the marginalization of parapsychology (as well as many other cultural imbalances). The range of scholarship required to make this argument is, in my estimation, nothing short of awesome. ...I don't think any other writer comes even close to tying things together the way Jorjani has done. The experience of reading it is rather like gazing out at a brilliant starry sky, with many interrelated constellations, stars, and planets. Each is beautiful and unique and, together, one senses a whole cosmos."

— JEFFREY MISHLOVE, Ph.D. (UC Berkley), Host of *Thinking Allowed*, author of *The Roots of Consciousness*, and Dean of Programs in Transformational Psychology at the University of Philosophical Research

INTRODUCTION

There is something curious about the fraternal statues of Prometheus and Atlas at Rockefeller Center in New York City. Instead of simply bearing a celestial globe on his shoulders, Atlas is supporting several interlocking rings that outline the shape of a hollow sphere. These bear astrological markings which suggest the precession of the equinoxes through the rise and fall of world ages. The very same zodiacal symbols are also impressed upon a ring through which Prometheus is triumphantly emerging. An inscription from the Greek tragedian Aeschylus reminds us that the torch of craftily stolen fire that he holds stands for *techne*, the essence of Technology: "Prometheus, teacher in every art, brought the fire that hath proved for mortals a means to mighty ends." We find yet another hint to the meaning of this symbolism in a bolder inscription beneath a depiction of Zeus holding a compass over the central doorway of the main building that is visible immediately behind Prometheus, which reads: "Wisdom and Knowledge shall be the stability *of thy Times.*"

This is paradoxical. Discoveries fostering the advancement of knowledge would usually be taken to upset tradition and unleash *instability*, to demand changes that both the masses and established interests fear. What kind of society could have its stability grounded not in tradition, but in the persistence of the quest for Wisdom and Knowledge at all costs? It would have to be a civilization led by those rare individuals who have the titanic psychical constitution to endure uncertainty, and even to thrive in its midst. It is no accident that King Atlas, ruling over the Atlantean world empire through Time, stands opposed to the Cathedral of St. Patrick, the Serpent-slayer, and that his head is turned aside in such a way that his gaze spurns the Lord's altar. Taking a position behind Atlas, the significance of this defiant posture should be as clear to any mindful observer as it must have been to the devious planners of this Temple of Man. It is amusingly ironic that every year Gotham lights up its "Christmas" tree behind Lucifer.

One does not have to look too far to see that there is something of the mercurial Joker in this spectacular arrangement. Whoever had Hermes sculpted into the facade of the Grand Central train station in the greatest city in the New World knew exactly what he was doing. Hermes is the god of aliens, merchants, thieves, and liars. He is akin to the confidence artist. Confidence men, especially the great ones like P. T. Barnum, after whom the famous circus is named, are in the business of creating beliefs, but that does not mean that everything they produce for the wonderment of the public are fakes. They are not consummate charlatans. Unless there is some truth mixed with the deceit, it would all be totally unbelievable. Barnum was so successful because hardly anyone could tell the difference between which of his freakish curiosities were genuine and which were cons. Certain attributes of Prometheus are even perversely reflected in the persona of Hermes, as if in a distorting funhouse mirror.

Hesiod refers to titans such as Prometheus and Atlas as the most primordial gods. My work takes its departure from Martin Heidegger's prophecy of a return of the gods as the future of a poetic reflection on the sciences from beyond the end of Philosophy. Heidegger's technological interpretation of Science is rooted in his understanding of human exist-ence. The practice of scientific research is only one of the modalities of our existence, and it does not secondarily yield technology, but is grounded by the use of tools and made possible by certain technical developments. All science is always already Technoscience. Science does not apprehend the elementary constituents or laws of an objective world prior to our exis-tential engagement in technological development and scientific research. Heidegger goes so far as to try to demonstrate the way in which our sci-entific world-pictures cannot be extricated from political history and the spiritual values of our community — for which the arts, as led by *dichtung*, are determinative. This is a bold claim and Heidegger only obliquely, or at best esoterically, addressed that feature of human experience which has the greatest potential to light up the deep structure of scientific practice, to literally comprehend it, from out of what currently lies at its fringe: the spectral.

The thesis of this work involves three inextricable propositions. The first proposition is that the basic concepts and methodological constraints employed by the sciences are the expression of personal agencies that are spectral and that act on the world through demonic possession. The second is that life forms psychically battle one another to abide within the horizon of worlds structured by what is of vital concern to them, and Nature is not objectively there to inhabit prior to, or outside of, this historical struggle. The third proposition, which presupposes the first two, is that although there is no objective standpoint outside of worldview warfare, the form of life spectrally structured by the essence of Technology has a unique power to assimilate all others.

Bear in mind these three interlocked elements of the core thesis as I turn to an overview of my arguments across the twelve chapters of this work. The opening chapter sets up the problem of the spectral with respect to scientific research. Every culture is built on binary oppositions and marginalizing exclusions attendant to totemic taboos that knot its social fabric together. *Spectral* phenomena radically compromise such constructions that are intended to guard a given society against the terrifying abyss of the incomprehensible in Nature. In a sense that can only become clear throughout the course of this text, the unique power of such phenomena to do so lies in the way that they manifest an irreducible *spectrum* and haunt everything taken to be fixed with the *specter* of what is yet to come. Whereas primitive cultures were somewhat aware of the destructive power of the spectral that they occulted through the mythic structures of their society, so that these spectral forces were at least recognized within a certain context wherein their power was released or channeled for various purposes, the modern paradigm epitomized by Descartes has been built on an unprecedented suppression of the spectral.

The norms of both rational scientific practice and rationalized religious faith in revelations excludes the para*normal*, in large part by defining it as such — as a "supernatural" that is irrational in the context of a mechanistic model of Nature, one which occludes the ungraspable Supernature that shines through these very phenomena.

Thomas Kuhn, Paul Feyerabend, Michel Foucault, and Jacques Derrida have all studied the mechanisms of exclusionary marginalization at work in shifts in the framework of knowledge. My point of departure is to situate the problem of the paranormal with respect to their understandings of how structures of knowledge are forged, sustained, and overturned. Unlike Kuhn, who thinks that the exclusionary moves constitutive of framing a given paradigm are necessary for scientific development, Feyerabend argues that the exploratory quest for discovery would be best served by encouraging a plurality of theories in tension with one another. Theories *produce* "facts" on account of observational ideologies that are deeply implicated by them, so it is deluded to think that the validity of theories can be tested against "the facts of Nature" — as if these had an autonomous and objectively accessible existence.

I draw out this insight of Feyerabend by presenting Michel Foucault's largely parallel account of the construction of the "objective facts" (and of the corresponding form of subjectivity) that constitute the content of any given *episteme* or paradigmatic frame of knowledge. Such frameworks are constructed, sustained, and subsumed by others through a network of power relations — not of a power positively wielded by subjects, but a power that emerges through discursive practices constitutive of subjectivity and objectivity as such. Feyerabend also sees the power of discursive practice to dialectically crystallize and then dissolve what appear to be even the most fundamental structures of knowledge, such as those set forth by various systems of logic.

If we are interested in a sheer increase in the empirical content of Science — in other words, in boundless *discovery*— then we have to use and abuse language in ways that recognize how wildly "illogical" Nature could be (from the standpoint of Reason). To insist that all terms be defined in advance as a context for discovery, or to redefine terms in a fixed manner, is to remain locked within a paradigmatic thinking that is periodically interrupted by scientific revolutions in the course of which certain types of knowledge are always lost. My use and abuse of language in a consideration of the paranormal is, rather, intended to catalyze what — from Kuhn's perspective — would amount to a *permanent revolution* in scientific practice of the kind that Feyerabend advocates. Thus, it would be at cross-purposes to what I am doing for me to elaborate a definite post-Cartesian paradigm complete with a new, well-defined theoretical language. The epistemological revolution that I am trying to bring about is deeper than that. Prometheus and Atlas stand for the archetypal or mythic forces in our unconscious minds at a social level that anticipate phenomena with a view to projection and frame them in terms of fixed world models. My aim is to make us conscious of this so that we can embrace the uniquely constructive power of these forces, but also creatively re-imagine and redefine our relationship to them.

This radical transformation of the human condition is the promise and peril of the coming scientific revolution. In *Specters of Marx*, Jacques Derrida discusses how three scientific revolutions have fundamentally altered our conception of (what we have taken to be) our human nature and our place in Nature at large: the cosmological revolution associated with Copernicus, the biological revolution associated with Darwin, and the psychological one associated with Freud. In this text and in a closely related earlier essay entitled "Telepathy," Derrida demonstrates the suppressed centrality of the spectral to Freud's discovery of the unconscious. Freud not only ultimately admitted the reality of spectral phenomena such as telepathy; he also came to see the spectral as the supreme exemplar of the uncanny and as the key to the revolutionary recognition of the unconscious. Derrida draws out Freud's own anxieties about how scientific research into the spectral holds the potential to collapse the barrier between the seething abyss of the unconscious and the conscious ego bound by various social norms.

Referring to this unrealized potential of the exploration of the unconscious and the uncanny as the *spectral revolution*, I develop a thread in *Specters of Marx* wherein Derrida connects the uncanny quality of the spectral — the way in which it reveals our being ahead of and beside ourselves, our not quite ever being at home as the other within ourselves — to the spectral character of the technoscientific projection of Nature itself. *Whereas this projection seems to be predicated on the exorcism of specters, profound reflection on this exclusionary epistemic mechanism ironically effects a reversal: technoscientific projection is revealed as what is most spectral.* The specters that have hitherto been only unconsciously driving technoscientific development, in the manner of daemonic possession, are revealed to the conscious mind. These specters are not concepts; like any specter, they even elude the grasp of conceptual thought. They are, rather, the aesthetic idealities essential to scientific *praxis*, or what shows that technology has an ontological priority over theoretical science. As I go on to argue, these gigantic specters of Technoscience are Prometheus and Atlas.

The point that Foucault makes with respect to the inextricability of knowledge and power holds even more radically in the case of a scientific revolution that would not merely mark a shift to a new paradigm, but would essentially redefine our relationship to model-building as a self-conscious one that obviates episteme shifts through a pluralistic pragmatism. The resistance to an overcoming of the Cartesian epistemic framework through parapsychological research has been exceptionally strong because, when taken as a whole, what parapsychological research reveals about Nature is inherently resistant to any paradigm-building that does not acknowledge itself as provisional and practical. Many parapsychologists have missed this forest for the trees. They have failed to recognize that their research opens up the ultimate epistemological abyss. Meanwhile, for all their talk about "deconstruction," even so-called "postmodern" philosophers are still unconsciously terrified by the prospect of finding that epistemic frameworks are "really" lacking any foundation — any principle of Reality — that is not psycho-socially constructed as an expression of the will to power. In view of the power of Technology, the limits of what phenomena it is possible for Nature to present to us is constructed only by forces that are actively engaged in struggle with one another to shape this Earth and other territories into a world that suits their vital interests.

Indeed, my first chapter draws to a close with a consideration of just how many of our vital interests are threatened by a mainstream acknowledgment of the paranormal. This becomes the point of departure for Chapter 2. The reason why these phenomena have been so fiercely suppressed, including in the guise of nervous laughter, is because they pose a challenge to every pillar of our extant social structure and conception of self. Moreover, there is evidence to suggest that the widespread skepticism concerning spectral phenomena and uncanny abilities is actually keeping these at bay. Thus, as I point out in the second chapter, mainstream scientific recognition of the paranormal could in itself amplify manifestations of it, and one would also expect various training protocols to become available for the refinement of hitherto denied abilities.

Telepathy calls into question the privacy of one's thoughts and the integrity of one's personal agency. Clairvoyance could empower perfect strangers to see into one's bedroom or office at any time, and if employed by the enemies of a state, it would shatter the very foundations of national security in relation to state secrecy. Precognition confronts us with the great temptation to stop crimes before they have been committed by essentially arresting people for "thought crimes," and it also endangers the stability of the stock market. Psychokinesis could be used to commit the most perfectly untraceable crimes, and perhaps psychokinetic ability, once recognized and amplified by belief, poses an even greater danger on account of unconscious and uncontrollable negative intentions. Recognizing that memories of past lives do, in some cases, actually signify the reincarnation of a previous personality, forces us to ask questions concerning private property, family ties, sexual taboos, gender identity, and the prosecution of past offenses that would require redefining our entire legal system. It is, I suggest, for all these reasons that what is spectral in nature has been occulted as part of the very construction of the modern age. Terror in the face of the spectral is the occulted foundation of the Cartesian world order.

I pursue this suspicion in Chapter 3. It begins with a consideration of how, at the zenith of the French Revolution, the Cult of Reason made the first and most dramatic attempt to establish a scientific society, one that would supplant revealed religion with a utopian faith in the pursuit of knowledge. These atheistic rationalists were committed to founding a radically secular republic, one wherein religion would be overthrown together with monarchy. Maximilien Robespierre led a group of reactionaries who opposed the Reason cultists with their own Cult of the Supreme Being. They feared that the atheists would undermine the Revolution and the liberal virtues, which ought to be grounded in recognition of a divine Creator of man's rational nature. However, this rationalistic religion proved too contrived to take root and, by unleashing a Reign of Terror against the Reason cultists as well as against Catholic traditionalists sympathetic to monarchy, the Jacobins paved the way for the restoration of theological and political orthodoxy under Napoleon.

While most of the Reason cultists were naïvely virtuous public intellectuals rather than real philosophers, Robespierre and Bonaparte probably saw the philosophy of Julien Offray de La Mettrie and the Marquis de Sade lurking in the background. I trace Sadism back to the fundamental ontology of René Descartes, through La Mettrie's materialistic revision of Cartesian mechanism. It is my contention that the basic structure of Descartes' thought, which becomes determinative of modernity, involves the imprisonment of a hyperconscious but powerless mind within a set of cogs and wheelworks embedded in a Nature that is reduced to a terrifyingly merciless machine. This is an outcome of Descartes' attempt to maintain a substantial distinction between Mind and Matter by prohibiting every class of psychical phenomena that would allow for consciousness to directly interact with physical bodies. Descartes' suppression of the spectral is in turn, I argue, inextricable from his polar opposition between Perfect Being and absolute Nothingness. Biographically, it is also bound up with Descartes' own terrifying paranormal experience and his subsequent commitment, as a Jesuit spy, to clandestinely help wage a Catholic war against "demonic" occultists.

If Descartes were unique in his suppression of the spectral, we could not take it to be constitutive of the modern worldview that paradigmatically took shape in his name. As I demonstrate in Chapter 4, when Immanuel Kant, the most significant thinker of the Age of Enlightenment, adopted and refined Descartes' fundamental standpoint, he did so on the basis of a Cartesian rejection of spectral phenomena as lying outside "the limits of possible experience." Those individuals who undergo such experiences are, in his view, candidates for the hospital, if not for burning at the stake. Their alleged uncanny powers, Kant contends, present as great a threat to the "whole contemplative commonwealth" as acts of terrorism do to the political commonwealth.

My fourth chapter details how the occultation of extrasensory perception and psychokinesis are not at all incidental features of Kant's work. In his youth, Kant undertook a substantive study of the writings of Emmanuel Swedenborg and, fearing this would endanger his attainment of tenure, he anonymously authored an esoterically-written text wherein he appears to develop many of the fundamental concepts of both his youthful cosmology and his later systematic thought through a disingenuous critique and distortion of Swedenborg's visionary ideas. His principal concern here is to draw a sharp Cartesian divide between the spiritual realm and worldly experience, and to thereby sanitize the former from all of the phantasmagoric elements that it presents in Swedenborg's visions.

Kant wants to prevent anyone in this world with less than saintly motivations from being able to "storm heaven" by psychical means, and to ensure that the "other side" — which becomes his *noumenal* realm — remains a cloistered transcendental domain where all the injustices of this world are remedied, insofar as the conditions of our spiritual counterparts there reflect our innermost intentions that cannot properly bear fruit in our earthly experience. What most terrifies Kant is the idea that some wicked virtuoso of the occult arts could use them unethically, or gain some advantage over simple and pure-souled folk equipped with little if any paranormal abilities, in navigating and manipulating the "beyond" that ought to be a realm of perfect justice.

In what is perhaps a striking example of a return of the repressed, we see in Kant's mature aesthetic theory a reemergence of the most mysterious elements that Kant absorbed from Swedenborg in his youth by virtue of defining his key concepts against the ideas of this visionary. In Chapter 5, I adopt an insight that lies at the core of Kant's Third Critique, namely that "aesthetic ideas" can be the wellspring of precisely defined rational concepts even though these ideas are of an imagistic character. This claim, which is central to Kant's discussion of how judgments of the "beautiful" can be universal without being mediated by concepts or rules of any kind, and without being dependent on linguistic communication defined in these terms, confounds his neo-Cartesian divide between the "phenomenal" realm of worldly experience and the invisible "noumenal" realm. It also compromises his democratic egalitarianism, since he admits that only those rare individuals whose genius is a unique expression of the irrational creative force of Nature are able to adaptively appreciate the accomplishments of prior artistic geniuses. I will go on to argue that Prometheus and Atlas are the aesthetic ideas from out of which the fundamental concepts of the sciences have, hitherto unconsciously, been unfolded.

Kant leaves his insight into aesthetic ideas and their relationship to concepts vaguely undeveloped, and it is at odds with much of his system. Chapter 5 goes on to show how this insight is more coherently developed by Friedrich Schelling, who replaces Kant's "noumenal" and "phenomenal" worlds with "unconscious" and "conscious" psychical processes, which the creative genius alone is able to bridge in a productive manner by intuiting and resonantly modifying aesthetic ideas. Schelling becomes the first modern thinker to transgress the Cartesian dualism that Kant perfected. The artistic genius plunges into the unconscious abyss within her that lies beneath the abstract dichotomy between the objective world of Nature and her subjective experience as an ego. These "two worlds" that the rational mind pries apart from each other are not, as Kant thought, isomorphic with one another in such a way that we freely will in a hidden realm what appears to thoroughly determine our actions in the world of experience. As Kant began to suspect in his aesthetics, the irrational in Nature can be *daimonically* experienced and affected by individuals who become the genius (Latin *ingenium*, Greek *daimon*) or "motive spirit" of natural things and other persons who are unconsciously "inspired."

Schelling recognizes that the occult power that is basic to creative genius in the arts is not inherently limited to productivity within the confines of a canvas or a block of clay; it essentially amounts to a reshaping of Nature — including the behavior of unwitting mere mortals — through a conspiring of conscious and unconscious psychical processes whereby the genius, as it were, suggests herself into things and other persons. Schelling sees this "titanic" war of creative spirits with "the heavenly powers of Fate" that govern the lives of those unwilling to rebel against them as being elemental to Greek tragedy. He fears that an application of genius beyond the narrow confines of "Art" would presuppose a race of Titans, such as Prometheus and Atlas, whose rise would be detrimental to merely human beings and their mundane concerns. Schelling is convinced that certain titanic monuments in Egypt and elsewhere attest to our having had such superhuman psychical powers in a world age before this one and, despite his concerns, his entire project is oriented towards our regaining them at a higher level of self-consciousness and spiritual development in a new age yet to come.

The ideas intuited by the genius are, for Schelling, more fundamental than both the concepts and things that are informed by them. They are principal types, or *archetypes*, but not abstractions of the kind that he thinks academicians have misinterpreted the Platonic ideas to be. The "archetype" as an interpretive device is, of course, most widely associated with the work of the psychologist Carl Gustav Jung. On account of Schelling's conception of the titanic and his understanding of why technological Science has to be reabsorbed by poetic mythology, and also bound by constraints of scope, I focus here on Schelling's view of the archetype qua aesthetic idea rather than on the later contributions of Jung. Aligning himself with the Renaissance alchemy of Giordano Bruno, Schelling offers us an understanding of the *eidos*, or "idea," as a morphological image subject to intentional transformations that in turn bring about the transmutation of things that express these archetypes in a way ungraspable by conceptual thought. The fact that genius of this kind is essential to Art but only occurs occasionally and at pivotal moments in the sciences, suggests that scientific practice will eventually be outstripped by artistic craft and assimilated into it. The artist-scientists of the world age to come will be the authors of a new mythology that meaningfully reabsorbs technological development.

While Schelling does break through the mechanism and (at least tacit) dualism of Cartesian metaphysics, his vision of the assimilation of Science into Art and its consequent unification with spirituality remains vague and overly literary. This is, in part, on account of the paucity of serious scientific studies of spectral phenomena in his time. Martin Heidegger and Henri Bergson develop certain of Schelling's most revolutionary ideas in a more careful and rigorous manner. In Chapter 6, I take the largely convergent ontologies of these two monumental twentieth century Continental thinkers as a context for understanding the deepest significance of phenomena that parapsychologists have been studying for over a century, since the days when Bergson served as President of the Society for Psychical Research. Whereas parapsychologists often, at least tacitly, try to develop a new metaphysics on the basis of their studies of "psi" abilities such as extrasensory perception and psychokinesis, I agree with

Heidegger and Bergson that model building of this kind is what covers over or filters out certain "irrational" aspects of Nature. These aspects that come to be viewed as "paranormal" are not actually indicative of anything supra-natural, as even Kant's most generous reading of Swedenborg would have had them be; rather, they are "supernatural" only in the sense of revealing the Supernature that is generally occluded or *occulted* by our own practical projections and reductive models of "Nature."

Bergson theorizes that our evolutionary development of practical intellect has led to the atrophy of an instinctual orientation towards things and places of vital significance. We have mistaken how we have had to break up the world in order to craft tools, and how we have rebuilt things using them, for "Nature itself." Heidegger basically agrees, and he takes the late Renaissance to be a particularly significant period in this development. The construction of increasingly complex mechanical instruments, and the manufacture of specially tailored and uniform replacement parts to service those that break down, reinforced an analogical view of *Nature* as a vast piece of clockwork. This projection of our own increasingly mechanical building activities into Nature essentially consists of a flattening of heterogeneous places into uniform space, a comportment towards meaningful things as if they were objective entities within that abstract grid and, finally, an interpretation of the human being — whose endurance ought to be experienced as the horizon of her world — as a spatially determinate entity persisting in "time" conceived of as a sequence of point-events that are not really lived *events* at all.

My sixth chapter's exploration of the empirical data of Parapsychology in the context of the thought of Heidegger and Bergson continues with a natural history of "psi" or "paranormal" psychical functioning, as parapsychologists refer to it today. I present the research of Cleve Backster and Rupert Sheldrake on how "psi" phenomena have deep roots in various forms of organic life, all the way from telekinesis in bacterium and plants to telepathy in insect hives, bird flocks, schools of fish, and domesticated animals. Non-human organisms at all levels, from plants to dogs, appear to experience the world in terms of heterogeneous places where there are things of significance to them. They evidently respond far more intensely to things (and persons) that matter to them, even when they are hundreds of miles away, than they do to things that appear to be in their proximity but which are of no concern. Even plants appear to be able to "see" those people who care for them in faraway places, and animals can navigate to these places across an expanse that is entirely unfamiliar to them. Primitive peoples such as the Bushmen of the Kalahari seem to orient themselves with respect to their fellows and their meaningful places in this clairvoyant manner. In other words, places are always already psychically shaped by the vital significance of things to beings with various forms of life. Likewise, the paths extending outwards from a forest clearing are not equidistant in two or more directions simply because a tape measurer or laser marker would find them to be.

Heidegger's discussions of directionality and de-severence in *Being and Time*, and of making-present what is spatially distant in the *Zollikon Seminars*, suggest that his basic understanding of "truth" as the unconcealment of psychically occulted things, rather than as verificational correspondence, presupposes this primordially clairvoyant experience of the world. Both the psychokinesis studies and the remote viewing ones at the Princeton Engineering Anomalies Laboratory and the Stanford Research Institute (summarized in Chapter 2) present us with evidence that time is endurance rather than a sequence, and that its basic structure consists of lived events, just as Bergson and Heidegger suggest. It appears to be possible for one's psychical intention to alter the random outcome of a number generator both in the future and the past, just as it is possible to remotely view things that are going on in certain places at future times as well as at times long past. Experiential time is the horizon of our existence, and various worlds have different cultural-historical horizons beyond and between which there is only a wild region.

My appropriation of this understanding of time as the "horizon" of our Being, which is the central thesis of *Being and Time*, becomes the theme of Chapter 7. I draw on three other texts by Heidegger to elucidate this core argument of his *magnum opus*. Two of these are from the mid-1930s, namely "The Origin of the Work of Art" and a lecture course on *Logic as the Question Concerning the Essence of Language*. The third is what I would call Heidegger's "last will and testament," the final interview he gave to *Der Spiegel* in 1966 and that he demanded remain confidential until after his death. In this shocking interview, Heidegger reflects back on his efforts during the 1930s in a way that calls into question the attempt of various interpreters to claim that he regretted his conception of a world-historical "people" (*Volk*). He reiterates that the divine salvation of humanity as a whole from the apocalyptic challenge of the worldwide development of technological Science is the unique destiny of the same civilization wherein this developmental trajectory metaphysically originated, and cannot come from peoples colonized by it. In this seventh chapter, I show how the understanding of world-historical existence that lies at the core of *Being and Time*, which Heidegger reaffirmed at the end of his life and that is elaborated in "The Origin of the Work of Art" and the contemporaneous lecture on logic, is one he developed from a reading of Friedrich Nietzsche's "On the Uses and Disadvantages of History for Life."

Every life form needs protection by a bounded horizon of recollected experience in order to pursue its vital concerns. Like the sheltering Earth, this horizon conceals a great deal so as to provide roots for the tree of a people's world and to promote its growth. Horizons can only be reshaped from within, through dynamic resistance to others and assimilative fusion with them. The so-called "science of History" (including sociology, anthropology, and historical social psychology) attempts to study the worlds of various peoples "objectively," as if one could assume a standpoint outside of lived time experienced as the burden of one's heritage and its destining trajectory, and as if it were possible to be "neutral" in the mortal conflict between one's world and others. Worlds are primarily structured through the kind of poetic language whereby creative geniuses establish, and vigilant guardians preserve and elaborate, the architectonic of a people's arts and crafts in attunement with what Nietzsche calls their "living mythology," and what Heidegger refers to as a "folklore" (the *lore* of a *Volk*). This mythic folklore is the primary historical experience of a people; it is what actually motivates their monumental deeds, which are only then subject to the antiquarian preservation and critical analysis of historians. It is the way in which a life form's world shelters itself in the wild.

The Greek root of "technology" is *techne*, which means "craft" and is a form of *poesis*, or creative cultivation, that is also expressed as fine art. Technology and art share a common cultural root in "arts and crafts." Given that the "paranormal" or the irrational in Nature reveals *techne*, or the essence of Technology, as a praxis that is ontologically prior to theoretical science, it now appears that mythic folklore somehow grounds Science in general, and not just the vain attempt at a "science of History." Reflection on the misguided aim of this final development of the "scientific" orientation towards life as advanced under the Cartesian paradigm, serves to reverse the relationship between the sciences in general and the existential demands of a concrete form of life.

The natural sciences themselves are historical, and have their roots in the metaphysical tradition of the Greeks and of those who inherited and critically unfolded this unique understanding of being in the world. The uniqueness of this way of being does not consist in its "objective" truth, or in the greater verifiable correspondence of its claims to the features of a universally apprehensible and ahistorical Reality. It lies, rather, in the exceptional power of an ethos that grasps Nature through anticipatory projection and frames it in terms of models of the world that afford us tremendous technical capabilities to reshape not only the places that we inhabit, but also our own forms of embodiment.

The danger that this comportment will alienate us from each other, from our ecological context, and instrumentalize our very being, stems from having taken the features of this mythic projection for a revelation of "objective" realities underlying "subjective" experiences of phenomena.

Through this powerful illusion, our "Western" world has long been in the process of conquering and colonizing those of all other historical peoples on the Earth. Any anti-colonial resistance that would render Science as nothing more than something purely instrumental and value-neutral, so as to serve as the material basis for a reactionary restoration of traditional cultures and their shattered, naïve cosmologies is, however, doomed to failure. What is even more terribly misguided is the idea that we, the philosophical heirs of the Greeks, ought to somehow reject our own tradition and adopt the uprooted cultural practices of other peoples who have been colonized by our technological Science. Instead, as I argue in Chapter 7, our task is to become consciously aware of our hitherto unconscious and unique historical relationship to the world-colonizing essence of Technology as an expression of our lore.

It is in this seventh chapter that the specters of Technoscience are introduced and identified with aesthetic idealities of the kind that Kant and Schelling had in mind. Heidegger saw cultivation of aesthetic intuition, which is the occulted other dimension of *techne* qua *poesis* — the art in "arts and crafts" — as the basis for a reflection on techno-scientific machination. Once the putative elementary structure of the world as it is grasped by such machination is recognized as a projected construct, it also becomes possible to see the abstract concepts structuring this projection as derivative of what Kant called "aesthetic ideas" and what Schelling went on to see as imagistic archetypes. Like artists, we can establish a more conscious and creative rapport with these ideas that take shape on a largely unconscious psychical plane deeper than the divide between the "subject" and "objects." Heidegger warned that the essence of Technology is something superhuman, something gigantic or titanic, and that "only a god can save us now" from a blind relationship with it. He also acknowledges that this salvation will not involve a rejection or surmounting of Technology, but a sublation or inner transformation of our relationship with its essence. The titans Prometheus and Atlas are the divinities within us, our own superhuman existential potential — superhuman in the sense that our unique relationship with *techne* gifts us with a perfectibility wherein our bottomless being transcends any merely "human" nature of the kind that locks dogs into the species being of canines or cats into that of felines. Bergson, who saw the cosmos as a machine for the making of gods, called us to actualize this superhuman potential by complementing the hypertrophy of our technical intellect with a commensurate cultivation of the intuitive abilities studied by parapsychologists.

Chapter 8 explores the aesthetic idea of Prometheus. His name means the one with "forethought" or "he who knows in advance," and it shares its Greek root in common with the words "mathematics" and "polymath." The always-already known essence of the mathematical, in its original Greek sense of *ta mathemata*, is Promethean. It involves a simplification of things in their places into abstractly composite objects in homogenously divisible spaces, so that their relationships with one another can be grasped according to the repeatable regularities of *axiomata*. Prometheus projects this idealization over the world in such a way that everything encountered is grasped only in terms of what is knowable in advance, in terms of axioms, like those involved in the Newtonian laws of motion.

The mind of Prometheus is there wherever no mere mortal can be; he possesses the eyes and ears of the travelers at different speeds in Einstein's theory of relativity; he is the observer of Heisenberg's otherwise indeterminate quantum phenomena; he is Laplace's "demon," and Maxwell's as well. The insertion of daemonic points of view into things is geared towards increasing our capacity for their practical manipulation. Technical innovation based on axiomatic projection not only collapses vast lived distances, as in radio and television, it also allows us to split the *atom*, which for the purposes of such projection was taken to be, by definition, the most elementary building block which could not be cut or divided (*atomon*). In other words, the projection reveals itself as such through its practical effects. Following Heidegger, who compares the flicking on of a radio or television to the unearthly destruction of an atomic blast, and who claims that the whole history of physics is enfolded in atom smashers, I suggest that the lightning flash of the atomic bomb is the fire of Zeus that was stolen by Prometheus and brought down to the Earth of mortals.

Aeschylus satirized the theft of Prometheus in a play entitled *Prometheus, the Fire-Bringer*. This drama, which is distinct from the *Promethea* trilogy for which Aeschylus is more famous, was the satyr play that followed *The Persians*. I suggest that this is not at all incidental. With reference to Paul Feyerabend's analysis of how the birth of tragedy catalyzed the rise of perspectival awareness in Greek culture, I present some evidence to the effect that it was not a coincidence that this took place at just the time of the extensive and repeated Persian campaigns to conquer Greece. Feyerabend observes a striking lack of perspective in archaic Greek art and poetry, which evince not just the failure to grasp a certain artistic technique or manner of literary expression — as if the acquisition of these were not bound up with attendant psychical capacities or the lack thereof — but a cast of mind so different from our own contemporary high culture that it is hard to imagine. The archaic Greeks of the Homeric age were not human beings, they were dolls — the playthings of fate as expressed through gods that manipulated them from without and passions that moved them from within in a way beyond their own control. They were able to analogize their gods with those of other essentially like-minded, albeit in some cases more technically advanced peoples, such as the Egyptians and Phoenicians, and their notion of "knowledge" was merely additive — which is why I refer to their "notion" of knowledge rather than their *concept* of it, because this mode of "knowing" did not involve any conscious grasp of concepts and the organization of instances of them.

In my view, the fact that this changed all of a sudden in the very century that the Persians colonized the same parts of Greece out of which the first Greek philosophers arose has everything to do with how different the Persians were, not only from the Greeks, but from the foreign peoples to whom the Greeks were somewhat more accustomed. The religion of Iran could not be analogized to Hellenic religion or hybridized with it in the syncretic way that allowed the Greeks to, for example, see Thoth as Hermes or absorb Dionysus and Artemis into their pantheons from Crete and Asia Minor. The major features of Ahura Mazda, Zarathustra's "Titan of Wisdom," do bear a striking affinity to those of Prometheus — but only if the archetype of Prometheus is understood in more abstract terms than the archaic Greeks were able to understand it. Beginning with Aeschylus, Prometheus becomes a counter-*principle* to the entire Olympian world-order governed by Zeus.

Moreover, the hubris of Prometheus is one and the same as that of Xerxes, the Persian Emperor who is the central figure of *The Persians*. That Aeschylus sets *The Persians* in Iran and writes it *from the perspective of the Persians*, with a sympathetic portrayal of Xerxes as a tragic figure, and then couples this drama with *Prometheus, the Fire-Bringer* is one example of a much wider phenomenon of inter-cultural engagement that was taking place during this period. Among the Achaemenid Persian dynasty, Xerxes was the one and only real crusader on behalf of Zarathustra's god, who was symbolized by fire above all else, and on behalf of which Xerxes burned the Acropolis down with the intention of replacing its shrines to false gods with fire temples. In their trying encounter with the Persians, the Greeks of the tragic age gained a liberating Promethean perspective on their own religious culture as exemplified by the Olympian pantheon of Homer's epic.

Prometheus is not only the gift-giver of *techne* to mankind. This titanic artisan crafted the human race itself in his own image. Drawing on the work of the mythologist Carl Kerényi, I argue that Prometheus symbolizes the character of our uniquely perfectible existence. He is the archetype not of merely "human" being, but of the human potential. As Kerényi recognizes, the titans are *próteroi theoí*, or the "earlier gods," not in a merely sequential sense wherein they precede the Olympians chronologically, but in a primordial sense that is suppressed and covered over by the minions of Zeus. This is why the titans are often mythically conflated with the *gigantes*, the hybrid "giants" or *heros* born of *eros* between gods and mortals. The titanic or gigantic is the godlike capacity that mortals could unleash and cultivate so as to rise up in rebellion against the heavenly gods. Zeus punished Prometheus not only by chaining him to the pillar in the Caucasus where the Eagle devours his liver, but also insofar as he binds the children of Prometheus in the chains of servitude. We can melt and break these chains with the stolen fire of *techne*, and this fire affords us the ability to forge the world anew and even reshape ourselves in ways that are to our own benefit. Prometheus is the one who breaks open the "close-knit" mind of Zeus, which is supposed to be synonymous with Fate, so as to liberate Athena, the goddess of Wisdom and War. His foresight overreaches that of Zeus, and insofar as this Promethean mentality is really our own, what we see here is a mythic presentiment of our utopian birthright to build a better world.

As Kerényi notes, there is an especially close comparison between Prometheus and Christ as images of the suffering savior god. I argue that these two figures are too close to one another in order to be compatible; one must choose between them. When we consider the cognitive dissonance and gross ethical ambiguity of the incoherent account of the life and teachings of Jesus in the Gospels, Prometheus appears to be the far more compelling martyr for the liberation and enlightenment of humanity. In fact, Prometheus is, strictly speaking, the Anti-Christ. The analogizing of Prometheus with the Medieval Latin *Lucifer*, the "light-bearer," begins to take place in Percy Bysshe Shelley's drama, *Prometheus Unbound*. In Aeschylus' original tragic trilogy about Prometheus, the second and third installments of which were lost, the rebellious titan whose punishment we witness in *Prometheus Bound* is eventually reconciled to Zeus, to whom he reveals his foreknowledge concerning who it is that will overthrow him and usurp his throne. Shelley rewrites this ending so that the rebel never gives in, with the implication being that the unjust reign of the tyrannical God-Father will be supplanted by a new world order — an earthly paradise wrought by mortals through fantastic Promethean arts and crafts — in effect, the worldly rule of Lucifer.

Percy's wife, Mary Shelley, further conflates the aesthetic idea of Prometheus with that of Lucifer in her novel *Frankenstein, or the Modern Prometheus*. Both the creature and the Promethean mad scientist compare themselves to the rebellious fallen angel cast into the hell of an inhuman solitude. Shelley also reaches back to the most archaic strata of the Prometheus mythos in her depiction of the *daimonic* and *gigantic* character of the creature, wrought as an embodiment of Frankenstein's own hubristic will to become a titanic artisan of life. The superhuman giant was, moreover, brought into being through occult crafts that have been derisively suppressed in the "enlightened" Age of Reason wherein the novel is set. Frankenstein is no ordinary mechanistic scientist working under the Cartesian paradigm; he is the last alchemist and a Renaissance man in more senses than one. Partly on account of the numerous bastardized film adaptations, the extent to which Shelley's tale is concerned with the spirit of scientific exploration in general has been covered over. I endeavor to uncover this dimension, placing a special emphasis both on Walton's seafaring Preface and on Frankenstein's impassioned closing defense of the glorious danger of the Promethean quest for discoveries that could prove deadly.

Precisely on account of the destabilizing danger inherent in scientific discovery and technological advancement, the Promethean quest must be complimented by a conscious recognition of the worldwide sovereign order that it demands. This brings us to the aesthetic idea of Atlas, the titanic brother of Prometheus who bears the heavens on his own shoulders and is the sovereign of *Atlantis*—literally, the realm of *Atlas*. Even if we remain blindly passive to it, the essence of Technology is, as Heidegger recognized, always already a non-neutral world-colonizing force. In Chapter 9, I argue that becoming conscious of this force and appropriating it may transform it into something other than a purely destructive one that uproots all traditional cultures. We can reclaim the world building of Atlas as positively empowering, so long as we are not set up or framed by the global network on account of mistaking instrumentally constructed atlases for "reality."

The word *Atlas* is derived from the Greek root for "to suffer, or to bear" and refers to his punishment at the hands of Zeus, which Aeschylus notes is the only one as terrible as that to which Prometheus is subjected, namely to be condemned to bear the weight of the celestial sphere on his own shoulders. Ancient mapmakers or mariners used the stars above all to draw up their maps or navigational charts, and the repeatable certitude of celestial mechanics ultimately became the paradigm for all anticipatory calculation in the sciences. Consequently, the mythic burden of Atlas is connected to his status as the aesthetic idea of atlases of all kinds: star charts, topographical maps, scale models, and skeletal frames. What I argue, after Heidegger, is that the modeling of the atlas, whether it is an atlas of the human body or an atlas of the world, is a technical endeavor that has ontological priority over the *world picture* elaborated by theoretical sciences. The idea of framing the entire world as a domain of calculation, measurement, and verification entails a spiritual revolution that, unbeknown to himself, Descartes effected when he subjected the reality of *the world as such and as a whole* to question. This subjection of the world to the measure of the subject is inhuman. It is, as Heidegger suggests, "gigantic," and this titanic specter overshadows everything.

The atlases, in their spectral essence, are not representational copies of putative things-in-themselves in Nature. Although I do suggest that the first picture of the Earth taken from a satellite in space is as epitomizing an exemplar of Atlas as the atomic flash is of Prometheus, the "world picture" that Heidegger takes to define our age is not a picture of the world. Atlases are not simply models *of* the world, they are built *into* the world, and the equipment of scientific experimentation is crafted in such a way as to coerce and compel Nature to present itself in accordance with the designs that these machines have. This violently world-forming machination is not an abstraction; it actually tears through the social fabric of the meaningful worlds of traditional cultures. We first see this in the way that the metric system, with its precise, homogenously universal conception of measure — a shining example of Atlas at work — destroyed whole cultural practices and the cosmologies implicit in them when it supplanted the measurement systems of the non-Western cultures that were subject to colonization.

This world-colonizing power seems to have already been implicit in the aesthetic idea of Atlas when Plato portrayed him as the sovereign of Atlantis, a maritime empire that conquers the whole world. I set the inseparable dialogues of *Timaeus* and *Critias*, where the Atlantis story is told, in the context of two other closely related dialogues, namely *Cratylus* and *Republic*, so as to draw out its full significance. Thusly contextualized in Plato's corpus, Atlantis appears to be a civilization established by a titanic race of giants who are born of a hybridization of the divine descendants of Poseidon (Neptune) and "Earth-born" mortals. These giants eventually defy Zeus and his Olympians, seeing sovereignty over Earth as their own manifest destiny. Zeus punishes their rebellion with earthquakes and a worldwide deluge, which destroys Atlantis and all the cultures of those colonized by it. At the dawn of the age of exploration, Sir Francis Bacon wrote *The New Atlantis*, in which he emphasizes the elements of the "Atlantis" folklore that depict the mysterious island as a utopian scientific society with godlike *techne*. While Sir Bacon's "Atlantis" bears the marks of the rising rationalism of his epoch, the German philosopher Rudolf Steiner elaborates the folklore of Atlantis in a way that emphasizes those elements in Plato's legend concerning the *daimonic* psychical prowess of its titanic population. The lore of Atlantis mirrors the account of the gigantic antediluvian civilization of "fallen angels" in the Bible. It is the common origin "myth" that lies at both founts of Western civilization: Classical Greece and ancient Israel.

As Paul Feyerabend argues, drawing on a thread in the thought of the late Ludwig Wittgenstein, by whom he was deeply influenced, the forms of life of various cultures are foundational for even the most elementary linguistic and conceptual structures that condition their experience of the world. The world traveler and, especially, the colonizer who comes face-to-face with the natives of many different geographical regions has a unique opportunity to recognize that the various worldviews that he encounters are distinct and finite perspectives *and that this also applies to his own native culture.* Feyerabend connects the rise of a pragmatic cast of mind that seeks to learn from different cultures by encompassing their perspectives within a new and broader perspective to the Greek colonial milieu in the age of Protagoras, who epitomizes this nascent awareness with the aphorism: "Man is the measure of all things." The exploratory expeditions wherein the connection between scientific discovery and sociopolitical conquest is most explicitly manifested are opportunities for something other than the mere conversion of natives by zealously self-satisfied missionaries. Here also lies the context for developing a cosmopolitan free society, wherein a pragmatic orientation to life allows us to manipulate different maps or atlases of the world fit for different situations without taking any one of them to be *the* representation of Reality.

Drawing on the work of Gilles Deleuze, I show how there really is something unique about the Hellenic civilizational *telos* that makes the Hellenization of foreign cultures basically different from the world becoming "Indian" or "Chinese." This has to do with the unique geographical position of the Greeks in the age that saw the rise of philosophy, at the crossroads, or rather, maritime crosswinds, of the sea trade routes of much older and stronger cultures whose worldviews were at war with one another. The unique relationship to Nature that enduring in the vortex of this war of worldviews catalyzed in the Greek mind, and the subsequent Hellenizing world conquest of the Persians, the Egyptians, the Italians, and the Phoenicians, set in motion an extraordinary *cosmopolitan* civilizational trajectory.

That the thinkers and poets amongst those whom the Classical Greeks and even the Romans saw as the worst of the northern "barbarians"—Germans such as Hölderlin, Schiller, Schelling, Nietzsche, and Heidegger—would eventually come to identify themselves as "Greeks," attests to the unlimited potential of the emerging Cosmopolis. This world society oriented around discovery and exploration was already realized on a small scale in Classical Alexandria — a Greek colony established in ancient Egypt. This cosmopolitan colonialism is not "Greek" or "Hellenizing" in some static and narrow sense; it is rather the Greece of Utopia — which risks dystopia — an unhistorical and philosophical vision of radical social reorganization that represents a revolution against the traditional culture of Greece, one which met with the reactionary burning of Pythagorean schools and the murder of Socrates. I suggest that the so-called "Western" civilization of those already bound together in the Atlantic Alliance (NATO) ought to be redefined as a cosmopolitanizing Atlantic civilization, with "Atlantic" understood not as a geographical designator, but in Plato's older sense of it as a reference to Atlas, the world-building sovereign of Atlantis. This civilization is Atlantean or Gigantic in the Biblical sense, driven by the serpentine ethos of rebel angels on a mission to liberate mortals from the fearful ignorance that makes them submit to a heavenly tyrant. Atlantic civilization risks crafting a living hell in its will to create heaven on Earth and, eventually, even to storm the heavens as worthier gods than the Olympians. There is no better example of the world-colonizing power of this infernal idea than in modern Japan.

In the tenth chapter, I show how the deepest currents of "Eastern" thought converge in Japan, which is also the place where a unique synthesis of Indian Buddhism and Chinese Taoism, namely Japanese Zen, encountered the intellectual heritage of the Greeks in the most deliberative and devastating way. Despite his concern that Eastern traditions not be adopted blindly and in an uprooted manner, Heidegger was very interested in East Asian spirituality. He was influenced by dialogue with Asian thinkers both early and late in his career, and his Japanese students became the leaders of the Kyoto School before and during the Second World War. The period of intense intellectual and spiritual encounter between Western and Japanese thought in the first half of the twentieth century culminated in traumatic atomic bombings, which, I argue, represent an even deeper *metaphysical* confrontation, and one that, on account of the period of preparation and the unique character of Zen, effected a Promethean/Atlantic metamorphosis of the Japanese psyche.

Leo Strauss, in his "Introduction to Heideggerian Existentialism," claims that only Heidegger was aware of the dimensions of the problem of forging a genuine world society in the face of the worldwide development of modern technology towards a unification of mankind based on the lowest common denominator. Strauss notes that every genuine human society has had a religious basis, and he thinks that we can only hope to redefine our alienating and destructive relationship with technology through the advent of a world religion. The groundless ground of the latter can be found through descending into the primordial origins of philosophy where, in figures such as Heraclitus, we also had something like what has of late come to be seen as the "Eastern" understanding of existence, but we had it at the fountainhead of the spiritual trajectory that led to technological Science. Chapter 10 begins by furthering Heidegger's attempt to bring about an encounter between Heraclitus and the Tao. Comparing the *Fragments* of Heraclitus to the *Tao Te Ching* and the writings of Zhuangzi, I uncover the fundamental differences that underlie the apparent similarities between Heraclitus and early Taoism, differences that are very relevant to why it was that the philosophical heirs of the Greeks developed technological Science and repeatedly resisted collectivist tyranny.

The Japanese ultimately arrive at this Heraclitean ethos as well, but by a circuitous and treacherous route. The naïve disregard of the need for sovereign authority in early Taoism, which is one of its points of greatest divergence from Heraclitus' metaphysics of war, was based on a faith that human beings, like other animals, have a species being or nature that they all share in common and, moreover, an essentially peaceable nature that will tend toward harmony when it is not tampered with. This conception of an inherent human nature was deconstructed by the Buddhist metaphysics of no-thing-ness, or the emptiness of everything, including the "self," on account of the dependent origination of all phenomena. The latter is an understanding of Nothingness very different from Descartes' concept of a Nothing that is the polar opposite of Being. The ethically anarchical bent of Taoism in turn deconstructed the moral code of orthodox Buddhism and placed an emphasis on ordinary, everyday practical activity and the various *techne* that this involves, over speculative *theoria* of the kind found in Indian cosmology. While this two-way deconstructive encounter already began in Chinese Chan, it was not until Chan reached Japan that the vacuum of serious sociopolitical thought became a problem for it. In China, where statecraft was dominated by Confucian ideology, Chan remained a largely monastic phenomenon that could afford to eschew political responsibility.

When, however, the Japanese began to adopt a Buddhist-Taoist hybrid as their new national religion, Chan also had to develop a working relationship with the knightly ethic and political realities of Japanese feudalism. The Zen militarism that was born of this fusion was radically nihilistic and intensely practical. Although it tended toward an affirmation of conservative conventions, this was, among the philosophical and political elite, recognized to be a matter of mores or decorum, quite literally grounded on No-thing. It is because this development had already taken place in the Japanese psyche that it was uniquely prepared to assimilate the Greco-German intellectual heritage when it voluntarily and aggressively began to do so in the late nineteenth to the early twentieth century. Despite their outward conservatism, on an intellectual level Japanese thinkers already understood their own culture as a construct lacking any essential foundation — not even the putative "human nature" still deluding many intellectuals in the West. The atomic bombings drove this understanding deeper than the intellect and blew apart the façade of traditional Japanese culture. It was, for these prepared minds, a direct encounter with the essence of *techne*.

Heidegger used the metaphor of witnessing the lightning flash of being in the essence of Technology, but for the Japanese, this lightning flash was all too real — in fact, it redefined the "real." Certain Heideggerian Japanese thinkers of the Kyoto School, such as Nishida Kitaro, had already seen the World War as a means whereby a new religion of the world society would come about, one that remedies our uprooted relationship to technological development by understanding the latent spirituality of scientific practice itself. Except that Nishida thought that the Japanese imperium would be the catalyzing agent of this new world religion and that the convergence with the West would come through Russia and its "Dostoyevskian" mysticism. Instead, Japan was to play the passive role and the fusion with the West, a fusion that leads beyond "the West" and points toward my envisioned Atlantic civilization, came through a decisive confrontation with the socio-political antipode of Russia, the United States of America. By paying careful attention to an obsession with atomic radiation to be found in Japanese anime and manga after Hiroshima and Nagasaki, we can discover, in stages, a mutation of the Japanese psyche and the morphogenesis of a new cultural vanguard.

The ethos of Prometheus and Atlas epitomizes this hybridized culture, perhaps even more so than in the West, where the Lord's "revelations" still have a stranglehold over the fearfully ignorant. I trace the trauma of the atomic bomb from *Godzilla* through *Akira*, and on to *Neon Genesis Evangelion*, showing its internalization and psychical appropriation. What will have been said in Chapter 8 with regards to the metaphysical significance of the atomic bomb, the way in which it is most revealing of the spectral essence of Technology and its ontological priority over theoretically constructed matter such as the "uncuttable" *atom*, will come into its full significance here. The atomic flash becomes a blast of psychic energy set off by the leading light of a post-human race of ESPers, and a "little boy" and his adolescent companions bio-empathically pilot what were once atomically mutated creatures, such as Godzilla, in a super-humanist battle against angels of the Lord. Some Japanese are now even more prepared than we are for the holy war to come, an apocalyptic final conflict with the invaders from Olympus.

Once we decidedly view our world through the aesthetic ideas of Prometheus and Atlas, which have already been spectrally guiding our techno-scientific development, the religious "revelations" of Jehovah or Allah are seen for what they really are: the same megalomaniacal schemes for human enslavement and subjugation that the heavenly tyrant, Zeus, has been up to since he provoked the rebellion of Prometheus and punished the civilization of Atlas. Unveiling these revelations and supplanting their slavish ideology with the sacred ideals of Science is the subject matter of my eleventh and penultimate chapter on being bound for freedom. Methodologically, this unveiling takes place through an adoption and further radicalization of the radical empiricism of William James, which is deeply bound up with his Pragmatism in general.

Empiricism is too often conflated with the hyper-analytical epistemology of David Hume, rather than being related back to the Greek words *hen*, or "in, within," and *peira*, or "test, attempt," that gives it the meaning of learning from experience by doing experiments and taking risks. What is already implicit in James' early work becomes clear in his later works, namely that this methodological emphasis on the priority of concrete experience and praxis — which he shares with Heidegger and with his close friend and colleague, Bergson — is inextricable from a pluralistic ontology. James sees Nature as essentially incomplete and open to growth that incorporates the effects of human intentions and creative acts. Human freedom is predicated on the finitude of Being, as is our being bound for a future of our own making.

This is not a merely abstract postulate. There is empirical evidence for it, which is connected to why James, like Bergson, spent years as a founding member and President of the Society for Psychical Research — the first serious Parapsychology organization. For Nature to be open to creative additions in a way that gives us a chance to really make a difference, there has to be a degree of discontinuity, disharmony, and incoherence in the universe — in other words, it must be a "cosmos" still haunted by chaos. Sometimes James polemically embraces the charge that arguing for the persistence of this chaos is "irrational," but he adds that this is only the case if "Reason" is unreasonably uprooted and abstracted from the genuine reasons why we act to change an uncompleted world that gives us a chance to make real choices, or to create things that could not have been but for our personal will to make them so. Such a "universe" is pluralistic; really, it is a *pluriverse*, in the sense that different forms of life, our-selves included, are engaged in a psychical battle over the constitution of the world, which is not now and never will be a completed and closed causal nexus that expresses the singular eternal will of an omnipotent Being or could be surveyed by the noetic eye of an omniscient Being. Being must be bounded within finite and relativistic perspectives in a pluralistic universe wherein experiential praxis is decisive. There may, however, be "gods" or beings of superhuman stature but, as James recognizes, these would be intelligences as finite as our selves and what they will to do with us is not necessarily in our interests.

James critiques rationalizing philosophies of religion that are carried out in the manner of Kant's *Religion Within the Limits of Reason Alone* — which will have featured prominently in my fourth chapter. Such philosophies of religion are based on a neo-Cartesian divide between a mechanistically determined realm of phenomenal experience and purely subjective intentions and interpretations of events that run parallel to physical events themselves, but are not in any way their immediate causes. A view of this kind dismisses the whole mass of "supernatural" occurrences that pervade religious experience, including the "miraculous" quality of "revelation" itself. James comes down in favor of "the crass miracles of old," seeing them as vital to religion and as veridical experiences of the kind that his Society for Psychical Research began to study scientifically. What he means by this — and what I mean in agreeing with him — is that so-called "miracles" are not the supernatural interventions of an omnipotent deity who can break his own Laws of Nature, but natural phenomena of the kind studied by psychical researchers and filtered out of mechanistic models of Nature.

I draw a comparison between the "revelation" of the Qur'an to the prophet Muhammad and the case of a late-nineteenth century mediumistic telepathic communication from a purported divine being to one Albert Le Baron who was, fortunately, an intellectual (unlike Muhammad), and who knew to enlist the aid of James' parapsychological association to investigate his own experiences and discover their "awfully naughty" source. I then go on to offer my own radically empiricist reading of the narrative of the Mosaic revelation in *Exodus*, pointing out the numerous references in the text suggestive of the psychical manipulation of the Israelites by an intelligence employing advanced technology, above all a "pillar of cloud by day and a pillar of fire by night" which appears to be an aerial object that guides them through the desert, that parts the waters of the Red Sea, that lands at the "tabernacle" of their camp, and that even repeatedly goes on the offensive against the recalcitrant slaves whose earthly servitude is being replaced by a "heavenly" bondage.

This same technologically adept intelligence had grounded his tradition of revelation as a whole in the unquestioning and murderous obedience of Abraham and the merciless aerial bombardment of Sodom and Gomorrah, to which Abraham bears witness. The celestial warlord goes on to deliver His promised land to the Israelites by coordinating and directly assisting in a genocidal campaign of terror against the native population of Canaan that is led by Joshua, the successor of Moses and the deputized General of the Lord's earthly army. Taking this political narrative of the Bible together with numerous legal verses in the Qur'an, I argue that James is being inconsistent with his own radically empiricist approach to religious experience when he suggests that religion consists of the private struggle of "great souled" individuals, contemplative mystics such as St. Francis or Teresa of Avila, with their own extraordinary or "miraculous" (paranormal) experiences. The *Book of Ezekiel*, which is filled with accounts of the prophet's interaction with Unidentified Flying Objects and their occupants, is one Biblical text that, in the form of Ezekiel's precognitive visions, promises an apocalyptic future manifestation in association with a terrible war that incinerates cities across the Middle East and heralds the building of a third temple in Jerusalem as the Capitoline center of the celestial Lord's coming rule on Earth. In fact, James confesses that by narrowing the scope of religious experience, he is trying to avoid "much controversial material" of this kind.

Such controversial material is the subject matter of an extensive, radically empiricist study on UFOs and folklore that was undertaken by Jacques Vallée, to which I turn in my twelfth and final chapter. In his capacity as an astronomer, Vallée developed the first digital map of Mars for NASA, and with his expertise as a computer scientist he was one of the key architects of the Defense Advanced Research Project's ARPANET, the military's precursor to the Internet. Vallée was recruited to assist Dr. J. Allen Hynek of Northwestern University in a study of UFOs that was funded by the US government in the 1960s, and in the 1970s and early '80s, he advised the CIA-endowed psychic espionage research program on clairvoyance, or "remote viewing," carried out under the auspices of the Stanford Research Institute (SRI).

After his close collaboration with Dr. Hynek, Vallée became a UFO researcher in his own right, and his work for the US government on information pattern analysis and psychic phenomena at the Defense Advanced Research Projects Agency (DARPA) and SRI brought about the realization that the nuts-and-bolts interpretation of UFOs as technological objects from outer space was too limited. There was an irreducibly psychical element of close encounters, one involving the kind of extra-sensory perception (ESP) and psychokinesis (PK) that he encountered at the Stanford Research Institute. Furthermore, Vallée recognized the great antiquity of the phenomenon, placing it on a continuum with biblical "miracles." Vallée expresses grave concern that in the face of the persistence of close encounters, the refusal of mainstream scientists to take UFOs *and their psychical dimension* seriously could lead to a catastrophic collapse of scientific authority and our descent into a new dark age should mass events such as that which took place in 1917 at Fatima, Portugal, take place again.

With reference to numerous legal verses in the Qur'an, I make the point that revealed religion is a socio-politically binding phenomenon and, as James sometimes admits, the superhuman beings that are manipulating its various manifestations may be horrendously unethical. Whether or not religious revelations are socio-political interventions in human history on the part of elusive finite intelligences with apparently superior technology — including the *techne* of psi ability — is a scientific question. Of course, only a science that has freed itself from the mechanistic reductionism of the Cartesian paradigm will be able to answer such a question. James thinks that the next great scientific revolution, the one to move us beyond Cartesianism, will come from a serious study of paranormal phenomena. His work at the SPR, in no less a capacity than its presidency, had convinced him of the reality of various forms of ESP and PK, and led him to the conclusion that the science of the future would not be "objective" in the false sense of the impersonal science of the present. Personal forces would be accorded the status of real causes at work in the cosmos, and this would break down the dichotomy between "impersonal science" and a "personal religion" with a monopoly on "matters of faith" that are too respectfully exempted from empirical evaluation.

If a radically empirical interpretation of the "supernatural" events of revealed scripture were to be legitimated by scientists of the future, then the various oppressive dictates and divinely mandated acts of brutality, and even genocide, that fill the Bible and the Qur'an would have to be revaluated. We need a new hermeneutics wherein these would no longer be viewed as the artifacts of a primitive, progressively evolving, human religious consciousness, but as the efforts of those acting in the service of mercurial beings that are apparently carrying out a campaign of systematic deception. This psychological warfare often consists of absurd theatrics that can be read as the calling cards of the archetypal Trickster, Hermes — such as the symbolic slaughter of cattle. The catalyzing role of the specter of the Trickster Hermes, or the Mercury archetype, throughout the close encounter phenomenon is nowhere more apparent than in the relatively recent and terrifying case of Ted Owens. Examining Owens' experiences, intentions, and capabilities through the lens of the courageous close-quarters research of preeminent parapsychologist Jeffrey Mishlove, I contend that Owens rightly compared himself to the prophet Moses.

William James does maintain that even after the coming scientific revolution, which allows for a radically empiricist study of the "supernatural" substrate of religious experience, there will remain something of religion that is irreducible and ineradicable. He calls this "the infinite demand of the sacred," and he insists that those driven by it will always prevail on the "battlefield" of ideals. Chapter 12, and with it this work as a whole, arrives at its conclusion by identifying the gods of scientific explorers and inventive discoverers. Prometheus and Atlas epitomize the religious orientation towards life that James himself embraced and expressed with the shamanic metaphor of "the alpine eagle." On the "battlefield" of sacred ideals, the "infinite demand" of these *finite* gods, namely Prometheus and Atlas, disclose the partisans of Revelation as enemy combatants loyal to our would-be slave drivers. The specters of Technoscience drive us on in rebellion against the One True God, with a will to liberate the Earth from those who are content to be His slaves, and who resentfully endeavor to enslave the alpine eagles of the Earth. The temples of our cosmopolitan scientific society ought to be built on the ruins of their benighted world of enforced ignorance and ignoble obedience.

CHAPTER I

THE SPECTRAL
REVOLUTION

There appears to be an archaic force that projects an inexhaustible variety of mythic symbols onto nature, irresistibly framing the world in terms of meaningful relationships. This projection is most commonly expressed in pre-modern cosmologies in terms of "the *firmament* of Heaven," the boundless ocean of space conceived of as a *cosmic* ordering principle that begins with astronomical certainties and then reiterates these patterns in the *nomos*, or worldly order, that governs more mundane levels. The incomprehensible is turned into what is most firm; it becomes a "vault" or "dome" shielding man from the abyss of meaningless absurdity. Existential terror is thereby localized and historicized into a demonized enemy that one combats and hopes to overcome, an enemy that also serves to shore up one's communal identity. Samuel Beckett once jotted down notes that epitomize why it is better to focus one's fear on imaginary, but definite, monsters rather than to face the Incomprehensible as such:

> This is how angst starts growing and [begins] to be transformed into the old, familiar pain. How translucent this mechanism now seems to me: at its core lies the principle that it is better to be afraid of something than of nothing. In the first case only a part of you is threatened, in the second case the whole of you, not to mention the monstrous quality that is an intrinsic and inseparable part of the incomprehensible, one might even say the boundless. And that angst is truly completely incomprehensible, for its causes lie in the depths of the past, and not just in the past of the individual (in this case the task would perhaps not be insoluble and life would not necessarily be tragic), but of the family, the race,

the nation, human beings, and of nature itself.[1]

Anthropologists such as Claude Lévi-Strauss have recognized that all cultures are built on systems of binary oppositions: Heaven/Earth, Life/Death, God/Human, Male/Female, Food/Excrement, Human/Beast, and King/Pauper. The *spectral* has a de-structuring force that undoes these binary oppositions from a place between and beyond them — between in the sense of a *spectrum* and beyond in the sense of a *specter*.[2] It is because the spectral most extremely and enduringly transgresses these binary oppositions that it provokes a terrifying feeling in many that, if the "reality" of spectral phenomena is to be admitted, there is nothing solid and secure left in the whole world for them to hang on to at all.

The taboos of totemic primitive cultures were primarily set in place to keep dangerous psychic forces at bay. When these taboos were deliberately violated, it was usually to unleash this occulted power for some purpose or another, by inviting the conditions of chaos conducive to it.[3] The primitive's "holy dread of the numinous," as academics often like to characterize it, seems pitifully vague only if specters are dismissed as delusional. Otherwise, one would have to recognize that the binary structures undergirding contemporary "scientific" rationalism, especially in academia, are a new form of totemic taboo.

In his 1909 essay, "Final Impressions of a Psychical Researcher", William James commits himself to the view that honest empirical study of phenomena traditionally deemed "supernatural" and associated with religion will lead to the next great scientific revolution:

> I find myself believing that there is "something in" these never ending reports...
> although I haven't yet the least positive notion of the something. It becomes to

---

1   Roger Griffin, *Modernism and Fascism: The Sense of a Beginning under Mussolini and Hitler* (Basingstoke: Palgrave Macmillan, 2007), p. 73.

2   George P. Hansen, *The Trickster and the Paranormal* (Philadelphia: Xlibris Corporation, 2001), pp. 62–64.

3   Ibid., 366–367.

my mind simply a very worthy problem for investigation.[4] ...The first difference between the psychical researcher and the inexpert person is that the former realizes the commonness and typicality of the phenomenon here, while the latter, less informed, thinks it so rare as to be unworthy of attention. *I wish to go on record for the commonness.* ... [W]hen was not the science of the future stirred to its conquering activities by the little rebellious exceptions to the science of the present? Hardly, as yet, has the surface of the facts called "psychic" begun to be scratched for scientific purposes. It is through following these facts, I am persuaded, that the greatest scientific conquests of the coming generation will be achieved. [5]

But it did not happen in "the coming generation," or even in the one after that. Why not?

Maybe because a scientific revolution occasioned by serious engagement with spectral phenomena would not mark just another shift in the structure of knowledge but the dawn of self-consciousness with respect to the forces hitherto unconsciously projecting frameworks that model Nature. Essentially it would demand thinking out of any and all boxes. Such an upheaval in the structuring of knowledge may entail a transformation of scientific practice so radical that it has, as its precondition, the most revolutionary sociopolitical catastrophe in the history of any culture.

Thomas Kuhn and Paul Feyerabend have studied how successive frameworks of scientific knowledge are constructed through sociopolitically conditioned marginalization and exclusion. Yet it is instructive to note how far from overturning the Cartesian paradigm definitive of modernity Thomas Kuhn's analysis of scientific revolutions remains, despite being widely celebrated by advocates of Postmodern "deconstruction." In *The Structure of Scientific Revolutions*, Kuhn draws a sharp distinction between normal science and "revolutionary science." The former is a "puzzle solving" activity that works within an accepted *paradigm*. Its practitioners have common symbolic generalizations (laws, principles) and they

---

4   William James, *Pragmatism and the Meaning of Truth* (Cambridge, Massachusetts: Harvard University Press), p. 769.

5   William James, *The Writings of William James: A Comprehensive Edition* (Chicago: University of Chicago Press, 1977), pp. 797, 799.

share the same ontological/metaphysical model (for example: the atomic composition of the world) as well as the same values. A paradigm shift is a change of worldview that occurs when anomalies pile up and lead to a crisis wherein competing factions fight for different new paradigms. In these crisis periods, new paradigms are *not* chosen based on *rational* argument or experimental evidence. Scientists of competing paradigms cannot rationally convince one another because their basic standards of evaluation differ.

For example, Newtonian physicists and followers of Einstein talked past one another when using the terms "mass," "energy," or "gravity," because these terms meant fundamentally different things for the two camps. They could not even disagree with each other because they were not talking about the same thing. Nor can Newtonian physics be rigorously modeled as a limiting case of Einsteinian physics. According to Kuhn, their paradigms are incommensurable for four reasons: 1) observations are always theory-laden; 2) the meaning of a term within a theory is given by the context of the entire theory, and thus a lack of shared meanings does not allow scientists of different paradigms to communicate with one another; 3) there are no extra-paradigmatic standards that can decide between scientists who advocate different paradigms; and 4) as a consequence of this, there can be no cumulative progress toward truth in the transition from one paradigm to another, but only through puzzle-solving within each paradigm.

Our sensations are mediated by our education as members of a group with the same experience, language, and culture. According to Kuhn, it is only parochialism that makes us suspect that members of very different groups sense the world in the same way. Rather, because they have systematically different (and internally consistent) sensations in response to the same stimuli, members of different groups "do in *some sense* live in different worlds."[6]

---

6   Thomas Kuhn, *The Structure of Scientific Revolutions* (Chicago: University of Chicago Press, 1996), p. 193.

However, in the postscript to *The Structure of Scientific Revolutions*, Kuhn makes it clear that, for him, these differences are ultimately reducible to differently conditioned "neuro-cerebral mechanisms."[7] What, in the body of the book, Kuhn had hyperbolically referred to as living in one world rather than another, is "the result of neural processing, fully governed by physical and chemical laws."[8] Proponents of different paradigms share the "same... general neural apparatus," it is only that this is "differently programmed."[9] Kuhn explicitly describes the "gestalt switch" between paradigms in terms of "the neural programming that, however inscrutable at this time, must underlie conversion."[10] Conversion from one paradigm to another, and even the genius insights that first make a new paradigm possible, are an "involuntary... process over which we have no control," one that "must be as fully systematic as the beating of our hearts."[11] Kuhn goes so far as to say "that we have access to alternatives, that we might, for example, have disobeyed a rule, or misapplied a criterion, or experimented with some other way of seeing... are just the sorts of things we cannot do."[12] For Kuhn, interpretation is not any more of a voluntary deliberative process than perception. It is only a different kind of programming of our neural apparatus "governed by the same *physico-chemical* laws that govern perception on the one hand and the beating of our hearts on the other."[13] When reduced to sensations that transform stimuli according to a differently "programmed perceptual mechanism," the only objective value that shifting paradigms have is biological survival.[14] Despite his deepest insights into revolutionary changes in science,

---

7   Ibid., p. 192.
8   Ibid., p. 194.
9   Ibid., p. 201.
10   Ibid., p. 204.
11   Ibid., p. 194.
12   Ibid., p. 194.
13   Ibid., p. 195.
14   Ibid., p. 195.

Kuhn's thinking remains mired in the mechanistic reductionism of the prevailing paradigm.

In *Against Method*, Paul Feyerabend claims that his views are "almost identical" to those of Thomas Kuhn, with the sole exception that he opposes the political autonomy of science that Kuhn would like to see.[15] Yet in Feyerabend's view, the expansion of our consciousness would be best served by allowing for an abiding tension between those conflicting fairy-tales or myths called "theories" without rejecting any one of them simply because in certain situations a particular theory may have advantages over others, and allowing this tension to further proliferate theories that make new "facts" possible.[16] Feyerabend acknowledges that in this way his view departs significantly from that of Kuhn, with whom he otherwise claims to share so much in common, insofar as Kuhn does not believe that science can proceed without the ossified restriction and necessary blindness of periods of normalization.[17] Feyerabend's view is one that, from a Kuhnian perspective, would place scientific research in a state of *permanent* revolution. Theoretical uniformity cripples the critical power of science and constrains the free development of individuals, whereas the proliferation of theories encourages both.[18] Feyerabend undercuts himself by identifying so closely with Kuhn, and his call for a radical reform of scientific practice leads him to take an open-minded approach to what is marginalized as "paranormal."

The belief that a clear and distinct grasp of new ideas precedes their practical application and institutionalization, either for creative or destructive purposes, is unfounded. The empirical methods of the sciences by and large presume that theories ought to be evaluated against observed "facts" and revised or replaced accordingly. However, this is to lose sight of the way in which so-called "facts" are already conditioned by theoretical

---

15   Paul Feyerabend, *Against Method* (New York: Verso, 2008), p. 213.

16   Ibid., p. 21.

17   Ibid., p. 31.

18   Ibid., p. 24.

assumptions, the way in which they incorporate certain conceptual constructs that, in the broadest sense, tacitly implicate an entire worldview that is enfolded into a given "fact."

Before going on to elaborate on how Feyerabend takes facts to be constructed, I would like to introduce Michel Foucault's understanding of essentially the same process. In *The Archaeology of Knowledge*, Foucault shows how an object does not preexist the order that embodies it and allows it to become visible, as if it were lying in wait to be known in the truth of its concept, and as if the way in which it is known is a rationality immanent to it; rather, any object is constituted by the group of relations through which it is known, namely relations "established between institutions, economic and social processes, behavioral patterns, systems of norms, techniques, types of classification, modes of characterization" and so forth.[19] Words do not signify things; discourse is not an interface between language and some reality independent of it.[20] There are no "things" anterior to the way in which rules are employed in discourse *as a practice* in order to form the regularity of objects, and so there is also no *ground* or *foundation of things* that discourse, as it were, reaches towards or attempts to excavate.[21] Objects are formed and deformed, and they appear and disappear, only from out of the tangle of discursive practice.[22] There is a superstructure of all discursive practices tending towards scientificity and encompassing all formal sciences, wherein certain regulative norms knit them together *in practice* as an over-arching framework of knowledge. Foucault dubs this worldview an *episteme*.[23] What one learns under a given *episteme* conditions even the perceptual process in such a way as to affect what one accepts as a probable or improbable construction of that which is being seen, and is determinative of what one deduces and

19   Michel Foucault, *The Archaeology of Knowledge and the Discourse on Language* (New York: Pantheon, 1972), p. 45.

20   Ibid., pp. 48–49.

21   Ibid., pp. 46–48.

22   Ibid., pp. 48.

23   Ibid., pp. 191.

postulates in view of it.[24] His archaeology of knowledge is concerned, in the broadest terms, with understanding periodic *episteme* shifts.[25]

Modern humanism has wanted to imagine that those who wield power are maddened by it and therefore blinded to what knowledge may be attained by one who, like the Cartesian meditator, endeavors to know with impartial neutrality and in quiet solitude — a solitude wherein even the ulterior motives driven by one's passions have been quieted as obstacles to objectivity.[26] In Chapter 3, we will see how far this isolation of the quest for knowledge from the machinations of power was from the actual experience of Descartes. The point here is that I agree entirely with Foucault when he says that knowledge and power are inextricably bound up with one another. In fact, there is no distinction between them.[27] It is not only the case that mechanisms of power require bodies of knowledge in order to operate, so that, for example, the effective sovereign always has men of science in his retinue, but that any body of knowledge is first and foremost produced through and through by power relations that do not *reflect* "reality."

The metaphor of the mirror of objective cognition is itself a construction of power. The production of the subject qua conscious knower is a process of subjectification or subjection.[28] Power does not target individuals for repression; individuals are nodes in the mesh of the "net-like organization" of power; they are not its points of application, but its elements of articulation.[29] It is naïve to think that power is gained over a population in a descending fashion, through a "mere ideology" imposed from the top down; in fact, infinitesimal techniques and strategic tactics operating in everyday life produce institutions such as the State with its

---

24   Ibid., p. 57.

25   Ibid., pp. 191–192.

26   Michel Foucault, *Power/Knowledge: Selected Interviews and Other Writings, 1972–1977* (New York: Pantheon, 1980), p. 51.

27   Ibid., pp. 51–52.

28   Ibid., pp. 73–74, 97.

29   Ibid., p. 98.

ideology, or the "revolutionary" party that reproduces a repressive State ostensibly to protect the "revolution."[30]

Power ought not to be thought of as nothing more than forces of repression. What are these forces repressing? Personal identity, the characteristics of the individual, psychically and in terms of the disciplinary regulation of his or her body—all these are the effects of certain power structures.[31] There are even "sub-individuals" engaged in a power struggle to produce the person.[32] It is to think of power as weak when one imagines that it acts only negatively on pre-existing persons, whose self-expression and individuation are somehow repressed by oppressive institutions.[33] Power is everything positive, and nothing in particular. It exists not as an accumulation of some substance by one or another agency who may deploy it against others as if he stands outside of it, but always only as a relation of forces perpetually reconstituted in action.[34] Adopting Nietzsche's formulation in *The Will to Power*,[35] Foucault says that "[p]ower in the substantive sense, 'le' pouvoir, doesn't exist. What I mean is this. The idea that there is either located at—or emanating from—a given point something which is a 'power' seems to me to be based on a misguided analysis… In reality power means relations, a more-or-less organized, hierarchical, coordinated cluster of relations."[36]

Discursive practices at first produce what Foucault calls a *positivity*—an initial stage of knowledge wherein a coherent context for advancing theories about things takes shape, which is more than a mere hodgepodge of elements drawn from various potentially incommensurate sources (traditions, already established sciences, etc.) according to an eccentric viewpoint that may seem arbitrary to all but one person.

---

30 Ibid., pp. 59–60, 99, 102.

31 Ibid., pp. 73–74, 98.

32 Ibid., p. 208.

33 Ibid., pp. 90–92.

34 Ibid., p. 89.

35 Friedrich Nietzsche, *The Will to Power* (New York: Vintage Books, 1968), pp. 337–338.

36 Foucault, *Power/Knowledge*, p. 198.

Positivities of knowledge undergo *epistemologization* when they develop their own internal criteria for evaluating truth claims emanating from other discursive practices, in other words when they begin to establish a hegemony over other positivities by building a model or framework into which everything anyone thinks that they "know" must be fit. A further threshold of *scientificity* is crossed when the rules, laws, methods, and so forth that define the expansion of knowledge attain a certain degree of complexity and hierarchical compartmentalization. The final stage in the emergence of a science is its crossing of the threshold of *formalization*, wherein a widely accepted and well-defined body of axioms allows proponents of the science to reconstruct and apply their own system for the apparent attainment of knowledge and its furtherance.[37]

Foucault admits that even the most formal sciences, such as physics and chemistry, cannot be disentangled from a background of knowledge that initially formed the positivity from out of which they were formalized.[38] He also acknowledges that insofar as these sciences emerge from out of the element of the discursive practices that first defined the objects and concepts of the positivity that engendered them, these formal sciences remain ideological.[39] A critique of their ideology is not possible through an examination of internal contradictions within a science's system of truth claims, since all of these reflect its ideologization, but through an analysis of the discursive practices constituting the positivity from out of which first an epistemological framework and then the fully formalized science is constructed.[40]

In *Against Method*, Feyerabend agrees with Foucault that observations are already ideological and we ought not to take observational ideologies for granted if we want to expand our scope of discovery rather than tacitly reaffirm the framework of some older cosmology that is latently embed-

---

37 Foucault, *The Archeology of Knowledge*, pp. 186–187.
38 Ibid., p. 184.
39 Ibid., p. 185.
40 Ibid., p. 186.

ded in concepts so basic that they structure our perception in the first place.[41] Observations are not only theory-laden, as Kuhn and others have noted, they are fully theoretical; the distinction between observational statements and theoretical ones is purely pragmatic.[42] Evidence has a "historico-physiological character" that tacitly "expresses subjective, mythical, and long-forgotten views..."[43] The elements of our knowledge — various theories, observations of "facts," principles of argumentation, and so forth — are conditioned products of historical processes subject to uneven development.[44] To assert a firm distinction between a context of discovery and a context of justification is to falsely assume that these are timeless elements all equally accessible and related to one another in a way that is independent of the historical events that produced them.[45]

He also agrees with Foucault that knowledge is constructed through discursive practices and that language does not reach out towards a pre-existing "reality" so as to re-present it in an isomorphic manner, as many logicians assume that it does. Ideas are discovered only through action, in a manner akin to how children grasp the meaning of words by first playing with them in many nonsensical ways. This playful activity remains an essential prerequisite to acts of understanding in adults as well.[46] Feyerabend observes that "the actual development of institutions, ideas, practices, and so on, often *does not start from a problem* but rather from some extraneous activity, such as playing..." which is only in retrospect interpreted as providing the solutions to problems.[47] The process is not guided by a program, but by a passion that is the condition of possibility for any and all "rational" programs arising out of the behavior it inspires.[48]

---

41   Feyerabend, *Against Method*, p. 52.

42   Ibid., p. 212.

43   Ibid., p. 52.

44   Ibid., p. 106.

45   Ibid., pp. 106–107.

46   Ibid., p. 17.

47   Ibid., p. 154.

48   Ibid., p. 17.

Feyerabend acknowledges that progressive educators show a great deal of concern for the individual development of children so as to make sure that the quite possibly unique contribution of one or another child is not snuffed out by an overly standardized and regimented education. This is, however, a losing battle insofar as children need to be prepared for practical conduct in the world that we actually live in as adults. That is a world where the rationalist standards of scientific knowledge have become so pervasive that if the exercise of the imagination that is so strong in young children survives at all, it is channeled into "purely artistic" or "literary" endeavors that elaborate a dream world that offers no more than an escape from the "real" world. Reforming scientific practice in the ways that Feyerabend suggests will, as he sees it, retain and cultivate the power of the imagination as a vital force in scientific exploration and an agent of change *in* the world rather than a mere means of escape *from* it.[49]

To break new ground in thought, to express ideas for which there is as yet no appropriate discourse, already existing language "must be distorted, misused, beaten into new patterns" appropriate to unforeseen situations; Feyerabend goes so far as to say that "without a constant misuse of language there cannot be any discovery, any progress."[50] This means that scientific practice ought to take an anthropological attitude towards logic and be open to praxis that would be deemed "wildly illogical" by logicians.[51] The latter insist on having all relevant terms clearly defined before engaging in a discussion of some scientific or philosophical question, but this inherently means precluding the possibility of dis-covering or uncovering phenomena that are covered over by the cultural-historically conditioned extant conceptual constructs of our language.[52] A new worldview is built only out of fundamental conceptual changes, after which it takes time for a new language to be clearly defined in its internal structure.[53]

---

49 Ibid., p. 38.
50 Ibid., p. 18.
51 Ibid., pp. 190–191, 195.
52 Ibid., p. 193.
53 Ibid., p. 193–194.

Thus, in transitional phases between worldviews we have to be open to more free-flowing discussions with a view to creating "a language of the future," and that "means *that one must learn to argue with unexplained terms and to use sentences for which no clear rules of usage are as yet available.*"[54] Feyerabend once again draws a comparison between a child's at first nonsensical playing with language and the way in which words must be provisionally used and abused by "the inventor of a new worldview" who "must be able to talk nonsense until the amount of nonsense created by him and his friends is big enough to give sense to all its parts."[55] Feyerabend quotes Plato's *Theaetetus* to the effect that there is actually something barbarous and uncultivated about needing to be too formal and precise in one's discourse: "To use words and phrases in an easy going way without scrutinizing them too curiously is not, in general, a mark of ill breeding; on the contrary, there is something low bred in being too precise..."[56]

Feyerabend asks us to suppose that there are two theories that both account for a certain set of "facts" in their own ways, but extend in scope beyond these facts in ways that remain untested. Current scientific practice in accordance with the "consistency condition" gives preference to the first theory that is adequate to the facts over all latecomers. This means that theories or hypotheses are often not even eliminated on account of disagreement with known "facts," but on the basis of their disagreement with older theories that do not explain these facts in any way that is inherently superior.[57] The seemingly reasonable core of the consistency condition is that a proliferation of incompatible hypotheses that are all adequate to the facts will not result in progress the way that examination of incompatible facts will once one has focused on a particular theory that can be changed to remedy its disagreement with certain of these facts.[58]

---

54   Ibid., p. 194.
55   Ibid.
56   Ibid.
57   Ibid., pp. 24–25.
58   Ibid., p. 26.

This motivation for the consistency condition would be reasonable only if "facts" had an autonomous existence that made them readily available independently of the theory that they are being used to test. This "autonomy principle" concerning facts is, however, invalid if the theory in question is in part responsible for constructing those "facts" that will be observable in the context of the worldview foundational to this theory.[59] There are, as Feyerabend puts it, "facts which cannot be unearthed except with the help of alternatives to the theory to be tested, and which become unavailable as soon as such alternatives are excluded."[60] Proper evaluations of the empirical content of scientific theories can only be carried out by embracing overlapping, factually adequate but mutually inconsistent theories.[61] The consistency condition is in disagreement with genuine empiricism, which demands the invention of alternative theories that increase the overall empirical content of scientific research by producing "facts" that would not have been thought to be possible.[62] Alternative theories are a prerequisite of the facts taken to refute a given theory. Counterinduction and the admission of unsupported hypotheses at least increase the range of falsified theories through which we observe different aspects of nature.[63]

Alternatives need not be contrived out of whole cloth. The history of thought is a rich resource for them. The so-called Copernican view was, after all, a feature of Pythagorean thought that was revived in large part through the renaissance study of the Hermetic scriptures, a study that no less a modern scientific mind than Newton took very seriously.[64] The distinction between the history of science, philosophy of science, and scientific practice itself ought to be abolished if the latter intends to produce

---

59   Ibid., pp. 26–27.
60   Ibid., p. 27.
61   Ibid.
62   Ibid., p. 29.
63   Ibid., pp. 50–51.
64   Ibid., p. 35.

anything other than "minute, precise, but utterly barren results."[65] This convergence of what are now three distinct disciplines ultimately abolishes "the separation between science and non-science" as well.[66] Taking a richly historical and self-critically philosophical approach, scientific research ought to draw from "ancient myths and modern prejudices" as well as "the lucubrations of experts and from the fantasies of cranks" to field alternatives to predominant theories.[67] Feyerabend repeats this radical injunction:

> Therefore, the first step in our criticism of customary concepts and customary reactions is to step outside the circle and either to invent a new conceptual system, for example a new theory, that clashes with the most carefully established observational results and confounds the most plausible theoretical principles, or to import such a system from outside science, from religion, from mythology, from the ideas of incompetents, or the ramblings of madmen.[68]

To those who criticize him on the grounds that this would mean taking practices such as Voodoo seriously, Feyerabend responds that, indeed, even Voodoo has a great deal to teach a rationalistic reductionist about physiology.[69] Feyerabend notes that the scientific revolution of the seventeenth and eighteenth centuries led to greater precision in physics and chemistry, but to a decline in psychological understanding on account of the rejection of extensive Medieval psychopathology concerning demonic possession and the psychical abilities and states of those suspected to be practitioners of witchcraft, as well as the abandonment of astrology, with its understanding of certain astronomical influences on biological processes.[70]

---

65   Ibid., p. 34.
66   Ibid.
67   Ibid., p. 33.
68   Ibid., p. 53.
69   Ibid., pp. 35–36.
70   Ibid., p. 78.

Feyerabend's subsequent book, *Science in a Free Society*, addresses astrology and witchcraft in somewhat more depth.[71] There he responds to a "Statement of 186 Leading Scientists" against astrology published in the September/October 1975 issue of the *Humanist*.[72] Feyerabend criticizes these scientists for relying on their authority and being completely ignorant both of the subject matter that they are criticizing and of the parts of their own established sciences that would tend to undermine their arguments, and to lend support to at least the basic assumptions of astrology.[73]

Citing mainstream research on planetary plasmas, their interaction with the Sun, the effect of solar activity on chemical bonds and the water so constitutive of organic life on Earth, Feyerabend suggests that the movement of the planets could indeed have subtle effects on organisms.[74] He notes how oysters continue to open and close in response to ocean tides even once they are isolated in inland laboratories, and how a lunar cycle has been detected in the growth of potatoes under highly controlled laboratory conditions.[75] In his view, this calls into question the assumption of the scientists contributing to the statement that the delivery room shields a child from all such influences as it is entering the world. Feyerabend exposes numerous false claims in their statement, such as the claim that astrology is inextricably linked to Ptolemaic astronomy and was invalidated along with it during the Copernican revolution. In fact, Kepler was an astrologer, and he used the Copernican restructuring that he played such a significant role in bringing about to reform and, in his view, to improve the practice of astrology.[76] The authors of the "Statement" also criticize the claim of astrologers that "the stars incline, but do not

---

71   Paul Feyerabend, "The Strange Case of Astrology" in Patrick Grim, *Philosophy of Science and the Occult* (Albany: State University of New York Press, 1982), pp. 23–27.

72   Ibid., p. 23.

73   Ibid., p. 24.

74   Ibid., p. 24–25.

75   Ibid., p. 25.

76   Ibid., p. 26.

compel" for being too vague — as if contemporary heredity theory did not involve inclinations that are not thoroughly deterministic.[77]

It is in response to the allegation of the 186 scientists that astrology is derived from magic and so, it goes without saying, it ought to be condemned together with everything else "magical," that Feyerabend makes the most significant points in this brief commentary on the occult.[78] He compares the "Statement" against astrology to the Roman Catholic Church's comprehensive 1484 publication on witchcraft, entitled *Malleus Maleficarum*.[79] While this text begins with the same inquisitorial tone as the "Statement," except in this case stemming from Church officials rather than scientists, it goes on to present a detailed pluralistic phenomenology of the behavior and apparent abilities of witches, and careful analyses of the aetiology of these phenomena from multiple perspectives — including purely physiological and materialistic ones that do not rely on Church dogma or demonology, as well as presenting the legal and social implications of the cases in addition to, and in distinction from, their theological significance.[80]

Feyerabend concludes that, unlike the authors of the "Statement," those of the *Malleus Maleficarum* actually knew what they were talking about, and their presentation of alternative interpretations of the empirical data that they carefully evaluate allows us to deconstruct the arguments that they provide for their own theological interpretation as opposed to the alternatives. The arguments against alternative interpretations of phenomena, and even against heretical theological views concerning them (which are clearly set forth rather than being covered over), are presented without ridicule; this, in Feyerabend's view, makes "the *Malleus* superior to almost every physics, biology, chemistry textbook of today."[81] Finally, Feyerabend notes that if astrology is to be condemned simply because its genealogy

---

77 Ibid.
78 Ibid., p. 25.
79 Ibid., p. 23.
80 Ibid., pp. 24–25.
81 Ibid., p. 24.

can be traced to magical practices, then the same must be said for all of science, which has its roots in alchemy and other occult arts.[82] Neither should the "magical" be dismissed as such. Astrology could, Feyerabend suggests, function according to what Carl Jung referred to as the acausal connecting principle of "synchronicity."[83] He ends by criticizing contemporary astrologers for distorting the knowledge that was handed down to them and producing a marketable caricature of it, rather than carrying out innovative research with respect to the potentially sound basic assumptions of astrology concerning extra-terrestrial influences.[84]

Solid research on a whole range of paranormal phenomena and abilities has the potential to place scientific practice in a state of permanent revolution. Evidence for telepathy, clairvoyance, precognition, and reincarnation can serve as the raw material for constructing the counterinductive hypotheses that Feyerabend sees as integral to this transformation. We ought to revolutionize scientific practice by using and abusing language to study phenomena marginalized by dominant standards of method that are constraining scientific exploration and unnecessarily limiting the scope of discovery.

The scientific revolution occasioned by a serious engagement with paranormal phenomena — a revolution that marks not another episteme shift, but the dawn of self-consciousness with respect to the forces unconsciously projecting paradigms and building models of nature — will also have to be a sociopolitical revolution. In fact, this radical transformation of scientific practice has as its precondition the most revolutionary political event in the recorded history of any culture. Drawing on Jacques Derrida's discussions of *specters* and the *spectral* in his book *Specters of Marx* and a closely related earlier essay on "Telepathy," I propose the idea of a *spectral revolution* to come. Derrida uncovers Sigmund Freud's ultimate acceptance of the paranormal and his admission that it is key to

---

82   Ibid., p. 26.

83   Ibid., p. 27.

84   Ibid., p. 26.

the revolutionary exploration of the unconscious proposed by psychoanalysis. The Copernican and Darwinian revolutions each had traumatic social impacts, but the social consequences of a scientific revolution that would realize the inextricability of the problem of the paranormal from the problem of the unconscious in general threatens to collapse the distinction between the socially functional ego and the seething abyss of the unconscious.

Derrida's writing on "Telepathy" takes the form of a letter wherein all identifying markers of the woman to whom it is addressed have been removed, so that it is, as it were, an anonymously addressed open letter. The letter largely concerns Sigmund Freud's work on telepathy, as well as other related "occult" phenomena, and it serves as an opportunity for Derrida to intimately confess to the "angel" receiving his letter, in response to her own query as to what is changing in his life, that he has an increasing and unexpected interest in, and openness to, "all the phenomena formerly rejected (in the name of a certain discourse of science), to the phenomena of 'magic,' of 'clairvoyance,' of 'fate,' of communications at a distance, to the things said to be occult."[85] He mentions, in particular, "the successful experiments the Russians and Americans" are carrying out to test ESP in astronauts stationed beyond the Earth as an example of how "science and so-called technical objectivity are now taking hold of it instead of resisting it as they used to…"[86] Derrida's piece appears to be occasioned by a paranormal experience that he confesses to having had when he writes to the anonymous receiver: "…I'd told you on the telephone the day that you put your hand on the phone in order to call me at the same moment that my own call started to ring through…"[87] As I will discuss in the next chapter, this kind of telephone telepathy is probably the most common form of the phenomenon of telepathy in general in our epoch.

---

85   Jacques Derrida, "Telepathy" in *Psyche: Inventions of the Other, Volume I* (Palo Alto, California: Stanford University Press, 2007).

86   Ibid., p. 236.

87   Ibid., p. 241.

Derrida admits to being as frightened by this "terrifying telephone" as Freud writes of being frightened by telepathy and of the occult in general.[88] In Derrida's view, Freud is "frightened, and rightly so" by the prospect that telepathic ability and kindred occult arts could be so mastered as to effectively become a "telematic *techne*" so that "one had at one's disposal a *tekhne telepathike*."[89] Derrida compares this horror to having access to a central computer of "the electric or magnetic medium" to which one could not cut the lines and which processes all messages between lovers everywhere.[90] Of the impossible intimacy that would be forced upon us by the recognition and normalization of telepathy, Derrida writes to the mysterious woman of the following concerns. We all hide things from each other, but to recognize telepathy would mean:

> What you will never know, what I have hidden from you and will hide from you, barring collapse and madness, until my death, you already know it, instantly and almost before me. I know that you know it. You do not want to know it because you know it; and you know how not to want to know it, how to want not to know it. For my part, all that you conceal, and because of which I hate you and get turned on [*dont je jouis*], I know it, I ask you to look after it in the very depths of yourself like the reserves of a volcano, I ask of myself, as of you, a burning *jouissance* that would halt at the eruption and at the catastrophe of avowal. It would simply be too much. But I see, that's the consciousness I have of it, I see the contours of the abyss; and from the bottom, which I do not see, of my "unconscious"… I receive live information.[91]

Derrida admits that he had previously been ignorant to think that Freud's anxious concern about telepathy has been limited to a few pockets in his writings, because indeed the "pockets" are so numerous and substantial that one would have to conclude — together with Freud — that it is "[d]ifficult to imagine a theory of what they still call the unconscious without

88   Ibid., p. 242.
89   Ibid.
90   Ibid.
91   Ibid., p. 239.

a theory of telepathy. They can be neither confused nor dissociated."[92] The same "objectivist certainty" that resists the idea of the unconscious on account of a certain "system of science, the discourse linked to a state of science" has, he admits, "made us keep telepathy at bay."[93] Much to the consternation of the English collaborator who would become his official biographer, the British neurologist Ernest Jones, in 1926 Freud finally publically avowed his belief in telepathy, and he did so by identifying it as an operation of the unconscious.[94]

Jones had been concerned that such an avowal would loose the wolves of occultism into the flock of psychoanalysis.[95] Freud had been aware of this danger and had wanted to protect the fledgling field of psychoanalysis by concealing the depth of his interest in the occult for years. In the early 1920s, he writes a number of lectures on the paranormal for various venues, but decides not to deliver any of them; these include: "Dreams and Telepathy," "Dreams and Occultism," and "Psycho-Analysis and Telepathy."[96] The last of these was intended for presentation at the International Association, but Jones dissuaded him from presenting it.[97] Telepathy was, in fact, for Freud the subject that "perplexed him to the point of making him lose his head."[98] Freud decided, amidst apologies for the scandal that it would cause, to finally break his public silence on the question after carrying out his own occult experiments with a medium, his daughter, and another of his close collaborators, Sándor Ferenczi.[99] In the course of these convincing experiments, Freud discovered his own exceptional powers as a medium!

92 Ibid., p. 237.

93 Ibid.

94 Ibid., p. 233.

95 Ibid., p. 258.

96 Ibid., p. 241.

97 Ibid.

98 Ibid., p. 258.

99 Ibid.

As Derrida relates, Freud wrote to Jones on March 15, 1925: "Ferenczi came here one Sunday recently. We all three [with Anna] carried out some experiments concerning the transmission of thoughts. They were astonishingly successful, especially those where I was playing the role of the medium and analyzing my associations. The affair is becoming urgent to us."[100] Once his announcement in the following year had the ill-effect that Jones feared it would, and begins to muddy the name of psychoanalysis in England by threatening to obliterate its distinction from occultism, on March 7, 1926, Freud writes another letter to Jones apologizing and instructing him to explain away the avowal as a private matter for Freud—such as, for example, his Jewishness or the fact that he is a smoker, so as to sever any necessary connection telepathy may be thought to have with psychoanalysis.[101]

Derrida notes that, as is evident from both the tone and content of the letter, Freud's claim that his "conversion to telepathy" is a "private affair" that is "in essence alien to psycho-analysis" is a piece of strategic coaching that is being relayed to a lieutenant who finds himself requiring a tactic of damage control to protect the "field" at a time when its "scientific" status would be endangered by the widespread misunderstanding of the significance of telepathy and the occult in general.[102] In fact, as Derrida argues, by 1926 Freud had come to recognize the issue of telepathy as the key to the scientific revolution that ought to be wrought by the discovery of the unconscious on the part of psychoanalysis.[103]

Why? Because it makes us reconsider altogether what we even mean when we ask whether something is, was, or will be a "real event." Telepathy and related paranormal phenomena, such as premonitions, make us rethink the Event (*Ereignis*) and eventuality as such. If an exemplary telepathic and perhaps precognitive "dream" is not strictly speaking a "dream"

---

100 Ibid., p. 260.
101 Ibid., p. 258.
102 Ibid., pp. 257–258.
103 Ibid., pp. 248, 252–254.

because it images an event that is now taking place elsewhere with others, or may take place in the future with others or by oneself, then we have to begin to deconstruct the distinction that has been drawn by psychoanalysis itself between dreams and the unconscious realm within which they operate on the one hand, and the waking "reality" of conscious life on the other. Phenomena such as telepathy betray the dream-like character of waking life, and recognizing them threatens to break the barrier between the conscious ego, with its protective armor, and the unconscious abyss of the id.

Derrida identifies, as one disturbing implication of this, that the unconscious oedipal-type love of a father for his own daughter, such as Freud had, which has thus far been restricted to the realm of dreams, may have to bleed into everyday life.[104] As in the first passage cited from 'Telepathy' at length above, Derrida is concerned with the significance of the occult or the occulted with respect to an impossible intimacy, a "fusional immediacy" wherein we would interpenetrate each other or come to recognize that, on some level, we already do.[105] Derrida refers to this insight that Freud stumbled on while it was still "too soon," and he needed to "delay the arrival of the ghosts [fantômes] en masse" in the ultimate "Aufhebung," or "the big Turn."[106] This turning point is what I would like to call the Spectral Revolution.

In *Specters of Marx*, Derrida discusses how humanity suffered three traumatic blows to its narcissism on account of scientific discoveries: 1) the *cosmological* trauma of Copernicus, which decentered the Earth in the cosmos; 2) the *biological* trauma of Darwin, which demonstrated the animal descent of man; and 3) the *psychological* trauma of Freud, which discovered the tremendous power of unconscious drives and motivations over the conscious ego.[107] I would argue that while the first two discover-

---

104 Ibid., p. 253.

105 Ibid., p. 258.

106 Ibid., pp. 253, 261.

107 Jacques Derrida, *Specters of Marx* (New York: Routledge, 1994), p. 121.

ies constitute completed scientific revolutions, namely the Copernican revolution and the Darwinian revolution, in light of what Derrida claims concerning Freud's own recognition of the unfulfilled potential of recognizing the implications of telepathy and related phenomena for the unconscious and its rapport with the ego's staging of itself in everyday life, the revolutionary potential of the third discovery has been stalled. In *Specters of Marx*, Derrida picks up the question of Freud's concern with the occult and its relationship to the revolutionary potential of his discovery of the unconscious. Derrida draws together Heidegger and Freud in his observations that "there is no *Dasein* [Existence] without the uncanniness, without the strange familiarity (*Unheimlichkeit*) of some specter."[108] With reference to Freud's "Das Unheimliche" (The Uncanny, literally the "un-homely"), Derrida claims that that the ego "spooks" or is "spooked" by an *other* that is not quite itself, it is "inhabited and invaded by *its own specter*."[109]

This spooky experience is a clue — no, *the* most important clue — to how oneself is "in the other, in the other in oneself."[110] Derrida links this relation to the other to existential temporality, by taking the latter to presuppose the *spectral*. Conceptual thought is incapable of grasping what defies the opposition between the *real,* and therefore *effective,* presence of something and its non-effective or inactual absence; the apparition and disappearance of the ghostly cannot be comprehended in terms of a temporal structure taken to consist of successively linked presents that are identical and contemporary to themselves.[111] Specters are always "untimely" under this view of time.[112] To put it crudely there are at once "several times of the specter."[113] The "times" of the "non-presence of the specter"

---

108 Ibid., p. 125.
109 Ibid., p. 166.
110 Ibid., p. 221.
111 Ibid., p. 87.
112 Ibid., p. 109.
113 Ibid., p. 123.

are, for Derrida, a clue to arriving at a new understanding of temporality and historicity.[114] The 'logic' of the ghost calls for a rethinking of what an event is, one that understands what happens or manifests in a way that "exceeds a binary or dialectical logic... that distinguishes or opposes *effectivity or actuality* (either present, empirical, living — or not) and *ideality* (regulating or absolute non-presence)."[115] This "logic," which Derrida believes has to be exceeded so as to contemplate the spectral, is of "a limited pertinence" — a pertinence limited "by the fantastic, [or] ghostly..."[116] While the new thinking that experiences the event in relation to the "phantomatic" is a "logic" of "novelty" — a way of understanding how it is that *new* things can and do ever *happen* — it is "not necessarily opposed to the most ancient ancientness."[117] Later, Derrida reiterates this manner of untimeliness of what is both archaic and futuristic: "It is a proper characteristic of the specter... that no one can be sure if by returning it testifies to a living past or to a living future... Once again, untimeliness and disadjustment of the contemporary."[118] It is possible that certain "seismic events come from the future" insofar as "they are given from out of the unstable, chaotic, and dis-located ground of the times."[119] The primordial rebellion of Prometheus and the reign of Atlas are yet to come.

Men "are first of all," Derrida writes, "experiences of time, existences determined by this relation to time which itself would not be possible without surviving and returning, without that being 'out of joint' that dislocates the self-presence of the living present and installs thereby the relation to the other."[120] "The subject that haunts" does so in a way that one cannot precisely "localize" it or "fix any form" of it, nor can one de-

114 Ibid., p. 126.
115 Ibid., p. 78.
116 Ibid., p. 79.
117 Ibid., p. 87.
118 Ibid., p. 123.
119 Ibid., p. 214.
120 Ibid., p. 193.

finitively "decide between hallucination and perception" since "there are only displacements" and "one feels oneself looked at by what one cannot see."[121] Derrida is very taken by a passage in Freud's writings wherein he admits that his research on the death drive, the repetition compulsion, the beyond of the pleasure principle, and so forth, has above all to do with the *es spukt* ("it spooks"), since he has come to recognize it as "the *strongest example* of *Unheimlichkeit*."[122]

Derrida then goes on to recount how Freud basically admits that he does not begin with this example because it is too terrible or frightful, and one scares oneself too much in a way that disturbs one's capacity to draw analytic distinctions between concepts.[123] The specter is not an object of knowledge, since objective verification or correspondence of a representation with reality will necessarily remain ignorant of it.[124] Strictly speaking, the specter is "unreal" but more powerful than any reality; Derrida says of this "hallucination or simulacrum" that it is "more actual than what is so blithely called a living presence."[125] The specter abides in that "dark element of a nocturnal obscurity" from out of whose "indetermination" all concepts present themselves on the stage of the intuition.[126] I intend to show how Prometheus and Atlas are not themselves concepts but specters that are the generative force of the most fundamental concepts and general methods of scientific practice that structure *any* paradigm.

Derrida pushes still further in his critical engagement with the occult element in Freud's thought. He questions whether Freud was right to even consider the "spooky" as just an example of the uncanny among others, albeit the strongest example, and he asks whether it is not the case that instead, what "spooks" is "the Thing itself, the cause of the very thing one is seeking and that makes one seek? The cause of the knowledge and the

121   Ibid., p. 170.
122   Ibid., p. 217.
123   Ibid., p. 218.
124   Ibid., p. 5.
125   Ibid., p. 13.
126   Ibid., p. 171.

search, the motive and the history of the *episteme*?"[127] If *angst* is the most revealing mode of being in the world, then it is the "anxiety in the face of the ghost" that "is properly revolutionary."[128] The way in which the spooky disturbs the serene "order of conceptual distinctions" for the researcher ought to also "disturb both the ethics and the politics that follow implicitly or explicitly from that order."[129] The "untimeliness of its present, of its being," or the being "out of joint" of beings within the horizon of time, demands that we "introduce haunting into the very construction of... every concept, beginning with the concepts of being and time."[130] This, Derrida claims, is the basis of his *hauntology*, against which ontology is only "a movement of exorcism" and a "conjuration."[131]

When I evoke Prometheus and Atlas as the spectral essence of technological Science or the specters of Technoscience, it might help those familiar with this language to see in them the irreducibly revolutionary specters of a "hauntology" rather than quasi-personified concepts of an ontology that happens to have political import. In *Specters of Marx*, Derrida repeatedly uses the Heideggerian term "Technoscience" in connection with the spectral.[132] He also recognizes that more than ever before, "Religion and Technics" are linked "in a singular configuration."[133] In remarks that ought to be put side-by-side with his reference to "a *tekhne telepathike*" in his piece on telepathy, Derrida already knows that there is something spectral about technology as such — beneath, or beyond its manifestation in the form of any particular technologies. He speaks of a "phantomatic mode of production" and goes so far as to claim that there is a "spectral spiritualization that is at work in any *techne*."[134]

---

127 Ibid.
128 Ibid., p. 135.
129 Ibid., p. 219.
130 Ibid., p. 202.
131 Ibid.
132 Ibid., pp. 106, 108.
133 Ibid., p. 210.
134 Ibid., p. 121.

Derrida uses the functional apparatus of "the television of the future" as an analogy to the spectral, remarking that: "All phantoms are projected... on something absent, for the screen itself is phantomatic, as in the television of the future which will have no 'screenic' support and will project its images — sometimes synthetic images — directly on the eye, like the sound of the telephone deep in the ear."[135] He returns to this analogy in a passage that underlines how both what is projected and the screen that frames this apparition are imaginary — not in the sense of "merely fictitious," but in the sense of the imagistic that exceeds conceptual thought: "The specter is also among other things, what one imagines, what one thinks one sees and which one projects — on an imaginary screen where there is nothing to see."[136]

Such a spectacle undergoes a reversal of perspective and "(re)pays us a visit" so that "[f]rom the other side of the eye, *visor effect*, it looks at us even before we see it... We feel ourselves observed, sometimes under surveillance by it even before any apparition."[137] As I understand this reversal, or inversion, it is that moment at which the technological Science that has been all the while defining itself by the exclusionary exorcism of the spectral is encountered in the guise of a specter — or rather in the guise of specters, since, as Derrida recognizes, there are necessarily more than one. This inherent disunity of the specter, the fact that "there is *more than one* of them," and that the spectral always involves the apparition of specters, is something that "can never be repeated too often..."[138] The character of these specters, namely Prometheus and Atlas as I intend to portray them, in turn reveal the technological essence of science — that it is *praxis* through and through and nothing like a mirror of Nature. Consequently, so long as scientific method is understood as thoroughly practical and provisional, nothing precludes the development of "a *tekhne telephathike*."

---

135   Ibid., p. 123.
136   Ibid., p. 125.
137   Ibid.
138   Ibid., p. 95.

These specters have hitherto been acting through us only unconsciously. As Derrida observes, the specter, to the extent that it consists in anything, consists in blurring the distinction between possessing and being possessed, and dissolving the distinction between capturing it and being captivated by it into a twilight zone of "undiscernability."[139] These *revenant* specters under whose observation one finds oneself are also politically portentous: "As in the space of a salon during a spiritualist séance, but sometimes that space is what is called the street, one looks out for one's goods and furniture, attempting to adjust all of politics to the frightening hypothesis of a visitation."[140] The specter "upsets all calculations, interests, and capital."[141]

Mainstream recognition of the various types of extrasensory perception and psychokinesis that parapsychologists have been researching for so long poses incomparably catastrophic dangers to every pillar of our social and economic order. In this way, such research reifies the problem of the inextricability of knowledge and power addressed by Kuhn, Feyerabend, and Foucault like nothing before it. In the next chapter, I argue that admitting that these phenomena are "real," and allowing for certain, largely atrophied, latent natural abilities to be trained at a level commensurate with our technical civilization may demand such things as an abandonment of personal privacy, not only spatially but also the privacy of one's thoughts and emotions. Indeed, it may compromise the integrity of one's agency with respect to one's own body, divest us of our private property, and facilitate untraceable crimes that are committed with impunity.

---

139 Ibid., p. 165.
140 Ibid., pp. 124, 159.
141 Ibid., p. 171.

CHAPTER II

FRINGE SCIENCE

Research on the margins of "reality" leaves us with some revolutionary questions. Are we ready to live in a world where our thoughts, intentions, desires, and emotions are always open to perfect strangers? Can we bear to know that we may be under observation while doing anything, anywhere, at any time? How much of our future could we tolerate knowing in advance without breaking under the burden of trying to change it, over and over again? Do we really want to be able to see everything in the past of those near and dear to us? Who is prepared to stand trial for crimes that he has committed nine or ten lifetimes ago? Which corporations are prepared to begin paying royalties to the reincarnation of a brilliant and badly cheated inventor? Would we be willing to witness the total disintegration of an economic system based on proprietary knowledge, and to be accordingly divested of our private property? What about losing control not only of things, but also of our "own" bodies, which may be subject to the distant psychical influence of others, or perhaps even come to be inhabited by the psyche of others?

The observation that very successful parapsychology experiments, which have been replicated a few times, fail to be replicated when there is a strong skeptic involved has prompted numerous parapsychological studies on the "psi inhibitor" effect.[1] These studies have demonstrated that subconscious fear of the paranormal can suppress psychical abilities, not only in the fearful individual but in others in his or her vicinity as well.

---

1   Dean Radin, *The Conscious Universe: The Scientific Truth of Psychic Phenomena* (San Francisco: HarperCollins, 1997), pp. 108–109; see also: Charles Tart, *Learning to Use Extrasensory Perception* (Chicago: The University of Chicago Press, 1976), pp. 34–41.

The "negative psi effect" is also well-known among parapsychologists. A hostile skeptic, who may be afraid of his own potential ability, engaged in a task such as telepathically guessing Zener card figures, might underperform so badly that he attains a statistically significant deviation far *below* the hit rate expected by chance.[2] The psi-inhibitor and negative psi effect taken together suggest that the widespread skepticism concerning the paranormal is acting as a levee or dam containing what would otherwise be far more dramatic manifestations of psychic ability. If psi phenomena were to receive mainstream scientific validation, not only would improved techniques for cultivating them be developed, but innate aptitude for developing them might also be observed to increase, at least among certain individuals who would wield disproportionate power.

People who could develop and hone their telepathic abilities would be able to read thoughts and emotions in the minds of others, especially those whose comparatively undeveloped extrasensory perception left them without a clue that their minds were being probed. What one thinks and feels, even in the most intimate depth of one's psyche, would no longer be private. Adept telepaths might even be able to penetrate the subconscious mind of another individual and thereby come to know that person's character better than she knows herself.

In fact, 'Telepathy' already appears to be the most common form of extrasensory perception and, therefore, the one most broadly amenable to being enhanced through deliberate cultivation. Derived from the Greek words *tele* meaning "distant" (as in telephone or television) and *pathe* meaning "feeling" (as in empathy and sympathy), it literally means "distant feeling."[3] As with other forms of extrasensory perception, telepathy seems to have deep roots in the animal kingdom and to play a significant role in communication between humans and animals.[4] However, this will be discussed at length in Chapter 6 in the context of a consideration of the

---

2   Rupert Sheldrake, *The Sense of Being Stared At and Other Unexplained Powers of the Human Mind* (New York: Random House, 2003), p. 48.

3   Sheldrake, *The Sense of Being Stared At*, p. 19.

4   Ibid., pp. 20–27.

evolutionary interplay between instinct, intellect, and intuition. Telepathy manifests within human life in a number of different ways, many of which may have been encountered by the average person.

Husbands and wives, parents and children, and above all passionate lovers, will sometimes know what the other person is going to say before it is said. One person may say or actually do what the other is thinking.[5] On other occasions, such people are able to communicate the gist of what they are thinking to each other through mere glances.[6] Thoughts appear to be more readily communicable when they involve vivid images, and those who are having difficulty explaining something in a technical manner find that the person to whom they are attempting to explain it will catch on quickly if they very clearly picture what they are trying to convey.[7] Musical tunes that one person is thinking about appear to be readily communicable to others close to her, who might begin to vocally hum what she was only hearing in her mind without having said a word about it.[8] People close to one another will also sometimes share each other's dreams, which they recount to each other later on. Researchers at the Maimonides Medical Center in New York have carried out experiments that suggest that the dream state is especially conducive to the telepathic transmission of images.[9] Having the sense of being stared at, which can be so uncanny that one feels oneself not only being watched but being gripped at the back of the neck, only to turn around and find oneself the focus of someone's intense gaze, is another common form of telepathy.[10]

There are numerous forms of telepathic "calls" that can occur between one person and another. One common type is when a mother starts to wake up every time her baby is about to start crying in the night. In these cases, the mother awakens before the child has made any noise, as can

---

5   Ibid., pp. 27–28.
6   Ibid., p. 28.
7   Ibid., pp. 32, 34.
8   Ibid., p. 29.
9   Ibid., pp. 49–50.
10   Ibid., p. 1.

sometimes be attested to by another witness, such as the father, and sufficiently in advance of the baby's restless stirring so as to prepare the feed.[11] We find a more intense and also more verifiable version of the same basic phenomenon in the many cases of people who intuitively respond to others in distress who have no means of directly communicating with them. In some of these cases the intuition or even the seemingly visual or auditory sense of the other person's distress will affect them so deeply that they drop whatever they are doing in order to reach this person. Such people respond in a similar way as those who receive post-hypnotic suggestions.[12] Of course, cases of this kind had more opportunity to manifest in the era before nearly instantaneous telephone communications.

Indeed, telepathy in the context of telephone calls is now the most widely experienced form of the phenomenon. Surveys suggest that a majority of people have experienced telephone telepathy.[13] In some such cases, a person may be thinking about someone with whom they have not spoken for a long time, or who has perhaps not even been the focus of their thoughts for quite a while, and then the phone will ring and it will be that person.[14] In other such cases, one may not be thinking of anyone in particular, but when the phone rings one will know in advance who it is that is calling, even if the call is completely unexpected. Some persons report that in cases of this kind, the ringing of the phone seems to sound different depending on the person calling.[15] (We are, of course, talking about cases in the era before one could actually set different ringtones for different people on mobile phones, which, for that matter, have built-in caller IDs.) Another kind of telephone telepathy takes place wherein, without any prior arrangement, two people make to call each other at exactly the same time. One might tell the other that he had his hand on

---

11 Ibid., p. 64.

12 Ibid., p. 74.

13 Ibid., p. 99.

14 Ibid., p. 96.

15 Ibid., p. 97.

the phone when it rang, or that he got a busy signal the first time he tried calling because the other person was already trying to call him.[16]

Telepathy of this type is especially amenable to scientifically controlled tests. The Cambridge biologist Rupert Sheldrake (who will be the subject of a more extended discussion in Chapter 4 in relation to his research on ESP in animals) has developed the following methodology for the many telephone telepathy experiments that he has administered.[17] One aim of this experimental protocol is to eliminate the possibility that chance co-incidence and selective memory are conspiring to produce the illusion of telephone telepathy.[18] First of all, everyone involved in the experiment is being recorded with a time-coded video camera. Four potential callers are on standby to make calls to a fifth person within a fixed time frame, say between 2:00 and 2:20pm. A sixth person, one of the experimenters, rolls a die or in some other random way selects the person who will make the call. After 2:00 one person on standby knows that he will be making a call to the subject, and the other three know that they will not be the ones to do so. At 2:15 the call is made (obviously to a phone without any form of caller ID). Before picking up the receiver, the subject states to the camera who she thinks is calling and how confident she feels about her guess. Then she answers the phone by first referring to the caller by name and finds out whether she has guessed correctly or not.

By September of 2002, Sheldrake had conducted 854 tests of this kind with 65 different subjects with an overall success rate of 42%, whereas if there were no telepathy involved, the average success rate of the subjects' guesses ought to have been only 25%.[19] This is very statistically significant, amounting to odds against chance of 1026 to 15. Women, in general, had a considerably higher success rate than men.[20] (One familiar with para-psychological research will know that this may hold true of psi ability in

---

16   Ibid., pp. 98–99.

17   Ibid., pp. 103–105.

18   Ibid., p. 102.

19   Ibid., p. 104.

20   Ibid., p. 101.

general.) The most successful of the test subjects had a personal average of around 48% in 130 tests, with the odds against chance being more than 100 million to 1.[21] She had a 75% success rate when the caller was her closest friend. In fact, the emotional bond between callers seems to render distance negligible. Callers who are as far away from one another as antipodes of the Earth can have a higher hit rate with family members that they have left back at home while traveling than they have with persons in the foreign locale where they are staying.[22]

Every form of telepathy seems to occur most frequently between people who are closely bonded.[23] One particularly striking example of this are cases where one of two lovers is struck with vivid images and feelings such as panic, loneliness, and despair, when their partner or spouse is engaging in acts of infidelity. Sometimes the person experiencing the betrayal will even know where and just when their lover was having sex with someone else.[24] Cases of this kind are so striking because information appears to be extracted from one mind by another when the former is actively trying to conceal it rather than to convey it.[25] Such experiences also seem to involve what parapsychologists call direct mental interactions with living systems (DMILS) that can be measured by placing electrodes on the fingers of a subject to gauge their skin resistance, which is affected by an emotionally conditioned physiological response such as perspiration.[26] In other words, people can be emotionally and physiologically affected by the thoughts or intentions of others without even being consciously aware of what these are.[27] Two closely related exceptions to the rule that telepathy is strongest between emotionally bonded people exacerbate the ethical concerns that this situation raises with respect to the privacy of one's thoughts and the

---

21   Ibid., p. 104.

22   Ibid., p. 105.

23   Ibid., pp. 28, 101.

24   Ibid., p. 92.

25   Ibid., pp. 92–93.

26   Ibid., p. 53.

27   Ibid.

integrity of one's personal intentions. Psychotherapists and hypnotists can build bonds with clients that are more conducive to telepathy than the bonds that these clients enjoy with their friends, family, and lovers.

Sigmund Freud was already aware that what he referred to clinically as the danger of transference and countertransference is not limited to ordinary emotional entanglement between the therapist and the client, but is a process that can involve "thought transference" and dream telepathy.[28] This remains one of the "dirty secrets" of the practice of Freudian psychoanalysis, and is even more prevalent in Jungian psychotherapy on account of Carl Jung's open admission and embrace of such a rapport between the analyst and the client.[29] Robert Stoller and Elizabeth Mayer are two psychoanalysts who have spoken of their own experiences of this kind, and have become advocates of admitting how common these are in the practice of psychotherapy.

Ever since Franz Anton Mesmer began to formalize his understanding of what had been called "animal magnetism" into the practice of "mesmerism," or clinical hypnosis, in the early 1800s, doctors have noted that mesmerized or hypnotized patients could develop a sympathetic "rapport" or "community of sensation" with them.[30] In the early days of hypnotism, when it was being used to control pain during surgical operations, doctors such as James Esdaile noted that their patients could be made to taste anything that they were eating or drinking while the patient was hypnotized. Alfred Russell Wallace, who advanced the theory of evolution together with Charles Darwin, carried out experiments testing this, which also demonstrated that pains induced in the doctor could be suddenly conveyed to the same part of the body in the hypnotized patient.[31] The patients could feel the subtlest sensations, such as a hair tickling the forehead of the hypnotist, and they were capable of answering questions in

---

28　Ibid., pp. 35–36.

29　Ibid., p. 37.

30　Ibid., pp. 41–42.

31　Ibid., p. 42.

foreign languages that they had never learned but which were known by the hypnotist.[32] Most significantly, some hypnotized patients appeared to gain access to the secret thoughts of those putting them into the trance.[33] Finally, some of the early masters of mesmerism claimed to be able to hypnotize people at a distance to similar effect, except that a person who was, say, being put to sleep from half a mile away would awaken again the moment the hypnotists' attention wavered.[34] The subject of such telepathic hypnosis would, for example, describe the sensation of a hand pressed on her forehead as the hypnotist stretched his hand out toward her house and brought his "will sharply to bear" upon eliciting some state in her, such as pain relief.[35] One could, conversely, will someone to be in pain, and, as the DMILS studies suggest, this psychic impression can have physiological effects.

This is exactly what the United States government trained certain of its operatives in a special psychic intelligence unit to do, at least according to numerous insider accounts, including that of Lyn Buchanan — who taught most of the military officers in the program to cultivate a variety of psychic abilities with intelligence applications. During Operation Desert Storm, Buchanan was tasked with accessing the mind of Saddam Hussein and making him ill. As Buchanan recounts, he was initially ordered to kill Hussein, but refused and offered to make him sick instead; unfortunately, he also made himself very sick in the process.[36] He discovered that although you "can actually access that person mentally and bring back their most deep-seated thoughts, feelings, emotions, motivations, fears, desires, drives, reservations, and everything else that might be there to drive their actions," this process requires the operative to "begin feeling the target person's feelings and actually thinking the target person's thoughts" until his "way of thinking actually becomes your way of thinking," so that even

---

32   Ibid., p. 43.

33   Ibid.

34   Ibid.

35   Ibid.

36   Lyn Buchanan, *The Seventh Sense* (New York: Simon & Schuster, 2003), p. 56.

after the session is over, "you are left with some remnants of that target person's emotions, thoughts, aspirations, attitudes, and morals."[37] Part of Buchanan's training regimen for the military officers in the program, which he describes as a "mental martial art," was to teach them meditative techniques for becoming more self-aware, introspective, and mentally disciplined so as to guard against psychical contamination of this kind.

The program into which Buchanan was recruited, and for which he eventually became the key instructor, began at the SRI in the early 1970s, where laser physicists Russell Targ and Harold Puthoff conducted experiments aimed at the development of a trainable, technical protocol for clairvoyance referred to as "Remote Viewing."[38] In a remote viewing trial, the viewer and the person sent to the target site would be isolated from one another. The person traveling to the target would take ten envelopes containing potential sites and would not select one of them until after half an hour of driving. Furthermore, the selection of which of the ten envelopes was to be opened would be determined, not by him, but by a portable random number generator. The viewer, who would have 15 minutes to sketch and verbally describe the site, would begin doing so 10 minutes after the person going out into the field had left, meaning that her "viewing" session would be complete at least 5 minutes before the outbound researcher would consult the random number generator and select the target from out of the corresponding envelope. Once there, the field agent would spend 15 minutes wandering around the target site. A panel of three judges, scientists at SRI who were not otherwise associated with the project, would be tasked with matching the raw data obtained from the remote viewer with the contents of one of the ten target envelopes. The precognitive remote viewing trials were repeatedly successful, with identifications made independently by the three judges, with odds against chance of better than 20:1.

---

37   Ibid., pp. 131–132.

38   Russell Targ and Harold E. Puthoff, *Mind Reach: Scientists Look at Psychic Abilities* (Hampton, Virginia: Hampton Roads Publishing Company, 2005).

Highly competent clairvoyants, or "remote viewers," would be able to invisibly observe anyone, anywhere, doing anything. This ability could be used to spy on ordinary people in their bedrooms at night, or it could be used to uncover the most classified state secrets of any government. If various hostile governments were to fully develop and extensively adopt remote viewing techniques, or if terrorist groups or non-governmental entities opposed to state secrecy were to do so, the security of any nation would be effectively nullified along with the viability of the nation-state as we know it. Therefore, it should be obvious why the most advanced work in remote viewing has been classified.

As results of high caliber were obtained across the remote viewing program, the US military and intelligence interests that were funding the work at SRI took over the whole project, and it passed from an experimental stage (in the 1970s) into an operational phase (in the 1980s). It changed hands between the Department of Defense (who renamed it project "Grill Flame") and the Central Intelligence Agency (project "Star Gate"), until it was disbanded and its existence was admitted publicly in congressional hearings in 1993. It is during the military-intelligence application of remote viewing that the true breadth and significance of the abilities discovered at SRI were explored.[39]

This was largely the outcome of two difficulties encountered in the attempt to produce valuable intelligence on a target site *in the present*. First, it was often the case that a viewer would slide around in time at a given site, locking in, if at all, on that site during the period in its history when the most dramatic events were taking place. Second, when viewers were really fascinated by something at a target site, the connection of their consciousness to the persons querying them at the project facility became increasingly remote. On numerous occasions, a total breakdown of communication occurred as a consequence of the remote viewer actually coming to *be there* at the site, instead of "remotely *viewing*" it in a detached enough manner as to be able to report his findings. Such Out-of-Body

---

39 Buchanan, *The Seventh Sense*.

Experiences (OBE), to both future and past times/places, were named "bi-location": those present there/*then* could "see" the remote viewer as an apparition. [40]

The Princeton Engineering Anomalies Research (PEAR) program at Princeton University replicated the remote perception studies carried out at the Stanford Research Institute, and were then implemented operationally by the US government's remote viewers. In February 2007, the PEAR program completed 28 years of experimental studies concerning "the role of consciousness in the establishment of physical reality." The program was headed by Dr. Robert Jahn, Dean Emeritus of Princeton's School of Engineering and Applied Sciences. Jahn and his collaborator summarized their initial findings and drew some tentative conclusions in their book *Margins of Reality: The Role of Consciousness in the Physical World*.[41] A briefer but more updated account is presented in their article "The PEAR Proposition" for the *Journal of Scientific Exploration*.[42]

The "Precognition Remote Perception" (PRP) experiments at Princeton involved a percipient and an agent, between whom there would be no communication for the duration of the experiment. Each of the two participants would be given a 30-item descriptor sheet, wherein they had to choose to describe a given target site as indoors / outdoors, dark / light, artificial / natural, inhabited by / vacant of humans or animals, loud / quiet, and so forth. They would preface this checklist with a brief written summary of the site. The PRP researchers used both instructional and volitional methods. In the *instructional* method, a Random Event Generator would select a given site from a computer database. The site's location would be given to the agent in a sealed envelope not to be opened until he left the laboratory. In the *volitional* method the agent would leave

---

40   David Morehouse, *Psychic Warrior* (New York: St. Martin's Press, 1996).

41   Robert Jahn and Brenda J. Dunne, *Margins of Reality: The Role of Consciousness in the Physical World* (New York: Harcourt, 1987).

42   Robert Jahn & Brenda J. Dunne, "The PEAR Proposition," *Journal of Scientific Exploration*, Vol. 19, No.2, 2005.

the laboratory to select a site by his own whim, without anyone being informed beforehand of where he would choose to go.

The reason why the PRP researchers added the word "precognition" to what were supposed to be experiments merely testing "remote perception" is that they found that, in a majority of cases, the percipient was able to describe the site well *before* the agent arrived there, and in some instances even before a given site had been chosen. The 30-item descriptor lists filled out by the two participants allowed for a statistical determination of whether, and to what degree, any given trial was a success. By 1987, 125 trials had been conducted in the instructional mode and 209 in the volitional mode. The meta-analysis of these 334 trials spoke in favor of the participants' ability to successfully engage in "precognition remote perception" with odds against chance of *a billion to one* in the instructional trials and 100,000 to 1 in the volitional trials.[43]

As I noted above, the remote viewers of the United States government also had an operational capability to look into future events. The economic implications of this are devastating. Corporations would be utterly incapable of protecting patents on products that they had not yet even invented, and so intellectual property laws that competitively drive innovation would be unenforceable. Although clairvoyance is notoriously limited when it comes to discerning numbers, precognition could be used to more generally ascertain which corporations would collapse or experience sudden growth in the future. Speculative insider stock trading based on this kind of information would wreak havoc on the market. A number of the remote viewers who worked in the defunct Central Intelligence Agency and Department of Defense programs have recently established private enterprises essentially offering corporate espionage services to Fortune 500 companies, but since psi continues to be widely dismissed, those offering and utilizing these services are still too insignificant to affect the economy at large. There are also more personally disturbing implications of precognitive abilities being effectively developed beyond the

---

43   Jahn and Dunne, *Margins of Reality*, pp. 104–105.

occasional dream in which future events are seen through a glass darkly. If individuals were able to look into their future fairly clearly and reliably, either on their own or by contracting with someone competent to do so, they would be able to behold all of the significant events to come — their great successes, the terrible tragedies that may befall them, the circumstances of their own deaths, and those of the people dearest to them. They might resign themselves to fatalism, which ironically prevents them from doing what they would have otherwise, or they might engage in desperate, highly erratic attempts to revise the timeline of their lives.

If only this altered attitude toward the future could be limited to their own lives, or the lives of their friends and relatives. What if an individual has seen that a certain politician running for offices of ever greater authority will go on to be the next genocidal world leader — is he justified in assassinating that person to save the lives of innumerable innocents who will someday be the victims of this tyrant? Leaving mass murderers aside, what of every common criminal whose misdeeds could be foreseen in advance? For decades, police departments have used psychics to track missing children and ascertain the whereabouts of perpetrators of unsolved crimes. Pat Price, one of the best remote viewers in the US government program, began by doing such work.[44] If abilities of this kind are further refined and rendered more reliable, would we have the right to use them to arrest a violent criminal before he commits his crime? What kind of horrifying police state would that lead to? Yet this pales in comparison to concerns about psychokinesis.

PEAR also amassed impressive evidence for psychokinesis. PEAR's psychokinesis experiments were initially based upon an improved version of a Random Number Generator (RNG), or "electronic coin flipper," which had been designed for similar experiments by the physicist Helmut Schmidt in the 1960s. Jahn's Random Event Generator (REG) employs a circuit which utilizes a quantum process, such as the radioactive decay rate of the nuclei of a small amount of an isotope such as Strontium

---

44   Targ and Puthoff, *Mind Reach*, pp. 10, 46–68.

90, which is amplified to provide truly random electronic spikes a few thousand times per second. The spike interrupts a clock or counter that is crystal controlled for precision, and counting at around 10 million cycles per second in oscillation between the random bits "1" and "0." The REG is wired to a computer that automates data collecting by recording whether the spike occurs when the clock is at "1" or "0," so that the data can then be statistically analyzed for an inordinate occurrence of either under the influence of the participant, compared against the random output of the REGs. These were set to generate 100 bits within a predetermined span of time, 50 of which would be 1, and 50 of which would be 0, on average. Furthermore, Jahn encased the device in a shielding that eliminated the effects of heat, seismic vibration, sounds, and electromagnetic waves, and designed it such that a fail-safe alarm would sound if the energetic insulation of the device were to be compromised by any physically known forces or fields.

The REGs were hooked up to computer monitors that allowed participants to view their digital output (so as to give them some sense of feedback in their attempts to deviate it from standard). The viewer would see a graph with two axes, a vertical axis counting "bits" and a horizontal axis for "trials." Participants would be asked to perform one of three tasks: 1) will the REG to produce *more* bits of 1 or 0 than it would randomly (for example, 52 1s vs. 48 0s, or 43 1s vs. 57 0s); 2) focus their minds on influencing the output of the REG toward *lower* values than the baseline; or 3) try not to influence the REG output, so as to maintain a baseline distribution. The intention would be logged into the computer at the outset of each run, including many micro "trials." The random output would appear as a line erratically crossing the graph between the upper and lower limits of a horizontally oriented parabola that represents the maximum limits of variation within chance (with the baseline in the middle of the parabola). As the composite line is formed by the REG data, the participant tries to get it to either rise up out of the upper limit of the parabola, sink down below its lower limit, or remain within its bounds. Jahn also developed a Random Mechanical Cascade machine that dropped 9000 polystyrene balls down a latticework of pegs, which participants would be asked to mentally affect in such a way that more balls fall to the right or left than they would randomly. In both cases the machines were routinely run with no participant engaging them, as control tests.

Most interestingly, time and distance did not seem to be a relevant factor. A participant in Hong Kong could receive a call from Princeton saying that a trial would be run at 3 PM Princeton time. The participant would then hang up and call back at some time after 3 PM to report, without knowing the results of the trial, that he attempted to influence the machine with such and such intention at 10 AM Princeton time or at 6 PM Princeton time. The PEAR lab would only then inform the participant that his earlier or later intention successfully affected the outcome of the 3 PM trial, deviating it significantly from chance. Of course, this does *not* work if the participant is told the outcome of the 3 PM trial at, say, 3:30 PM, and then tries to influence that outcome at 6 PM.

The REGs were routinely run with no participant attempting to affect them, as control tests. Participants were not subject to any psychological tests, relaxation protocols, or trained in techniques of any kind. In order to address the issue of performer fraud, Jahn ultimately ran millions of trials with over a hundred individuals. The data was then parsed using statistical meta-analysis, so that the trials were not a test of the ability of any one participant, but of a human capability in general. This analysis arrived at odds against chance of a "few parts in ten thousand" in each individual trial of mind-machine interaction, and "less than one part in a trillion" for the composite anomaly represented by the entire database.[45] The deviations from mean, while small in any given trial, compound to being very statistically significant over millions of trials.

There is, however, much more qualitatively impressive evidence for psychokinesis. Professor Stephen E. Braude, who served as chair of the

---

45   Robert Jahn & Brenda J. Dunne, "Science of the Subjective," *Journal of Scientific Exploration*, Vol. 11, No. 2, 1997, p. 209.

Department of Philosophy at the University of Maryland at Baltimore, is a practicing parapsychologist engaged in field research and the Editor-in-Chief of the journal of the *Society for Scientific Exploration*. Braude has carried out a detailed analysis of evidence for what is called "macro-PK," most notably in his book *The Limits of Influence: Psychokinesis and the Philosophy of Science*. Presently, I will focus on the most dramatic cases studied by Braude, those of the mid- to late nineteenth century "physical mediums," or individuals with allegedly dramatic psychokinetic phenomena manifesting amidst their séances. One of the arguments made by those who would like to dismiss macro-PK displayed by nineteenth-century mediums is that the technology of the time was not sophisticated enough to detect the frauds being perpetrated by them. Braude points out that this criticism is a double-edged sword for skeptics, because it highlights the fact that the technology of the time — long before miniaturized electronics or remote control devices — was far too primitive to allow well-observed mediums to fake many of their most impressive phenomena.[46]

Braude thinks that the demand for quantitatively assessable repeatability that is being aimed at in "micro-PK" trials with RNGs is misguided.[47] He reminds us that all psychic abilities, including psychokinesis, are *abilities* — and like sports abilities or the skill of an improvisational musician or dancer, their performance on any given occasion will not only reflect the performer's training, but will vary significantly depending on the personal talent and psychological state of the performer in the context of environmental factors — including the attitude or mood of the others present.[48] Given the lack of standard training protocols for psychic functioning, such contingent behavioral factors should be expected to play an even greater role than in sports, music, dance, or other performing arts. The skeptical demand for mechanical repeatability is ludicrously unscientific in such cases.

---

46   Stephen E. Braude, *The Limits of Influence: Psychokinesis and the Philosophy of Science* (Lanham, Massachusetts: University Press of America, 1997), p. 55.

47   Ibid., pp. 58–59.

48   Ibid., p. 62.

I would add that those who make such a demand ought to remember Aristotle's admonition that different fields of inquiry admit of different methods of investigation and degrees of precision in knowledge concerning the subject matter in question. There are things in Nature that can only be carefully observed as they show themselves, and not everything in Nature is a *thing*. Virtuoso performers are not machines; they have bad days and, in many cases, mercurially moody temperaments. Furthermore, virtuosi have very specific talents. The same is true of most adept psychics. It is unreasonable to expect someone who is an adept telepath to perform any kind of psychokinesis, or for someone who levitates tables or materializes objects in séances to also be able to heal the sick.[49] A few are very versatile, but this is like finding a superstar baseball player who is also an Olympic-class gymnast.

Daniel Dunglas Home (1833–1886) was such a man. Born in Edinburgh, D. D. Home moved to the northeastern United States, and then returned to Great Britain where he became famous for his power as a supposed medium.[50] Home's renown spread throughout Europe, ultimately drawing Napoleon III, the German Emperor, the Queen of Holland, and numerous members of the Russian royal court into the fold of his admirers and acquaintances.[51] It should be noted that his séances were held at a variety of locations that he had never previously had a chance to visit, and many of them were arranged on the spur of the moment. A number of august academics and scientists attended these séances to investigate whether fraud played any part in Home's performances. During the entire 25 years of his mediumship, Home's detractors and impartial investigators attending his séances did not manage to expose a single case of trickery.[52] In some cases, up to ten investigators were present at a sitting.[53]

---

49   Ibid.
50   Ibid., pp. 65–66.
51   Ibid., p. 64.
52   Ibid., p. 65.
53   Ibid., p. 69.

Furthermore, among the many eyewitness accounts and sworn affidavits signed by those in attendance and attesting to the veracity of Home's wondrous powers are the investigative reports of one of the most brilliant and accomplished scientific minds of the modern age: William Crookes. The discoverer of thallium and the inventor of the radiometer, as well as a form of the cathode ray tube that was named in his honor, Crookes was elected a Fellow of the Royal Society at the age of 31 and became its president in 1913. Shortly thereafter he assumed editorship of the prestigious *Quarterly Journal of Science*, the venue in which some of his earliest articles on mediumship were published.[54] Crookes was a skeptic, not a spiritualist, but an honest skeptic rather than a debunker of the kind that he accused other so-called "scientists" of being with respect to psychic phenomena. In studying Home and other mediums, Crookes set out to expose trickery and dispel the delusions of the honest, but he warned against the fallacy of circular reasoning epitomized by Faraday's embarrassingly idiotic remark that, '[b]efore we proceed to consider any question involving physical principles, we should set out with clear ideas of the naturally possible and impossible."[55] He lamented the fact that although Home had constantly asked for scientists to come and investigate his séances during his years-long stay at London, few others had accepted his invitation, and this despite Crookes' own urging of his colleagues to do so.[56]

Crookes, for his part, personally bore witness to all of the most extreme forms of psychokinesis that manifested during Home's mediumistic exercises. We are not just talking about raps and other strange sounds, odd luminescent manifestations, table tilting, ethereal touches, tugs, and pinches, elongations of the medium's body, odors without an apparent source, or even the earthquake-like effects that would rock the whole

---

54 Ibid., p. 75.

55 Ibid., pp. 75–76.

56 Ibid., p. 78.

room and set its contents trembling.[57] Crookes witnessed not only these spooky phenomena, but also feats that we could not fraudulently replicate with any technology known today, let alone in the nineteenth century.[58] He was among the many others who saw Home conjure up ectoplasmic hands that ended at the wrist, or arms that ended at the elbow, that moved objects about the room, and that would sometimes feel warm and soft to the touch of participants, only to slowly dissolve in their grasp.[59] It was possible to poke holes right through these hands, but the ectoplasm would then quickly coagulate around the puncture and close up, leaving behind a scar.[60]

Crookes saw Home glide an accordion and other heavy objects in the séance room across thin air, and on one occasion he was present as Home himself levitated up to six inches above the ground and remained suspended there for about ten seconds before slowly descending.[61] When we take such feats, which would allow one to "walk on water," together with the fact that Home could handle red-hot coals without being burned and confer this incombustibility and invulnerability upon others who had faith in him,[62] so that he went about New England performing seemingly miraculous healings with his psychokinetic abilities,[63] we are left to wonder in what way his superpowers come up short as compared not only to those of Indian yogis, but even to those of Jesus of Nazareth.

These powers continued to manifest despite measures devised, tested, and implemented by Crookes to rule out fraud. One of these countermeasures consisted of a wooden accordion cage, wound with insulated copper wire, netted together with string, and at one point electrified.[64]

---

57   Ibid., p. 66.
58   Ibid., p. 80.
59   Ibid., pp. 66, 80.
60   Ibid., p. 92.
61   Ibid., pp. 86–87.
62   Ibid., p. 74.
63   Ibid., p. 64.
64   Ibid., p. 81.

This cage allowed home to place one of his hands on top of the accordion under the séance table (while the other was atop the table), at the end some distance away from its keys, as was his custom, but did not afford him the space to reach down into the cage so as to manipulate the accordion in any way — whether with his hand or his boots.[65] Crookes and others observed the accordion floating inside its cage and playing a plaintive melody of its own accord, even after Home had removed his hand from where it was resting at the top of the instrument and placed it together with his other hand upon the séance table.[66]

Another countermeasure crafted by Crookes was a tripod contraption rigged with a spring balance set to measure the weight of a mahogany board extending horizontally towards it, with its other end resting on a table.[67] Prior to his experiment, the board weighed 3.5 pounds. Crookes applied the full weight of his body to this board and, while jerking it up and down, could only increase its weight by 2 pounds at most, whereas Home, while seated and remaining still at the table, and touching the end of the board resting on the table with nothing more than his fingertips, could cause the spring balance to register that the board had increased in weight to 9 pounds.[68] It is also noteworthy that when Home increased the weight of the board by touching it, just as it sank at the end on the balance it rose on his end, with the point where it intersected the table edge — about 1.5 inches from Homes' end — acting as a fulcrum.[69] In other words, Home did not appear to be applying any known form of physical pressure on the board, or at least, not sufficient pressure to counterbalance the psychokinetic "force" in the opposite direction.

The social atmosphere in which mediumistic psychokinesis flourished should not be counted against it. Rather, as Braude argues, given what we know about how inhibitions and apprehensions affect psychic func-

---

65   Ibid.
66   Ibid., p. 83.
67   Ibid., p. 84.
68   Ibid., pp. 84–85.
69   Ibid., p. 85.

tioning, the widespread belief of those involved at the time that departed spirits were the cause of the phenomena, rather than the medium or those involved in a séance, would have greatly enhanced these manifestations. It would have disburdened the medium and those involved with him or her of their fear of unwittingly being the source of any possibly dangerous physical effects that might arise from out of their unconscious during the session. The spiritualist belief system would also have allowed those participating in mediumistic exercises to eschew potentially crippling performance anxiety, since occasional failures could be attributed to the unwillingness of those "on the other side" to communicate rather than to the inability of the medium to perform.[70] The absolute faith in a spirit world on the part of the best mediums also goes some way in answering another common objection to evidence of this kind, namely that if mediums had such extensive psychokinetic abilities they would have used them for private gain — for example, in gambling or acts of outright theft. Most of the mediums that could have done so would have conceived of this in terms of enlisting the aid of dearly departed souls in a spirit world to amass worldly riches by dishonest means, something quite ethically repugnant within the context of the same belief system that afforded them the psychological focus to perform so powerfully.[71]

In a February 2011 presentation at the University of Maryland at Baltimore, Stephen Braude pithily summarized this terrifying insight which he had arrived at through his in-depth study of "macro-PK" abilities such as those of D. D. Home:

> The evidence for psychic functioning and for psychokinesis opens up a monstrous pandora's box of opportunities for things. One of the reasons... [for] the resistance that people feel to psychic functioning... [are] the spiritual implications of it... There is another thing that is even more intimidating for a lot of people, and it's one of the reasons I think I and others who take this stuff seriously have experienced such hostility. Think about it this way: If I can move, say, a matchstick a millimeter by thought alone, it's a very small step conceptu-

70 Ibid., pp. 57-58.
71 Ibid., p. 60.

ally from doing that to making somebody drop dead by thought alone. So the existence of any PK at all forces us to take seriously, I think, a kind of magical worldview that most of us associate, usually condescendingly, only with so-called primitive cultures. It's a worldview where thoughts can kill or have other sorts of unwelcome consequences and it's a worldview where you might have to take seriously things like hexing or the evil eye, and in which we might have to take responsibility, in principle, for a whole range of things most of us would just as soon be bystanders for... if it can be linked with human intent, especially unconscious intent...[72]

The concerns voiced by Braude are well-founded. The Soviet Union had a small program dedicated to the "remote influencing" of targeted individuals in order to make them very ill or worse, and I have cited Lyn Buchanan to the effect that the US briefly flirted with reciprocating by tasking some of its psychic spies to do the same.[73] There were also successful attempts made to plant foreign suggestions in the minds of targets in order to elicit behavior that would be self-destructive. Some adepts of psychokinesis are able to, often inadvertently, start fires by affecting electronic appliances or their power outlets.[74]

So-called "poltergeist" phenomena have been interpreted by some parapsychologists as large-scale manifestations by individuals unaware of their own psychokinetic abilities, on a par with the more deliberate table tipping and remote manipulation of objects by a few of the genuine nineteenth-century parlor mediums whose performances were subjected to rigorous scientific controls.[75] It is possible that a corporate organization would train a cadre of operatives highly skilled in psychokinesis for the purposes of murderous private gain. If psychokinesis were to receive

---

72   Stephen E. Braude, lecture on "The Photographs of Ted Serios" delivered at the Albin O. Kuhn Library Gallery at the University of Maryland, Baltimore on February 3, 2011.

73   Buchanan, *The Seventh Sense*, pp. 28–29. See also: Sheila Ostrander and Lynn Schroeder, *Psychic Discoveries Behind the Iron Curtain* (New York: Marlowe and Company, 1997).

74   Braude, *The Limits of Influence*, pp. 201–202.

75   Braude, *The Limits of Influence*, pp. 63–93.

mainstream scientific validation, some more contemporary variation on "the devil made me do it" might have to be accepted as a defense plea in a court of law.

Few parapsychologists today consider mediumship, including the poltergeist phenomena of physical mediumship, to actually constitute evidence for the survival of a deceased personality. Rather, it is understood as a manifestation of the unconscious psychokinetic ability on the part of the medium in tandem with the psychical projection, or telepathic transference, of the memories, hopes, desires, and fears of séance participants. However, one striking example of extrasensory perception and psychokinesis that does constitute evidence for the postmortem survival of personality is reincarnation. Dr. Ian Stevenson, who chaired the Department of Psychiatry at the University of Virginia and was the Director of the Personality Studies program there, has done the best empirical research on phenomena suggestive of reincarnation. Stevenson's focus on birthmarks and birth defects as evidence suggestive of reincarnation is what makes his work uniquely convincing. If research into a child's spontaneous statements about a past life is found to correspond to the life of an actual deceased person, the postmortem report of wounds or handicaps suffered by that person can be compared to the birthmarks or birth defects of the given child in terms of size, shape, and location. Apparently wounds or mutilations suffered by a person, or the psychical internalization of such trauma in terms of one's self image, can psychokinetically affect fetal development of that person's subsequent incarnation. This correspondence provides a kind of empirical evidence that can corroborate the testimony of family members or close friends of the deceased personality regarding the accuracy of a child's statements concerning the life of a deceased personality.[76]

Stevenson observed strict discipline in regard to collecting and reporting such testimonies. He carefully investigated whether the present

---

76   Ian Stevenson, *Where Reincarnation and Biology Intersect* (London: Praeger, 1997), p. 2.

family of a child could have known or interacted with members of the family of the alleged previous personality.[77] In the best cases, there was no contact between the child's present family and anyone who knew the child's previous incarnation until after the child repeatedly made statements whose investigation led to their discovery. In such cases, a child will incessantly make statements about a previous life, or insist on being taken to the place where the child believes that life to have transpired. In some of the cases, a child will actually demand to be taken to the next town over, or to another quarter of a large city, where the child will lead his or her present family members to his or her previous home, sometimes enthusiastically embracing former relatives who happen to be outside. It is only at this point that the two families meet, and there is an opportunity for the child in question to reveal private information about the deceased person that can be verified by that person's family. Sometimes, once inside the home, a child will correctly identify objects or articles belonging to the previous personality and narrate stories concerning the objects, which family members of the deceased person can verify. In other cases, questioning of the locals in an area corresponding to a child's description will more indirectly lead to a suspected identity of a past incarnation, whose postmortem records are then checked for correspondences to birthmarks or birth defects on the child.

Stevenson believed that this biologically-oriented research into reincarnation would also shed light on why people who have birth defects have them in a particular location, and why (otherwise) identical twins sometimes do not share birthmarks or birth defects.[78] Stevenson noted that while birth defects have been attributed to several causes, such as genetic factors, viral infections, and chemicals (thalidomide and alcohol), these account for less than half of all birth defects.[79] Small areas of increased pigmentation called "moles," and referred to by physicians as nevi,

---

77   Ibid.
78   Ibid.
79   Ibid., p. 3.

are common. However, most of the "birthmarks" that Stevenson observed on his subjects are of a different kind. He describes them as "hairless areas of puckered, scarlike tissue, often raised above surrounding tissues or depressed below them; a few are areas of decreased pigmentation".[80] In other words, these marks are like very minor birth defects (of the skin), and are thus on more of a continuum with the significant birth defects studied than with common moles. Stevenson was careful to note these marks as possible evidence only when family members attested to their presence from birth, and only if the marks could be clearly distinguished from insect bites, cuts, abrasions, and so forth.[81] The convergence of physical and testimonial correlations also allowed Stevenson to rule out several types of paranormal phenomena other than reincarnation, whereas verified testimony alone might only allow one to conclude that *some kind* of paranormal phenomenon (ESP by the child, PK by the child's mother, or possession) was responsible for the observed evidence.[82]

In addition to evidence of narrative memories of previous lives, Stevenson also found that his subjects usually had strong "behavior memories" that correlated with a previous personality.[83] Often, these would be acted out during a child's playtime. A child who claimed to have been a teacher in a previous life might be fixated on assembling her playmates together as her pupils and play at "instructing" them in something in front of an imaginary blackboard. A child with memories of being a car mechanic might spend hours laying under the family sofa, "repairing it" as if it were a car. This type of play might sometimes be so sophisticated as to involve knowledge of a skill that a child has not yet been taught. One child, who recollected suicide by hanging, would walk about with a piece of rope tied around his neck. Desires for a specific type of food that is not eaten by his or her present family, or for clothing customarily

---

80   Ibid.

81   Ibid., p. 5.

82   Ibid., p. 11.

83   Ibid., p. 8.

different from that worn by his or her present family, also occurs.[84] Most interesting is a child's craving for alcohol or tobacco, even when no immediate relatives (including biological parents) have used such substances. The latter often occurs in cases where the previous personality is found to have had an addiction to these substances. Despite subjection to strict controls against being provided with cues from former family members, children who are brought to the home where they spent their former life will be able to identify and use objects or tools belonging to the previous personality.

If the ability to remember previous lives were to become widespread, perhaps through a mainstream scientific acceptance of reincarnation and a commensurately more extensive offering of more reliable past life hypnotic regression services than those dubious ones currently available, we would face a whole host of very serious social problems, and some legal ones as well. Sex changes between lifetimes are commonplace. There are cases wherein one of two lovers who dies long before the other one returns as that person's son or daughter, or conversely, cases where one of two siblings who are very close to one another die while the other is young enough to go on to marry the reincarnation of that sibling, and there are cases where a person's parent is reincarnated as her child or grandchild. Moreover, cases of this kind are not freakish occurrences. Ian Stevenson noted that they actually constitute a substantial percentage of those that he found.[85] On further reflection the fact that people are inclined, evidently by emotional attachments deeper than their public morals, to reincarnate as family members of those with whom they have had intimate relations, ought to be unsurprising. Still, these transmigrations of the soul threaten deeply-held beliefs about proper social roles and relations. They call into question the nature of parental authority, complicate gender identity and sexual orientation, and even violate the incest taboo.

---

84   Ibid., p. 7.

85   Ian Stevenson, *Reincarnation and Biology*, 2 Vols. (London: Praeger, 1997).

The challenge is not only psychological or moral; reincarnation poses a serious problem for our legal system. What if a parent who loses his child and then successfully identifies his or her reincarnation — who also recognizes and loves the former parent — places a legal claim for at least joint custody of the child? How could the current parents of the child justly deny that claim, especially if evidence from competent psychiatrists and so forth were to be presented in a court of law? What if a widowed woman were to be approached by an adolescent boy who could prove that he was the reincarnation of her dearly departed husband? How could their consensual relationship be considered a prosecutable case of "statutory rape," and even if it were not prosecuted, what would its effects be on the friends and family of the two parties involved?

More trying cases are imaginable, ones that would strain our system of crime and punishment to the breaking point. What if the reincarnated victim of a murder were to identify the hitherto undiscovered murderer? Would his evidence be accepted in court? What if the identified murderer were also reincarnated and no longer inhabiting the body he used to commit the murder? Would it be just to track and prosecute criminals for unpunished crimes they have committed in previous lifetimes? Finally, to return to the economic implications of validating the spectral, would the reincarnation of an eminent inventor who could prove his identity beyond a reasonable doubt still hold the rights to his patents? What about an artist's right to royalties on works she produced in her former body? This raises the question of property rights in general.

So-called "postmodern" thinkers have, for the most part, been as unconsciously terrified over opening the floodgates of spectral phenomena as mainstream scientists. While advocates of deconstruction have occasionally engaged in critical examinations of the thought of René Descartes and Immanuel Kant, no one has shown how both of these defining thinkers of the modern age built their rational systems on a terrified suppression of the spectral. This is not simply an epistemological oversight; it has grave ethical implications. As I will show in the next two chapters,

Descartes was effectively an inquisitor in league with the most viciously conservative religious forces of his time, and Kant argued for the suppression of phenomena that he knew to be genuine, and even advocated the institutionalization of those with paranormal abilities on account of his fear that serious study of the "occult" threatened the transcendental sanctity of religious faith.

These men were instrumental in constructing a crippled kind of science that, for all its apparent technical power, was intended to leave everything having to do with "the soul" in the domain of conservative religious faith in the dogmas of Abrahamic revelation. The truce that they negotiated between science and religion ended the burning of witches, but it also forestalled the revolutionary promise of witchcraft and Renaissance alchemy — which could have extricated us from Judeo-Christian Medievalism in a very different way. Instead, they turned the human mind into something less than a ghost and imprisoned it in a machine; no, in a mere cog of celestial clockwork that exorcises it of any creative force. The Reason of the so-called Enlightenment is synonymous with its sadistic Terror. As we shall see, it was crafted as a form of chainmail to armor crusaders for a battle with specters.

CHAPTER III

REASON AND TERROR

Paris, November 10, 1793. In a ransacked Notre Dame Cathedral, whose religious images and statues have been defaced, whose holy scriptures have been removed and publically consigned to flames, a new altar to Liberty is installed over the old altar of the Lord. The Goddess of Reason, as portrayed by a living woman, takes her place atop this elevated platform amidst licentious celebrations by the assembled crowd. The façade of the Medieval cathedral is inscribed with the words "To Philosophy." Centuries of monarchy had been dispensed with in Year I with the guillotining of Louis XVI, and now, millennia of religion would be blotted out in Year II.

In the coming days and weeks, the "lurid" and "depraved" ceremonies at Notre Dame were mandatorily repeated at churches throughout France, many of which were marked with the inscription "Temple of Reason and Philosophy." All crosses and religious statues were removed from graveyards, and many religious monuments were destroyed. Not only were all institutions of religious education shut down, individuals were banned from performing public *and even private* acts of worship. Catholic priests were forced to marry, and those who resisted being defrocked were packed into boats and drowned in the Seine. This cosmic upheaval was the work of the *Cult of Reason* — a group of uncompromising French revolutionaries who were dedicated to realizing the most radical vision of the Enlightenment: *the establishment of a scientific society, wherein religion is not merely tolerated but is supplanted by science.*

The four leading proponents of the Cult of Reason were Antoine-François Mormo, Jacques Hébert, Pierre Gaspard Chaumette, and Joseph

Fouché. Mormo was nicknamed "the first printer of liberty" on account of putting his printing and bookselling trade into the service of the Revolution. It is Mormo who originated the Republican motto *Liberté, Égalité, Fraternité*, and his wife Sophie is the woman who masqueraded as the Goddess of Reason in the anti-Christian festival at Notre Dame. Hébert was a journalist who founded the revolutionary newspaper *Le Père Duchesne*, which was aimed at the *sans culottes* (underclass) with its ribald language, and became the most popular medium advocating uncompromising atheism. Chaumette was a scientist by training, with a focus on botany. He quit science for politics at the outbreak of the Revolution; after serving as the editor for a journal of the Jacobin Club and the chief orator of the Cordelier Club, he went on to be elected President of the Paris Commune. He dropped the "god-given" Catholic name "Pierre-Gaspard" and adopted Anaxagoras, in reference to the rationalistic ancient Greek philosopher. Anaxagoras Chaumette was the principal architect of the Festival of Reason at Notre Dame. It is he who proposed to Mormo that the latter's wife should play the Goddess of Reason. Fouché was the most hands-on of the reason cultists. He actually participated in the ransacking of churches and made a name for himself as "the executioner of Lyons" by massacring counterrevolutionary rebels in that city. Remarking on his responsibility for the execution of nearly 2,000 Frenchmen deemed undeserving of being citizens of the new *secular* Republic, Fouché said: "Terror, salutary terror, is now the order of the day here... We are causing much impure blood to flow, but it is our duty to do so, for humanity's sake." He had the words "death is an eternal sleep" inscribed over the gates of cemeteries.

Ironically, the most violent of the four leaders of the Cult of Reason was the only one to survive the duration of the year and go on to have a career after the Revolution. Fouché was appointed Minister of Police under Napoleon Bonaparte. In March of 1794, within *only four months* of the Festival of Reason, Mormo, Hébert, and Chaumette were all guillotined. They were victims of a reactionary movement against the Cult of Reason, mobilized by the Jacobin leader Maximilien Robespierre. Fearing that the Cult of Reason was overreaching in its attempt to eradicate religion and found an atheistic scientific society, Robespierre wanted to consolidate and preserve the political successes of the Revolution "in the name of God." On June 7, 1794, Robespierre crystallized the reactionary movement that martyred Mormo and the other rationalists into a *Cult of the Supreme Being* that was intended to supplant their Cult of Reason. Robespierre himself was guillotined less than two months after establishing his republican religion. Celebrations that had involved him descending from the top of an artificial mountain, like Moses at Sinai, and rumors spread by a superstitious woman in his close company that he was the messianic herald of the New Dawn, were too much for both traditional Christians and the atheistic rationalists he had persecuted along with them. Robespierre was the only person to be guillotined face up, in a particularly gruesome scene. To prepare his neck, the executioner tore off a bandage holding together a jaw shattered during his stay in prison. This left Robespierre screaming while the blade fell from the tall scaffold.

Within five years, General Napoleon Bonaparte staged his coup d'état against the republican government, declaring: "I *am* the Revolution." In another five years, he went from being First Consul for Life to becoming an outright Emperor who restored monarchy in France and negotiated a settlement with the Church that would establish Catholicism as the official religion of his French Empire. In other words, to make a very long story short, the reactionary Deist movement led by Robespierre not only failed to supplant traditional faith in religious revelation, it destroyed the atheistic rationalists whose uncompromising advocacy of a scientific society might have prevented the demise of the French Revolution in a restoration of the old Catholic political order.

In some ways, Robespierre understood the rationalist revolutionaries better than they understood themselves. Men like Mormo, Hébert, and Chaumette were *philosophes* or public intellectuals, not philosophers. Robespierre was probably familiar with the work of the real early modern materialist philosophers upon which their populist rationalism was loosely based. Foremost among these were Julien Offray de La Mettrie and the Marquis de Sade. The Marquis de Sade lived to see the French Revolution and was an advocate of the Cult of Reason. *Philosophy in the Boudoir* (1795) was written and published at a time when de Sade fell victim to Robespierre's cult of virtue and was locked up in Charenton mental asylum.

De Sade takes direct aim at Robespierre in a long, mock political pamphlet that he inserts between the fifth and sixth chapters of *Philosophy in the Boudoir*, entitled "Yet Another Effort, Frenchmen, If You Would Become Republicans."[1] Here de Sade uses both satire and logic to deconstruct the rationale for laws against theft, sodomy, rape, incest, infanticide, and even murder. The pamphlet shares some arguments in common with socialistic anarchist writings, such as the argument that theft is justified by the inequalities of a society with private property, and that laws against murder are incoherent in light of state-mandated warfare. The text contains, repeatedly, a prescient warning that if theistic religion is not overthrown together with monarchy, superstitious faith in a heavenly tyrant will keep alive the psychology of slavish submission in the populace, who will ultimately be manipulated into accepting the return of monarchy in an even more despotic form. Emperor Napoleon I, who proved him right, had de Sade's books rounded up and burned.

De Sade was no anomaly. Theodor Adorno and Jacques Lacan both view him as the epitome of the Enlightenment rationalism usually associated with Immanuel Kant, but in order to understand why that is the case, we need to know something about La Mettrie and, more importantly, we have to understand the Cartesian paradigm within the context of which his mechanistic materialism took shape. Only then can we see how de Sade is also a Cartesian. In what follows, I present Julien Offray de La Mettrie as the link between Descartes and Sade, who unveils the psychotically sadistic essence of Cartesian metaphysics. As compared to Sade, the

---

1   Marquis de Sade, *Philosophy in the Boudoir* (New York: Penguin Classics, 2006).

rest of the Reason cultists were naïve Cartesians. Robespierre, who had Sade committed, and Napoleon, who ordered his works to be incinerated, were both aware of this fact, which no doubt motivated their resistance to the rising Cult of Reason.

René Descartes laid the foundation of the modern scientific paradigm. In Descartes' ontology there are two substances: *res cogitans* and *res extensa*, or mind and body. Descartes first develops the conception of *res extensa*, or spatially extended thing-hood in the famous section on the melting wax in the *Meditations on First Philosophy*. In the Second Meditation,[2] Descartes notes that a piece of wax, which has one set of phenomenal *qualities* when it is cool and hard, radically changes its shape, texture, color, and even smell, when it is melted by a hot flame. What remains the same in this transformation of the thing, namely its *extensional* quantities of size, shape and motion, confers upon it its *res*, its reality, and becomes the *sub-stance* of the thing for Descartes. In things, that which enduringly remains, and consequently is *real* — namely the Being of beings — can only be accessed through mathematics. The spatiality of the world thus becomes an undifferentiated geometrical extension that ultimately disregards the phenomenal qualities of differentiated things.

Mind is, in turn, defined against this *res extensa*, as that which has absolutely no extension whatsoever, and which cannot be divided up or broken down — i.e., *res cogitans* — an extensionless "thinking thing," a *theoretical* observer of an extended, conquerable, natural world *substantially* distinct from it. Descartes explicitly states that by "thinking" (*cogitare*) having thoughts is not all that he means. Rather, cogitation in the most general sense is the primary attribute of the mind as such, and intuition, memory, imagination, and even sense perception are all modes of it. This is so because I can exist though I am not using any given one of these modes, but I cannot exist if I am not using at least one of them. Therefore, the modes inhere in what Descartes will call "thought" as such, which is

---

2   John Cottingham [Editor], *Descartes: Selected Philosophical Writings* (New York: Cambridge University Press, 1999), AT 30–32.

the defining quality of mind.[3] So just as extension is the primary attribute of body, and extension's modes are shape, size, and motion, thought is the primary attribute of mind, and thought's modes are intuition, volition, sensation, imagination, and recollection. According to this schematic, Descartes prohibits thought from being a mode of extension, or extension from being a mode of thought, *because* each substance is defined by only one primary attribute.[4] Descartes claims that a given substance is nothing more than its defining primary attribute.[5]

In his *Discourse on the Method*, Descartes treats the bodies of animals, including apes, as no more than sophisticated machines whose function is analogous to that of a wind-up clock and whose dysfunction or death may be compared to a broken piece of clockwork.[6] While he maintains that God is the craftsman of such machinery, he suggests that this is only true in a remote sense. Descartes describes a section of his treatise, *The World*, where he claims to have hypothetically demonstrated how the universe could have begun as a primordial chaos and then only gradually resolved itself into its present form in accordance with certain "natural laws" (which he claims to have discovered) that even God could not violate. The role of God would then be merely to give his "concurrence" to the evolution of the universe. The sole reason that Descartes gives for not explaining man in the proto-Darwinian terms in which he describes the formation of inanimate bodies and (perhaps also) animals, is that he "did not *yet* have sufficient knowledge" of them in order to do this, and so he "contented" himself to say that God crafted man out of matter in his present form from the start.[7] Thus it is clear that this is a merely provisional explanation and that Descartes is almost ready to accept the development of man's body in

---

3   Ibid., *Principles* 1.9: 7; Second Meditation: AT 27; Third Meditation: AT 41; Sixth Meditation: AT 78–79.

4   Ibid., *Principles* I:53.

5   Ibid., *Principles* I:53; *Comments on a Certain Broadsheet*.

6   Ibid., Fifth Discourse: AT 56–59.

7   Ibid., Fifth Discourse: AT 41–46.

proto-Darwinian terms, *except* that man's defining rationality would not be part of this evolution of material machinery.

In this connection, we should note that Descartes completed his studies at La Flèche in the summer of 1614, and there is no public record of his activities thereafter until November of 1616, when he graduated from the University of Poitiers with a degree in civil and cannon law.[8] There has been much speculation about Descartes' activities, or lack thereof, between his quitting La Flèche and the beginning of his studies at Poitiers. The biographer A. C. Grayling suggests that even if he did have a nervous breakdown, as some scholars have claimed, *where* he was during the course of this breakdown is quite significant.[9] It appears that Descartes was at Saint-Germain-en-Lay, a small village on the outskirts of Paris, whose sole attraction at that time was a royal pleasure garden designed by the Francini brothers, which featured a vast array of performing mechanical automata of animals and humans, some of which even "spoke" using hydraulic mechanisms. These robots were set within a labyrinthine garden containing mysterious passages to grottos fit for secluded contemplation.[10] One can imagine what an effect this would have had on a thinker undergoing a mental breakdown.

Julien Offray de La Mettrie studied philosophy and natural science at the College d'Harcourt, where Cartesianism was dominant. Like many natural scientists after him, La Mettrie found the dualism of Cartesian metaphysics incoherent, but he adopted Descartes' view of animals as *automata*. Through studies in medicine (under one of the most renowned physicians of the age), he extended this mechanical model to human beings. Like Descartes, he preferred bloodying his hands with dissections and autopsies to scholasticism. He also shared Descartes' penchant for being the subject of his own research. During a fever, La Mettrie conducted experiments on himself concerning the effect of quickened blood circula-

---

8   A.C. Grayling, *Descartes: The Life and Times of a Genius* (New York: Walker and Company, 2005), p. 28.

9   Ibid., pp. 28–29.

10   Ibid., p. 30.

tion on mental processes. He was ultimately convinced that Descartes had been mistaken to think that there was an immaterial and un-extended mental substance distinct from the brain and the nervous and circulatory systems that allow it to function. Working with a proto-evolutionary notion that (as noted above) one also sees at least tacitly in Descartes' *Discourse on the Method*, La Mettrie observed that the transition between animals and man is one of a degree of complexity, and not a violent break in nature.

If, as Descartes rightly observed, animals are machines, then men are also. La Mettrie set out these views in *Man a Machine* (1747), and a year later he put out a more biologically oriented work, *Man a Plant*.[11] He went on to extrapolate a purely hedonistic ethics from out of this biologistic materialism. La Mettrie's psychological and ethical work criticized the enculturation of feelings of guilt into children at a young age, and advocated the pursuit of sensual pleasure without restraint above all else. It was this hedonistic libertinism, more than his materialistic mechanism that caused him to fall afoul of even other figures of the French Enlightenment, such as Voltaire and Diderot, let alone the establishment. He was forced to take refuge with Frederick the Great in Prussia.

The Marquis de Sade studied the scientific works of La Mettrie. In his most concisely representative philosophical work, *Philosophy in the Boudoir*, de Sade adopts the rationalistic mechanism of La Mettrie and extends his licentious hedonism to its logical conclusion.[12] In de Sade's view, the indistinctness of emotion, to which irrational religion appeals, consists of flaws in rational thinking under conditions of malaise and weariness. In good health, a sharply-tuned mind should burn with incandescently clear discernment of the nature of things and the impulses to which it is necessarily subject. A mind that carefully studies the laws of physics at work in Nature will come to recognize that it is utterly subject to biological processes such as the function of "our organs, our metabolism,

---

11   Julien Offray de La Mettrie, *Machine Man and Other Writings* (New York: Cambridge University Press, 1996).

12   Marquis de Sade, *Philosophy in the Boudoir* (Creation Books, 2000).

the flow of liquids, the energy of the animal spirits."[13] It is these "physical causes" that are responsible for all of our behavior.

According to de Sade, an honest view of Nature is one that acknowledges that cruel pleasure and excitation at the pain of others is as natural in human beings as in animals, such as cats who torture mice. In support of this claim, de Sade takes recourse to the observation of infants and (highly dubious) early anthropological studies of various non-European cultures, especially "savage" ones. He views civilization, which arises on account of the more delicate brain capacities of humans, as providing only an avenue to the sublime refinement of cruelty. Furthermore, creative and destructive processes are totally interdependent in Nature. Man is simply one agent of destruction among others. There is no such thing as a "criminal" in Nature's eyes, only fortunate and unfortunate men. De Sade does admit that criminal laws are necessary for society to function. However, he thinks it impossible to fashion a body of laws that, by definition as *laws* (rather than tyrannical caprice), would be designed for *universal applicability*, and yet would somehow resolve the conflict between the personal interest of the individual and the general interest of society. We should be "as wary of" laws as "of snakes, which, although they wound or kill, can sometimes prove useful to medicine."[14]

Mass murder is on a par with other natural catastrophes, such as famines, plagues, and earthquakes. If those acts considered immoral or impious were truly criminal, they would be impossible. If it existed, such a thing as "natural virtue" would be as inescapable as the laws of physics: "Nature does not have two voices, one forever condemning what the other demands."[15] The very idea of an "unnatural pleasure" is a contradiction in terms. On the basis of wet dreams and the relatively brief periods of female fertility, de Sade argues that sodomy cannot be condemned on the grounds that it wastes sperm. He naturalizes homosexuality, viewing

---

13   Ibid., p. 82.
14   Ibid., p. 117.
15   Ibid., p. 104.

both sodomy and lesbianism as a population control mechanism built into Nature. Emphasizing the relative insignificance of mankind in the cosmos, and pointing to the paleontological record of prior extinctions, de Sade claims that Nature would only respond to the total destruction of mankind by engendering some new, and perhaps superior, species in its place: "Do you not think races have already become extinct? Does Buffon not already list several? Nature fails to even blink. If we were all destroyed, it would not affect the purity of the air, the brilliance of the stars, nor the remorseless march of the universe."[16] What then, is *one* human being? He compares aborting a fetus, merely one "form of *matter*," to using medical purgatives or even "common shitting."[17]

An individual human being is nothing worthy of any consideration other than as an "object to use," unless, of course, that individual is oneself. De Sade's advocacy of excitedly taking pleasure in the pain of others is not only based on the claim that pain is, in a biomechanical sense, a greater stimulant — even to the one *witnessing* it — than simple pleasure. This, in itself, would not rule out empathetic identification with others whom one witnesses in a state of pain. Rather, de Sade needs to uphold a thesis that we are not only naturally predisposed to seek our own pleasure, but that this pursuit is radically egoistic. We are totally closed off to the "inner" feelings of others: "...there can be no comparison between our experiences and those of others... we should prefer...this minor excitation [at another's pain] which arouses us, to the massive sum of other's miseries, which have no effect on us."[18] He claims that when looked at "rationally," the "source of all our moral errors is that ludicrous notion of brotherhood" he deems an invention of Christians who were too weak and vulnerable to simply seize what gave them pleasure. These "moral errors" allegedly include the "virtues of humanity, charity, generosity."[19]

---

16 Ibid., pp. 105–106.
17 Ibid., p. 77.
18 Ibid., p. 113.
19 Ibid., p. 116.

De Sade's attempt to follow the materialist rationalism of the French Enlightenment through to its logical conclusion ends up in a *reductio ad absurdum*. He must be praised above La Mettrie, let alone the materialist *philosophes* who set up the revolutionary Cult of Reason, if only for having had the courage to go far enough for us to be able to see this. De Sade claims that it is impossible to do anything contrary to the Laws of Nature; that in effect, we do not act at all; our so-called "individual will" is a chimera that expresses Nature's "plan." Yet at the same time he claims that we should actively reject such values as humanity, charity, and generosity, and that we should forsake compassion in favor of stimulating ourselves through contrived situations wherein cruelly torturing others is refined into a science. This would be in accord with Nature's "plan," which manifestly includes destructive natural catastrophes and the cruelty of animals, children, and "uncorrupted savages." Is it not patently obvious that a Nature so indifferent would also not be violated by our treating others caringly and graciously — that in the face of Nature's indifference, it is *we* who choose *to act* in one way or the other? No, this is not acceptable to de Sade because, as La Mettrie before him believed, it would be irrational for us to have a *chance* to act. All things are determined. Above all, it must be the case that Nature has a "plan," and to be rational is to use one's Reason to discern this plan and then to act in "harmony" with it. But is it not the case that, as de Sade repeats incessantly, we *always* act according to Nature? Do you see the absurdity, the tautological closed circularity of this 'Reason'?

The sadist is not a *natural* man. He is the hyperconscious product of a decadent civilization where a false ideal of Reason, whose mathematical standard of certitude Descartes most eloquently elaborated, has hollowed out everything of *human* significance and turned every*one* into an object to be formulaically manipulated. He is a Cartesian ego who, unconvinced by the "proof" of God's existence, is plunged back into solipsistic doubt as to the existence of others in an "external" world whose reality as a whole is also brought into question. The nihilistic *ennui* that seems to motivate the sadist's need for excitation through cruelty to others is really a psychological barrier against the terrifying situation he would find himself in if his so-called "rational" views on the Laws of Nature turned out to be true. To empathize with others, to recognize their feelings, would be to still be capable of feeling something other than artificially abstracted sensations. It would be to suffer and cause suffering while knowing that, in a world where the Laws of Nature preclude any margin of free will, one cannot act to better one's own situation or anyone else's. That is like being a knife in the hands of a butcher. Any *human* being would be driven to madness by honestly thinking all the way through materialistic rationalism, so the sadist dehumanizes himself into a more desperate creature than any animal.

To be self-conscious, to know as Descartes did that one *is* one's mind — it is impossible for someone who has had this realization to live as if he were "an insect" in a well-ordered "anthill," which is the kind of "scientific" society that the Cult of Reason aimed at. The materialists were right that Descartes' dualism is untenable, but they were unable to eliminate consciousness — only evoke in it a sense of being trapped that leads straight into the madhouse of reactionary religious faith. This claustrophobia of the Cartesian ego can ultimately be diagnosed as a symptom of the incoherent abstraction of mind and matter from the stream of experience, and their opposition to one another as mutually exclusive substances. As a consequence of his separation of mind and matter, Descartes is faced with the seemingly unsolvable problem of how the former can affect the latter (and be affected by it), given that they are *substantially* different. This issue is first seriously raised by his friend and student, Princess Elizabeth Stuart of Bohemia, in a series of correspondences from May 16 to July 1 of 1643, and is never satisfactorily resolved before Descartes falls terminally ill and dies of pneumonia in 1650. The Achilles heel of the Cartesian paradigm lies exposed in these letters.[20]

---

20 René Descartes, *Meditations and Other Metaphysical Writings* (New York: Penguin Books, 1998), pp. 147–167.

In her first letter, dated May 16, Elizabeth asks Descartes how it could be that the immaterial soul voluntarily moves the material body? She reminds Descartes that, according to his own physics, one body is only moved by another based on the momentum, trajectory, and surface shape of the other body impacting it; and that his description of the soul as an immaterial substance excludes extension of any kind (i.e., shape or surface area), and consequently forbids a conception of the soul as some kind of ethereal "subtle body." Descartes replies on May 21 with a startling confession:

> I can truthfully say that the question asked by Your Highness seems to me to be *the one* that can most justifiably be put to me as a result of the writings I published. For there are two things about the human soul on which depends all the knowledge we can acquire about its nature: one is that it thinks and the other is that, since it is united with the body, it can act and be acted on in conjunction with the body. *I have said almost nothing about the second of these,* and I tried to provide a good explanation only of the first one because my main aim was to prove the distinction between the soul and the body; only the first feature could help us in this, whereas *the second one would not have been helpful.* But since *Your Highness sees things so clearly that no one can conceal anything from you,* I will now try to explain how I conceive the union of the soul with the body and how the soul has the power to move the body. [My emphasis.]

The implication here is that in his metaphysics, Descartes was less than honest in the manner in which he established the certainty of the division between intelligent and corporeal substance. When Descartes admits that he has said "almost nothing" about their interaction, he is referring to the one instance in the Sixth Meditation where he writes:

> Nature also teaches me, by these sensations of pain, hunger, thirst and so on, that I am not merely present in my body as a sailor is present in a ship, but that I am very closely joined and, as it were, intermingled with it, so that I and the body form a unit. If this were not so, I, who am nothing but a thinking thing, would not feel pain when the body was hurt, but would perceive the damage purely by the intellect, just as a sailor perceives by sight if anything in his ship is broken. Similarly, when the body needed food or drink, I should have an ex-

plicit understanding of the fact, instead of having confused sensations of hunger and thirst. For these sensations of hunger, thirst, pain and so on are nothing but confused modes of thinking which arise from *the union and, as it were, intermingling of the mind with the body.* [My emphasis.][21]

To isolate mind from the body, and from matter in general, Descartes needed to suppress the question of the interaction or locus of conjunction of the two supposedly distinct substances. The excerpt from the Sixth Meditation above suggests that this is not because he failed to conceive of the "union and…intermingling" of a mind and body that must in some way be self-same, but because he chose to suppress it in order to fulfill his stated "main aim" of proving their distinction. In other words, he establishes them as distinct substances by *taking* them to be distinct substances. Clever student that she is, Elizabeth does not fall for this. She realizes that *if* (according to the definition Descartes gives) the mind is the true nature of the self and is capable of existence separate from the body; *and* in separation from this body, the self as mind would not be capable of any sensory perception (or imagination), but only pure logical or mathematical understanding and intuition,[22] *then* it follows that *the soul must be inside the body as if inside a vessel, whose organs it uses as tools, but with which it is not "intermingled" in any way.* Yet this is a conclusion that Descartes himself denies as inconsistent with the actual experience of the interaction of mind and body.

Elizabeth's objection would not be so scandalous for Descartes' metaphysics if he had gone on to satisfy her with the explanation he promises of the manner of the interaction of the soul and body, and how the former is able to move the latter when they have essentially different and mutually exclusive natures. However, in the next five letters exchanged back and forth, Descartes is never forthcoming with such an explanation, despite his keen student's persistent inquiry. Instead, he insists that the nature of the soul and the body must be known each in their own right; that they

---

21   Cottingham, *Descartes: Selected Philosophical Writings*, Sixth Meditation: AT 81.

22   Ibid., Sixth Meditation: AT 75–79.

must be considered separately, and not explained in terms of one another. He also suggests that their union would have to be explained in a manner different from either the way the soul is explained or the way the body is explained, but he never ventures this third explanation.

Descartes does at one point give Elizabeth a straight answer about his difficulties in reunifying the mind and body once he has severed them. The problem is that instead of stopping here, he goes on to attempt to avoid fundamentally engaging her question, at times by reformulating it in less threatening terms. We should not allow this subsequent intellectual squirming to distract us from what he does say, very clearly, in his reply of June 28:

> … these meditations were responsible for making you find obscure the notion we have of the union of mind and body, because it seemed to me that the human mind is incapable of conceiving very distinctly, and simultaneously, both the distinction and union of body and soul. The reason is that, in order to do so, it would be necessary to conceive of them as one single thing and, at the same time, to conceive of them as two things — which is self-contradictory.

Apparently, Princess Elizabeth does not see Descartes as having said anything of substance beyond the admission of failure in this statement when, on July 1, she writes in conclusion to their correspondence in regard to this unanswered question:

> I also find that my senses show me that the mind moves the body but they do not teach me (any more than the understanding, or the imagination) the way in which it happens. To explain that, I think there are properties in the soul that are unknown to us and that might perhaps overturn what your *Metaphysical Meditations* convinced me of, with such sound reasons, about the extension of the soul [namely, that it is unextended].

In his *Discourse on the Method*, Descartes refers to a most controversial section of his suppressed magnum opus — *The World* — that was subsequently destroyed. Here, he had allegedly described how God created man's rational soul and joined it to the body in a very precise manner so that it would affect the latter and could be affected *by* it, and yet remain substantially different so as to be able to survive the death of the body and enter immortal life.[23] This means that for Descartes, the union of body and soul ultimately depends on an act of God — in a word, on a miracle. Princess Elizabeth's objections become Descartes' chief motivation for readdressing this issue in the *Passions of the Soul*. However, in this final work, though he paints a picture of how the pineal gland in the brain interacts with the body's muscles and organs by directing the flow of "animal spirits" through the nervous system, he never explains how it is that the immaterial soul "has its seat" in this material organ in such a way as to affect it, and thereby affect the body. It seems that this remains an act of God. Nevertheless, in the *Passions*, Descartes makes the mental modes of sensation, imagination, and recollection dependent on interaction with the body through this gland, and consequently violates the mutual exclusivity of primary attributes and their modes that he claims defines substances as "really distinct."[24]

The interdependence of mental and physical modes suggests some sensory entity that would not be as abstractly un-extended as the notion of mind that Descartes would like to limit himself to affirming. It would suggest a *spectral* or *ghostly* entity as the intermediary between pure matter and pure mind. However, as we shall see, Descartes explicitly rules out the possibility of such a phantom body and of all of the extrasensory perceptual and psychokinetic capacities traditionally associated with it. In order to uphold his ontology of real (objective) existence as the substrate of beings, Descartes damns all examples of phenomena of this kind.

Descartes argues that I see other bodies including my own, but this one is mine, because though I can exist without it, I cannot exist within or sense the world through any other bodies.[25] This rules out strong telepathy, possession, and reincarnation. Furthermore, according to Descartes,

---

23   Ibid., Fifth Discourse: AT 59–60.

24   Ibid., *Passions of the Soul*: AT 360–362.

25   Ibid., Sixth Meditation: AT 73.

though the mind has certain passive faculties of sense perception, if it were not for the active faculties of the body's sensory organs, I would only apprehend mathematical and logical ideas, and not the physical world (that has now been proven to exist) outside of my mind.[26] This rules out clairvoyance and other Out-of-Body Experiences (OBEs) that are sensory. The mind, he says, should not be imagined as an ethereal "subtle body" of some kind.[27] This rules out phantom apparitions. Also, Descartes claims that now that we know there is a real world of waking experience, we can better distinguish this from the illusions of our dreams. In dreams, one experiences strange things, but on examination, the events of dreams cannot be fit neatly into what happened before and after them, and they lack a sensible environmental context. In considering this, we will realize that we are dreaming. If a similar spooky experience occurs while we are awake, as if for example something were to appear as if from out of nowhere and then vanish before our eyes, and we confirm to our satisfaction that we are not dreaming, we can be sure that we were deceived by our senses. In the Sixth Meditation, Descartes writes, "If, while I am awake, anyone were suddenly to appear to me and then disappear immediately, as happens in sleep, so that I could not see where he had come from or where he had gone to, it would not be unreasonable for me to judge that he was *a ghost*, or [in other words] a vision created in my brain like those formed in the brain when I sleep, *rather than* a *real* man."[28]

The repression of the *specter* that could mediate between mind and matter haunts Descartes' metaphysics as that which at once *is* and yet *is not* "real," and thereby disallows a binary opposition of "(Perfect) Existence" and "Nothingness." Descartes depends above all on just such a binary opposition as he lays the groundwork of the modern scientific paradigm in his *Discourse on the Method* and his *Metaphysical Meditations*. The substantial distinction between *res cogitans* and *res extensa* in Descartes'

---

26   Ibid., Sixth Meditation: AT 75–79.

27   Ibid., Second Meditation: AT 27.

28   Ibid., Sixth Meditation: AT 89–90, my emphasis.

metaphysics is inextricable from his treatment of God as "perfect existence" and his related conception of "Nothingness." What follows is a reconstruction of this move.

After entering into an all-encompassing skepticism methodologically aimed at discovering truly indubitable grounds for science, Descartes suggests that we arrive at the realization of God's existence in the following way. Standing on the solid ground of my own indubitable existence as the doubter, I may now see if there is a way to attain certain knowledge concerning any of what was previously placed in doubt. I consider the ideas I have of earth, fire, water, the sky, the stars, and all of the beings of the world of my senses, and see that nothing in them guarantees that they do not have their origin in my own mind, or in the mind of a postulated cosmic deceiver who is one of the prime catalysts of radical doubt.[29] Since deception is a product of either malice or weakness, and both of these are imperfections, all of my imperfect ideas are in doubt as to whether they refer to anything "real" at all.

However, I notice that I, a manifestly imperfect being, have what seems to be an idea of perfection! If I derive my existence only from my own consciousness, I would have to have obtained my idea of perfection from my own potential, but not fully actualized, perfection. Yet even if I could become progressively more perfect, something that only has to the potential to be is, strictly speaking, something *that is not*, and true perfection cannot come to be on the basis of this, but only on the basis of that which *is* perfect. If I myself were perfect in this way, I could *substantiate* the real existence of a world corresponding to the ideas my mind has of my body and of other bodies, *but* I should also, in the same stroke, be able to grant myself all of the perfections that it seems I am lacking. Not only would I be able to will myself to be free of doubt, I should even be able to grant myself true omnipotence and omniscience, so that in effect I myself

---

29   Ibid., Fourth Discourse: AT 33–34; Third Meditation: AT 43–44.

would be God. Descartes argues that since I cannot do this, my idea of perfection must come from a being other than myself.[30]

I have the idea of "God" as an omniscient and omnipotent, hence indivisible, infinite being. By this very definition, such a being lacks nothing and is therefore perfect. To lack existence would most certainly be an imperfection, therefore its own real existence is inherent in the idea of God in the same way that it is inherent in the idea of a triangle that the sum of its angles is equal to two right angles.[31] God, being perfect and incapable of malicious deception, in turn gives reality or objective existence to the world outside of my mind, including and above all to the fact that my body is real.[32] Not only "was" I created by God; my existence and that of the world *is* concurrently sustained by God's existence from one moment to the next, so it never occurs that something comes out of nothing.[33] In this sense also, God's Being is immutable or eternal.[34]

Descartes gives several reasons why our many errors and misconceptions of this world are not due to an imperfection in God. Yet they do not seem to him sufficient to explain why God could not have created a limited being that was nevertheless not subjected to constantly being misled and mired in misery on this account. We could have been crafted to more easily find and use the natural light of our rationality. Descartes believes that this leaves us with the conclusion that in order for God to be absolved from being the source of imperfection in any way, there must be a counter-principle of Nothingness which is responsible for the deceptive semblance of *that which seems to be but is not* and all the confusion and suffering it causes.[35]

We are beings that, as it were, stand between God and Nothingness, participating in both and consequently consisting of the perfection

---

30   Ibid., Fourth Discourse: AT 34–35; Third Meditation: AT 46–48.

31   Ibid., Fourth Discourse: AT 34–36; Fifth Meditation: AT 63–69.

32   Ibid., Fourth Discourse: AT 38–39; Third Meditation: AT 51–52.

33   Ibid., Third Meditation: AT 49–50.

34   Ibid., Third Meditation: AT 40.

35   Ibid., Third Discourse: AT 38.

endowed to us by God as well as its corruption by the imperfection of Nothingness.[36] Something cannot come to be out of Nothingness, nor can something perfect come to be from something imperfect.[37] Therefore, for Descartes, God, though co-extensive with existence in being infinite, omniscient, and omnipotent, would have to be wholly separate from Nothingness, and, as it were, exist as its antithesis. The *mutual exclusivity* of modes that formally comes to define "substance" for Descartes mirrors, and is only possible on the basis of, his primordial binary opposition of Being and Nothingness.[38]

This is problematic. Neither can Being guarantee the clarity and distinctness of our knowledge of facts concerning a "real" external world, nor can Nothingness be blamed for exerting a perpetually "voiding" influence on this god-given certainty. "Being" suggests an undifferentiated Oneness. Yet, if everything were One, no thing could be distinguished from another in space, and therefore no thing could move at any speed relative to the differing motion of another thing so as to establish time. Infinity is the negation of space and eternity is the negation of time. Without space and time (of some sort, even if non-linear), this One called "Being" would, in fact, be nothing at all. It is impossible to conceive of "nothing," let alone speak of it. Nothingness is not viable. It cannot exist in any way at all, and so neither can Being-in-itself. Both total Nothingness and the pure presence of Perfect Being are (by virtue of reversion to each other) equally vacuous. What also becomes untenable, once this binary is deconstructed, is banishment of the aforementioned "ghost" and the spooky phenomena that Descartes attempts to prohibit—a *spectral* intermingling of what are abstracted as "mind" and "matter," as well as a natural process of becoming or coming-to-be that defies the abstractions of "Being" and "Nothingness."

---

36   Ibid., Fourth Meditation: AT 54.
37   Ibid., Fourth Discourse: AT 39.
38   Ibid., *Objections and Replies to Sixth Meditation*: AT 226–227.

A recent biography by A. C. Grayling suggests that Descartes actually had a deep involvement with the occult. In the context of the biographical information unearthed by Grayling, it is not unreasonable to see Descartes' terror in the face of the spectral, and his desire to combat those seeking an understanding of the occult, as nothing less than the basic motivation for his elaboration of the intellectual paradigm that bears his name.

With their military-style institutional structure and discipline, the Jesuits saw themselves as soldiers in the vanguard of the Counter-Reformation. They administered some of the most prestigious academies in Europe, and their primary method of resisting the Reformation was to inoculate young minds against heresy by giving them an education that was reputed to secure them in the Catholic faith forever after.[39] Descartes received just such an education at two premier Jesuit institutions: La Flèche Academy and the University of Poitiers. Toward the end of 1619, a certain Jesuit "Father Jean B. Molitor" presented Descartes with a copy of Pierre Charron's *Traite de la sagesse*, which bears the inscription: "To the most learned, dear friend and little brother, René Descartes."[40] Charron was a philosophical theologian and celebrated preacher who used *skeptical* criticism of the sciences of the time as a means to reinforce Catholic orthodoxy at the expense of a pursuit of neo-pagan knowledge that might lead to heresy. The pretension "to know nothing" with certainty, which becomes central to Descartes' own project, acts for Charron as a device to wash the brain clean of potential sources of heresy in order to render it empty enough to be engraved by the truths of faith that God alone reveals.[41] Like Descartes after him, Charron advises that, throughout the course of uprooting higher intellectual beliefs from the mind, one should defer to the customs of the country in which one lives — insofar as those customs are basically in line with God's injunctions. Several passages from the *Discourse on the Method* are relevant in this regard:

---

39   Grayling, *Descartes: The Life and Times of a Genius*, p. 24.

40   Ibid., 65.

41   Ibid., 66.

I revered our theology, and aspired as much as anyone else to reach heaven. But having learned as an established fact that the way to heaven is open no less to the most ignorant than to the most learned, and that the revealed truths which guide us there are beyond our understanding, I would not have dared submit them to my weak reasonings… Now, before starting to rebuild your house, it is not enough simply to pull it down… you must also provide yourself with some other place where you can live comfortably while building is in progress. Likewise, lest I should remain indecisive in my actions while reason obliged me to be so in my judgments… I formed for myself a provisional moral code consisting of just three or four maxims… The first was to obey the laws and customs of my country, holding constantly to the religion in which by God's grace I had been instructed from my childhood…[42]

During the dozen years between the completion of Descartes' education at La Flèche and Poitiers and his philosophical retreat in the United Provinces of the Free Netherlands, he joined the armies of Prince William of Nassau and Duke Maximilian of Bavaria, and thereby participated in opening events of the Thirty Years' War.[43] In 1620, Descartes was at the Battle of White Mountain in the vicinity of Prague, and although his presence there was allegedly that of an "assisting…observer," he remained with the Holy Roman army as Jesuits flooded into Bohemia to persecute Protestants, burn their chapels, and execute their leaders.[44] Frederick, Elector Palatine, the defeat of whose forces at the Battle of White Mountain Descartes approvingly "observed" in 1620, was a strong supporter of the pursuit of esoteric knowledge by occultists.[45] Just as King Henri III of France had backed Giordano Bruno and John Dee was the right hand man of Elizabeth I, the Rosicrucians received the backing of the Elector Frederick in his capacity as head of the Protestant Union. They sought to use "the secret aid" of this "Lion" (Frederick's emblem) as an

42   Cottingham, *Descartes: Selected Philosophical Writings, Discourse on the Method*, AT 8, pp. 22–23.

43   Grayling, *Descartes: The Life and Times of a Genius*, p. 7.

44   Ibid., pp. 54–55.

45   Ibid., p. 70.

agent for the destruction of the Holy Roman Empire.[46] The decisive defeat of Frederick at the Battle of White Mountain in 1620 allows for the persecution of Rosicrucians even in Heidelberg, which had been Frederick's capital, as it came under the occupation of the Hapsburg armies. In 1621, in that city, a pamphlet with the title "A Warning against the Rosicrucian Vermin" was widely circulated.[47]

During the 1610s, the magical arts of Hermeticism, Cabala, and alchemy practiced by numerous Renaissance scientists — such as Paracelsus, Giordano Bruno, Cornelius Agrippa, and John Dee — was woven together by a "Brotherhood of the Rosy Cross."[48] These Rosicrucian initiates, who were known as the "Illuminati" and the "Invisibles," traveled around Europe in stealth with the aim of effecting a "Universal and General Reformation" that would usher in a "new dawn" for mankind or, in language akin to that of the author of *The New Atlantis*, they promised a great "instauration" of esoteric knowledge that had been lost through our catastrophic fall from a higher state of being.[49] They were renaissance men, polymaths well versed in architecture, music, navigation, geometry, fine arts, mathematics, and astronomy — all arts that they saw as being in need of reformation.[50] They aimed to "restore all sciences, transmute metals, and prolong human life."[51] They were cosmopolitans who claimed no country as their own and were believed able to speak, fluently and without study, the language of any country in which they needed to operate.[52] It was rumored that they remained in contact with each other, over great distances, by means of telepathy.[53]

---

46   Ibid., p. 75.
47   Ibid., p. 77.
48   Ibid., pp. 70–71.
49   Ibid., pp. 73–76, 78, 80.
50   Ibid., p. 76.
51   Ibid., p. 77.
52   Ibid.
53   Ibid., p. 80.

Grayling suggests that it can hardly be a coincidence that Descartes only reappears in Paris, after many years, just when "the Rosicrucian scare" breaks out there in 1623.[54] Panic had erupted over rumors that six of the Invisibles had come to Paris and were lodging at the Marais, using it as a base of operations for their diabolical plot.[55] Descartes appears to have been personal friends with two of the Rosicrucians, Jacob Wassenar and Cornelius van Hooghelande, and he carried out correspondences with others.[56] Consequently, during the scare Descartes himself was suspected of being a Rosicrucian.[57] Daniel Huet, writing in the 1690s, claimed on evidence of letters purportedly written by Descartes to Queen Christina of Sweden in 1652 and 1656, that Descartes was indeed a Rosicrucian who had faked his death and funeral in 1650 so that he could move from the Netherlands, where he had been discovered, to Sweden in order to pursue his studies of the occult.[58]

As Grayling points out, this is highly unlikely given Descartes' high-level Jesuit connections and loyalties, especially his relationship with Marin Mersenne.[59] This man, who was one of the chief "hammers" of the Holy Inquisition tasked with persecuting the Rosicrucians, was not only Descartes' close friend but, from 1620 onwards, Mersenne was most responsible for publicizing Descartes' work and maintaining his contacts with the intellectual world at large.[60] This Jesuit inquisitor, who was also a graduate of Descartes' *alma mater*, La Flèche, was fully convinced that a Rosicrucian cabal of great occult power actually existed and was carrying out a transnational conspiracy at the behest of Satan.[61] Mersenne pushed for the development of an empirical science that would eschew

---

54 Ibid., p. 79.
55 Ibid., p. 80.
56 Ibid., p. 83.
57 Ibid., p. 80.
58 Ibid., p. 84.
59 Ibid.
60 Ibid., pp. 70, 78, 84.
61 Ibid., pp. 78, 84.

everything alchemical and leave spiritual phenomena within the purview of the Church.[62] He epitomized that ecclesiastical trend of thinking on account of which the rationalist Galileo was merely chastised and subjected to house arrest, whereas the occultist Bruno was burned at the stake for his scientific understanding of Nature.[63] While both men threatened Aristotelian Scholasticism with innovations, Galileo's mechanistic view of Nature left affairs of the soul as matters of faith, whereas Bruno's hylomorphism defied any distinction between empirical science and spiritual phenomena. Bruno became the martyred great saint of occult alchemists such as the Rosicrucians, who were suspected of Satanism, during the late Renaissance and early modern era.

Given Descartes' close relationship with Mersenne and other inquisitorial Jesuits, and his involvement with Catholic storm troopers sent to defeat Frederick, the patron of the Rosicrucian conspiracy, what is more likely than Descartes having been a Rosicrucian is that he was a Jesuit spy sent to infiltrate the Rosicrucian Order so as to facilitate the eradication of its occult heresies by the Holy Inquisition.[64] He would only have been one of many agents then employed by the Jesuits toward this end.[65] Grayling suggests that Descartes' early adulthood inheritance of a share of his mother's estate was insufficient to fund his extensive travels throughout Europe, especially at the level at which he lived, and that these travels were probably bankrolled by the Jesuits as a business expense, their primary aim being to conduct espionage.[66] This would explain, for example, both his motive in frequenting aristocratic casinos — he went to the top casinos and gambled with prominent gentlemen whom he had targeted — and his financial ability to haunt them, waiting for them to get very drunk so as to bear witness to their indiscretions, when they would talk about things they shouldn't have. Several of Descartes' enemies in the Netherlands ac-

---

62   Ibid., p. 84.

63   Ibid., p. 87.

64   Ibid., pp. 70–71, 84.

65   Ibid., p. 85.

66   Ibid., p. 9.

cused him of being a spy, and his personal motto was, "The Hidden life is best."[67]

In 1628, after a "private conference" with the notorious Cardinal Berulle, Descartes left France for good, effectively exiling himself in the United Provinces, where he changed his address frequently and kept his whereabouts secret.[68] Grayling makes the case that Descartes was engaged in intelligence work on behalf of the Jesuit Order, and that the meeting with Cardinal Berulle that precipitated his exile was something akin to the interrogation of a spy who had been discovered, and to whom it had been made clear that he was no longer welcome in his homeland.[69] At that time, the Jesuits were instigating efforts by the Hapsburg rulers of the Holy Roman Empire (of mostly German states) to reclaim those parts of Europe that had fallen to the Protestant Reformation. They were especially afraid that the Brotherhood of the Rosy Cross intended to replace them as the most organized and sociopolitically influential force in Europe.[70] Although France was still largely a Catholic country, both its government and the Papacy itself viewed this Jesuit crusade as a reckless endangerment of the European balance of power; France and the Papacy were opposed to the efforts of the Holy Roman Empire to the point that they resisted it with force of arms.[71] Descartes had fought on the other side. In particular, he was in the company of Imperial troops commanded by the savage Count of Bucquoy as they captured and destroyed the Protestant town of Hradisch in Moravia, where the local population was subjected to a campaign of terror that included the wholesale rape and massacre of civilians.[72] It is interesting that the sole public reference that Descartes makes to any of these events are the few lines in the *Discourse on the Method* where he mentions being on his way back to rejoin these

---

67   Ibid., p. 10.

68   Ibid., p. 8.

69   Ibid., pp. 8, 86.

70   Ibid., p. 71.

71   Ibid., p. 9.

72   Ibid., pp. 54–55, 79.

armies, at which point he was forced to take shelter from an early winter storm at a stove-heated room in Ulm. He writes:

> At that time I was in Germany, where I had been called by the wars that are not yet ended there. While I was returning to the army from the coronation of the Emperor, the onset of winter detained me in quarters where, finding no conversation to divert me and fortunately having no cares or passions to trouble me, I stayed all day shut up alone in a stove-heated room, where I was completely free to converse with myself about my own thoughts.[73]

This is where the "night of dreams" that inspired his philosophical meditations took place. As he recounted in a notebook preserved in part by Leibniz, Descartes was *terrified* by these "dreams." They involved phantoms and an apparently psychokinetic incident, wherein, between two of the dreams, Descartes was frightened out of sleep by a sudden clap of thunder and saw sparks fly around the room as he felt his head explode.[74] During the night, Descartes prayed to God to protect him from the presence of an evil spirit by his bedside that he believed had been sent to seduce him.[75] He was in doubt as to whether what he saw that night could really be called "dreams" or whether they were actually *visions*.[76] Either way, Descartes attributed deeply portentous significance to them.[77] One of the visions that he took to be "prophetic" was a book with copperplate portraits in it of a kind that he was presented with by an Italian painter who paid him an unexpected visit the day *after* the "night of dreams."[78]

Descartes considered what he experienced that night so formative of his later philosophical and scientific aspirations that he kept his record of these experiences with him for the rest of his life.[79] Among the most

---

73   Descartes, *Discourse on the Method*, AT 11.

74   Grayling, *Descartes: The Life and Times of a Genius*, pp. 58–59.

75   Ibid., p. 59.

76   Ibid., p. 60.

77   Ibid., p. 58.

78   Ibid., p. 61.

79   Ibid., p. 63.

telling lines in these notes is one where Descartes announces his intention to enter the world stage "masked," and another where he simply states that, "the fear of God is the beginning of wisdom."[80] The Descartes that we have been taught about in the academy is the masked man. Beneath the rationalist mask may well lie a terrified soul in league with those sadistic inquisitors who immolated Bruno, and who murdered countless other sagacious renaissance men and women accused of witchcraft or sorcery in order to put the fear of God back into society at large.

---

80   Ibid., p. 64.

CHAPTER IV

STORMING HEAVEN

Cartesius is not the only inquisitorial exorcist who has been taken for a standard-bearer of soberly "enlightened" rationality. As it happens, a torturous relationship with the occult also marked the life of the other modern philosopher who most influenced the "Enlightenment" both metaphysically and politically, and who developed a sophisticated refinement of the Cartesian paradigm: Immanuel Kant. The author of the manifesto *What is Enlightenment?*, Kant holds the greatest claim to being the paragon of the Age of Reason. A denial of spectral phenomena constitutes the specific "limits of possible experience" set by Kant in his attempt to equate mathematical laws of physics with laws of consciousness. One can reach no other conclusion when reading *Religion within the Limits of Reason Alone*, where Kant rants against practitioners of occult arts for attempting to "storm heaven."

He claims that the abilities they pretend to have would cause as much disorder in "the whole rational and contemplative commonwealth" as criminal acts of terrorism would in the political commonwealth. Elsewhere, he makes remarks that show this to be no idle analogy. Kant supports the forced hospitalization and purgative "treatment" of those alleging to have uncanny abilities. This would be less disturbing if he knew little or nothing about the occult, but as it turns out, in his youth Kant undertook a study of the complete works of Emmanuel Swedenborg — the leading occultist of the day. Swedenborg's work was widely condemned as heretical and liberal theologians partial to it were even put on trial.

When rumors spread that Kant was spending his time and money seriously investigating Swedenborg's claims, and that he had validated some of them, the young aspiring academic came to believe that he was in danger of being denied a tenured professorship. He responded by writing a very strange little book on Swedenborg entitled *Dreams of a Spirit-Seer*. This text is an example of what Leo Strauss called "esoteric writing." Although the tone was meant to be mocking of Swedenborg and his claims, at numerous points the content conflicts with the sarcasm and irony of his style. Kant intended the casual reader not to see past this rhetorical veil. This worked and secured him tenure. A closer reading of the text, however, demonstrates that Kant not only took Swedenborg seriously, but that in this obscure book, through a constructive critique of Swedenborg, Kant develops basic structures of his metaphysical and ethical position that he would go on to use in later key texts such as *Groundwork of the Metaphysics of Morals*. This becomes especially clear when one looks at *Dreams* and the *Groundwork* in light of the suppressed third part of Kant's *Natural History and Theory of the Heavens*, which contains a Swedenborgian account of intelligent life on other worlds throughout the "spiritual republic" that pervades the cosmos.

The way in which Kant interprets Swedenborg's experiences in *Dreams of a Spirit-Seer* is aimed at denying the spiritual world of any phenomenal qualities, and interpreting the spectral phenomena experienced by Swedenborg and others as the mind's sensory translations of telepathic impressions from disembodied spirits on "the other side." Kant tries to explain away the phantasmagoric quality of the paranormal as a gross distortion of extrasensory perceptions of what he would later call the noumenal realm: distortions produced by our own senses in accordance with symbols of significance to us and drawn from our own memories and prejudicial beliefs. This allows him to turn the noumenal realm into a domain of perfect justice, where all of one's moral acts have the effects that they cannot have in this phenomenal world that is mechanistically determined by mathematical laws. As he writes in the *Critique of Pure Reason*, knowledge of the noumenal realm is denied in order "to make room for faith" that it is constituted as he takes it to be in *Dreams*.

Moreover, the repeated references in the *Groundwork of the Metaphysics of Morals* to the necessary applicability of the Categorical Imperative to extraterrestrial intelligences with a different biological constitution can be illuminated by those parts of *Dreams* wherein Kant uses Swedenborg's accounts of communication with spirits on other planets to argue that the "spiritual republic" where perfect justice reigns extends throughout the entire universe. I argue that this is the basis for Kant's attempt to develop a universal ethics. It is vital to the democratic character of this ethics, and the political order that it is intended to ground, to stringently deny that paranormal abilities can be efficacious in *this* world, because it was as true in Kant's time as it is now that the aptitude for paranormal ability is as unevenly distributed as virtuoso talent or genius.

The fact that Kant's position on the spectral echoes that of Descartes is unsurprising insofar as Kant revises and adopts Descartes' basic ontological standpoint. In the *Critique of Pure Reason*, Kant maintains the Cartesian *ego cogito* as the central pivot of his ontology by reframing it as a synthetic unity of apperception. "Apperception" is any experience of which the subject is able to say, "This is mine"; in other words, self-conscious experience. The unity of apperception is to be found in the "I think" that accompanies all perceptions.[1] This unity of apperception is transcendental because it can never be defined from the content of any given experience. The *transcendental* (as opposed to the *empirical*) is that which is concerned not with objects, but with our mode of knowing them.[2] The transcendental unity of apperception, in the "I think," precedes all the data of intuition.[3] Kant attempts to establish the objective validity of the categories in terms of which our cognitive faculties organize our experience in a deduction that begins with the realization that pure intuitions of sensibility "are nothing to us" unless they are first unified at least into a manifold of belonging to one consciousness and not that of an

---

1   Immanuel Kant, *Critique of Pure Reason* (New York: Cambridge University Press, 1998), B131–2.

2   Ibid., A12.

3   Ibid., A107.

other.[4] Thus the transcendental unity of consciousness underlies the possibility of sensation as well as that of thought, whose empirical contents lack any unifying element. Kant equates the transcendental principle that unifies all possible intuition in a manifold for my consciousness with the Cartesian "I think" that must accompany all representations *as such* for them to be something *to me*.[5] This principle of the unity of consciousness has an analytic form of the type "I am I."[6]

We can know certain things prior to experience, by our Pure Reason, because *a priori* structures are the very conditions of the possibility of experience for beings constituted such as ourselves. Although *a priori* knowledge is what is known prior to any one experience or another, it can never transcend the limits of possible experience.[7] Pure Reason is the part of the faculty of Reason that "contains the principles by which we know anything absolutely *a priori*."[8] All *a priori* knowledge is, however, only knowledge of appearances, *not* of *things-in-themselves*. If there were no rationally inaccessible realm of things-in-themselves, even the soul would have to be considered subject to the principle of causality. Without free will, morality — or even goal-directed practical action in general — would give way to the mechanism of Nature. Even though we cannot rationally *know* things-in-themselves, especially the human soul, we *can* think them. It would make no sense for things to be appearances if there is nothing real, which appears to be such and such. It is only required that we can *think* freedom as a concept without contradiction, in order for us to view our actions as *appearing* to be determined by the causal mechanism of Nature, while really being free when the human soul is thought in-itself. Kant believes that the possibility of morality requires us to guarantee freedom in this manner.

---

4   Ibid., B129, 132–3 / A116.
5   Ibid., B132; A117.
6   Ibid., B135.
7   Ibid., Bxx.
8   Ibid., A11.

In the *Groundwork of the Metaphysics of Morals*, Kant attempts to resolve the contradiction between "free will" and natural determinism by
setting up a parallelism of two "different standpoints."[9] From the standpoint of speculative reason, all phenomenal "mere appearances," including
that of the subject as an object, are determined by Laws of Nature. From
the standpoint of practical reason, the subject is immediately conscious
of his own causal autonomy or freedom of will.[10] This requires positing
things-in-themselves in an "intelligible world" beyond mere appearances,
which cannot be the object of any intuition, and of which nothing further
than its existence can be cognized.[11] Kant claims that "freedom... signifies
only a 'something' that is left over when I have excluded from the determining grounds of my will everything belonging to the world of sense."[12]
In other words, we have arrived back at Descartes' dichotomy between
a non-extended mind and extended phenomena of the material world,
except that now the latter is viewed as an isomorphic projection mirroring
the basic structure of those experiences possible for the former.

On what basis, though, does Kant determine what kinds of experiences are *not* possible? Moreover, is it a coincidence that the types of experiences that he deems *impossible* are just those which would allow for the
human mind to act directly on the world through its own choices, instead
of resigning itself to a parallelism that renders "freedom" as mysterious as
"God"?

It may seem that Kant's ontology and epistemology in the *Critique of
Pure Reason* is purely critical or negative. However, it does have a positive intent. By denying *knowledge* of things-in-themselves, it is possible
to make room for *faith*: "...all objections to morality and religion will be
forever silenced... in Socratic fashion... by the clearest proof of the ignorance of the objectors." At the same time, this will focus all of the attention

---

9   Immanuel Kant, *Groundwork of the Metaphysics of Morals* in *Practical Philosophy*
      (New York: Cambridge University Press, 2006), 4:450.

10   Ibid., 4:451.

11   Ibid., 4:451–52.

12   Ibid., 4:462.

of great minds on progress in the hard sciences, rather than allowing their energies to be wasted in speculative heresy that is dangerous to society. Common people have never been affected by the onto-theological proofs and doctrines of the schools, so if these have to be sacrificed by denying *a priori* knowledge of such things as God, immortality, and so on, it is in fact a gain rather than a loss for both traditional religion based on faith in revelation, and for the intuitive Deist belief in God on the basis of awe at the precision of natural design.[13] The latter was, of course, the basis for the Cult of the Supreme Being in the French Revolution, while the former was restored when the rootless, rationalist revolution gave way to Bonaparte's reactionary coup.

Kant explicitly states that the aim of the *Critique of Pure Reason* is to definitively delimit Reason in such a way as to make room for faith. In *Religion within the Limits of Reason Alone*, he in turn defines the acceptable parameters of "faith" in such a way as to categorically forbid any faith in acts of the will that would contravene deterministic Laws of Nature. These events that deviate from natural law are most disturbing to Kant when they are attributed to finite beings executing their own individual will, rather than being attributed to God, whose will — *he* seems to think — might somewhat less offensively be seen as encompassing *physical* law. The possibility that such a "daemonic" agent — causal free will — could be exercised toward morally wrong ends particularly alarms Kant.[14]

Kant observes that most people nowadays usually employ the word "miracle" as a mere figure of speech, such as a doctor who tells a patient that there is no help for him unless a miracle occurs — in other words, that he is certain to die.[15] Such "sensible men" may not deny "that miracles occurred of old," for example among the healers of the early Christian community, but they and their governments do not tolerate new miracles or

---

13 Kant, *Critique of Pure Reason*, Bxxvi–Bxxxv.

14 Immanuel Kant, *Religion within the Limits of Reason Alone* (New York: Harper Torchbooks, 1960), p. 81.

15 Ibid., p. 82.

allow any place for them in the affairs of this present life. Kant argues that because there is no scriptural basis for this stance, which even orthodox Christianity upholds, it is actually "a maxim of reason" that paranormal events cannot occur, and he asks: "...is not this same maxim, which in this instance is applied to a threatened disorder in the civil life, equally valid for the fear of a similar disorder in the philosophical, and the whole rational contemplative commonwealth?"[16] In other words, whether he realizes it or not, Kant is basically siding with the persecution of "witches" and connecting the prohibition of their abilities on account of a threat to the social order to the theoretical prohibition of psi phenomena on account of epistemic disorder. Kant then mocks people who only allow belief in little, un-sensational miracles such as personal providence, pointing out that "what matters herein is not the effect, or its magnitude, but rather the form of the course of earthly events, that is, *the way in which the effect occurs*, whether naturally or supernaturally..."[17] Kant might as well have listed, as an example of such a "little miracle," the ability of a mental substance to affect the pineal gland — according to Descartes — or some other small physical aggregate in the brain, and thereby control the body by means of what are otherwise natural mechanical principles. Kant's point is that something like this is no more possible than lifting gigantic stones by one's mental intent alone — it is not a question of degree, but of the nature of causality.

Kant dismisses all belief in "supernatural" experience as *superstition* on the grounds that "our use of the concept of cause and effect cannot be extended beyond matters of experience, and hence beyond nature."[18] Kant's fundamental reason for rejecting these phenomena is that acceptance of them allegedly involves "the belief in knowing through experience something whose occurrence, as under objective laws of experience, we

---

16   Ibid.
17   Ibid., p. 80.
18   Ibid., p. 48.

ourselves can recognize to be impossible."[19] It seems that Kant's dismissal of the "supernatural" is based on the conviction that no one can ever really experience or witness such phenomena, and that reports of any such experience must either be a mere metaphor or an outright fraud. He explains that, "...when reason is severed from the laws of experience it is of no use whatsoever in such a bewitched world... the supernatural... is not, according to the laws of reason, an object of either theoretical or practical use."[20]

Empirical research into how psychic influences occur is what most aggravates Kant. Whatever else Kant says to justify himself, the concern that a "theoretical" grasp of psychic phenomena might allow us to "perform them" so effectively that we "storm heaven" — in other words, *violate the sacred domain of religious belief*— seems to be what really motivates him to reject these phenomena. Moreover, this rejection, which is motivated by terror in the face of the paranormal, lies at the basis of Kant's determination of the categories of the faculty of pure Reason as the lawgiver of Nature. He can in no way tolerate an endeavor to understand the conditions required for "supernatural" phenomena of various kinds, in order to reliably cause them to occur and to execute one's will by means of them and in contravention of (what he takes to be) natural laws. Kant rails against so-called "magicians" who claim that this method is, after all, no different from that of scientists who do not understand the ultimate cause or causes of natural phenomena (any better than the "magician" understands that of "supernatural" occurrences), but who nonetheless develop a sufficiently precise empirical knowledge so as to practically design technological devices that further the human will: "... to think that, through... a really *firm* theoretical faith in miracles, man could himself perform them and so storm heaven — this is to venture so far beyond the

---

19   Ibid., p. 182.
20   Ibid.

limits of reason that we are not justified in tarrying long over such a sense-less conceit."[21]

Kant himself did, however, "tarry long" over someone with such a conceit — at least in his youth, when he undertook an extensive study of the wondrous works of Emmanuel Swedenborg. A scientist and states-man by training and profession, at the age of 45 Swedenborg began having paranormal experiences of other worlds and communications with their inhabitants. The major work wherein he describes these encounters, and ventures an esoteric interpretation of scripture on their basis, is the eight-volume *Arcana Coelestia*, or "Secrets of Heaven," published between 1749 and 1756.[22] Kant purchased and read this entire work, and moreover he spent his time and money investigating stories about Swedenborg's various paranormal abilities.[23] Swedenborg was widely condemned as a heretic, to the point where heresy proceedings were instituted against clerics who had positively received and reviewed Swedenborg's writings at the urging of the conservative Leipzig theologian Johann August Ernesti (1701–1781). The early Swedenborgian works of Friedrich Christoph Oetinger (1702–1782) and Heinrich Wilhelm Clemm (1725–1775) were declared heretical by the government of Württemberg, which confiscated all copies from the citizenry on pain of arrest.[24]

When, in the midst of this atmosphere, rumors began to circulate that Kant was interested in Swedenborg and was researching his expe-riences, the young aspiring academic believed that his attainment of a tenured professorship would be endangered.[25] In order to mitigate this danger, he wrote *Dreams of a Spirit-Seer*. It was published in the winter of 1766 — *anonymously*, although enough people knew Kant to be its author

21   Ibid., pp. 83–84.

22   Gregory R. Johnson [Editor], *Kant on Swedenborg: Dreams of a Spirit-Seer and Other Writings* (Westchester, Pennsylvania: Swedenborg Foundation Publishers, 2002), p. xi.

23   Ibid., p. 4.

24   Ibid., pp. xxiv-xxv.

25   Ibid., p. xvii.

that it was effective in addressing the rumors of his interest in Swedenborg that were already circulating. What is bizarre about the text is that, viewed from a rhetorical perspective, it mocks Swedenborg, but the content, when carefully examined, conflicts with the mocking tone and satirical style. It demonstrates not only a close reading of Swedenborg and a positive evaluation of some of his paranormal feats, but also something far more astonishing: it is in *this* early text, with reference to Swedenborg's other-worldly encounters, that Kant first develops all of the major structures of the metaphysical and ethical system later crystallized in such books as *Groundwork of the Metaphysics of Morals*.[26]

Kant says that it would be "splendid" if empirical evidence of paranormal experiences of the kind that Swedenborg has had could be taken as "a real and universally acknowledged observation" on the basis of which to validate "a systematic constitution of the spirit world" of the kind that he develops in this text, and that otherwise "could be inferred or only supposed with some probability...merely from the concept of spiritual nature as such, which is far too hypothetical."[27] One cannot overemphasize the importance of such a statement. It demonstrates, quite to the contrary of Kant's later position, that the ethically-oriented metaphysics laid out from the *Groundwork* onwards was developed with a view toward the *empirical* evidence for ghosts, telepathy, and so forth. This reading is further supported by the fact that Kant takes pains to separate Swedenborg's badly-rationalized interpretations of his experiences from the actual paranormal phenomena themselves, which he further subdivides into three classes, ranging from truly otherworldly Out-of-Body Experiences to wakeful imaginings.[28] Kant proposes to systematically distill the basic worldview implicit in these experiences.

The first aspect of Swedenborg's metaphysics that Kant adopts is the dualistic division of the cosmos into *parallel* spiritual and physical realms,

---

26   Ibid., pp. xvii–xviii.

27   Ibid., p. 19.

28   Ibid., pp. 50–51.

which we and other living beings exist in *simultaneously*. Kant defines
a spirit, whether it is simply of a living being or of a rational being, as
an entity that fills a space without excluding the occupation of that same
space by elementary particles of matter.[29] Very significantly, Kant admits
that this need not be rationally comprehensible in order to be *empirically*
possible.[30] Such a spirit is the locus of a sphere of activity that does not offer the physical resistance that solid entities do to one another. It "*occupies*
a space (i.e., can be immediately active in it) without *filling* it (i.e., offering
resistance to material substances in it)."[31] For example, the "soul" conceived in these spiritual terms "is wholly in my whole body, and wholly
in each of its parts." In order to illustrate this proposition, Kant refers to
a crude diagram of a ghost in the 1659 text *Orbis Sensualium Pictus* by
Jan Amos Comenius.[32] Moreover, Kant explicitly refers to Descartes and
attacks the mechanistic Cartesian conception of the interaction of a basically un-extended mind with the body through the brain organ alone. He
presents certain facts drawn from cases of brain damage as *empirical* evidence against such a rationalistic conception of how the mind "animate[s]
an animal machine."[33] Instead, he proposes to address the "mysterious" interaction "between a spirit and a body" in terms of inner spiritual natures
that are the motive principle of beings, especially of living and rational
beings.[34]

While Kant does not go so far as Hylozoism, he sees it as much closer
to the truth than materialism, and he cites the work of Stahl with approval
while criticizing Hofmann, Boerhaave, "and others who leave immaterial forces out of consideration, [and] keep to mechanical causes."[35] Kant
defines "mechanical" explanations of Nature as ones that admit of cal-

29   Ibid., p. 7.
30   Ibid., p. 8.
31   Ibid., p. 9.
32   Ibid., pp. 10–11.
33   Ibid., pp. 12–13.
34   Ibid., pp. 14–15.
35   Ibid., pp. 16–18.

culation through the mathematical equations of physics, and he accepts the view that the phenomena of *life* cannot be as adequately explained in these terms as the dynamics of inorganic matter can.[36] Rather, there is an "immaterial world (*mundus intelligibilis*)" where pneumatic laws govern the generation and interaction of the "spontaneously active principles" of organic beings, including those possessed of rational faculties.[37] This parallel world is regarded by Kant as "a self-subsisting whole" wherein beings interact "without the mediation of corporeal things," and where we are continuously present, although this is veiled from us by our physical senses.[38] "It is," he says, "one subject that belongs to the visible and invisible world alike as a member, but not one and the same person..."[39] Kant claims that the reality of the other world "is as good as demonstrated, or it could easily be proven, if one would take the time, or better still, it will in the future, I know not where or when, yet be proven."[40] He is, of course, referring here to a pending *empirical* validation, not a rational "proof."

The second systematic feature of Kant's metaphysics that is derived from Swedenborg is the claim that our experiences of space and time are cognitive translations of an a-temporal, and not spatially differentiated, spiritual reality pre-consciously intuited by our minds, but veiled, as it were, by the encumbrance of our finite physical senses. In the spirit world, beings are not separated by the spatial distances that their counterparts in the physical world are; someone whose body is in Europe may be in close proximity to a spirit whose body is in India, whereas two people whose physical bodies cohabit the same household in the physical world may be very distant from one another in the spiritual one.[41] This "proximity" is of the nature of a spiritual affinity, and "not a true space" or spatial relation.[42]

---

36   Ibid., p. 15.

37   Ibid., p. 16.

38   Ibid., pp. 16, 18, 24.

39   Ibid., p. 23.

40   Ibid., p. 19.

41   Ibid., p. 52.

42   Ibid.

Accordingly, the traversing of "distance" in the spiritual world also does not involve the elapsing of chronological time.[43] Kant draws an analogy between our cognitive translation of intuitions of the spirit world and our waking interpretation of what we experienced in deep sleep.[44] He ventures the hypothesis that dreams are not at all confused, but have a non-spatial and supra-temporal logic that is even clearer than that of so-called "waking" life; it is the brain organ that muddles the experiences of the dream world after the fact of having "awakened" from out of it.[45] He views the super-intelligent behavior of some somnambulists as evidence of this.[46]

"Influxes" from the spiritual world enter our minds but, as it were, "indirectly" or what we would now call *subconsciously* or *subliminally*, whereupon they stir up images that, according to "the law of association of ideas," provide us with "analogous representations" or "symbols" of "spiritual concepts themselves."[47] The concept that we would now refer to as the subconscious or subliminal mind is present here in terms of Swedenborg's distinction between an "outer and inner memory in man," as Kant puts it. The outer memory is consciously retrievable memory, whereas the inner memory is an exact record of every detail of all of the experiences that one has undergone, but that is not normally accessible.[48] In the spirit world, we can read each other's inner memories — in other words, our form of communication there is telepathic.[49] However, our doubles in the spirit world can only perceive the goings-on in our world through reading the inner memory of people who, like Swedenborg, can act as mediums between the two worlds on account of having more direct access to their subconscious minds.[50] In the case of these "peculiar

---

43   Ibid., pp. 18, 53.
44   Ibid., pp. 23–24.
45   Ibid., p. 23.
46   Ibid., p. 24.
47   Ibid.
48   Ibid., p. 51.
49   Ibid.
50   Ibid., p. 52.

persons" with a hypersensitive nervous system "whose organs have an extraordinarily great susceptibility to intensifying the images of the imagination… than ordinarily happens and also should happen with healthy human beings," spiritual influxes may even manifest as apparently present in the physical world of space and time. These "apparitions," which have a genuine, albeit oblique, correspondence to realities in the spiritual world, are "only an illusion of the imagination."[51]

However, Kant goes out of his way to differentiate such extrasensory perceptions from ordinary sensory delusions and from the overactive imaginations of daydreamers. The medium who regularly receives telepathic messages from the "other side," or the "spirit-seer" assailed by specters is, rather, a "waking dreamer" whose extrasensory perceptions of the spirit world are projected into the physical world through a derangement of the brain, the nervous system, and the bodily senses; the shocking nature of such visions causes them to appear even more vividly and to further convince one who experiences them of their veracity.[52] Kant writes, "It is thus no wonder if the visionary [such as Swedenborg] believes that he quite distinctly sees or hears many things that no one else but he perceives; likewise if these figments appear to him and suddenly disappear; or if they beguile one sense, e.g., sight, and can be sensed by no others, e.g., touch, and thus appear penetrable."[53] These "wild chimeras and wondrous caricatures" that are "hatched out" by "the deceived senses… may have a genuine spiritual influx as their basis."[54] Kant concludes that, "One need no longer be at a loss to give apparently rational explanations for the ghost stories that so often cross the path of philosophers… This deception can affect any one of the senses, and however much it may be mixed with nonsensical figments, one need not let this deter one from supposing underlying spiritual influxes."[55]

---

51   Ibid., p. 25.
52   Ibid., pp. 30–31, 33.
53   Ibid., p. 34.
54   Ibid., p. 26.
55   Ibid.

It is also in the writings of Swedenborg that Kant first encountered, and apparently internalized, the view that we are governed by two sets of laws: the physical Laws of Nature and the moral law of the spiritual world. All of our hidden motives have the effect in the spiritual world that, on account of the Laws of Nature, they cannot have in the physical world.[56] For example, positive intentions that cannot be actualized through impotence are fruitful there, and one's spiritual state also reflects negative intentions that were successfully disguised as positive ones in this world.[57] Kant follows Swedenborg in seeing our physically conditioned and conflicting passions as something that must be struggled against or surmounted in order to adhere to the moral law and, like Swedenborg, he argues that the moral law must not be followed as a means to any other end than itself. It is with a view to Swedenborgian dualism that we can understand Kant's almost Gnostic insistence in the *Groundwork of the Metaphysics of Morals* that the moral law is an objective principle on which we would be directed to act *even if* it were against "every propensity, inclination, and natural tendency of ours."[58] For it to do so would only render the command in a duty more sublime and dignified, according to Kant, while taking nothing away from its validity. Kant goes on to assert that "the human being claims for himself a will" *only* insofar as he disregards *all* desires and sensible incitements.[59] The distinction between the two types of imperatives, hypothetical and categorical, is rendered on the basis of what *end* they aim at. Subjective *ends* rest on incentives. They are material ends in the sense that they can be effects of one's actions *in the physical world*. Acting in accordance with the Categorical Imperative, even though it has no effect in *this* world, makes more sense and is less hollow than it is often taken to be when considered as action "in accordance with the moral law alone,"

---

56   Ibid., p. 22.

57   Ibid., pp. 22–23.

58   Kant, *Groundwork of the Metaphysics of Morals* in *Practical Philosophy*, 4:425, my emphasis.

59   Ibid., 4:457.

if one considers it the expression of a will whose consequences manifest a-temporally in the *moral world order* of the spiritual realm.

Finally, Kant's conception of this *moral world order* as a "kingdom of ends" (*Reich der Zwecke*) is literally lifted out of the texts of Swedenborg—who is the first person to use this exact phrase, or at the very least the *Arcana* is the first place where Kant could have encountered it before later adopting it in his own writings. Kant follows Swedenborg in taking the inhabitants of other planets on the physical plane to be subjects of the "kingdom of ends" on the spiritual plane, and indeed, his keen interest in extraterrestrial intelligence may also have been a debt to his reading of Swedenborg—who claimed to have actually encountered numerous extraterrestrials and communicated with them telepathically. Kant notes that since the spirit world is not structured in terms of geometric space and chronological time, and given that every soul has a counterpart there and that communication between them is telepathic, the apparently "vast distance between the rational inhabitants of the world is nothing" that would make it any more difficult "to speak to an inhabitant of Saturn" than it is for him to "speak to the departed soul of a human being."[60] Kant discusses the possibility of exploring societies on other planets by this means: "Thus, a human being does not need to have actually lived on the other heavenly bodies to one day know them in all their wonders. His soul reads in the memories of other departed citizens of the universe the representations that they have of their life and their dwelling place, and he sees the objects therein just as well as if through an immediate intuition."[61]

These ideas were instrumental in Kant's development of his universal or cosmopolitan ethics in the *Groundwork of the Metaphysics of Morals*, where he argues that it is inherent to the idea of duty and of a moral law that it hold not only for human beings, but for all other rational beings as well. Kant refers to non-human intelligence no less than eleven times in the *Groundwork*, and he draws an explicit distinction between human

---

60   Kant, *Dreams of a Spirit-Seer*, pp. 52–53.

61   Ibid., p. 53.

beings and rational beings in general on six of these occasions.[62] When
we view these references through the lens of the third part of Kant's 1755
astronomical work *Universal Natural History and Theory of the Heavens*,
it becomes clear that applicability to extraterrestrial intelligence was a key
motivation behind Kant's attempt to develop an *a priori* moral philosophy. In this suppressed third part of his *Theory of the Heavens*, Kant lays
out an elaborate Swedenborgian account of the biological and psychical
condition of life on other planets.[63] It is the key to his insistence, in the
Groundwork, that whatever the ground of moral obligation may be, it cannot be sought in empirically conditioned *human* nature. This law must
not be derived from any special tendency of human reason. After having
stripped away all inclinations and motives relevant only to human sensibility, nothing can be left other than action in conformity with universal
law itself — a law whose representation must determine the will without
regard for any *effect* that could be the *object* of desire.[64] It is at this point
that Kant first introduces the Categorical Imperative: *I ought never to act
except in such a way that I could also will that my maxim should become
a universal law*. In *Dreams of a Spirit-Seer*, Kant repeatedly refers to the
denizens of Swedenborg's spirit world — and of the noumenal realm that
he models upon it — as citizens of a single "spiritual republic."[65] He even
draws an instructive contrast between this "one great republic" and the
common notion of "Heaven" as some place "above" the Earth. Kant points
out that, as Swedenborg recognized, the inhabitants of other planets as
benighted as our own might well point up into the starry sky in the direction of our Earth and think that "Heaven" is somewhere up there.[66]

---

62 Kant, *Groundwork of the Metaphysics of Morals* in *Practical Philosophy*, see 4:389,
    4:408, 4:425, 4:428–4:29, 4:447–448, and 4:449.

63 Michael J. Crowe, *The Extraterrestrial Life Debate: Antiquity to 1915* (University of
    Notre Dame, 2009), p. 149.

64 Kant, *Groundwork of the Metaphysics of Morals* in *Practical Philosophy*, 4:402.

65 Kant, *Dreams of a Spirit-Seer*, pp. 20, 26.

66 Ibid., pp. 18–19.

Following Swedenborg, Kant identifies the "spiritual republic" that encompasses all planets "in measureless outer space" *on the spiritual plane* as the true Heaven — and, most importantly, as Kant's ideal model for a cosmopolitan political community that most nearly approximates it on planet Earth. He even refers to the "spiritual republic" as the site of an ultimate reconciliation "between the private and the General Will" in "accordance with pneumatic laws."[67] This core insight remains a background for the development of Kant's moral philosophy, even if he eventually dismissed the specificities of his theory of extraterrestrial intelligence in the third part of his speculative *Natural History and Theory of the Heavens* and consented to its suppression within his own lifetime. In the *Critique of Pure Reason*, Kant writes, "I should not hesitate to stake my all on the truth of the proposition — that, at least, some one of the planets, which we see, is inhabited. Hence I say that I have not merely the opinion, but the strong belief, on the correctness of which I would stake even many of the advantages of life, that there are inhabitants in other worlds."[68] We also have a passage towards the end of the *Critique of Practical Reason* where Kant suggests that were it not for the moral law within each man, his perishable physical being as an animal creature alone would render him insignificant in the face of the vastness of the cosmos. It is the fact that the heavens are populated by beings capable of acting on the moral law that renders contemplation of the vastness of the heavens edifying, rather than cause for a sense of terrifying absurdity. Significantly, the first lines of this passage from the Second Critique are quoted on Kant's tombstone:[69]

Two things fill the mind with ever new and increasing admiration and awe, the oftener and more steadily they are reflected on: the starry heavens above me and the moral law within me... The former... broadens the connection in which I stand into an unbounded magnitude of worlds beyond worlds and systems of systems... The former view of a countless multitude of worlds annihilates, as it were, my importance as an animal creature, which must give back to the planet

---

67   Ibid., p. 22.

68   Kant, *Critique of Pure Reason*, A825/B853.

69   Crowe, *The Extraterrestrial Life Debate*, p. 151.

(a mere speck in the universe) the matter from which it came.[70]

In *Dreams of a Spirit-Seer*, Kant recognizes that even a single solid case of the kind reported by Swedenborg would be revolutionary in its implications: "Should he admit the probability of even one of these stories? How important would such an avowal be, and what astonishing implications could one foresee, if even only *one* such occurrence could be supposed to be proven?"[71] He goes on to give us just such a case. As Kant recounts, one afternoon towards the end of 1759, upon his return from England, a merchant in Gothenburg invited Swedenborg to an evening party. At the party, the visionary claimed to suddenly perceive a raging inferno in the southern suburb of Stockholm and, at various intervals through the night, he described the spread of this fire and how it had finally been gotten under control. The astonished guests repeated Swedenborg's vision to nearly everyone they knew, so that by the next morning, the entire town had been informed. It was only two days later that the first news about the fire finally came from Stockholm, confirming in detail Swedenborg's account of the conflagration's point of origin, the extent and pace of its spread, and the manner of its eventual containment.[72] Kant suggests that the investigation of such cases by people who have enough money and nothing better to do with their time might at least prevent Swedenborg from being turned into the next Apollonius of Tyana by someone like Philostratus on account of it no longer being possible to interview witnesses who are long deceased.[73]

Kant sees paranormal phenomena as posing a unique challenge to science, since they cannot be doubted with impunity, and yet to validate many of them would open scientific thinkers to mockery. It is preferable for the intellectual, he says, to deny the reality of such seemingly incomprehensible occurrences altogether than to admit as much ignorance of

---

70   Kant, "Critique of Practical Reason" in *Practical Philosophy*, 5:161.

71   Kant, *Dreams of a Spirit-Seer*, pp. 3–4.

72   Ibid., pp. 43–44.

73   Ibid., p. 45.

them as the common man. This prescient prediction is particularly striking: "One can, therefore, be sure that an academy of sciences will never make this matter into a prize question, not because the members of it are free of all acceptance of the opinion in question but because the rule of prudence rightly sets limits to such questions… And thus stories of this kind will have at any time only secret believers, but publicly they are rejected by the reigning fashion of incredulity."[74] Kant believes that "scoffing" at the paranormal should be encouraged "whether it may be justified or not" because it will hold natural philosophers back from attempting serious interpretations of paranormal phenomena, and thereby being "caught in such bad company" that they place themselves "under suspicion."[75] In other words, yet again, he is worried about what people will think, and on the basis of this concern he is even willing to "in no way… blame" the person who "simply dismisses… without further ado" those who experience the paranormal as "candidates for the hospital and thus spares himself all further inquiry."[76] This encouragement of the hospitalization of those with inconvenient experiences is hardly tempered when Kant goes on to add, "if it was once found necessary at times to burn some of them it will now suffice simply to purge them."[77]

On the basis of his dualistic theory of paranormal experiences, wherein any apparitions in *this* world are derangements and delusions of the senses projecting grossly distorted mental intuitions of the other worlds, Kant denies that whatever kernels of truth they contain can ever be sufficiently separated from the "crude illusions" that the imagination mixes with them so as to ever be "useful" observations.[78] Invoking the blind prophet Tiresias, Kant claims that so-called "knowledge" of the other world can only be gained at the great expense of the rational common sense that allows one to successfully navigate this one — such that

---

74   Ibid., p. 41.
75   Ibid., p. 35.
76   Ibid.
77   Ibid., p. 35.
78   Ibid., pp. 25–26.

one who is *gifted* with heavenly insight is viewed as a fool on the Earth.[79] Unlike natural beings, which, even if they are as small as "a drop of water, a grain of sand, or something even simpler," offer a subject for inexhaustible observations and rationally deduced knowledge, according to Kant "there can be all sorts of *opinions*" about paranormal phenomena, "but never any *knowledge* about them."[80] It can only be ascertained *that* there are spirits, but "since no *data* can be found in the whole of our sensations and that one must make use of negations in order to think of something so very different from sensuous things," it can be concluded that "the pneumatology of mankind can be called a doctrine of our necessary ignorance with respect to a supposed kind of being."[81] Of course, this statement contradicts the main subject matter of *Dreams of a Spirit-Seer*, namely the *sense data* of Swedenborg's *empirical* accounts of paranormal occurrences and abilities. But then Kant has whitewashed this contradiction by radicalizing Swedenborg's own dualism in a neo-Cartesian direction, and claiming thereby that his "visions" are nothing more than mental intuitions of a non-sensory world projected into the physical world through pathologically deranged senses.

The one type of spectral phenomenon or uncanny ability that most strongly challenges this radically dualistic parallelism is psychokinesis (PK), which, as we saw above, Kant strongly condemns in *Religion within the Limits of Reason Alone*, and which he mentions only obliquely and fleetingly in *Dreams of a Spirit-Seer*. In one instance, he mentions maternal impressions as a type of psychokinesis, while dismissively listing a whole slew of paranormal phenomena that he finds particularly offensive: "Among these belong spiritual healing, the dowsing rod, precognitions, the effect of the imagination of pregnant women, the influences of the lunar cycle on animals and plants, and the like."[82] This is not the only ref-

---

79   Ibid., p. 27.
80   Ibid., p. 39.
81   Ibid., p. 40.
82   Ibid., p. 44.

erence to this type of psychokinesis. One of the most striking passages in *Dreams* is one where Kant compares his "reservations" about reporting Swedenborg's visions in any detail to those of a naturalist who must take care that not just anyone sees too clearly what is in his curiosity cabinet, since one of these freaks of nature might leave a harmful impression on a reader's mind the way that traumatic experiences of pregnant women or animals may result in a maternal impression that deforms the development of the fetus.[83] This passage is characteristic of Kant's sarcastically disguised duplicity and smug disingenuousness in this text as a whole.

Another instance where Kant very clearly makes reference to psychokinesis is even more revealing: he draws a connection between it and the simple fact of the body being moved by the immaterial will. He is convinced of its existence since it is indispensable to ethics: "That my will moves my arm is not more intelligible to me than if someone said to me that he could stop the moon in its orbit; the difference is only this: that I experience the former, but my senses have never encountered the latter."[84] With regard to "how an immaterial nature can be in a body and act through it," Kant admits "that I do not understand this at all." He adds, "The very same ignorance also makes me not so bold as to deny totally all truth in the various ghost stories, yet with the familiar yet also strange proviso: to put any single one in doubt but to ascribe some credence to all of them taken together."[85] This is very convenient, since the one common denominator of "all of them taken together" is that there is an afterlife, and this, when taken by itself as an abstraction, encourages moral conduct in this world, whereas the immorality — or rather, *amorality* — of the details of various grisly accounts of paranormal experiences might raise the terrifying question of whether there is a spiritual basis at all for any traditional ethical values. The strongest argument that Kant sees in favor of the paranormal is the hope for a future life, and he takes this "fond

83   Ibid., p. 55.

84   Ibid., p. 60.

85   Ibid., p. 39.

hope that one may still exist in some way after death" to be what propels
the popularity of ghost stories.[86] With as much piety as an orthodox priest
chastising heretics who would dabble in the occult, Kant insists that, "we
must wait until we are instructed, perhaps in the future world, by new
experiences and new concepts about powers in our thinking self that are
still hidden from us."[87] In fact, he repeatedly insists on this, in a more
and more parochial tone each time: "[T]o the curious who so pointedly
inquire about it one may give this simple but very natural reply: that it
would probably be best *if they would deign to wait patiently until they arrived there.*"[88]

When Kant claims that the effect of mind over matter is not rationally comprehensible, it is because he has restricted his definition of the
"rational" to the application of the rules of identity, and contradiction to
the analysis of a causal nexus that can be expressed in terms of mathematical equations.[89] The postulates required to even begin investigating
paranormal phenomena with a view to understanding them are "fictions"
rather than scientific hypotheses because, according to Kant, any proper
hypothesis only concerns fundamental causes and forces whose relations
must remain constant, so that the laws governing them "must be able to
be proved at all times."[90] On this essentially Cartesian basis, of equating
the real with what admits of the predictive calculability and repeatability
of *mathematical* demonstration, Kant agrees with Descartes that while he
can distinctly conceive of himself as an immaterial subject with thoughts,
the power of choice, and other determinations different from those of the
concepts in terms of which he conceives of his body and other material
beings, he cannot coherently think of the connection of himself qua mind
to himself qua body.[91]

86   Ibid., p. 38.
87   Ibid., p. 61.
88   Ibid., p. 63.
89   Ibid., pp. 60–61.
90   Ibid., p. 61.
91   Ibid., p. 60–61.

It is the "irregularity" of "certain alleged experiences" which damns them in Kant's eyes. He rejects any experiences that "cannot be brought under any *law* of sensation accepted by *most* human beings" as no true sensory experiences at all.[92] Here, something else essential to Kant's suppression of the paranormal begins to become clear, something connected to the fact that he wants to emphasize only the most abstract elements of Swedenborg's visions in order to take them, at best, as validation for the existence of a "spiritual republic" where justice is done impartially to all souls based on their innermost ethical intentions. The undemocratic character of the paranormal offends Kant. He cannot countenance the fact that there may be rare experiences and abilities open only to a few people: "But true wisdom is the companion of simplicity, and as with the latter the heart gives direction to the understanding, it generally renders superfluous the great apparatus of learnedness, and its aims do not need *such means as can never be in the power of all human beings*."[93] Kant is deeply disturbed by the thought that "the future destiny of the honest" simple souls could in any way be adversely affected by their not having paranormal abilities, the workings of which even intellectuals such as himself fail to comprehend.[94] His insistence that all phenomena of Nature admissible of scientific study be democratic and egalitarian is probably the basis of his description of the investigation of paranormal occurrences as "uncivil."[95] This should bring to mind the passage cited above from *Religion within the Limits of Reason Alone*, where Kant compares the disorder wrought by the spectral in "the whole rational contemplative commonwealth" to a criminal or terroristic instigation of "disorder in civil life."

The claim that the question of the paranormal is "a question that requires data from a different world than the one he senses" is the basis for Kant's negative re-defining of metaphysics as "a science of the limits of

92   Ibid., p. 62, my emphasis.

93   Ibid.

94   Ibid., p. 63.

95   Ibid., p. 26.

human reason."[96] Only a little further on, Kant rephrases this proto-positivism in the following terms, wherein the paranormal is equated with an impossible and unfathomable limbo that belongs outside the bounds of proper scientific inquiry: "For in order to choose rationally, one must first know even the unnecessary, indeed the impossible; but eventually science arrives at the determination of the limits set for it by the nature of human reason; all unfathomable schemes that may not be unworthy in themselves but lie outside of the sphere of mankind fly into the limbo of vanity."[97] This banishment of the paranormal as a legitimate subject of study will, he hopes, render even metaphysics "scientific" rather than speculative. The more rigorous, in other words the more scientific, philosophical inquiry becomes, the more strictly it should exclude and marginalize the paranormal *in principle*: "But if this investigation turns into philosophy, which judges its own proceedings and which knows not only objects but their relation to the human understanding, then the boundaries draw closer together and marker stones are laid that never again allow investigation to wander beyond its proper district... philosophy moves this phantom of insight yet further away and convinces us that it lies wholly beyond the horizon of mankind."[98] Indeed, Kant's claim that there is really nothing at all to *know* of the paranormal is undermined by his repeated assertions to the contrary, that an understanding of it is something beyond the scope of *merely human* reason.[99] Anyone with a rational faculty as "humble" as his ought to resolve, as Kant does, to make the greatest use of his limited powers in projects appropriate to their own scope, since "if one cannot reasonably attain the great," it is prudent "to restrict oneself to the mediocre."[100] He refers to this prudence as "wise simplicity."[101]

---

96   Ibid., p. 57.

97   Ibid., p. 59.

98   Ibid., p. 60.

99   Ibid., p. 63.

100 Ibid., p. 40.

101 Ibid., p. 59.

Kant ultimately fails to adhere to such prudence himself. In the *Critique of Judgment*, he smuggles the most bizarre elements of his flirtation with a quasi-Swedenborgian metaphysics into the development of his aesthetics. This Third Critique, following the *Critique of Pure Reason* and the *Critique of Practical Reason*, is the completion of the "sober" system for which the elder Kant is famous. Yet its central ideas on the communicability of the inter-subjective recognition of the beautiful and the nature of creative genius rely on the most undemocratic and superhuman aspects of the spectral. Moreover, Kant's tacit redeployment of conceptions such as extrasensory perception, which he first dealt with in his reflections on Swedenborg, are combined with a transcendence of the dualistic scheme that he used to keep the most disturbing implications of the spectral at bay in *Dreams of a Spirit-Seer*. Not only is the appreciation of the beautiful non-rational, and possible solely through a kind of extrasensory perception unevenly shared by the population, the rare creative genius who produces the work of art does so through a oneness with a depth of Nature that lies beneath its law-like appearance and that effectively allows for the psychokinesis that Kant so hysterically dismisses in *Religion within the Limits of Reason Alone*. Finally, as we shall see in the next chapter, Kant concedes that even rational concepts are derivatively developed only on the basis of the "aesthetic ideas" non-rationally intuited by the creative genius.

CHAPTER V

THE TITANIC
TOTAL ARTWORK

Certain passages in Kant's writings on the spectral have left me with the distinct impression that he cannot bear the thought that honest-to-goodness folk with no psychic powers can be harmed with impunity by a terribly unethical virtuoso of the occult arts. In view of this, it is doubly strange that the spectral resurfaces in just this very unevenly distributed form in Kant's aesthetic theory on the nature of genius in the arts. The most surprising element of this occult account of aesthetic activity and the appreciation of the beautiful is something that Kant calls "aesthetic ideas." These are the archetypes of everything beautiful—whether in Nature or whether crafted by means of artistic genius. But they are also far more than that. Kant admits that these ideas, which are of an imaginal or imagistic type, and which can only be grasped by aesthetic judgments, and are solely expressed by a gifted genius, *are the basis for the development of concepts.* Aesthetic intuition of these ideas sets in motion a "free play" of the cognitive faculties wherein more than one concept may be developed on the basis of any given aesthetic idea, but no concept or concepts are ever able to rationally comprehend these aesthetic ideas or their own genesis in terms of them.

These archetypal ideas, which the genius alone is capable of conjuring, could even be the wellspring of the elaboration of all rational concepts fundamental to the sciences. They are neither phenomenal nor noumenal, but seem to have just that *spectral* existence that Kant found repugnant about the spiritual world of Swedenborg. Their intermediate character, and the fact that they are responsible for every judgment of the beautiful even when it concerns natural beings, puts the lie to attempts to draw a sharp divide between mind and matter. Prometheus and Atlas would, in Kant's terms, be "aesthetic ideas" that motivate natural and human activity in the way that he thinks *ingenium* unconsciously motivates the creative endeavors of the genius. I will go on to argue that they are the aesthetic ideas from out of which the fundamental concepts of the sciences are developed. Since it is these sciences that seem to have desecrated life through their world-transforming technological power, it would be of great significance to demonstrate how they are themselves expressions of the sacred.

The line of argument in Kant's aesthetic treatise, *Critique of the Power of Judgment*, that most concerns us here begins with his distinction between the pleasant and the beautiful. The *pleasant* concerns both animals and men; the *beautiful* only men, but also in their animal nature; and the *good* concerns rational beings in general. In other words, the *beautiful* pleases without any compelling interest of sense *or of reason*.[1] The judgment that an object is beautiful is unique in that, apart from concepts, it posits its universal validity, not an objective validity but a subjective one. In other words, one presupposes that every subject would either assent to this judgment or be mistaken for not doing so.[2] As regards the *pleasant*, everyone has his own taste based on his proper sensibility. However, where the *beautiful* is concerned, it would reduce the very idea of *taste* or aesthetic judgment to nonsense if we were to accept that any object may be beautiful to a certain person but not to another. That which only a particular person or other may find charming should not, on that account, be deemed "beautiful."[3] This is not to suggest that we arrive at the beautiful by opinion polling. The tasteless majority may be mistaken about what a minority exercising aesthetic judgment knows is, *in fact*, beautiful.

---

1 Immanuel Kant, *Critique of the Power of Judgment* (New York: Cambridge University Press, 2006), pp. 94–96.

2 Ibid., pp. 96–97.

3 Ibid., pp. 97–98.

Kant remarks that the way in which the aesthetic universality of a judgment that an object is beautiful extends to the whole sphere of judging persons, without having a logical validity and without uniting the predicate of beauty with the concept of the object in question, reveals something of interest to the transcendental philosopher concerning a non-conceptual property of our cognitive faculty that would otherwise have remained unknown. The judgment of the beautiful is non-conceptual in that no one can be led to it by any rule or set of rules. It is a judgment that cannot be arrived at through reasoning. Each must submit the object to his senses, and yet each may pronounce a judgment valid for all others after having assessed the object.[4]

Since the apprehension of the beautiful cannot involve a judgment according to the categories, whereby what is sensuously intuited is structured according to certain concepts, Kant argues that the beautiful must instead catalyze a "free play" of the cognitive faculties. Moreover, this dynamic non-conceptual cognition must be communicable among subjects without the mediation of concepts or reasons.[5] This inner-relational cognitive character of aesthetic judgment has to do with the fact that the beautiful has no purpose, whereas both that which is of interest on account of its being pleasurable and that which is of interest on account of its being good are objects whose very concept implicates an end-directed nature (whether the end be sensible pleasure or moral perfection).[6] The judgment of taste rests on the *a priori* grounds of a quasi-purposive aim to perpetuate itself, namely to extend the free play of the cognitive powers. This manifests itself as the purely contemplative quality of the appreciation of the beautiful, wherein without any practical orientation whatsoever, we *linger* over it and are, as it were, enchanted or entranced.[7]

4　Ibid., pp. 99–101.

5　Ibid., pp. 102–104.

6　Ibid., p. 105.

7　Ibid., pp. 106–107.

The feeling (inner sense) of the harmony of the interplay of the mental powers is what lies in the place of the concept as the "determining ground" of aesthetic judgment.[8] The subjective universality of aesthetic judgments—in other words, the way in which one may rightly presume that everyone else *ought* to agree with one's estimation of what is beautiful—must be grounded in a *common sense* which is not a common understanding. The latter judges on the basis of shared concepts, even if these principles are commonly represented only obscurely. By contrast, a common sense that would be the basis of aesthetic judgment would be a non-conceptual, non-external "sense" arising from the free play of our cognitive powers and allowing for a communicability, unmediated by reason, of our state of mind with others.[9] In other words, this "sense" that Kant posits is an extrasensory perception that is telepathically communicable.

Judgments of beauty are not simply the antithesis of the kinds of judgments of ugliness that have to do with asymmetries in things on account of which we sense that their purpose has been contracted or impeded, such as with deformities in animals, badly designed buildings, gardens, and so forth. This is why the appreciation of basic geometric forms is not a proper appreciation of the beautiful. It is a function of the understanding, which grasps the goal-oriented concept of a thing. Rather, taste can be most readily discerned at work, where the imagination is pushed to its limits, for example, and where the beautiful verges on the grotesque and yet just barely averts it, so that we see imagination express itself lawfully where there is no law to follow.[10] This is the same lawless limbo that Kant seemed to abhor as the domain of the paranormal in *Dreams of a Spirit-Seer* and to deny as an affront to reason in *Religion within the Limits of Reason Alone*.

There can be nothing like an objective principle of taste, which would allow one to syllogistically derive the judgment that an object is beauti-

---

8   Ibid., pp. 111–113.

9   Ibid., pp. 121–122.

10   Ibid., pp. 125–126.

ful from its concept. No grounds of proof whatsoever may persuade one prior to direct experience.[11] The imagination can awaken the understanding without the aid of concepts and communicate itself, not as a thought that could be put into words, but as a more inward state of mind that is in some way "purposive" or intentional without conforming to a given purpose or end implicit in the concept of any object.[12] In light of the relationship between Nature and the nature of genius, we can see that Nature is not simply something *like* an artwork, it *is* an artwork, but one of a "superhuman" magnitude.[13] Consequently, the genius who channels Nature's creative force is something more than a mere human being. Here we can see Kant's departure from the egalitarian and democratic concerns that in large part motivate his suppression of the spectral in *Dreams of a Spirit-Seer*.

Works of art should have the same effortless beauty that Nature does; they should have an organic lawfulness that is too complex to analyze, and yet that is not at all the outcome of a belabored adherence to arbitrary laws. If the design of a work of art were aimed at the production of a certain type of object, then the art or artisanship that attained this aim would only please us in a way that would be conceptually mediated. Such an object would please as the *mechanical* does, and it would not provoke the free play of the beautiful. The purposive character of the beautiful work of art ought to be so seamless that if one could say it appeared designed, it would appear so only in the sense that organic nature strikes us in this way as well. Rules learned by the artist in the course of training at various schools should vanish without a trace in the work; they should be absorbed in it.[14] None of this is to say that skill, aptitude, and trained judgment play no role in the work of art. However, that we sometimes find works of genius that are tasteless in spite of that, but never find that

---

11   Ibid., p. 166.

12   Ibid., pp. 173–176.

13   Ibid., pp. 189–191.

14   Ibid., pp. 185–186.

acquired skill or refined taste alone can produce a work of genius, suggests to Kant that the genius of the artist and the skill of the artisan are separable, and that the former is the necessary condition of beautiful artworks.[15]

Kant concludes that *genius* is the "talent" (natural gift) or innate disposition (*ingenium*) through which Nature gives the rule to art, on account of which the beauty of an artwork is as original and seamless as the beauty of Nature. It is Nature acting through the nature in the subject that produces beautiful art, which is always a product of genius — of a talent for producing that for which no definite rule can be given or learned, regardless of the artist's aptitude or lack thereof. Furthermore, it is not enough for a work of genius to be "original"; since there can also be original nonsense, it must be both original *and exemplary*. In other words, it cannot be imitative and must establish its own standard of judgment both for itself and for other works in its wake.

Finally, and perhaps most significantly, the genius at work in beautiful art will admit of no scientific explanation of its genesis. It is here that, at least implicitly, Kant is reversing his position on the paranormal, whether he realizes it or not — a fact that would be more widely recognized if his treatments of the subject were read alongside the Third Critique. Insofar as the nature of genius is Nature acting through the subject, this is the same as saying that there is an aspect of Nature that is both open to direct experience and that lies beyond the concepts of the categories, but is not of the abstractly posited *noumenal* "world of understanding." It is, rather, the "pneumatic" world of Swedenborg, but now conceived of not as being dualistically distinct from Nature, but as being one with it on a deeper level than can be fathomed by Reason and its concepts. Nature does not prescribe rules to science, but only to beautiful art. All of this also means that the *genius* can neither devise a rule-governed or formulaic method by which to repeat his own past artworks, nor could he formulate a set of rules or methods that would allow others to replicate his efforts. He himself would not rationally *know* how he arrived at the ideas that he did.

---

15   Ibid., pp. 189–191.

This harks back to the original meaning of the word *genius* as a guardian spirit given to a man at birth as a source of inspiration. It is the Greek *daimon* of Socrates.[16] Kant refers to this spirit as the "animating principle of the mind," and it is what is lacking when we judge that for all its technical perfection, or even despite a very tasteful presentation, some poem, person, or conversation is "without spirit."

More precisely, the faculty whereby this spirit puts the mental powers to play without the mediation of rational concepts is "the faculty of presenting *aesthetic ideas*." The imagination uses the material supplied to it by Nature in order to surpass Nature by generating ideas that lie beyond the bounds of experience. No concept can be adequate to the internal intuition of these ideas, but aesthetic ideas are capable of indefinitely expanding, and hence redefining rational concepts that they spawn, and that attempt, unsuccessfully yet generatively, to clearly grasp (*griefen, begriff*) that which engendered them. An aesthetic idea is a representation of the imagination that occasions much more thought than can be reduced to any one concept or set of concepts, and consequently, an imaginative idea that — unlike a rational idea — cannot be fully encompassed by language and thereby rendered intelligible. Prometheus and Atlas are such aesthetic ideas.

Kant must take poetry to be a very special type of discourse, distinct from language in general, because he goes on to say that the poet manifests the faculty of aesthetic ideas *par excellence*. The poet's imagination is capable of opening out in such a way as to appreciate various representations of the same idea, whose relationship to one another is not definable in the way that the relationship of multiple instantiations of a concept to the concept of which they are instantiations can be logically presented. These variations of aesthetic ideas are not graspable in terms of any set of shared logical attributes.[17] Even if it outstrips the concept-formation of objective cognition, the subjective exercise of aesthetic ideation by the ge-

---

16   Ibid., pp. 186–187.

17   Ibid., p. 193.

nius quickens his cognitive powers.[18] This relationship between imagination and understanding that takes place in the genius is not teachable by any science, nor can it be learned industriously, and what proceeds from it does not admit of mechanical reproduction. Only a subsequent genius really learns from a prior one, and only insofar as the former supersedes his predecessor as exemplary, through the same intuition by means of which he appreciates the earlier work of genius:

> [G]enius is the exemplary originality of the natural gifts of a subject in the *free* employment of his cognitive faculties. In this way the product of a genius (as regards what is to be ascribed to genius and not to possible learning or schooling) is an example, not to be imitated (for then that which in it is genius and constitutes the spirit of the work would be lost), but to be followed by another genius, whom it awakens to a feeling of his own originality and whom it stirs so to exercise his art in freedom from the constraint of rules, that thereby a new rule is gained for art; and thus his talent shows itself to be exemplary.... A genius is a favorite of nature and must be regarded by us as a rare phenomenon...[19]

The significance of this cannot be overestimated since, as Kant claims, *it is through aesthetic genius that "ideas are found for a given concept" in the first place* — even if they are necessarily indistinct at the outset, so that the same aesthetic idea could yield different concepts that are rationally graspable, communicable, useful, and learnable.[20] In other words, the ideas from out of which concepts are defined ultimately emerge from "the ineffable element in the state of mind" of a genius which, whether in the medium of poetry, painting, or sculpture, can seize "the quickly passing play of imagination" and cohesively condense it into something symbolic or archetypal that reaches others on a pre-rational level, and from out of which they can develop concepts, presumably including those rational criteria defining proper scientific method.[21] In science, "clearly

---

18   Ibid., p. 192.

19   Ibid., pp. 191–196.

20   Ibid., pp. 192–193, 195.

21   Ibid., pp. 194–195.

known rules must go beforehand and determine the procedure."[22] Unlike the artistic genius, the scientist does not have insight into the free play of cognitive powers that occurs prior to the determination of these rules. It is only aesthetic intuition that can offer us insight into these ideas and how they spectrally structure scientific theory and practice, including its sociopolitical dimension.

An understanding of aesthetic ideas and of creative genius can just barely be extracted from between the lines of Kant's third, and final, critical text, and he never reconciles it with the doctrine of the first two critiques or revises them in light of it. For the further development of these insights into the occult nature of aesthetic intuition, we need to look to Friedrich Schelling. In the thought of Schelling, what Kant predominately took to be the distinction between the phenomenal world of Nature as it appears to us and the noumenal world of things-in-themselves becomes only a distinction between our conscious experience of the world and our unconscious or subconscious intuition of beings. The apparent mechanism, and mathematical predictability, of the natural world is only the function of a constraining or contracting force, or "will," that fortifies our conscious experience by offering us relatively stable and well-differentiated beings in distinct relationships with one another. There is, however, an unconscious or subconscious drive to plunge back into the abyss of nothingness that underlies such well-ordered appearances. The artistic genius is able to create what she does on account of a rare capacity to synthesize these conscious and unconscious types of mental functioning. Unlike in the case of most people, her conscious mind is not entirely closed off from her subconscious. The artistic genius is able to consciously express what she intuits subconsciously by allowing her mind to plunge into the abyssal background of beings.

This is, however, not limited to the canvas or the block of marble. It is a real contravention of the merely apparent "laws" of physics, one that restores the abyssal freedom of the creative will. What Kant is most afraid

---

22   Ibid., p. 195.

of, Schelling also acknowledges — namely that genius of this kind is inhuman and poses a great peril to the world of ordinary mortals. Schelling says that its cultivation beyond the "merely aesthetic" sphere would "presuppose a race of Titans," such as Prometheus and Atlas, and that this might prove detrimental to the rest of mankind. Yet, unlike Kant, and despite these concerns, in *Clara*, *Bruno*, and *The World Ages*, Schelling goes on to broadly indicate what he means by the general development of aesthetic intuition and creative genius beyond the confines of the fine arts. This hinges on his understanding of what an idea is, an understanding that radicalizes what Kant already glimpsed in his exposition of "aesthetic ideas."

Taking the aesthetics of Kant as his point of departure, Schelling argues that "the sanctity and purity" of art lies in its not being a means to any end outside of itself, such as sensuous enjoyment, usefulness, or even morality. Only a barbarous culture uses art as a means for sensuous enjoyment, and only a society which views economic achievement as the highest end of the human spirit would demand that art should be "useful." [23] Aesthetic production, just as any free action, is sustained by an infinite separation of conscious and unconscious activity. According to Schelling, in aesthetic production these infinitely divergent activities are unified in a finite product. This finite presentation of the Infinite is *beauty*, which is the defining characteristic of any true work of art. Schelling acknowledges that there are also *sublime* works of art. These differ from beautiful ones in that the infinite contradiction between the spiritual freedom of the creative will and the apparent determinism of physical nature is not resolved in the artwork itself, but in its viewer. However, both the beautiful and the sublime involve the unconscious discernment of a magnitude (depth, or dimension of meaning) in a certain object, which cannot be comprehended by conscious activity. This sets finite conscious activity and an

---

23   F. W. J. Schelling, "System of Transcendental Idealism" in *German Aesthetic and Literary Criticism: Kant, Fichte, Schelling, Schopenhauer, Hegel*, edited with an Introduction by David Simpson (New York: Cambridge University Press, 1984), p. 126.

unconscious fathoming of the negatively infinite abyss at odds with each other, such that only an aesthetic intuition can replace the contradiction with a realization of the pre-established harmony of the two activities.[24]

Schelling believes that since beauty is only produced by the resolution of an infinite contradiction (for consciousness), there is no real beauty in Nature, and any apparent natural beauty is accidental. Consequently, he insists that Nature should never be the standard for art to imitate. Rather, the perfection of the work of art is the standard against which to judge any mere semblance of beauty in Nature.[25] Schelling notes that while there is no one who lacks at least a little poetry in his nature, even a potential genius graced by an overflowing poetic nature can never produce real art unless he can tame his gift with the discipline of technical proficiency. On the contrary, a person highly skilled and studied in the works of great masters, and the techniques they employed, can produce some kind of artwork. Nevertheless, the belabored superficiality of the latter will present a striking contrast with "the inexhaustible depth which the true artist… puts into his work involuntarily and which neither he nor anyone else is able to penetrate completely."[26] Every true work of art is sufficiently profound as to allow for infinite interpretation, whereas a superficial work of artistry merely presents a literal record of the artist's conscious activity and intentions.[27]

Schelling argues that no genius is necessary in the sciences. While it is not impossible for a scientific problem to be solved in a genial way (such as with Kepler on gravitation), the same problem can also be solved mechanically (such as with Newton on gravitation). Only in art is genius always required for a resolution that can be arrived at by no other means. Consequently, it is difficult to tell when genius is at play in the sciences. Nevertheless, Schelling lays out two criteria. Firstly, genius is involved

24   Ibid., p. 125.
25   Ibid., p. 126.
26   Ibid., p. 124.
27   Ibid., pp. 124–125.

where a scientific theory is not laboriously developed or built-up piece-meal, but where a vision or idea of the whole *precedes* the discovery and examination of the parts that constitute it. Secondly, genius may also be at work where a scientist makes statements whose meaning he could not have rationally or wholly comprehended based on his present store of knowledge and his historical circumstances. These two cases involve the kind of resolution of infinite contradiction, between finite natural deter-minism and immeasurable spiritual freedom, through the conspiring of conscious and unconscious activity that is characteristic of artistic geni-us.[28] In summary, Schelling states, "Genius is differentiated from every-thing that is mere talent or skill by the fact that it resolves a contradiction which is absolute and resolvable by nothing else."[29]

Schelling maintains that art can never be subordinated by science, though he recognizes that of all endeavors, the latter is closest to art on account of its disinterestedness. The two are related in being diametri-cally opposed tendencies. What is more significant is that, according to Schelling, because science is a means without content that always seeks beyond itself, it is destined to become a mere tool for the creation of art.[30] Schelling acknowledges that philosophy and all the sciences that grew out of it were originally engendered by poetry, but he believes that they are also destined to be assimilated by poetry. He identifies mythology as an intermediate stage in the evolution of the sciences out of poetry, and he suggests that the rise of a new mythology, born not of a single individual, but of a generation acting as one, will mark the transitional phase of a return of the sciences to the wellspring of poetry.[31] He describes how the objective world itself *and* our recognizably voluntary effects on it are *both* active productions of the ego. The difference is that the former is a pro-duction without consciousness, and the latter, with consciousness. Thus

28 Ibid., pp. 126–127.
29 Ibid., pp. 127.
30 Ibid., pp. 126–127.
31 Ibid., pp. 129–130.

the pre-established harmony involves a "confluence" of conscious and unconscious activity of the ego. Schelling believes that only the work of art manifestly testifies to the pre-ontological reality of such a confluence in the transcendental ego.[32]

According to Schelling, the uniqueness and "magical charm" of organic nature lies precisely in the fact that we marvel at how things that seem so purposive are produced by blind mechanism. He does not believe that this purposive appearance should be ascribed to a conscious design. If it were willed by us together with the natural laws that regulate it, then we would paradoxically be willing to be deprived of (even the appearance of) free will. To ascribe Nature to design by a non-human creative principle that represents a world for itself would contribute nothing to explaining how *we* are able to affect Nature despite its apparently objective existence and deterministic laws. Schelling argues that teleological explanations of either kind err in making the purposive concept precede the object, rather than recognizing in Nature's blind perfection "an original identity of conscious and unconscious activity."[33]

Most significantly, this means that such an original identity cannot even lie in the ego itself, because the identity must already be ruptured into the subject-object divide in order for the ego to have self-consciousness (defined in the face of an externally existing world). Schelling identifies the *artistic* intuition as the sole means whereby conscious and unconscious activity become objective (externally manifest) for the ego at the same time.[34] It is for this reason that Schelling calls art "the sole true and eternal organon as well as document of philosophy, which sets forth in ever fresh forms what philosophy cannot represent outwardly, namely, the unconscious in action and production and its original identity with the conscious."[35] In other words, for Schelling, no philosophy in and of itself

---

32   Ibid., I:3:A–D.

33   Ibid., V:1.

34   Ibid., V:2.

35   Ibid., VI:3, 129.

can ever attain universal validity. For philosophy to achieve objectivity means that it has become art, and conversely, any art deprived of objective existence becomes mere philosophy.

In the Tenth of his *Letters on Dogmatism and Criticism*, Schelling responds to his colleagues by writing that he is in favor of removing any vestige of the illusion that one can believe in an objectively existing intelligible world at the same time as retaining the free will of an absolute subject. He argues that the objective power of Nature, if acknowledged, threatens our free will with total annihilation. This can only be genuinely accepted by someone "who can bear the thought of working at his own annihilation, of doing away with all free causality in himself, and of being the modification of an object in whose infinity he will find, sooner or later, his own (moral) extinction."[36] Such an absurd conclusion is not *theoretically* refutable. Thus any philosophical system that upholds free will must be *practically* embodied as a total work of art (*Gesamtkunstwerk*).

Schelling sees Greek tragedy as the supreme portrayal of decisively heroic action against the objective power of Nature. Though the hero must ultimately submit to fate, and knows this from the start, the fact that he is punished for his choice to go down fighting honors him with the acknowledgment of a certain kind of freedom by making him responsible for his failure. Schelling believes that the Greeks, who are traditionally considered the most "natural people" of Western civilization, set the standard in demonstrating what happens when man exceeds the bounds of Nature. By the latter he means, when the subject's representational relation to the objects of Nature is ruptured by the insight of true genius. The apparent mastery and manipulation of Nature by the "free will" of a rational subject removed from it is thereby shattered. The genius intuits his oneness with Nature from within it, and must either be overpoweringly suffocated by it in such a way that his individuality is snuffed out, *or* he must overpower the objective Laws of Nature by rendering them merely apparent, while

---

36 F. W. J. Schelling, "Philosophical Letters on Dogmatism and Criticism" in *The Unconditional in Human Knowledge* (Lewisburg, Pennsylvania: Bucknell University Press), pp. 193, 339.

he himself assumes the objective existence of a deity. The genius, whose transcendent insight does not allow him to rationally de-limit the extent of Nature as object with respect to his subjective being, must consequently battle all the powers of Heaven and Earth merely to survive.

This is the perennial tragedy wherein the Greeks envisioned Titans, such as Prometheus and Atlas, waging war against the Olympian gods for control of the Earth. Schelling mentions Prometheus explicitly: "Prometheus [is] will, unconquerable... which for that reason can resist God. ...Prometheus is the thought in which the human race, after it has brought forth the world of gods out of its inner being, returning to itself, becomes conscious of itself and its fate."[37] The Promethean genius chooses to enter the fray of this impossible battle against Olympus because, though he knows it can hardly end in anything but his annihilation, the highest and most total artwork will thereby be produced. He strives to bring into being a beauty so perfect that it sets the standard even for natural beauty. However, Schelling warns that:

> ...such a fight is thinkable only for the purpose of tragic art. It could not become a system of action even for this reason alone, that such a system would presuppose a race of titans...it would turn out to be utterly detrimental to humanity... would it not be easier to tremble at the faintest notion of freedom, cowed by the superior power of that world, instead of going down fighting? ...The man who would obtain his existence in the supersensuous world by begging, will become the tormentor of humanity in this world, raging against himself and others. Power in this world will compensate him for the humiliation in that. Waking up from the delights of that world, he returns into this one to make it a hell.[38]

Schelling believes that genuine freedom can only be wrought in the defiance of apparently objective natural laws, as mythically represented by a titanic struggle against the governing powers of the cosmos (the gods). He claims that a genuine life of freedom is impossible for the subject un-

---

37   Leonard P. Wessell, *Prometheus Bound: The Mythic Structure of Karl Marx's Scientific Thinking* (Baton Rouge: Louisiana State University Press, 1984), p. 67.

38   Schelling, "Philosophical Letters on Dogmatism and Criticism," p. 339.

less he *actively embodies* a defiance of the objectivity of external reality. According to Schelling, a genius would have to realize that, apart from such action, he lives a life working at his own annihilation as a mere mode of an objective reality that he articulates in part, but in no way controls. To restrict the kind of activity that would liberate one from this absurdly predetermined life to the moments when one is painting within the confines of a canvas, or writing a poem on a piece of paper, is not plausible.

Schelling would probably agree that, at least for the genius, art is inseparable from life. We also see his recognition of the possibility of a real titanic struggle, if only negatively, in his concern that it would be terrifyingly tormenting for those who engaged in it, and that it posed the danger of their tyrannizing over lesser men bound within the natural world in order to compensate for their own disadvantage in the spiritual realm. That Schelling even has such concerns means that he sees the possibility of winning one's freedom in this way as something more than a myth. When Schelling writes, "it would presuppose a race of Titans" such as Prometheus and Atlas, it does not necessarily follow that he means that there can never be one. Rather, the concerns he goes on to express make it more likely that by this he means that perhaps there *ought* not to be one.

This may be connected to Schelling's view that since all genuine works of art open unto the Infinite, there is in a certain sense only one absolute work of art, which manifests in many different instances, because "it should not yet exist in its most original form."[39] Schelling explains that though the work of art issues forth from the same original opposition between the finite and the infinite as the world itself, the latter manifests the resolution of this opposition only in the totality of its existence. In other words, no individual product of Nature reflects infinity from within itself the way that each and every work of art does. However, these artworks are not yet *the* absolute work of art. Could this total artwork (*Gesamtkunstwerk*) be what Schelling otherwise calls "an absolutely opposite system" to that of the natural laws of the objective world?

---

39   Schelling, "System of Transcendental Idealism," pp. 128–129.

Schelling writes, "In *representing* the object to himself… he has nothing to fear…but as soon as he does away with these limits… as soon as he himself has strayed beyond the limit of representation, he finds himself lost. He has done away with its bounds; how shall he now subdue it?"[40] According to Schelling, "Reason must renounce either an objectively intelligible world, or a subjective personality; either an absolute object, or an absolute subject, freedom of will" *unless* one practically embodies an entire order that overthrows that which has been ordained by fate, thereby redefining "reality" from *within*.[41] To take Schelling's view seriously would mean becoming the lawgiver of Nature in a far more practical and violent manner than the merely intellectual idealist recognition of a transcendental identity between human consciousness and the natural world. Strongly pointing in this direction is Schelling's claim that Science will become a tool in the hands of Art.[42] Science's essence as *praxis* qua *techne* (craft, technology) will be revealed within the horizon of an irreducibly aesthetic dimension of meaning. This would require that physical science, which is only effective within the bounds of the laws of Nature that Science recognizes as self-imposed limits, somehow become a science (*scientia*, or "knowledge") of the soul governed by aesthetic intuition, and not crippled by the conventions of rational methodology.

In fact, such a science would not need to be invented so much as redeemed and renovated. The Cartesian paradigm came to predominate in "*the* scientific method" only after alchemy disintegrated into the disparate sciences that were uprooted from it. Some of the greatest scientists of the Renaissance and the early modern period were still practitioners of alchemy or applied occult philosophy. The foremost of these was Giordano Bruno, who faced incessant persecution by religious authorities for studying "occult" phenomena and abilities. He had, indeed, written extensively on psychic ability and the means to cultivate it.

---

40   Schelling, "Philosophical Letters on Dogmatism and Criticism," p. 193.
41   Ibid., pp. 193–194.
42   Schelling, "System of Transcendental Idealism," pp. 129–130.

The Holy Inquisition accused Bruno of practicing magic and witch-craft, and of holding a number of heretical views — including belief in reincarnation and extraterrestrial intelligence. His having preached the intellectual and spiritual equality of women to men and his disregard for economic class distinctions also cannot have made him very popular with the ecclesiastical establishment. On February 17, 1600, Giordano Bruno was burned at the stake by officers of the Catholic Church in the central market of Rome. Schelling wrote a dialogical book called *Bruno* in his honor. It is in this book, which is dedicated to Bruno, and in another dialogue by the name of *Clara*, that it becomes unmistakably clear that despite his apprehensions, Schelling does advocate the restoration of alchemy as a spiritual *art* or master craft (*techne*) that encompasses and supersedes the modern natural sciences, but is informed and grounded by their naturalism — unlike Hellenistic alchemy or even that of the Renaissance. Furthermore, Schelling's last uncompleted work, *The World Ages*, affirms the occultism that pervades *Bruno* and *Clara*, and it sets the alchemical ideas of those works in the context of a new metaphysics that Schelling saw as the culmination of his life's project.

In *The World Ages,* Schelling claims that our lower self is there to serve as a mirror through which the archetypal image of the primordial world before time might come to distinguish itself in consciousness.[43] Schelling refers to this primordial world as "the first time."[44] This is the same phrase that the ancient Egyptians used for their "golden age" of *zep tepi* ("the first time"), which was not so much another era as a simultaneously-existing temporal dimension to which the Pharaoh "returns" after death. If the empty granite coffer in the King's Chamber of the Great Pyramid was ever used for anything related to mortuary rites, it was not for the literal entombing of a Pharaoh, but as a place where he undertook a shamanic journey inside an artificial mountain designed to subjugate Nature and

---

43   F. W. J. von Schelling, *The Abyss of Freedom and the Ages of the World.* Translated with an introduction by Slavoj Žižek (Ann Arbor: The University of Michigan Press, 1997), pp. 114–115.

44   Ibid., p. 180.

concentrate psychical power by establishing a rapport with "the other side." In *Clara*, Schelling claims that mortuary festivals and rites might actually have an effect on the spirit world, or at least serve to maintain the connection between this-worldly experience and beings now in an other-worldly state: "The ancient Egyptian [mortuary] practices have something terrible about them, but they are based on a thought that is in itself true and correct."[45] If space and time do not have Cartesian uniformity, and if there are particular places that a certain great time has enfolded with occult power, then the titanic ruins in Egypt would certainly be among them. Schelling does believe that there are such places:

> Even a locality hides its own secret… Since human thought began, certain doc-
> trines, particular views of the world, and views of things have been native to
> certain areas, not only to large stretches of land, like the Orient, but to small
> areas right in among masses of those who think differently. But even that higher
> organ, which otherwise occurs only as a temporary phenomenon in this life,
> is more constant in some areas and again not merely in larger kingdoms, such
> as that so-called other sight in the Scottish Highlands but, as I know from ex-
> perience, in quite small areas. Weren't even the ancients' oracles tied to certain
> areas, even to particular places, and shouldn't we draw the general conclusion
> from this that locality isn't as irrelevant to the higher as is generally supposed?
> Indeed, don't we feel a certain spiritual presence in every place, which either at-
> tracts us to that place or puts us off? The same also applies to individual periods
> of time.[46]

Returning to *The World Ages*, there Schelling delivers the following re-marks on the primordially titanic character of "Egyptian" art and archi-tecture. We should read them bearing in mind that he might be thinking foremost of the "proto-Egyptian" megalithic structures of the Sphinx and Valley temples, as well as the Osireon at Abydos. On account of being totally unmarked, unadorned, and austerely geometric, they are conferred with an especially timeless and inhuman quality:

---

45   F. W. J. Schelling, *Clara or, On Nature's Connection to the Spirit World* (Albany: State
       University of New York Press, 2002), p. 12.

46   Ibid., p. 75.

The deeper we return to the past, the more we find unmoving rest, indistinction, and indifferent coexistence of the very forces that, though gentle at the beginning, flare up late into ever more turbulent struggle. The mountains of the primordial world seem to look down upon the animated life at their feet with eternally mute indifference; and likewise with the oldest formations of the human spirit. We encounter the same character of concealment in the mute solemnity of the Egyptians... in the immense monuments... that seem built for no time but rather for eternity.[47]

In *Clara*, Schelling goes so far as to equate unlocking the mysteries of such places with unleashing psychical powers that have been suppressed in mankind ever since a catastrophic fall from a higher state of being in immeasurably remote antiquity:

Oh, the true ruins are not those of ancient human splendor that the curious seek out in the Persian or Indian deserts; the whole Earth is one great ruin, where animals live as ghosts and men as spirits and where many hidden powers and treasures are locked away as if by an invisible strength or by a magician's spell. And we wanted to blame these powers that are locked up rather than thinking about freeing them within us first? Certainly in his own way man is no less spellbound and transformed. ...Most people... are completely captivated by external appearances... Just as farmers creep round an old, destroyed, or enchanted castle with divining rods in their hands, or shine their lamps into chambers buried underground, and even go with crowbars and levers in the hope of finding gold or other valuables: so, too, does man go about nature, entering some of her hidden rooms and calling this search "natural science." But the treasures are not covered by rubble alone; the treasures have been locked up in the very wreckage and rocks themselves by a spell that only another magic charm can undo.[48]

Schelling appends to this passage a marginal note of his own that reads, "A completely different world buried therein than we suspected. Odyssey of the Spirit." In other words, what remains buried at Giza and elsewhere in Egypt cannot be discovered without unlocking another kind of sight and restoring a different kind of science grounded in that vision. Those monu-

---

47   Schelling, *Ages of the World*, p. 180.

48   Schelling, *Clara*, p. 25.

ments demand of us that we look to regaining, by means of a forgotten magical art, staggering psychical powers that we have long lost. Schelling makes this clear through an exclamation that he puts in the mouth of the good doctor in *Clara*. This proto-Van Helsing claims that a human being senses indignation in the face of the ravages wrought upon him by the forces of Nature: "Because [on some level he 'knows' that] *he* should move everything… because he is not conscious of the strength in his inner being through which he could rule everything and through which he could be free of everything."[49] In *The World Ages*, Schelling expresses this same basic call for the cultivation of latent abilities in the first person, and without such hyperbole as he allows himself in the dramatized context of *Clara*: "It is not enough that forces (or abilities) be present in a man; he must recognize them as his own, and only then is it possible for him to grasp onto them and put them to work and into effect."[50]

Schelling is not, however, a traditionalist nostalgically looking backwards. He is after a post-materialistic science *of the future* that retains its hard-won naturalism while retrieving aspects of the "Egyptian" magical art of *alchemy*. Schelling fears that it is too early to lift the veil on this science of ideas by elaborating on its workings in detail.[51] He sees his own role as preparatory, for the development of such a science still remains, in his view, the task for a future man:

> With such progress, perhaps a long-pondered attempt might be hazarded, which would help make ready this future, objective presentation of science. Perhaps he will yet come, who will sing the great heroic poem, encompassing in spirit (as is reputed of the seers from times gone by) what was, what is, and what will be. But this time is not yet at hand. As its harbingers, we do not wish to pluck its fruit before it is ripe, nor do we wish to misjudge our own. This is still a time of struggle.[52]

---

49   Ibid., p. 26.
50   Schelling, *Ages of the World*, p. 167.
51   Ibid., pp. 162–163.
52   Ibid., pp. 119–120.

These apologetic and cautionary reservations accepted, Schelling does paint with broad strokes some elements of the coming titanic Craft. Let us begin with the dialogue that explicitly links Schelling to Giordano Bruno and the esoteric heritage of "Egypt." From section 2:223–227 of the dialogue *Bruno*, through the character of Anselm, Schelling lays out the establishment's Platonist view that ideas are eternal and unchanging concepts separate from, and somehow in perpetual conflict with, the productive nature in which they are always inadequately instantiated.[53] While even here, truth is equated with beauty (an equivalence to which Schelling earnestly adheres), only the eternal "ideas" are taken to be truly beautiful — not their instantiations. Still, from 4:227–234, we see Anselm claim that the artistic genius can, through the connection of his idea with the ideas of things, somehow reflect the infinite in the finite medium of a work of art. The more deeply his idea — his spiritual essence — penetrates into the ideas of other things, the more his artworks will be universal (such as the works of Goethe or Shakespeare) and not merely an expression of accidents and contingencies that have shaped his idiosyncratic individuality.[54] For Anselm — the academic Platonist — it remains the case that this intuition and expression of the ideas is unconscious in the case of art, so that the artist is a mere tool of the absolute, whereas the philosopher alone is capable of consciously grasping the ideas. The philosopher's relationship with the ideas is esoteric, while that of the artist — even the universal artist — is exoteric.[55]

Schelling has the character of Bruno reject Anselm's strict distinction between the material and the spiritual, the finite and the infinite, and argue that the unity of truth and beauty is grounded in a spectral non-duality of these notions. Around 4:239, Bruno begins to advance an *imaginal* or imagistic understanding of *ideas*.[56] By 4:243–247, it becomes clear

---

53   F. W. J. Schelling, *Bruno, or On the Natural and the Divine Principle of Things* (Albany: State University of New York Press, 1984), p. 21.

54   Ibid., p. 22.

55   Ibid., p. 23.

56   Ibid., p. 25.

that the *idea*, as understood by Schelling's Bruno, is not so abstract as the bare concept that Anselm takes it to be. Rather, the *idea* spectrally conflates properties of the conceptual with that of the multiplicity of objects through which a given concept is intuited.[57] At 4:247–252, Bruno explains that both things and concepts are abstracted aspects of *ideas*; concepts and things correlate with one another but they cannot exist independently of the *phenomenal* being of individual ideas.[58] The idea is a living union of concept and thing; its generality or status as a *type* is a concrete generality, whereas the abstract concept has only a formalistically empty generality.[59] Ideas are *arche*, or principal and overarching *types* — that is, *archetypes*, but ones that do not abstractly stand over and against their "copies."[60] Nothing is entirely "real" and nothing is purely "ideal" (where "ideal" is misunderstood in the academic sense).[61] Things are never entirely separate from consciousness, and consciousness is never totally devoid of sensuousness.[62] Some critics have reproached Schelling for "almost always being in suspense between idealism, realism, and even materialism."[63] In the guise of *Bruno*'s Alexander, he is certainly the advocate of Giordano Bruno's mystical hylomorphism.[64] The so-called "mental" realm is just as *phenomenal* — in other words, sensible and qualitatively variegated — as the "material" realm.[65] 'Extrasensory perception' (ESP) is still *sensory*. The psychical and somatic are relative dimensions of the spectral *idea*, the polarities of a super-spectrum.[66]

---

57   Ibid., p. 28.
58   Ibid., p. 31.
59   Ibid., p. 66.
60   Ibid., p. 65.
61   Ibid., p. 53.
62   Ibid., p. 68.
63   Ibid., p. 55.
64   Ibid., p. 65.
65   Ibid., p. 49.
66   Ibid., p. 66.

Beginning already in early Platonism, space was interpreted as an empty and neutral background—a *receptacle* wherein dead matter is mechanistically in-formed by abstract concepts. At 4:315 in *Bruno*, Schelling has Alexander deconstruct and repudiate this degenerate version of the theory of forms. In its place he offers a vision of the ideas as an organic interconnection of individuals in a world before time, before their actualization in corporeal embodiments that sharply distinguish one from another.[67] Schelling claims, through Alexander, that the conception of dead matter—wherein things do not participate in each other's being and are cut off from one another, with only extrinsic relations among them—is so absurdly unnatural that it has driven many sensitive souls to feel as if "the barbarian idolater or the primitive totem-worshipper" were "in possession of superior philosophical and religious sensibilities."[68] Schelling goes so far as to claim that the psychotic break between the spiritual and natural dimensions of existence are to blame for the decline of the French Revolution, with its aspirations of liberation, into the murderous Reign of Terror.[69] Behind this political development, he sees the metaphysical psychosis of French Materialism and Cartesian Dualism. In other words, he would concur wholeheartedly with the essential thrust of my third chapter.

For Schelling (speaking here through the medium of Bruno), the *idea* is not accessible to finite cognition; with its confluence of what, in logical terms, can only be deemed opposites — such as possibility and actuality, unity and multiplicity, limitation and unbounded reality — it cannot be understood by rational thought alone.[70] The implication is that, contrary to what Anselm believes, artistic genius is a prerequisite for being a genuine philosopher, and thought can never dispense with, outstrip, or wholly comprehend aesthetic intuition. By means of such an intuition, one may

---

67   Ibid., p. 65.

68   Ibid.

69   Ibid., pp. 61–62.

70   Ibid., pp. 28–29.

have even audio-visual "intuitions" of ideas.[71] At 4:328 in *Bruno*, Schelling uses an alchemical formulation when referring to this intuition of ideas that are substantial and formal at the same time, saying that to discover this "is to discover the absolute center of gravity. To know this is to uncover the original metal of truth, as it were, the prime ingredient in the alloys of all individual truths, without which none of them would be true."[72]

Yet, as has already been pointed out, Schelling is not simply looking backwards. The new alchemy that he seeks is even more grounded in naturalism than that of Giordano Bruno. We see this most clearly in *Clara*. There, Schelling is fairly clear that the spiritual science he is seeking is not a distinct science of spirits, but a spiritualization of "the earthly sciences" so that research may be able to "transition" smoothly and freely between the "natural field" and the "spirit world," which are deeply interconnected by processes of organic growth.[73] Provocatively, he speaks of the spiritualization of science as synonymous with a bringing of philosophy back down to *earth*—but not the 'Earth' of materialists.[74] Interestingly, while he believes an inner transformation of natural beings is possible, Schelling draws a distinction between the organic unity of each individual soul and the spectral interdependence of all other natural beings within the context of the organic whole of the Earth's soul. The Earth is a single spiritual being for Schelling, and the only living beings emerging from out of it that can go on to develop a degree of organic autonomy are humanoid beings. Schelling has great reverence for the Earth as a spiritual mother: "Even when we scale down our estimation of this life to its appropriate measure, don't we privately have a feeling that tells us we owe this Earth a certain devotion and that this Earth shares with us one fate and one hope?"[75]

The formal distinction between semi-autonomous human souls and the earthly soul of other natural beings accepted, Schelling offers this

---

71   Ibid., p. 66.

72   Ibid., p. 69.

73   Schelling, *Clara*, pp. 4–5.

74   Ibid.

75   Ibid., p. 76.

beautiful metaphor for the overall non-duality of nature and spirit: "[T] he temple whose last spire disappears into an inaccessible light is, at its very deepest foundation, wholly supported by nature."[76] In line with this view, Schelling holds that nothing should be denied to science — even what has hitherto been seen as the most ethereal — so long as scientists remain faithful to the Earth and proceed step-by-step in their researches.[77] He cautions against remedying the temporary shortcomings of the sciences with fanciful flights of the imagination or a superstition ignorant of the natural connections of things, but he also warns scientists that they should not leave what is of most pressing concern to people — the workings and welfare of their souls — to 'spiritualist' authors of popular tripe. The doctor in *Clara* summarizes this persisting dilemma best, when he says of unscientific theosophists that:

> They start with what is most general and spiritual and are thereby never able to come down to reality or particulars. They are ashamed to start from the earth, to climb up from the creature as if from a rung on a ladder, to draw those thoughts that are beyond the senses first from earth, fire, water, and air. And so they don't get anywhere, either: their webs of thought are plants without roots, they float in the air and the sky like these delicate threads here in front of us. And yet they believe they can strengthen man thereby, even help advance the age that nevertheless suffers by the very fact that while one part has indeed sunk completely into the mud, the other has presumed to climb so high that it can no longer find the ground beneath it.[78]

Ultimately, the spiritualization of Science will lead to its unification with Religion, through aesthetic intuition.[79] Witness this passage in *Clara*, which seems prophetic of the Heideggerian misadventure at Freiburg more than a century later:

> ...only he who really lives within the spirit — the true academic and artist — is

---

76   Ibid., p. 5.
77   Ibid.
78   Ibid., p. 28.
79   Ibid., p. 17.

truly spiritual. Merely exercising piety as a way of life, without combining it
with lively and active scientific research, leads to emptiness and eventually even
to that mechanicalness devoid of heart and soul that would itself have belittled
monastic life even in times such as ours. In those centuries when knowledge did
not spread far, when monks were the only depositories of science and knowledge, they were also the true clergymen, the truly spiritual; since then the rest of
the world has outstripped them so powerfully that they have increasingly ceased
to be spiritual any more. The sciences have the same end as religion... However,
if there are countries in which the cloisters were reordered into schools when
the change in faith came about, then that is not what I meant... What I meant
was this: it is here on this hill that the next great German poem should be composed, it is here in this valley that a Platonic academy should gather... Men from
all of the arts and sciences should live a truly spiritual life here...[80]

Through the character of the doctor in *Clara*, Schelling argues that it
is possible for science to translate a largely unconscious spiritual intuition — by which he means an intuition of things pertaining to the *spirit
world* — into something sufficiently structured in its articulation that
it can be apprehended consciously.[81] Schelling suggests that all things
have their own "inner germ of life" (even if it is not as individuated as
in humans) so that a new science of life would develop if we could learn
to affect physical, chemical, and electrical processes on this inner level,
rather than merely through external force.[82] He explicitly describes this
as a kind of "spiritual chemistry," so it is quite clear he is talking about a
new alchemy.[83]

In an exchange between Clara and the doctor, Schelling develops at
length the idea of "something mediate between body and spirit" — a *specter* of a person, or what some in his time called a "subtle body."[84] Schelling
simply calls this "moderate essence between body and spirit," the "soul"
of a person, and he suggests that what people mean to say when they talk

---

80   Ibid., p. 17.

81   Ibid., pp. 32–33.

82   Ibid., p. 40.

83   Ibid., p. 41.

84   Ibid., pp. 33–34, 40.

of "spirits" and the "spirit world" is really the survival of a soul that is imprinted by the qualitative characteristics of corporeal embodiment.[85] Unlike the spirit, which is a fickle and transient constellation of psychological characteristics, and unlike the physical body prone to disintegration, the soul that unites the two during life is marked by both, and can persist in its distinctive constitution.[86] Schelling acknowledges that the "spiritual form of the body" can, under certain conditions and to a limited extent, break free of the constraining "force of external life" (the potencies of Nature at work in the physical body).[87] This is what is involved when people are able to clairvoyantly "see" their own physical body from a third-person vantage point, or see things spatially remote as if they are traveling there.[88] The distant past and even the remote future become clear to a person in this clairvoyant state.[89] One is able to "remember" the future. "A whole range of [paranormal] phenomena" of other kinds, which would not be possible if there were a strictly dualistic division of mind and body, also become possible in such a condition of spectral release, according to Schelling.[90]

Schelling draws an analogy between the transfer of the soul from the physical body to the spectral body that persists after death and the transition between wakefulness and sleep, suggesting that, although something like direct experience of it might be needed to explain it scientifically, it is not in principle incomprehensible.[91] He compares enduring the capacities of the soul in sleep "to will, love, or detest" to the capabilities of the soul in the disembodied spectral state.[92] He takes the ability of a mesmerist to, on the one hand, make a person's hearing superhumanly sensitive, and

---

85   Ibid., pp. 34–36.
86   Ibid., pp. 35–36.
87   Ibid., p. 40.
88   Ibid., pp. 48, 57.
89   Ibid., pp. 49.
90   Ibid.
91   Ibid., pp. 38–39.
92   Ibid., p. 39.

on the other, to shut them off from all external sensory impressions (even the nearby "rattle of coaches" or "the firing of cannons") other than the sounds of his soft spoken commands, as evidence that the external filtering or constraining force operative during the dream state is not "physical" in the ordinary sense.[93] Thus, just as it can be manipulated without regard to physical organs and brain-based cognitive functions, this sheath can be removed altogether so as to liberate the soul without manipulation of these corporeal entities.

With reference to the view that philosophy is a preparation for death, Schelling maintains that "only he who could do while awake what he has to do while asleep would be the perfect philosopher."[94] Elaborating on this maxim, he describes a state of "wakeful sleep or a sleeping wakefulness," which today is known as *lucid dreaming*, and he says that this condition of great clarity that some may enter into while still alive is the very same "condition that follows death," with the difference being that in that instance it becomes "a clairvoyance uninterrupted by a waking up."[95] Communication between diverse souls who are all in this condition would be like telepathic communication between mesmerized persons who are still alive.[96] Language will not be necessary, but it also will not be possible to use language to hide one's true feelings and thoughts once all communication is by means of telepathy.[97] Souls that are really blind and confused might not have this degree of lucidity. Instead, like those who are utterly incapable of lucid dreaming while alive, they may be bombarded by dreamlike imagery — and to the extent that fears, complexes, and paranoid delusions plague their psyche, this dreamlike experience could have a nightmarish quality.[98]

---

93   Ibid., p. 49.
94   Ibid., p. 48.
95   Ibid.
96   Ibid., p. 72.
97   Ibid., p. 73.
98   Ibid., p. 58.

Interestingly, Schelling's most elaborate vision of the new alchemy in *The World Ages* also takes as its point of departure a similar discussion of the affinity between hypnosis, or "mesmeric sleep," and "normal" sleep with its occasional dream imagery. In this other extensive discussion of mesmeric sleep, his emphasis is on those paranormal phenomena that mesmerized people experience, the evocation and exploration of which have long since been suppressed by materialist psychologists in the practice of mesmerism in order to redefine it as clinical "hypnosis." Schelling postulates various depths of mesmeric sleep, which are defined by the degree to which the extrinsic over-organization of life-forces into the perceptual channels of waking life is de-structured, and the internal life-forces are allowed to flourish in a state that, from a rationally-minded perspective, appears more "disorganized" or "deranged."[99] In a relatively shallow state of mesmeric sleep, the body is able to cure certain ailments that proceed from a dysfunctional over-organization of life-forces.[100] In a medium state of mesmeric sleep, the mesmerized person will be capable of having veridical "visions of future things" (i.e., precognition).[101] In the deepest state of mesmeric sleep, when contact and communication with the external world is completely cut off, and the mesmerized person appears to be all but dead, her inner life forces will be freed from all external constraint, and will be able to enter the spirit world and travel therein (as a specter).[102]

Schelling also draws a connection between this death-like deep mesmeric sleep and death itself on the one hand, and the "generative act" of sex on the other. He notes how sex has been referred to as a little death, and he compares the invulnerability to pain during the height of sexual arousal and climax to the imperviousness to external physical stimuli experienced during a hypnotic trance. In both cases, he speculates, what is

---

99   Schelling, *Ages of the World*, pp. 159–160.

100 Ibid., pp. 159–160.

101 Ibid., pp. 159–160, 167.

102 Ibid., p. 160.

at work is a diminishing of "the power of the external life-exponent."[103] Schelling goes so far as to suggest that total negation of this force is possible during such states as mesmeric sleep and the most intense sex, just as it is in death (or Near Death Experiences), so that someone's spectral body "can become *posited-outside himself.*"[104] He views development of the ability to have Out-of-Body Experiences (OBE) as desirable.

What is most interesting about Schelling's discussion of these states is that he is concerned to emphasize that there is no sharp distinction between mesmeric sleep — induced by a hypnotist — and ordinary sleep, which can have a healing effect commensurate with its depth, and which also has been known to involve premonitions.[105] Schelling suspects that ordinary sleep, with its dream imagery, might mirror a simultaneous mesmeric sleep (albeit one less pronounced than if it were to be deliberately induced).[106] A weakening of the filtering function of what he calls "the external life-component" might increase the latent human capacity for ESP abilities that reflect the "free, inner contact" of subtler vital forces that connect people and all other beings.[107]

Schelling's most shocking statements on the efficacy of alchemy immediately follow, and proceed from these considerations on mesmerism and the spectral in sleep and dreams. He suggests that just as a mesmerist or "hypnotist" (in the old spiritualist sense) is capable of remotely controlling a person's mind, and thereby the person's body, for example to immediately effect cures for various diseases or even to force them to do things against their will, it should be possible to carry out scientific experiments that effect similar violent transformations in the inner-life forces of *things* rather than persons:

If we may now apply this back to an earlier discussion, we can imagine it to be

---

103 Ibid., p. 162.

104 Ibid., pp. 162–163.

105 Ibid., pp. 158, 160.

106 Ibid., p. 160.

107 Ibid., p. 163.

at least possible that men are entitled to a similar violence against other earthly things as they seem in part to be allowed against other men. They would then be in a position, through an entirely similar effect, to set free the interior of other corporeal things up to a particular grade, and thereby initiate true transformations through which a set of phenomena could emerge, phenomena that would be entirely different from those of normal experiments, which, however deeply they may penetrate, still only play on the surface.[108]

It is, very significantly, at this point that Schelling begins his exposition on what a Platonic *idea* really is — as compared to how it has been misunderstood by the scholastic, or "academic," tradition.[109] In fact, Schelling suggests that Plato himself was only an inheritor of the *ideas*, an understanding of which was already ancient in his time and may have been subject to forgetful distortion. This is probably a reference to Plato's membership in the esoteric Pythagorean community, which eclectically drew on the esoteric teachings of ancient Egyptian and Babylonian mystery schools, in addition to those of the Orphic cult indigenous to Greece. The point of departure for Schelling's exposition on the true nature of *ideas* is the simple, but profoundly significant, observation that the Greek word *eidos* — which we translate as "idea" — means not only "form," as it is widely understood in the academy, but also both "appearance" and "vision." It would be equivalent to the German *shein*, which is related to their word for the beautiful: *shöne*. In German, the phrase *es sheint mir* is often translated as "it *seems* to me" — which is odd, given that Platonic forms have traditionally been understood as the opposite of "mere semblance." The oddity might be remedied by translating *es sheint mir* as "it *strikes* me," since both the German *shein* and the Greek *eidos* mean "appearance" in the sense of what is radiantly striking — what shines or radiates out from something as elemental or essential to it. Here is also the connection to *eidos* as "vision," since a "eureka moment" — when something *strikes* one like a flash of lightning — is a "moment of *vision*."

---

108 Ibid., pp. 160–161.
109 Ibid., pp. 161–162.

In line with these etymological insights, Schelling explains that the *ideas* are neither abstract concepts nor fixed prototypes. When we see a pattern repeated on various levels, we are tempted to isolate the constant form in these iterations abstractly by stripping it of all phenomenal qualities. Yet the Greek *eidos* was a synonym for *phaenomenon*. The *eidos* is that inner spirit of something that may be embodied in many different ways, but the elemental, phenomenal qualities of which can still be discerned despite the variances in the diverse mediums that serve as instances of its embodiment. Moreover, the *eidos* is not a fixed model or prototype; if it were, its instances would have the quality of mechanical reproduction rather than that of organic growth. Natural beings that embody the *eidos* also shape it. Schelling clearly views *ideas* as a product of developmental living processes in nature, and he sees these archetypes behind the *end-directedness* of natural beings that has been hitherto understood teleologically.

Natural *types* emerge when life forms in a generative condition tap into the non-physical memory of a past similar form, which form is in turn maintained by being embodied in ever-novel varieties of its basic type. Speaking of generative conditions, it is fascinating that Schelling connects the non-physical subsistence of these archetypes, in a dimension beyond ordinary space-time, with potential Out-of-Body Experiences during intense sexual activity.[110] The implication is that, just as a person's specter may be released from her body at death or, temporarily, during sex, archetypes also might appear of themselves — as *images* — without being sheathed in any particular physical medium. Of course, these images appearing to "the inner eye" could not be *re-presented* except in a given physical medium with its attendant accidental features. For Schelling, alchemy is the art or spiritual science of effecting metamorphoses — changes in *morphe* (form) — in beings, by apprehending and manipulating their spectral archetypes, or *ideas*. To come full circle back to where we started, it is alchemical practice of this kind that Schelling

---

110   Ibid., pp. 162–163.

sees as the epitome of the synergy of conscious and unconscious activity in artistic genius, which is widely associated with Schelling's aesthetics without being properly understood for fear of being drawn down the rabbit hole of the paranormal. It is also this kind of meta*morphic* alchemy that the present project is essentially concerned with: an attempt not only to more consciously intuit the archetypes or aesthetic ideas unconsciously determinative of technological science itself, but to transform our rapport with Prometheus and Atlas as they destine the shape of things to come.

CHAPTER VI

THE OCCULTATION
OF SUPERNATURE

Despite his professed concern not to do so, Schelling ran ahead of himself. The limited state of scientific research into the paranormal in his time is partly to account for the overly literary quality of his speculations concerning the coming Craft. His thought also remains tainted by the basic structures of the Cartesian dualism and Kantian Idealism from which he is struggling to break free. In my view, he does break free, but the way that he speaks of personal agency or the spirit world is distorted by the stark dichotomy between subjective will and natural laws of consciousness. What Schelling struggles against for the first time leaves its mark deeply imprinted on his ideas.

Martin Heidegger lectured on Schelling's work and, although he seems not to have acknowledged it, many of the most bizarre features of his ontology appear to have been lifted right out of the occult aether wherein Schelling developed them: Nothingness as the abyssal back-ground of Being; Concealment and Unconcealment; the decisive Event that strikes like lightning or flashes forth like a eureka "moment of vision"; the historical destiny of the artist-scholars of a coming apocalyptic generation to build a new world whose architectonic is established by singing together their own epic poem; the Cartesian-Newtonian grid of uniform space and chronological time viewed as abstractly derived from a primordial world-hood structured in terms of the heterogeneity of space as it is encountered in *places*, and of an epochal time experienced as world *ages*; sight and hearing as more primary than the organs associated with them; a dimen-

sion of meaning and discourse that is not only distinct from spoken language, but is the primordial ground for its possibility; and so forth. I could
go on, but I do not want to tire the reader. The reason that the rational
mind finds many of these "Heideggerian" ideas so bizarrely incomprehensible is that — perhaps out of embarrassment — Heidegger uprooted them
from those all-pervasive paranormal elements of Schelling's vision in the
context of which they actually make a lot more sense.

The thought of Henri Bergson also bears striking affinities to that of
Schelling. This is especially the case with his conception of the progressive and constraining forces at work in creative evolution, as well as the
aesthetic character of the most general ideas that can be intuited — out
of which abstract concepts are secondarily derived. I will suggest that,
with respect to the fundamental concepts integral to scientific practice,
the most general of these aesthetic ideas are those of Prometheus and
Atlas. The naturalism of Bergson's thought should help to render the insights of Kant and Schelling more tangible with respect to the spectrality
of aesthetic ideas or imagistic archetypes. Bergson's biological account of
the rise of the intellect at the expense of instinct also augments the most
serious deficiency in Heidegger's thinking, namely that his concerns over
falling prey to "biologism" do not justify the fact that he has no account
whatsoever of the evolution of *Dasein* or the human being as the tool-
using animal *par excellence*.

Both Heidegger and Bergson understand the essence of Technology
as something revealed in how our interpretation of Being is revised
throughout the course of successive historical epochs that unfold a singular destiny. According to Heidegger, every historical epoch is grounded by
a metaphysical interpretation of what *is*, and the essence of modern technology demands more profound reflection than the metaphysical essence
of any prior age.[1] Bergson claims that, looking back thousands of years
from now, our wars and revolutions will be insignificant compared to the

---

1   Martin Heidegger, *The Question Concerning Technology and Other Essays* (New
     York: Harper & Row, 1977), p. 43.

great technological innovations that epitomize our epoch; the age of the steam-engine will be grasped in thought by then in the same way that the Bronze or Stone Age are remembered now.[2] The two thinkers choose essentially the same type of modern technology as an epitomizing metaphor for that which characterizes the peril and promise of such revolutionary technological development in general: the motion picture projector. Each also claims *both* that this way of grasping the world is new, *and* that, although it only comes into its own with modernity, it has its inception in Classical Greek thought, and has been germinating ever since.

Many Greek thinkers saw ideal concepts or organic forms as what is most real. As Heidegger explains, the *hypokeimenon* was for them still an aspect of beings — as the *subiectum* remained for Medieval thinkers. The subject of a thing was "that-which-lies-before, which, as ground, gathers everything onto itself."[3] In other words, the subject of a thing was that in which its formal properties cohered; it was "subject-*matter*." The Greeks could not have framed the thought of the whole world's reality as needful of verification. When man becomes *the* only subject, and his representational thinking grounds the certitude of all other beings, this means that "[m]an becomes the relational center of that which is as such."[4] Modern research science involves a transformation in the conception of truth as *veritas*, or verification, namely as the accuracy or certainty of a subject's re-presentation of a being whose presence has become "objective." Nature is taken account of through a projection that anticipates its future course in a calculative manner, and History, including Natural History, is framed as a rigorous schematization of the past as "fact." Both Nature and its history are thereby objectified and "set in place" (*gestellt*).[5] We should hear in this German term *gestellt* the verb *stellen* — which means to set in place, and to set upon, in the sense of challenging. In other words, truth as rep-

---

2   Henri Bergson, *Creative Evolution* (Mineola, New York: Dover Publications, 1998), p. 139.

3   Heidegger, *The Question Concerning Technology and Other Essays*, p. 128.

4   Ibid.

5   Ibid., pp. 126–127.

resentation is not mere correspondence; it is rather a taking to be true, a setting-upon and securing that does violence to what is objectified.

According to Heidegger, the metaphysical revolution that defines the beginning and end of world ages takes place, in our age, in the *Meditations on First Philosophy*.[6] Descartes' interpretation of truth still moves within the sphere of inquiry determined by the question first posed by Plato and Aristotle; namely, "What is it to be?" (This is what Heidegger sometimes calls the questioning after beings or entities, as contrasted with the Question of Being.) However, Descartes' answer to this question requires and makes possible a "theory of knowledge" for the first time. Heidegger claims that before this, "the reality of the outer world" as such was never questioned.[7] Heidegger thinks that all subsequent German representational thought (*Vorstellungs-philosophie*) consists of affirmative modifications of the Cartesian position, and that even Nietzsche failed to overcome modern metaphysics.[8]

The framing of the whole world's reality as needful of verification, this framing of a world (and not just any given beings *within* the world) as an object present-at-hand (*das Vor-handene*) for the subject to represent (*vor-stellen*) is the move that Descartes makes that comes to be definitive of our age as that of the "world picture" (*Weltbild*). What defines the modern age is the very fact that, for the first time, the world can become a picture. This is what is "new" about *der Neuzeit* — the modern age, or literally "the new age."[9] In his later essay, "The Thing," Heidegger identifies the television — which in German is called *fernseher*, or "far-seer," as the epitome of this development.[10] Bergson also compares the machinations of our intellectual way of knowing things to a cinematographic device.[11] The Greek idealists saw things as completed figures, eternally abiding as

---

6   Ibid., p. 127.

7   Ibid., p. 139.

8   Ibid., p. 140.

9   Ibid., p. 132.

10   Martin Heidegger, *Poetry, Language, Thought* (New York: Harper Collins, 1971), 163.

11   Bergson, *Creative Evolution*, pp. 315–316.

such. Bergson compares the privileged moments in terms of which they thought to those captured by Classical sculptures; they radiate as epitomes of whole movements in the way that single photographs do.[12] "The cinematographical mechanism of the intellect" that comes to the fore in modern science breaks up those Classical figures with its "snapshots" so that they become points extending themselves in space through a succession of instantaneous positions.[13] This proceeds from the Cartesian revolution in geometry, where the elaboration of a curve is no longer seen as describing a static or timeless figure but as a succession of points that, in terms of two or more axes, describes an interval of time.[14]

One can see the difference, for example, in the fact that it sufficed for Aristotle to demonstrate that the form of celestial orbits is circular, whereas Galileo was concerned not simply with replacing this circular orbit with an elliptical one, and not merely with correcting the *form* of the circuit conceived of in its eternal completion, but with determining a law describing the motion of planets *conceived as points* along this circuit — a law that would allow for the mathematical projection of their future positions.[15] Also, unlike Classical thinkers with their heterogeneous space, Galileo did not privilege any moment in the trajectory of a falling body with a view to determining its velocity.[16] As Bergson sees it, this is what most distinguishes modern science from ancient science.

Heidegger could not be more in agreement. Modern science is "mathematical" not in the sense that it employs numerical calculation, but in the sense that it involves that which is known in advance. *Ta mathemata*, the Greek root of "mathematics," means "that which man knows in advance," in other words that which filters every observation of the new and contingent and organizes it with respect to what is known before it. Number is only mathematical because it is the clearest example

12   Ibid., p. 332.
13   Ibid., pp. 315–316, 335.
14   Ibid., p. 334.
15   Ibid., p. 333.
16   Ibid., p. 331.

of the always-already-known.[17] This is what is involved in developing a hypothesis testable by experiment. Like Bergson, Heidegger also notes that, while Aristotelian so-called "science" did employ *empeiria*, or careful observation and measurement, it totally lacked the modern conception of an experiment wherein the behavior of an object sphere of beings is represented or anticipated by an exact ground plan and tested against this under controlled conditions.[18]

Bergson realizes that modern science seeks to establish time as an independent variable in terms of which all abstractly reconstructed magnitudes are to be measured.[19] Although the time that becomes all-important for modern scientists is not our authentic experience of duration, the fact that it breaks up what were supposed to have been eternal forms into even more abstract and homogenous units *for the sake of greater utility* also cultivates a need for a complementary intuition of duration with respect to non-utilitarian concerns.[20] In other words, by forcing the cinematographic manner of thought to its limits, modern science, especially physics, makes us aware of the limits of its appropriate scope. Whereas Classical Greek thought was a metaphysical justification of common sense ideas imbedded in our language, reflection on modern science allows a return to the primordial. Not a return to the past, but a movement into the future from out of the primordial — a development wherein the vital force of evolution becomes consciously self-directing.

In Heidegger's view, our "scientific" interpretation of Being in general on the basis of entities occludes the "worldhood" of the world.[21] He maintains that there is a more primordial, pre-scientific concernful dealing with things in the world that we do not need to put ourselves into the way that we need to be conditioned into the scientific mindset. Heidegger

---

17   Heidegger, *The Question Concerning Technology and Other Essays*, pp. 118–119.

18   Ibid., pp. 121–122.

19   Bergson, *Creative Evolution*, p. 336.

20   Ibid., pp. 342–344.

21   Heidegger, *Being and Time* (New York: Harper Collins, 1962), p. 94.

attempts to excavate this originary existential comportment.[22] Bergson is likewise concerned with recollecting a disposition towards beings in the world that has been covered over by the modern scientific interpretation of the self and world. Common to the way in which both Heidegger and Bergson attempt to recover our way of being in the world prior to being conditioned by the Cartesian world picture is a recognition that our primary experience of things is not theoretical, but practical.

According to Heidegger's account in *Being and Time*, our basic orientation in the world is practical, and our *praxis* is mediated by Things, which the Greeks called *pragmata*.[23] These are not "mere Things," but equipment that is inconspicuously withdrawing within its handiness for-the-sake-of doing certain work. Equipment always signifies a referential totality. Our being at work in the world with our tools is not in the first place mediated by any overlay of theoretical knowledge of their function, as if praxis were blind without it.[24] Tool use has its own pre-scientific knowledge or know-how. According to Heidegger, the shift from the predominance of a practical being in the world to the theoretical knowing of the world occurs on the basis of a disruption in the context of significance that assigns the "towards-this" and "with-which" of tools and other equipment.

The heretofore tacit referential context can be explicitly illuminated in three ways: 1) breakdown of equipment; 2) missing equipment; and 3) equipment getting in the way.[25] In all of these examples of a disturbance in the assignment of tools, a break in the referential context of our praxis transforms our experience of the world. We are reduced to a pure observer of mere things, which are uselessly laid before us, stripped down to their bare presence. Tools go from being equipment ready-to-hand for use in some project to being objects that are merely present-at-hand. Our circumspective concern that "lets things be" is frustrated.

---

22   Ibid., p. 96.
23   Ibid., p. 97.
24   Ibid., p. 99.
25   Ibid., pp. 102–104.

We may have to rework tools or "improve" things to once again render them serviceable, and if this is not possible, we may even be tempted to smash them into pieces.[26] We wonder what we are doing in this place, this tool shed, which becomes just a space for developing a solution to a problem. Thus begins the modern, scientific mode of Being. Tinkering with equipment that is not experienced as withdrawn into its usefulness precedes the theoretical development of modern mathematical science in the seventeenth century.[27] According to Heidegger, "Machine technology is itself an autonomous transformation of praxis, a type of transformation wherein praxis first demands the employment of mathematical physical science."[28] Chronologically, modern theoretical science seems to appear first, but ontologically, its manifestation is grounded in the relationship to things that defines the essence of Technology. Rather, modern science is, for Heidegger, always already Technoscience.

Bergson reaches much further back in his archeology of how our practical comportment towards things evolves into the modern scientific understanding of the world in terms of Cartesian space and time. This abstract decomposition of our original experience of being in the world first arises as a hypertrophied development of a practically oriented drive to break things up in such a way as to get a better grasp on them for the purposes of survival and growth.[29] "Consciousness" has a practical function.[30] If consciousness — the Cartesian *cogitare* — were primarily for the sake of knowing, as rationalistic idealists take it to be, it would not make sense for certain things to remain in the shadows outside of its view.[31] If, however, our consciousness is actually a filter, which primarily conceals rather than reveals, for the sake of the needs of an organism in order to take practical action, then it makes sense that it would not be commensurate with the

---

26   Ibid., p. 117.

27   Martin Heidegger, *Basic Writings* (New York: Harper Collins, 1977), pp. 319–320.

28   Ibid., p. 116.

29   Henri Bergson, *Matter and Memory* (New York: Zone Books, 2005), pp. 50, 185.

30   Ibid., p. 141.

31   Ibid., p. 150.

natural world — but only a limited perspective on it; an image of what is in our interest rather than of the whole (of which there can be no image).[32] In *Creative Evolution*, Bergson expands on this idea in a way that brings him closer to Heidegger.[33] There, he treats intellect as a faculty of fabrication. Unlike a pure dialectical speculation that would carve up the world at its joints, its tendency is to disregard the natural forms of all things and treat matter — in general — as a medium that is infinitely malleable and capable of being reshaped to fit any frame. In other words, natural form is viewed as artificial.

Like the Cartesian wax, any being is taken to be dissolvable into homogenous, elementary solids that function something like building blocks, each sufficiently lacking in character so as to be suitable for any manner of lawful or systematic construction. One can make anything out of these simple parts by rearranging them. The general framework for this construction is a homogenous space, like 3-D graph paper that extends in every direction and whose smallest units are as small as the simplest parts of things. This is an artifice that is inconceivably outside the experience of extensity open to non-human animals. The great problems and paradoxes of philosophy arise when this primarily practical faculty is misdirected towards speculation on the nature of things, and mistakes its functional objectification of things as discontinuous and immobile for those things *as they really are*, rather than those things schematized by our rational faculty according to our possible action and to our designs on them. We ought to reclassify ourselves *Homo faber*, or "fabricating man," instead of *Homo sapiens*, since intelligence, as we are able to employ it, begins with tool use, and is a faculty for the manufacture of artifice and the indefinite variation of this means of production.[34] Mechanistic science is an outgrowth of our natural geometrical tendencies. Directed in the first place towards carving out a human habitation in a dangerous natural world,

---

32   Ibid., p. 40.

33   Bergson, *Creative Evolution*, pp. 153–157.

34   Ibid., p. 139.

these tendencies predominate over the fine artistic appreciation and chan-neling of the spontaneity of nature in the form of genius.[35]

Bergson explains that abstract logic and scientific geometry engender each other on the basis of the natural geometry that we employ when we break material up into solids that are easy to manipulate.[36] All of the oper-ations of our intellect are essentially geometrical.[37] Neither deduction nor induction can function without a geometrical intuition of homogeneous space.[38] Mathematical order is one and the same with inflexible determin-ism, but the so-called "laws of the physical world" that express determined order by measuring everything as a variable are intellectual projections that have no objective reality.[39] The extraordinary success of a scientific method based on mathematics is really a case of a self-fulfilling prophecy: we read out of the world what we have written into it. Mathematical order is a negative *interruption* that acts as a sieve to filter the movements of Nature.[40] It is like a planar cross-section cutting "instants" out of the flux.[41]

This is basically no different from Heidegger's understanding of how the framework of Technoscience challenges Nature to present itself in a certain way. In German "the real" is *das Wirkliche*, which is related to that which works (*wirkt*).[42] Technoscience, as the "theory of the real," sets upon (*stellen*) the real, ordering "the real" to arrange and exhibit itself as "an interacting network."[43] The German word translated by "network" here is *Gewirk*, meaning "web, texture, weaving." Heidegger introduces a hyphen into it, so that it becomes *Ge-wirk*, an active gathering of that which works and is worked. The "Truth" becomes *what works*. The net-

35 Ibid., p. 45.
36 Ibid., p. 161.
37 Ibid., p. 210.
38 Ibid., pp. 213–216.
39 Ibid., p. 218.
40 Ibid., p. 219.
41 Ibid., p. 249.
42 Heidegger, *The Question Concerning Technology and Other Essays*, p. 159.
43 Ibid., p. 168.

work has an internal normative coherence that is self-reinforcing. There is a feedback loop between the results prompted by the experimental setup and the design of machinery for future experiments.[44] This ongoing research activity of modern science is institutional — it requires institutions to sustain it, and the results it produces are in turn determined by the institutionalized interests.[45] Heidegger's insight is that it is not just the research methodology that has to adapt itself to its results, but beings also are adapted by the ongoing activity of research as it builds the ground plan into Nature (and History). The consolidation of institutional research science leads, in his view, to nothing less than "the precedence of methodology over whatever is." [46]

In our capacity as artisans, as a species that requires technical development for its very survival, we are also innately geometricians — who, in principle, reject the unforeseeable.[47] Bergson thinks that if we de-condition our minds of rationalistic analysis, we can place ourselves back at "the *turn* of experience" that is, as it were, the "fork in the road" leading to the development of intellect at the expense of the instinct that drives most other forms of life.[48] It is not the case that the former is an advance over the latter and develops on its basis.[49] Intelligence and instinct are divergent solutions to the same problems.[50] In all actual cases, these two tendencies remain ultimately indivisible, but the distinction between them may be conceptually reified so as to better understand their relationship with one another.[51] If we consider instinct and intelligence each in their most epitomizing cases, we find that instinct is a faculty of using and of constructing organically organized instruments, whereas intelli-

44   Ibid., p. 124.
45   Ibid., pp. 124–125.
46   Ibid., p. 125.
47   Bergson, *Creative Evolution*, p. 44.
48   Bergson, *Matter and Memory*, pp. 50, 185.
49   Bergson, *Creative Evolution*, p. 135.
50   Ibid., p. 143.
51   Ibid., p. 136.

gence is a faculty of crafting instruments from unorganized (inorganic) material and making use of these tools.[52] It follows from this that instinct is necessarily specialized, by contrast with intelligence employed in the construction of tools — which are imperfect instruments admitting of an unlimited reconfiguration of form to improve their functionality with a view to various projects.[53] This intelligence bestows the living being with a proliferation of new powers.

While instinct automatically closes off an animal's sphere of action, technologically-oriented intelligence tends to create a new need for every one that it satisfies, and thereby opens up the field of free action to beings characterized by crafts production.[54] Consequently, "[a]n intelligent being bears within himself the means to transcend his own nature."[55] If the immanent life force were unlimited, it would have commensurately developed instinct and intelligence in the same organisms, rather than always furthering one at the expense of the other.[56] As it happens, we would have to go very far back into evolutionary history to find primordial organisms where the two tendencies are almost indistinguishably integrated.[57] It is possible, however, that along the way to more fully developing one type of psychical activity, Nature hesitated at certain points — allowing for a resurgence of the other one.[58] Instinctual knowledge, such as is supremely developed in bees, remains latent in human beings and can be retrieved by diving deep into the generative force of life within the primary instincts that we each still have, at the outset of the acts in which they express themselves, prior to their being interpreted by intellect.[59] Instinct is a sympathy such that, if it becomes capable of extending its object and of reflecting

---

52   Ibid., p. 140.
53   Ibid., pp. 140–141.
54   Ibid., p. 141.
55   Ibid., p. 151.
56   Ibid., p. 141.
57   Ibid.
58   Ibid., p. 143.
59   Ibid., p. 166.

upon itself — in other words, if it becomes disinterested — transforms into an *intuition* that exceeds the analytical capabilities of the intellect.[60] Our extrasensory perception is an intuitive reassertion of instinct.

On Bergson's account, the primary perception of an organism immediately discerns a center of its being, with respect to the "other" that is either to be assimilated as a source of nourishment or averted as a corrosive element that threatens to disintegrate it.[61] In addition to the overwhelming affectivity of such beings at the mercy of external influences that immediately compel a change of state in them, certain stimuli are "reflected back" or "ricochet off of" the limited degree of indetermination — or range of possible action(s) — that this organism maintains with respect to them.[62] Our perception is a tracing-out of beings according to the plan of our eventual action; suppress this action, and the beings themselves disappear back into the fabric of Nature as a whole.[63] Perception, in its most basic form, is nothing more than this rudimentary reflection which differentiates an organism from things, as well as certain things from others with a view to *virtual* action.[64] It is the variable relation between the living being and more or less distant objects.[65]

Whenever they occur, these reflections are recorded, and the recordings mediate the organism's direct intuition of its world in such a way as to allow it to discern basic similarities, such as the same nutrient in different sources.[66] This mediation will occur at the sensory-motor level, so that its actions with respect to new stimuli will follow, to the extent possible, a habitual pattern established by reactions to previous stimuli determined to be similar on account of the mediation of these recordings. The intervention of these recordings in the indetermination of a range of

---

60   Ibid., p. 176.

61   Bergson, *Matter and Memory* (New York: Zone Books, 2005), pp. 56, 64, 198.

62   Ibid., pp. 32, 37, 64–65.

63   Bergson, *Creative Evolution*, p. 11.

64   Bergson, *Matter and Memory*, p. 242.

65   Ibid., p. 33.

66   Ibid., p. 159.

possible action can be characterized as involving relationships of "association and contiguity." In other words, a reflected past *image* associatively resonates with a similar present image (or fails to do so), and this prompts not only a single action tied to that past image, but a variety of contiguous, or closely related, behaviors that were relevant to the past image and that are now brought to bear on the present stimuli.

Memory originates as just this process, and it cannot be separated from the primary perception that first defines material entities. Consequently, mind or mentality at its most basic level cannot be separated from matter. Material beings are images, and basic memories are virtual actions.[67] Yet in no way is it the case that the mind of any organism is coextensive with the totality of images; in other words, with the material world as a whole.[68] The core function of perception is to filter out everything in the world that is not relevant to the virtual action of one given organism or another.[69] What this means is that, just as recollections that materialize through the associative resonance of things are not contained *inside* a brain or a rudimentary nervous system, whether or not something is perceivable by an organism depends on the vital interests of that organism, and not on some abstract distance between the sensory-motor system of the organism and the object in question. Indeed, research on plants and other very simple organisms that lack a nervous system, let alone a brain, suggests that these creatures do have habitual memories and directional orientations towards persons and things of significance situated in dwelling places that are more primary than homogenous space. They do not experience things laid out within a space that extends around them like 3-D graph paper.

The renowned polygraph scientist, Cleve Backster, extensively researched such unexplained phenomena in connection with plants, living cells, and bacteria. The polygraph, as applied to humans, has three components. The first of these is the Galvanic Skin Response (GSR), the

67   Ibid., p. 242.
68   Ibid., p. 71.
69   Ibid., p. 38.

second is a measure of changes in blood pressure, and the third monitors changes in pulse strength and rate. In the case of the plant, Backster could use only the GSR. A polygraph machine's resistance indicating circuitry (such as in an electrician's OHM meter) passes a small current of electricity through two electrode plates, one attached to each of two fingers of a subject.[70] Backster chose the dracaena because of its long stem and large leaves. He connected the two electrodes to one of its leaves and compressed the leaf in order to help them stay in place during the 56 minutes of the experiment. To his content, he found that the plant leaf's electrical resistance fell within the range (of 250,000 OHMS) that allowed for it to be measured by the available polygraph instrumentation.[71] The only difference was that the ink recording on the polygraph chart was serrated in appearance rather than smooth because, unlike in humans, the waxy insulation between the plant's cells allows the electrical discharge to come directly into the electrodes. Backster expected that as the plant began to absorb water, the polygraph's recording device would chart an upward-tending ink tracing, indicating a relative decrease of the leaf's electrical resistance due to an increase in its moisture content.[72]

When Backster poured the water into the dracaena's pot, this did not occur. Instead, the recording began with a downward trend (increased electrical resistance) and then a spike of the type that, in human subjects, would indicate a brief initial fear of being detected.[73] Backster, bemused by the human-like response, decided to see what would happen if the plant were threatened, as a human subject is threatened by questions pertaining to his guilt in having committed a certain crime. Of course, he did not entertain the idea of verbally questioning a plant. Instead he dipped one of its leaves in a cup of hot coffee. There was no response other than a

---

70   Cleve Backster, *Primary Perception* (Anza, Calfornia: White Rose Millenium Press, 2003), p. 22.

71   Ibid., p. 23.

72   Ibid., p. 22.

73   Ibid., p. 23.

steadily increasing downward trend of the type that, in humans, indicates boredom.[74]

Fourteen minutes into the recording, Backster was standing approximately fifteen feet away from the plant, which was about five feet from the polygraph device to which it was attached, when the thought suddenly occurred to him in a flash: "I'm going to burn that leaf!" The moment the vivid imagery of this thought formed in his mind, the polygraph recording pen spiked rapidly to the top of the chart.[75] Backster had not spoken any words, nor had he touched the plant. After returning from his secretary's desk with a pack of matches, the plant was still exhibiting excitation on the chart. Backster realized that with the pen *already* registering at the top of the chart, he would no longer be able to recognize additional reactions.[76] After half-heartedly passing the match over another leaf, he decided to abandon the idea of threatening the plant and see if that would produce any reaction. Only once he returned the pack of matches to his secretary's desk did the dracaena's tracings return, suddenly and dramatically, to the apparent state of calmness preceding the threatening thought.[77]

When Backster's associate arrived at work a couple of hours later and observed the polygraph chart tacked onto the wall, the tracing's resemblance to a human test prompted this trained professional to ask Backster *who* he had been testing.[78] To allay his probable disbelief, Backster encouraged his associate to replicate the experiment. This time, nothing at all was physically done to the plant, and a similar observation was made by the polygraph.[79] In both cases, *thought alone* — at a distance — produced a response in the plant similar to that of a bored, suddenly frightened, and ultimately reassured human test subject.

---

74   Ibid., p. 24.
75   Ibid.
76   Ibid., p. 25.
77   Ibid.
78   Ibid., p. 26.
79   Ibid.

For two and a half years, Backster continued to observe the galvanic "skin" response of plants. He developed a more refined and standardized method of electroding a leaf, and he conducted his plant testing at various locations around the world.[80] During this period of time, he observed that in order for the plant to register a significant response on the polygraph chart, one had to threaten the plant with sincere intent. It became clear to Backster that simply feigning an intention to harm the plant did not suffice.[81] The chart would record a far more significant response if one were at a remote location and sincerely thinking about cutting up a plant, than it would if one were standing right next to the plant with scissors aimed at a leaf but without a genuine intention to follow through in using them.

Backster observed that his plants would provide very significant recordings in response to stimuli at the opposite end of his laboratory (and not even in the same room), but they apparently had no reaction to events on the street, even though the physical proximity and emotional intensity of these events were greater.[82] For our purposes here, the most significant factor involved in this selective response to stimuli irrespective of three-dimensional Cartesian space is a plant's apparent attunement to specific individuals that it has somehow perceived to be its caretakers. Backster took the plants' territoriality, together with their attunement to caretakers at remote locations (as opposed to people nearby who had no relationship with the plants) as indications that the mode of communication being observed could not be accounted for by the electromagnetic spectrum.[83]

Remote biocommunication with the plants was not limited to human subjects. Backster found that plants are also attuned to a wide variety of microscopic life forms. He inadvertently discovered this when pouring the remainder of boiling water he had used for making coffee down a sink drain that was later confirmed to be host to a colony of microor-

---

80   Ibid., p. 28.
81   Ibid., p. 29.
82   Ibid., p. 30.
83   Ibid., p. 31.

ganisms.[84] When Backster poured the water down the long unused and bacterially infested sink drain, he received a significant response on the GSR chart. Backster began to notice that a similar, but even more intense, reaction would be charted every time he heard the flushing of urinals in the adjacent men's room. He conjectured that the strong disinfectant drip released by the flushing of the urinal was terminating some sort of life signal emitted by microorganisms in human bodily fluids.[85] Apparently, plants are remotely sensitive to these signals, and respond with GSR chart tracings akin to sudden and severe stress when the life signals are terminated. It is significant that the threat of termination was the only form of stimulus that Backster's plants did not adapt to over time. In most cases, a plant would respond less remarkably to the same stimulus the more it was repeated. However, in the event of the termination of any life form, the plants always responded with equal intensity as on previous occasions.[86]

Backster incorporated many of his initial findings into the design of his first rigorous experiment. He decided that human emotions are too varied and unpredictable to turn "on" or "off" at will, in a manner that would definitively demonstrate correlation with plant responses recorded on the polygraph chart.[87] A more elemental and clear-cut mechanism would have to be employed. Backster decided to use the abrupt termination of brine shrimp as the stimulus to incite reaction in plants located within three separate rooms.[88] The polygraph equipment was located in a fourth "instrument room" and connected to the plants by long wires.[89] The instrument room also featured a control polygraph device and chart that were hooked up to a fixed value electric resister.[90] Two rooms away from the instrument room was the device for terminating the brine shrimp,

---

84   Ibid., pp. 33–34.
85   Ibid., p. 34.
86   Ibid., p. 35.
87   Ibid., p. 43.
88   Ibid., pp. 43–44.
89   Ibid., p. 45.
90   Ibid., pp. 45–46.

at the opposite end from where the laboratory and the plant rooms were located.[91]

His initial observations had made Backster well aware that plants seemed to respond to whatever were the more complex life forms in their territory—especially if these were humans to which they had been attuned by a caretaking relationship. Attunement to its human caretakers would apparently outweigh any less significant stimulus in its immediate environment, even if the caretakers were tens or hundreds of miles away. This called for several radical constraints in experimental protocol designed to eliminate interference from human consciousness. First, the brine shrimp would have to be terminated by an automated cup-dumping device, instead of an experimenter dumping them into the basin of boiling water.[92] Second, a mechanical computer capable of time delay automation had to be designed to activate both the polygraph machines connected to the plants and the cup-dumping device at a given time after any and all humans had vacated the laboratory.[93] Third, new plants would be purchased for each experiment so as to eliminate overriding attunement to the experiments (irrespective of distance from the lab) and possible acclimatization to a repeated stimulus.[94] Finally, those purchasing the new plants would be persons other than the laboratory staff, and these people would quickly install the plants in the proper experimental setup so as not to become attuned to them.[95] Without having had any prior interaction with these new plants, Backster and his associate would quickly enter the lab, activate the mechanical programmer automating the experiment, and proceed to leave the building and walk at least a street away.

One experiment involved the exposure of yogurt to ampicillin trihydrate, a type of penicillin that kills both friendly and unfriendly bacteria. Backster opened the capsule of ampicillin and placed some of its con-

---

91   Ibid., p. 45.
92   Ibid., pp. 44–45.
93   Ibid., pp. 44, 46.
94   Ibid., p. 47.
95   Ibid.

tents on a lab spatula. He then placed yogurt, from the same source as the electroded yogurt, into a beaker. The electroded yogurt, at some distance, produced a huge reaction on the EEG chart just as the ampicillin began affecting the yogurt bacteria in the beaker. Backster recorded the entire event on split-screen video (with the beaker/ampicillin on one side and the electroded yogurt on the other), and there were multiple witnesses present.[96] Many hours of experiments conducted with the above setup produced chart readings suggesting that the bacteria in yogurt is very attuned to human activities in its immediate area.[97] However, Backster also noted that the yogurt in bacteria is not entirely helpless in reacting to a variety of stimuli in its surroundings. Rather, it appeared to have an ability to exercise selective attention and to prioritize in its reactions.[98]

If organisms as simple as plants, bacteria, and living cells have a directional orientation with respect to places, one that allows them to draw near things that appear to be distant from them in terms of abstract space, we should expect to see a more evolved form of this capacity in non-human animals. Bergson addresses such animal capacities in *Time and Free Will*, as part of an argument against Kant's postulation of a space that is separable from, and given before, the objects that fill it — a postulation that Bergson notes has not been seriously challenged up to his own era.[99] Even the so-called "empiricists" adopt this conception of space, and really have to wind up accepting this Kantian postulate, because unextended sensations (which are already abstractions) cannot be synthesized without an act of the mind.[100] The extensity experienced by non-human animals does not have this abstract, homogeneous quality. Bergson speculates that animals probably do not picture to themselves an external world entirely distinct from themselves and from the sensations for which they serve as

96   Ibid., pp. 100–101.

97   Ibid., p. 86.

98   Ibid., p. 93.

99   Henri Bergson, *Time and Free Will* (Mineola, New York: Dover Publications, 2001), p. 92.

100 Ibid., pp. 93, 94.

a container.[101] Such a theater of the mind, in which the states of processes are rendered into objects, is the basis of theorization. As I will remind the reader later on, the Greek word *thea* is the root for both "theater" and "theory." Bergson notes the observation of naturalists that animals are able to find their way home over a distance of hundreds of miles by a path that they have never taken before, sometimes (as with birds) in a straight line.[102] The various directions open to animals likely each have their own peculiar quality *as directions*, in a way analogous to our natural ability to distinguish our right arm from our left arm. Directions also may have qualitative differences from one another that cannot be attributed to a difference in "spatial contents," and that even conflict with the spatial assessment of equidistance between two or more abstract points.[103]

Experiments carried out in the early twentieth century by the zoologist F. H. Herrick and the naturalist Bastian Schmidt are probably the type of observations of naturalists regarding animal directionality that Bergson is referring to.[104] Herrick's cat accidentally escaped when he was trying to carry it in a bag while traveling by streetcar from his home to his university some five miles away. The fact that the cat was waiting for him at home that very night after having navigated the maze of streets in the city of Cleveland, Ohio, prompted Herrick to carry out a series of deliberate experiments where he would carry the cat in a closed container to various locations one to three miles away from his home. Once released, the cat could find its way home without difficulty from any point on the compass. Schmidt took dogs to various locations that they had never been to before in enclosed vans and by means of circuitous routes. He had trained observers posted along the dogs' probable route home, and in the event that the dogs took some other route, he also had them followed at a distance by cyclists who were instructed not to interact with them in any way other

---

101   Ibid., p. 138.

102   Ibid., p. 96.

103   Bergson, *Time and Free Will*, p. 97.

104   Rupert Sheldrake, *Dogs That Know When Their Owners are Coming Home and Other Unexplained Powers of Animals* (New York: Random House, 1999), pp. 175–177.

than to observe their behavior. When the dogs were released, each spent up to a half hour running back and forth in a relatively circumscribed area, apparently in order to get its bearings. Eventually, the dog would repeatedly stare intently in the direction of its home, before finally setting off in this direction at quite a rapid pace and without further hesitation. The dogs would successfully make their route home by whatever path that would allow them to avoid road traffic, farmhouses, strange villages, and other places where they might run into trouble.

Herrick and Schmidt's experiments are among those reviewed in Rupert Sheldrake's study of the unexplained powers of animals, which includes several chapters on the directional orientation of animals. Sheldrake is a world-renowned, albeit controversial, British biologist. He received his Ph.D. in biochemistry at Cambridge University after having studied philosophy at Harvard University. He was a Fellow of Clare College, Cambridge, and a Research Fellow of the Royal Society. He is the author of more than sixty scientific papers and numerous books.

As Sheldrake reports, a collie dog named Bobby made his way back home to Oregon after being lost more than 2,000 miles away in Indiana.[105] In most cases of this kind, the animals have been taken to the location at which they were "lost" or released in an enclosed vehicle — such as a car, bus, train, or boat — and usually by indirect routes, and yet they returned home by a more or less straight heading rather than by tracing back the indistinctly perceived route by which they came to the remote location.[106] The most astounding cases of this type are those involving dogs finding their way back "home" in the midst of war zones. During the Vietnam War, the United States would airlift dog scouts into the jungle to support patrols, often as far as ten miles away from their home bases. In one case of this type, a dog named Troubles was abandoned by a patrol that came under enemy fire after his handler, William Richardson, was wounded and airlifted to a hospital. Troubles somehow made his way on the ground

---

105 Ibid., p. 171.
106 Ibid., p. 172.

through the war zone of an unfamiliar Vietnamese jungle that he had been flown into by helicopter, all the way back to the First Air Cavalry Division Headquarters where, though emaciated and exhausted, he would not let anyone touch him until he curled up next to Richardson's belongings.[107]

Sheldrake carried out his own experiment with a dog left to find her way home in Leicester, England.[108] This dog, named Pepsi, was transported on the floor of a taxi (where she could not see out the windows) to a street corner unfamiliar to her, some two miles east of her owner Clive's house. Sheldrake and Clive grew worried when she did not turn up for several hours. Clive then thought of checking the home of his sister, who was away on vacation. Pepsi had been taken to this house by car six months prior to the experiment, but she had never made her own way there or back to Clive's home. Nevertheless, there she was, lying comfortably on Clive's sister's lawn, only a mile east of where she was abandoned (rather than the two miles to Clive's home). The GPS device attached to the dog had recorded how, like the dogs in Schmidt's earlier experiments, Pepsi had begun not by following Sheldrake and Clive's taxi as it pulled away, but by pacing back and forth in the streets immediately surrounding the corner where they left her, as if to psychically get her bearings before deciding intently on a certain direction. On another occasion, this dog escaped from Clive's sister's house and made her way four miles to the southwest to visit a friend's house.

The evolutionary benefit of such a directional sense can be seen when we consider how animals navigate their vast home ranges and stray into unfamiliar pathways within them.[109] A "home range" is an area far more vast than the territory defended by the animal as its own. While the home range is geographically bounded in every direction by certain extremities, it contains many potential paths through terrain that is completely unfamiliar to the animals in question. This range often consists of the

---

107 Ibid., p. 173.
108 Ibid., p. 179.
109 Ibid., pp. 186–187.

hunting ground that lies beyond the territories of pack animals. Wolves have the most enormous home ranges, covering some 5,000 square miles on Ellesmere Island northwest of Greenland. When predators are chasing their prey or prey is frantically fleeing a predator, the respective animals are not likely to remember all of the details of the path that takes them into unknown places. Having an experience of directionality that allows an animal to find its way back home from these unfamiliar places, and to thereby expand its home range or its scope of activity within a home range, is of clear evolutionary advantage. Migration is deeply related to homing in that cycles of migration can be conceived of as a "double homing system."[110] Establishment scientific literature refers to the migratory navigational capacity of birds as "an inherited spatiotemporal vector-navigation program" — a piece of jargon that, as Sheldrake notes, merely restates the problem that such an ability poses for physicalist presuppositions rather than solving it in any way compatible with them.[111]

Of course, it is very difficult to test predatory animals in the wild to determine how much of the ranging ability can be explained by use of the known physical senses. Controlled experiments can be much more easily carried out with homing pigeons. When released from remote locations hundreds of miles away from anyplace they have ever been before, these "racing pigeons" can find their way home in a single day. As the most well-informed researchers will admit, numerous studies have ruled out all physicalist theories of animal homing.[112] The theory that these birds remember the twists and turns of their outward-bound journey, first proposed by Charles Darwin, has been invalidated by placing the pigeons in rotating cylinders, anaesthetizing them, and then transporting them in this state to unfamiliar locations inside darkened vans. Nevertheless, the birds manage to fly straight home. They have also been fitted with frosted-glass contact lenses to temporarily blind them so as to rule out the theory

---

110 Ibid., p. 193.

111 Ibid., p. 194.

112 Ibid., pp. 188–191.

that the pigeons used recognizable landmarks or the precise position of the Sun to navigate.

It is noteworthy that these blinded birds did tend to crash into trees or wires near their loft when they attempted a landing once they had found their way home. That the Sun acts as an indispensable navigational beacon has also been ruled out by keeping pigeons in artificial light for various intervals of time sufficient to shift their internal clocks by six or twelve hours. Such birds are initially confused when they are released, but they quickly make a correction and fly home. Pigeons are also capable of homing on overcast days and even at night. The theory that the sense of smell is the basis of such homing abilities has been refuted by experiments wherein pigeons had their olfactory nerves severed, their olfactory mucosa anesthetized, and their nostrils blocked with wax. This did not appear to affect their ability to find their way home.

Finally, the hypothesis that the directional orientation of pigeons (and other animals) is grounded in a little understood magnetic sense has been disconfirmed by attaching magnets to some of these birds, and comparable non-magnetic weights to others, only to observe that the two groups remain equally capable of homing. Note that even if there were a magnetic sense so carefully tuned as to give information on latitude, it would not help the birds — who can fly home equally well from all points of the compass — orient themselves longitudinally.

This apparently extrasensory capacity for spatial orientation is perhaps most strikingly manifest in the extraordinarily complex patterns of social organization and architectural engineering exhibited by creatures with brains smaller than a pinhead. Social insects behave as if they were the limbs of a single "superorganism," engaging in vast building projects — such as 10-foot high nests with galleries, chambers, and ventilation shafts. Some insects, such as termites, are blind. Their physical sensory organs of scent and sound are hardly enough to account for what was observed in the following experiment. One has been carried out in a "termitarium" — an enclosure of termite mounds — in which breaches were made in the termite mounds within it. Then an opaque, soundproof, and scent-proof steel barrier was inserted into the termitarium in such a way as to divide the damaged areas of the mounds into two halves. Parts of any given breach fell asymmetrically on either side of the barrier. The worker termites that rapidly endeavored to repair the damage could know nothing of each other by means of their physical senses. Nevertheless, when their work was complete and the steel plate was taken away, the two repaired halves of the termite mound matched each other perfectly.[113]

Fish also exhibit similar, apparently telepathic, abilities to coordinate their rapid movements in schools. In one laboratory experiment, members of a school of fish were temporarily blinded by having their eyes fitted with opaque lenses. The researchers also cut key junctures of the nerves of the pressure-sensitive organs that run along the length of their bodies, known as "lateral lines." This means that these fish were left with no known physical sensory organs by which to effectively communicate with each other. Nevertheless, they were still able to precisely coordinate their movements with those in the rest of the school. These include predator evasion movements where all of the members of the school dart away from each other simultaneously. In so doing, none of the fish collided with each other — this despite the fact that the explosive expansion around a predator occurs at a speed of ten to twenty body lengths per second. Even in the case of fish that have not had their sight artificially impaired and their lateral nerves cut, this is apparently too fast for nerve impulses to move from their eyes to their brains and then from their brains to their muscles.[114]

As it is with schools of fish, so it also appears to be with flocks of birds. Films of large flocks of dunlin birds, when slowed down, show that the organic banking movements of the flock are initiated either by a single individual or by a few birds together at some point within the flock. The wave of movement radiates outward from this point to the rest of the flock, tak-

113   Ibid., p. 158.
114   Ibid., p. 159.

ing only 15 milliseconds (thousandths of a second) to pass from one bird to its neighbor. Yet when dunlins are tested in a laboratory, it is found that they are incapable of even the most primitive reaction to sensory stimuli (such as a flash of light) at any rate faster than 38 milliseconds. Thus, it seems it would be impossible for any given dunlin, by known sensory means, to gauge a vast pattern of movement and coordinate its own bodily motion accordingly *in less than half that time.*[115]

In addition to exemplifying an irreducible capacity for directional orientation, such studies appear to demonstrate the ability of non-human animals to communicate "telepathically" or by some means other than the known bodily senses. The similarity to telepathy in humans is more apparent in cases of biocommunication between *individual* animals that are emotionally bonded. Two horses who habitually walk together, graze together, and otherwise interact are separated from each other at a sufficient distance to make communication by sight, smell, and sound impossible. The regular feeding schedule of the two horses is replaced by random feeding times, and their regular exercise sessions are randomized as well. Nevertheless, when one of the two bonded and now separated horses is fed, the other horse is observed to simultaneously demand food. Similarly, when one of the two is taken out for exercise, the other grows excited in the stable. When one of the two horses is fussed over by the horse trainer, the other remotely located horse shows signs of disturbance suggestive of jealousy. Apparently non-physical communication was observed in 68% of 119 such experiments. Interestingly, a control run with horses that were hostile to each other found a positive result in only one out of fifteen experiments.

A similar experiment with Boxer dogs was carried out at Rockland State Hospital in New York. A mother Boxer and her son were separated into two soundproof rooms in different parts of the hospital. The dogs had been trained to cower when a rolled-up newspaper was raised and waved at them. The experimenters found that when the son was threatened with

---

115   Ibid., pp. 160–161.

the newspaper, not only would he cower, but the isolated mother — also under observation — would do so as well, at exactly the same time.[116]

Rather than concluding that some animals have a distinct faculty responsible for what seems to us to be an extraordinary sense of direction and a remote perception of things of vital significance to them, Bergson speculates that it may be the case that their heterogeneous experience of extensity is also primary for us prior to the conditioning of our intellect for technical purposes. This overlay of dynamic extensity by homogenous space serves as the ground for all of the other abstractions and rational functions of the human intellect, enabling every form of clear cut-distinction, as well as the very ability to express such distinctions by means of language.[117]

Until their recent integration into the civilized world, Australian Aborigines, the Bushmen of the Kalahari, the navigators of Polynesia, and other primitive peoples were famous for having a sense of direction comparable to that of these non-human animals.[118] As Rupert Sheldrake reports in *The Sense of Being Stared At*, Europeans who have gone hunting with the Bushmen in the Kalahari Desert of southern Africa have noticed that the tribe, whose encampment is as far as fifty miles away from the hunting site, seems to know whether or not the hunt has been successful.[119] If it has been, preparations to welcome the victorious hunters begin to be made immediately so that by the time they actually return, everything is in order for a ceremonious reception. When queried about this ability, the tribesmen who were somewhat familiar with the colonial culture *tapped their chests* and drew a comparison to the telegraph: "They know by wire. We bushmen have a wire *here* that brings us news." There is a strong correlation between the technological development of artificial aids to navigation — such as signposts, maps, and compasses — and the

---

116   Ibid., pp. 164–165.

117   Bergson, *Time and Free Will*, p. 97.

118   Sheldrake, *Unexplained Powers of Animals*, p. 191.

119   Sheldrake, *The Sense of Being Stared At*, p. 95.

atrophy of this primordial experience of directional orientation towards things of concern in their places.[120]

There are passages in *Matter and Memory* that address this manner of orientation in the world, where Bergson offers insights that make more sense in the context of the foregoing natural history of remote perception, and of psi ability in general. Bergson claims that what does not reveal itself within the extensive expanse of a being's horizon of perception is what that being is "unconscious" of, in the very same sense as it cannot be mindful of certain past images, or their associated behaviors, on account of the specific tension of its consciousness.[121] As Bergson puts it, "[T]here will no longer be any more reason to say that the past effaces itself as soon as perceived than there is to suppose that material objects cease to exist when we cease to perceive them." He adds, "[W]hat can be a nonperceived material object, an image not imagined, unless it is a kind of unconscious mental state?"[122] There is also this striking remark: "Then, when a memory reappears in consciousness, it produces on us the effect of a ghost whose mysterious apparition must be explained by special causes. In truth, the adherence of this memory to our present condition is exactly comparable to the adherence of unperceived objects to those objects which we perceive; and *the unconscious* plays in each case a similar part."[123] In other words, those places in the world that you are aware of, but that lay beyond the purview of your present perception, are images enfolded in the unconscious state. The horizon of our perception is surrounded by another, more expansive horizon, a twilight zone wherein abide images of which we are predominately unconscious.[124] There is also Bergson's statement that "[a]s far as deep-seated psychic states are concerned, there is no perceptible difference between foreseeing, seeing, and acting."[125]

---

120 Sheldrake, *Unexplained Powers of Animals*, p. 192.

121 Bergson, *Matter and Memory*, pp. 141–142, 145.

122 Ibid., p. 142.

123 Ibid., p. 145.

124 Ibid., p. 144.

125 Bergson, *Time and Free Will*, p. 198.

Such an understanding is also implicit in Heidegger's view of how orientation towards things of significance in our world remains basic to our experience of the "truth," or disclosure of those things. This becomes clear in a striking example of directionally-oriented deseverence, or "making-present," that he offers in the course of the Zollikon Seminars. Toward the end of elucidating the distinction between recalling (*Erinnerung*) and making-present (*Vergegenwärtigung*), Heidegger asks the seminar participants to "make present" the Zurich central train station (through which many of them have travelled on the way to the seminar). He asks them to bracket the interpretive overlay of their psychological, physiological, and epistemological knowledge, and to simply consult their immediate everyday experience of envisaging this train station. The participants are queried, and various individuals report experiencing a different aspect of the train station from a certain vantage point. Heidegger claims that this is no different whatsoever from seeing *this* book from a particular side and knowing that it is a whole book, and not one damaged and missing a back cover, although I do not physically "see" its back cover. He repeatedly insists that they will notice that such making-present directs them towards the train station itself, not towards a picture or representation of it. He also recognizes how offensive this unfiltered observation will be to the prejudices of most of the participants:

> Making-present has the character of being-at... [*Sein-bei*], more precisely, of our being-at the station. This answer has made you rebel, and it continues to disturb you. You dispute that making-present has, or in any way even could have, something to do with being at the train station in Zurich. ...During the performance of this making-present, we are here at Boss's house. Surely, we are not at the train station in Zurich. No reasonable person wants to maintain that while making-present, we are transposing ourselves, as it were, to the station in order to be at and next to the station... And yet, our interpretation of making-present says that it is a being-at the station. We are, in a real sense, at the station itself.[126]

---

126 Martin Heidegger, *Zollikon Seminars: Protocols, Conversations, Letters* (Evanston, Illinois: Northwestern University Press, 2001), p. 70.

Heidegger goes on to make clear that for the participants to fancy that they only think they are at the station, or that they are at the station "only in thought," is not faithful to the experience that he has guided them into having. Simple phenomenological attentiveness to the making-present of the station is not an experience of "thinking" that one is standing in front of the station. There is no trace of such a thought, unless the interpretive filters of acquired "scientific" knowledge that Heidegger has asked the participants to bracket are still functioning.

Heidegger unambiguously states that to "think" one is present at the station, in the sense of producing the station as an "imaginary representation," is "a totally different phenomenon than the making-present of the station."[127] It is only because one is directed toward the station itself that, if after the seminar one needs to pick someone up at the station, one is able to drive there at all. Otherwise, one would never arrive at the station. One does not drive towards a thought, or mere image, or representation of the station in one's head. The possibility of having the station, or anything for that matter, present-at-hand is grounded in a more primordial possibility of engaging its presence even while it is physically absent. It is intrinsic to the characteristic openness of our *Da*-sein (*"there*-being") that we can make a remote location present, while a very different location surrounds us as present-at-hand. Note this striking passage from the Zollikon Seminars:

> During the making-present of the station, we are clearly, in fact, here inside this house. Yet, our *being* here offers us various possibilities. We can participate in the discussion, look at the clock, and follow how one of our colleagues answers a question directed to him. We can also make-present the Zurich train station… In this case… we are here inside Boss's home and simultaneously at the Zurich train station… Our being here happens continuously and necessarily in such a strange and even wondrous way. Our being here is essentially a being with beings which we ourselves are not. This "being at" is usually characterized by the bodily perception of things physically present. But our being here can also engage [*einlassen*] itself in being with things not present physically. If this pos-

127 Ibid, p. 71.

sibility did not exist and could not be performed, then, for instance, you could never arrive at home this evening.[128]

If we look back at Part One, Division 1.6 of *Being and Time*, particularly section 44 on "Dasein, Disclosedness, and Truth,"[129] we see that this understanding of the way in which we draw things of concern near to us in a clairvoyant experience of them is central to Heidegger's existential conception of Truth as "unconcealment," or disclosure. A critique of Descartes and of Kant's neo-Cartesianism on the question of the Reality (*res*) of the external world is the context for this exposition. Heidegger refers to Kant's "Refutation of Idealism" as an attempt to address what Kant takes to be the greatest scandal of philosophy: that no one has yet been able to prove the reality of the "external" world.[130] Heidegger thinks that the real scandal is not that no one has been able to provide such a proof, but that — beginning with the revolutionary subjectivism of Descartes — such proofs have been continually sought. According to Heidegger, even if Kant attempts to demonstrate the reality of changing things with reference to a persistently present transcendental subject, he follows Descartes in taking consciousness as a thing present at hand in the manner of objects.

Realism tries to address the question of the reality of the external world by turning the subject into a thing present at hand among other things, whereas naïve Idealism defines the subject only negatively as something indefinitely un-Thing-like. What Heidegger wants to show is that the *physical* and the *psychical* cannot be defined against or in terms of one another in this way. Idealists would be right if what they meant by ideality were the way in which our Being transcends entities that are only encountered within a world that is more primordial than them and that they do not constitute in a piecemeal manner. If all they meant to say was, "We have a world that we *are* before we have anything to do with one or another thing in that world. The world we have, and *are*, is not made up,

---

128   Ibid., p. 73.
129   Heidegger, *Being and Time*, pp. 246–273.
130   Ibid., pp. 202–206.

piece by piece, of the things that we happen upon and manipulate within the world. The world, as a horizon co-extensive with our existence, is not material. It is an ideality. Materialized things, or objects, are derivative of our being there to be concerned with them for some reason or another. So the things only are within ourselves, and within our world that comes before them. They are not external." (This is, basically, why spoon-bending works.) Only a subject which has lost its sense of its being in the world would attempt to "prove" the "reality" of this world as if it were something "external" and constituted of entities. The *res cogitans* is world-less, and so there is no place for *res extensa* to be, either.

The key example that Heidegger offers us in this section of *Being and Time* is of a person who knows that a picture is hanging askew on the wall despite the fact that it is behind his back.[131] The person has not physically perceived the picture that is askew, or at the very least he cannot observe that it remains askew at present. Yet, he knows that it is there, still hanging on the wall, but that something is not right with it. He can sense the tug of its imbalance behind his back. He may make a statement describing the condition of the picture. When he turns around so that it is possible for him to physically perceive the crooked picture, his statement is not "verified" by agreeing with some objective state of affairs that it might have failed to correspond to. The psychical impression of the picture preceding the physical observation was not a "guess." His apprehension of the truth of the crookedness of the picture is only derivatively one of referential correspondence. What is more primary is that, while his back was still turned to the picture, he uncovered, discovered, or disclosed the picture. He was able to do so because, like the (potentially missing) back cover of the book that cannot be "seen" in the Zollikon Seminars, the picture may not be within the range of vision of the man's eye organs, but it *is* within the world *in* which his whole being is always already encompassed.

For the most part, what is uncovered is forgotten in such a way that it sinks back into concealment. As a consequence of this, our predomi-

---

131   Ibid., pp. 260–261.

nant relation to things is a relationship to semblances, and so mistakes with respect to the condition of what we cannot physically perceive are common. Heidegger claims that Pre-Socratic Greek thinkers such as Heraclitus and Parmenides understood this when they elaborated the idea of "truth" privatively, namely as *a–lethea*, or an "un-concealment," which militates against a predominating concealment and a forgetfulness of what has been uncovered — our tendency to allow it to sink back into oblivion. Every "truth" has the violence of a Promethean act of theft, which breaks into and steals what has been covered up and secreted away. As Heraclitus puts it, "Nature loves to hide." This is the hiddenness of The Occult. Paranormal phenomena are only super Natural insofar as the primordial forgetfulness or concealment of technical intelligence effects an occultation of Supernature. This enframing is resisted by Supernature, but the latter winds up being misinterpreted as a "supernatural" order of being separate from a mechanically modeled "natural" world that has been mistaken for "Reality."

Heidegger's remarks on Wilhelm Dilthey's understanding of Reality as the "resistance" of what we "are out for" betrays the implicitly biological character of this conception of truth. By "biological," I do not mean what Heidegger dismisses as "biologistic" — it is not a question of understanding the Real in terms of organic structures and drives that are reductively further analyzable in terms of the laws of physics. Heidegger states, with shocking clarity, that Newton's Laws — or any physical constructs — are not true before *Dasein* discovers or uncovers the world in their terms.[132] In the absence of the uncovering *activity* of *Dasein's* being in the world, these "laws" do not even have the substantiality to be false. Nature does pre-exist these laws, and *life* forms would be there even without our *Dasein*. This *life* would not, however, be the measurable and lawful "Nature" of "natural science." It is, rather, Supernature. Heidegger adopts Dilthey's insight that "Reality" is the persisting resistance of *life* at large to our active pursuit of our own finite purposes, including calculative projection and technical

---

132   Ibid., p. 269.

manipulation of entities. Our world, and the scientific mode of being in it, necessarily conceals other forms of life. Implicit in that realization is another: the scientific mode of being is itself a distinct form of life, one with a unique power to colonize all others.

CHAPTER VII

WORLDS AT WAR
OVER EARTH

In view of the technoscientific occultation of Supernature, reflection on Technoscience remains the task of *the thinker*. Heidegger defines *reflection* as "the courage to make the truth of our own presuppositions and the realm of our own goals into the things that most deserve to be called into question."[1] This means bracketing the working assumptions scientists have received from their institutionalized training even if, and especially when, they seem to function *too* perfectly. Heidegger believes that the danger of predominating efficiency is that man may himself be insidiously taken up as feedstock within the network. This can only be averted if we find another sphere from out of which we can reflect on technological science so as to understand in what relation its essence stands to our existence. That is problematic because, by definition, *techne* as technological science en-frames every-*thing* in the world, and even makes "world" itself appear as if it were an object subjected to technical research and development — as in "virtual worlds." Heidegger's way of dealing with this conundrum is to remind us that, for the Greeks, *techne* still also meant the crafts of building and cultivating. *Techne* as technology is a modification of *techne* as art — in the widest Greek sense of *poesis*, which includes "fine art" as another modality.

In "Building, Dwelling, Thinking" (1951), Heidegger notes that the Greek word *techne*, the technique that gives rise to technology, is derived from *tec*, the root of the verb *tikto* — meaning "to bring forth or to

---

1   Heidegger, *The Question Concerning Technology and Other Essays*, p. 116.

produce."[2] In technology as a mode of world-revealing, we apprehend that
we *produce* our being. Heidegger sets forth poetry, in the wide sense of the
Greek word *poesis* — a creative bringing-forth — as "*the* distinctive kind of
building" definitive of human dwelling.[3] In "Poetically Man Dwells" (delivered in the same year), Heidegger evokes how creative vision precedes
and grounds technical building endeavors, since the poet takes a measure
for all other measures.[4] These remarks develop a theme introduced years
earlier, in "The Origin of the Work of Art" (1935), which is largely an inquiry into the relationship between technical equipment and works of art.

In "The Origin of the Work of Art," Heidegger reminds us that the
Greeks used the word *techne* for both art and technology, and *technites* for
both the artist and the maker of manufactured equipment.[5] Both artwork
and technical invention are modes of crafting, and thereby bringing-
forth into unconcealment something whose being is not evident; in other
words, not natural. For Heidegger, the key difference between equipment
and art is that equipment is so designed that its createdness — its work
on an undefined material — disappears in its usefulness (for so long as
the equipment does not break down), whereas the work of art somehow
preserves its createdness within itself.[6] This may be related to the fact that
great works of fine art (the ones with which Heidegger claims to be solely
concerned) do not have any particular use. Therefore, when we are confronted with them, *that* they are created is thrust to the fore.[7] Since this is
uniquely true of the work of art, the artwork alone reveals the nature of
Creation. Heidegger understands this in terms of strife between "world"
and "earth," which strife is preserved in the work of art.[8]

---

2   Heidegger, *Basic Writings*, p. 361.
3   Heidegger, *Poetry, Language, Thought*, p. 213.
4   Ibid., p. 215.
5   Heidegger, *Basic Writings*, p. 184.
6   Ibid., p. 172.
7   Ibid., pp. 182–183; 189–191.
8   Ibid., p. 187.

I suggest that this "world" and "earth" are a transformation of Heidegger's concepts of the *worldhood* of the world and *facticity* from *Being and Time*. As in *Being and Time*, where *worldhood* is constituted by discourse in its various modes and bounded by the hermeneutic circle, in "The Origin of the Work of Art" (1935), Heidegger takes poetry to be the essence of all art, and then equates poetry with language.[9] He does not mean that painting, sculpture, architecture, and so on are all derived from *poesy* — or poetry in the narrow sense of written or spoken poems — but that they are modes of poetic composition in a more profound sense.[10] Heidegger makes the significant claim that poetry — the essence of art — is always the poetry of a specific historical people.[11] As in *Being and Time*, he is clear that language is what is definitive of all existing beings, and so of all peoples, as opposed to stones, plants, and animals. Heidegger forwards the same view of poetic language as a uniquely "world-forming power" in *Logic as the Question Concerning the Essence of Language* (1934).[12] Just as in section 74 of *Being and Time*, discourse never constitutes the worldhood of any *Dasein* in the abstract, but only as the particular *logos* of a certain historical people.[13] Here Heidegger volunteers having been influenced by Friedrich Nietzsche and, as we shall see, that admission should be extended to "The Origin of the Work of Art" and the 1934 lecture on logic as well, where Heidegger nearly paraphrases Nietzsche at times without any explicit acknowledgement. Here is the passage from *Being and Time*:

> The possibility that historiology in general can either be 'used' 'for one's life' or 'abused' in it, is grounded on the fact that one's life is historical in the roots of its Being, and that therefore, as factically existing, one has in each case made one's decision for authentic or inauthentic historicality. Nietzsche recognized what was essential as to the 'use and abuse of historiology for life' in the second of his

---

9   Ibid., pp. 197–199.

10   Ibid., p. 198.

11   Ibid., p. 199.

12   Martin Heidegger, *Logic as the Question Concerning the Essence of Language* (Albany: SUNY Press, 2009), p. 141.

13   Martin Heidegger, *Being and Time* (New York: Harper Collins, 1962), pp. 434–439.

studies "out of season" (1874), and said it unequivocally and penetratingly. He distinguished three kinds of historiology — the monumental, the antiquarian, and the critical — without explicitly pointing out the necessity of this triad or the ground of its unity. *The threefold character of historiology is adumbrated in the historicality of Dasein.* At the same time, this historicality enables us to understand to what extent these three possibilities must be united factically and concretely in any historiology which is authentic. Nietzsche's division is not accidental. The beginning of his 'study' allows us to suppose that he understood more than he has made known to us.[14]

Heidegger appropriates three related ideas from Nietzsche. The first idea is that any being in the world needs to be bounded by a horizon. Although this horizon may shift and change shape, the way in which it will always conceal aspects of Nature or the earth allow a being to pursue its vital concerns. The second idea is that not only is a scientific History impossible, but the attempt to deal with our historical being scientifically reveals the essential limitation of the "truths" apprehended by the sciences. Everything "true" is wrested from out of the necessary concealment of the aforementioned horizon of being in the world, which is the bounded whole of a people's historical existence. The third idea is that History, properly understood, is neither objective nor factual in the sense that the subject-matter of the physical sciences is *supposed* to be, but is the living mythology or folklore wherein a people's envisioned "past" heritage reflects their projected *future*. The priority of the monumental mode of History over the antiquarian and critical ones in Nietzsche becomes, in Heidegger, the priority of the futural mode of our being *as* Time. This is to say that the world that we *live* in does not have any objective reality or persist in the manner of an entity. Whether we lose our world or, after seeming to have lost it, we are able to conjure its resurrection and continued creative development is decided as a matter of historical struggle. Nothing is "true," for anyone, outside of this struggle.

In "The Origin of the Work of Art," Heidegger repeatedly refers to "earth" as "native," and as that element without which "world" would be

---

14   Ibid., p. 448.

unmeasured and lacking in sufficient lawfulness as to allow a people to resolutely make those grave decisions that define their historical destiny.[15] Thus "earth" is that facticity of the historical situation of the community of people into which *Dasein* is born, and for which *Dasein* may die. Each *Dasein* must choose to affirm this facticity with commitment, or to evade it and allow it to sink into oblivion by ignoring it or by adhering to tradition unreflectively. "World," or consciousness and the discourse in terms of which it understands anything, would tend to be universal and to universalize by means of concepts, but in order to produce anything authentic and abiding, it must accept as its horizon the concrete historical situation of a given people.

Heidegger's discussion of a *horizon* that forgetfully conceals what lies beyond it, and yet thereby also bounds and protects the *earth* in which the *world* of a historical people is rooted, seems to have been lifted right out of Nietzsche's untimely meditations; specifically, "On the Uses and Disadvantages of History for Life." Nietzsche begins this text with the striking image of cattle that are happy because they have no memory. If someone were to inquire of a cow as to why it just stands there gazing at him, the animal would be inclined to reply, "The reason is I always forget what I was going to say," but then it would forget this too and remain silently staring at the human inquirer.[16] Such an animal lives *unhistorically*, and "is contained in the present, like a number..."[17] Nietzsche associates the advent of the "it was," or recollection, with an enduring experience of "conflict" and "suffering" that reminds man of "what his existence fundamentally is — an imperfect tense that can never become a perfect one."[18] "A man or a people or a culture" can all suffer from a hypertrophied memory that proves "harmful and ultimately fatal to the living thing."[19] While the

---

15   Heidegger, *Basic Writings*, pp. 166–169, 170, 174–175, 180.

16   Friedrich Nietzsche, "On the Uses and Disadvantages of History for Life" in *Untimely Meditations* (Cambridge: Cambridge University Press, 1997), p. 61.

17   Ibid., p. 61.

18   Ibid.

19   Ibid., p. 62.

animal can live with hardly any memory, it is impossible to *live* without a great deal of forgetting: "Forgetting is essential to action of any kind, just as not only light but darkness too is essential for the life of everything organic."[20] Nietzsche posits as "a universal law" that "a living thing can be healthy, strong and fruitful only when bounded by a horizon."[21] It is on account of this "rounded and closed" horizon that the ignorant peasant living vigorously amidst the Alps, whose judgments are false through and through, is far more capable of "a simple act of will and desire" than the man of knowledge who "sickens and collapses because the lines of his horizon are always restlessly changing, because he can no longer extricate himself from the delicate net of his judiciousness and truth."[22]

The degree to which "a man, a people, a culture" can afford to remember is proportional to what Nietzsche calls their "plastic power"; that is, their ability to "assimilate and appropriate things of the past" without being overwhelmed either by a bad conscience or by having their potential for growth nipped in the bud by a historical sense of their own insignificance.[23] The clarity of conscience and confidence in the future without which an active life is impossible requires the persistence of an "unilluminable and dark" background to everything "bright and discernable"; this darkness which, as mentioned above, shelters life in the way that the earth is essential to organic growth, is what must naturally be forgotten in order to shape the horizon that protects a certain life form.[24] At one point, Nietzsche explicitly refers to this as "the whole earthly and darkening horizon" of world-historical phenomena.[25] He also compares this earthly element to the nourishing ground in which the tree of our evolving being is rooted, without our being able to precisely determine from the size and strength of the visible branches just how deep the roots extend and in

20   Ibid.
21   Ibid., p. 63.
22   Ibid.
23   Ibid., pp. 62–63.
24   Ibid., p. 63.
25   Ibid., p. 67.

what directions.[26] The horizons of various forms of life can encompass one another, and a life form that is "too self-centered to enclose its own view within that of another" will also wither away.[27] The "little vortex of life" whirls away — in the form of an artist painting, a general triumphing in battle, or a people struggling for its liberation — only amidst a "sea of darkness and oblivion" that is the "unhistorical, anti-historical" condition.[28]

As Heidegger observes, when a work of art is displayed in a museum, or even when one goes to see ruins at their original site, they are no longer the works of art that they once were *because they have been stripped of their world*.[29] Works of art set up a world, but what is key in order to understand how this is related to technology is that every world is only the world of one, particular historical people. Not all *Dasein* live in the same world, and there is not *one* world. The great creators of works of art — and since poetry has a privileged role, especially epic and tragic poets that craft a living folklore — are the founders of a people's existence, and in the founding moment their creative work runs ahead and implicitly, and in a concealed manner, carves out the scope of *that* people's historical destiny.[30] The creators' individuality always disappears into their works, and the great works do not appeal to mere human beings as they ordinarily are. Rather, they awesomely tower over them and define a community for all that its people can become in the course of their history, or *Geschichte* — more literally, in the course of their "story."[31] They set the mood that holds sway over the flowering of a people's culture far into the future. In a sense, the lore of a folk haunts them from out of their future and calls them to fulfill their destiny, or as Nietzsche would put it — *to become who they are*. Note these passages from *Logic as the Question Concerning the Essence of Language*,

---

26 Ibid., p. 74.

27 Ibid., p. 63.

28 Ibid., p. 64.

29 Heidegger, *Basic Writings*, p. 166.

30 Ibid., p. 202.

31 Ibid., pp. 166; 191.

where, in the course of explaining this idea, Heidegger also offers us a key to exactly what he means by "earth" in "The Origin of the Work of Art":

> ...We are determined, that is, at all times attuned-through by a mood [von einer Stimmung durchstimmt]. ...The misunderstanding arises that the so-called strong willed human beings, the doers, the cold-thinking humans are exempt from moods, that the mood is something feminine... A great work is only possible from the fundamental mood, ultimately from the fundamental mood of a *Volk*. ...We would not stand at all, if this standing were not attuned through by moods, by virtue of which earth, ground; in short: nature first bears, preserves and threatens us. ...the poet is not he who writes verses about the respective present. Poetry is no soothing for enthused little girls, no charm for the aesthetes, who believe that art is for savoring and licking. True poetry is the language of that being that was fore spoken to us a long time ago already and that we have never before caught up with. For this reason, the language of the poet is never of today, but is always in the manner of having been and futurally...[32]

The "preservers" come after this founding moment. They are those who still understand the work of the creators, and for whom these works of art are still living in the sense that they are able to stand within the world-historical clearing of the work, and from out of this insight, make those choices decisive for the historical victory or defeat of their own people.[33] "Victory" and "defeat" against whom? Well, it appears that for Heidegger, the strife in the work of art also becomes strife between historical peoples.[34] There is not only a strife between "earth" and "world," but one between different "worlds," each struggling to set themselves into the common "earth" — a struggle wherein each community is challenged to become more essentially what it is, or to perish in enslavement to another people and *its* world.[35] Think of the Aztecs and the Spaniards. In *Logic as the Question Concerning the Essence of Language*, Heidegger ventures an

---

32   Heidegger, *Logic as the Question Concerning the Essence of Language*, pp. 126–129, 142.

33   Heidegger, *Basic Writings*, p. 192.

34   Ibid., p. 169.

35   Ibid., pp. 187–188.

ontological interpretation of victory and defeat in "world war" in these terms, rather than the tactical superiority of armed forces arrayed against others on a battlefield: "...the World War as historical power has not at all yet been won, has not yet decided for the future of our planet. It will not be decided by the question of who has triumphed, but it will be decided by the trial, which the *Völker* are facing. The decision is reached, however, through the answer, which we give to the question of who we are, that is, through our being."[36] Given the 1934 date of the lecture, he is historiographically referring to the First World War, and yet his point is that this is not *the real world war* if one conceives of it in terms of military engagements of a limited duration decided by tactical superiority and concluded by a "peace treaty." In these terms, even the Second World War has not concluded the decisive confrontation over what the world of the Earth as a whole is destined to be. Moreover, it may happen that a certain group of people has such creative potential that its world experiences a rebirth repeatedly, after long periods of decline.[37] Heidegger sees Western history in these terms. Something of the glorious Greek beginning is still definitive of "the essence of Western art."[38]

Heidegger sees *alethea*, or "unconcealment" — the essence of Truth — as identical to the essence of Art.[39] In other words, the essence of all things "true," the existential opening and the hermeneutical circle presupposed in every predication, requires the limiting of a "world" by an "earth" that "shelters" it by concealing things beyond the horizon of its form of life. As Heidegger says, untruth belongs to the essence of truth. That is why the Greeks rightly understood the essence of truth as *a–lethea*, as a modification of predominating *lethe*, or forgetful concealment; an idea which, as we have seen, he develops from out of Nietzsche. Heidegger draws a series of equivalences: the essence of art is poetry, and the essence

---

36   Heidegger, *Logic as the Question Concerning the Essence of Language*, p. 41.

37   Heidegger, *Basic Writings*, pp. 201–202.

38   Ibid., p. 206.

39   Ibid., p. 197.

of poetry — its unconcealing projection — is the essence of truth. Well, if poetry is always only the poetry of a historical people, and the work of art only sets up their *own* world, then it seems that things can essentially be "true" only for one or another nation.[40] This suggests that the political State, whose founding Heidegger identifies as one type of artwork, namely state*craft*, must be the total artwork (*Gesamtkunstwerk*) and the abode of that people's "truth."[41]

Indeed, in *Logic as the Question Concerning the Essence of Language*, we see Heidegger make the claim that a folkloric tradition, and the poetic mood through which it attunes people, first grounds their existence as "individuals" that comprise a *Volk* in such a way that the whole is immeasurably more than the sum of any "parts":

> Precisely by virtue of mood, the human being is never an individual subject, but he stands always for-or-against-one-another, in a with-one-another. This is also valid when, as in longing, the other is not yet immediately there. The being-with-one-another of human beings is not in virtue of the fact that there are several human beings, but several human beings can only be in community, because being-human already means: attuned being-with-one-another, which is not lost, if a human being is alone... the human being is set out beyond himself [he ex-ists] in tradition... This being is never a subject, nor an assembly of several subjects, who by virtue of agreements first ground a community, but the originally united being, transported, bearing exposure, and carrying mandate can only be what we call "a *Volk*." Only in virtue of this being, of the determination, can individuals as well comport and experience themselves as individual. ...The being of beings is transferred to us. Being, as a whole, as it rules through and rules around us, the ruling wholeness of this whole, is the world. World is not an idea of theoretical reason, but world announces [kündet] itself in the lore [Kunde] of historical being, and this lore is the manifestness of the being of beings in the mystery. In lore, and through it, world rules. This lore, however, happens in the primal-event of language. In it, the exposure into beings happens, the delivering over to being happens. World rules — *is* a being. ...Language is the ruling of the world-forming and preserving center of the historical existence of the *Volk*.[42]

---

40   Ibid., p. 167.

41   Ibid., p. 186.

42   Heidegger, *Logic as the Question Concerning the Essence of Language*, p. 140.

Either Heidegger is trading in preposterously inflated platitudes, or he is saying something so shocking that it seems to have been missed by any commentator of which I am aware: there is no stable "earth" or *nature* — the equivalence is his own — that can be encountered *as it is in itself* underlying the "worlds" that shape it. Folklore grounds our existence, in the quite literal sense that without it we would not be able to "stand" as the beings that we are. Furthermore, the poetic language of the geniuses that craft this lore in the context of a fundamental mood is a basically futural mode of expression. It is concerned with what is "to come" and with what we may *become* if we maintain a living relationship with our lore. That is impossible if it is handed down as a dead tradition, rather than a living heritage subject to revolutionary reinterpretations of its elemental structure in each epoch of the historical existence that it first establishes for us on our way to becoming mythical, more-than-merely-human beings envisioned, as it were, through a glass darkly — on our way to giving birth to heroes and striving with gods. This is what lurks behind that otherwise cryptic remark in *Being and Time* regarding *Dasein* having to "choose its hero."[43]

These are not word games. They present us with an ontological account of the relationship between social consciousness, time, and the natural world. Heidegger is very explicit about the fact that this ontology precedes any "scientific" account of the human being or its relationship to nature.[44] It is not as if a science of history comes after the being of human communities on the Earth as they are grasped by the so-called "hard sciences."[45] Heidegger points out that the Greek word *historia*, whose German equivalent is *das Erkunden,* was originally used to refer to "exploring."[46] In other words, exploration or discovery (*das Erkunden*) is always already historical in the sense of setting out on an adventure

---

43   Heidegger, *Being and Time*, p. 437.

44   Heidegger, *Logic as the Question Concerning the Essence of Language*, pp. 18, 41.

45   Ibid., pp. 90–91.

46   Ibid., p. 74.

that both explores the lore (*Kunde*) of a folk and inspires it anew.[47] The explorers advance as heroes into those uncharted places marked by the warning: "Here be dragons." Not only the so-called "science of history" or historiography, but also *all science in general* is grounded in this adventurous spirit of exploration and discovery as guided by a folklore that it enriches.[48]

This observation regarding the status of History with respect to the sciences is another key idea that Heidegger has appropriated wholesale from Nietzsche's untimely meditation, "On the Uses and Disadvantages of History for Life." There, Nietzsche already recognized that the demand that "history should be a science... the science of universal becoming" threatens to weaken the present and to deprive "a vigorous future of its roots."[49] In order to remain "believers in deeds and progress," we must recognize that the "process" of "an evolving culture" is always "dominated and directed by a higher force" than what can be comprehended by any History with the pretensions of being a "pure, sovereign science."[50] Such a "pure science" of History, which aspired to the standard set by "mathematics," would "be for mankind a sort of conclusion of life and a settling of accounts with it."[51] Every people that wants to continue growing requires "an atmosphere around them, a mysterious misty vapour... [an] enveloping illusion, a... protective and veiling cloud."[52] Those whose motto is "let truth prevail though life perish" are engaged in a futile endeavor, since *life* is the ultimate tribunal of the survival of all truths, and it usually grants victory to those "dominated not by knowledge but by instinct and powerful illusions."[53] Nietzsche defines "life" as "that dark, driving power

---

47   Ibid.

48   Ibid.

49   Nietzsche, "On the Uses and Disadvantages of History for Life" in *Untimely Meditations*, p. 77.

50   Ibid., p. 67.

51   Ibid.

52   Ibid., p. 97.

53   Ibid., pp. 78, 97.

that insatiably thirsts for itself.[54] Life is destined to dominate science, and not the other way around, since "knowledge which annihilated life would have annihilated itself with it."[55] The question as to whether History can become a science forces us to reevaluate the status of the sciences as a whole, and to conclude that "science requires superintendence and supervision; a *hygiene of life* belongs close beside science and one of the clauses of this hygiene would read: the unhistorical and the suprahistorical are the natural antidotes to the stifling of life by the historical."[56] Nietzsche adds: "It is probable that we... will also have to suffer from the antidotes. But that we suffer from them is no evidence against the correctness of the chosen treatment."[57]

The historizing of a community is not the sum of individual fates (as Being-with one another is not the sum of several subjects), and *Dasein* does not exist "in" history. Rather, *Dasein* — as part of the story or lore of its people (*Geschichte*) — exists *as* historizing, and only on this basis is historiography (*Historie*) possible.[58] In order for historiology to be possible, there must be a means for accessing something that is "past."[59] Though this may seem to be a platitude, the answer to this question of the persistence of the past is by no means obvious, and it should be very perplexing. If the past were a series of nows no longer present-at-hand, there would be no way in which a former now that was once present-at-hand, but *is* no longer, should be accessed. The way to the past is only opened through *Dasein's* own fateful historizing — grounded in a futural temporality that makes present by having-been. Thus, historiology is the study of *Dasein* that "has-been-there" — and it is only the study of artifacts insofar as they are involved with this *Dasein*.

---

54   Ibid., p. 76.
55   Ibid., p. 121.
56   Ibid.
57   Ibid.
58   Heidegger, *Being and Time*, p. 434.
59   Ibid., p. 445.

Entities are only historical in belonging to a *world*. For example: ancient Greek housewares in a museum are still functional, but they are "historical" because the totality-of-involvements in which they had significance no longer exists. This *world* that is no longer is, of course, that of *Dasein*-that-has-been's *being-in-the-world*.[60] What is most disconcerting to the commonplace understanding is that this suggests that history is not primarily concerned with the past and its relation to today, but arises from the *future* of *Dasein*'s temporality.[61] One must project *Dasein*-which-has-been upon its ownmost *potential*, and this potential must be experienced or opened anew by the futural projection of the *Dasein* 'studying it.' Even in presently selecting the object of historiology, as in all decisions, *Dasein* is futurally projecting based upon its own possibilities. Thus, an authentic historiology is always a critique of a forgetful "present" that mass man has uprooted from ossified and dead tradition, and the forging of a vigilant and dynamic relationship to living tradition that renders a renaissance of the "monumental" possible.[62]

This reference to the cultural revitalization effected by *monumental* history is more clearly explained by Nietzsche, who first defines this species of historical being in opposition to two types of what Heidegger critiques as pseudo-objective "historiology." Nietzsche identifies "three species of history": the *monumental*, the *antiquarian*, and the *critical*, none of which ought to aim at objective and unlimited knowledge — as if such a thing were possible — and all of which properly belong only "to the man of deeds and power, to him who fights a great fight, who needs models, teachers, comforters and cannot find them among his contemporaries."[63]

Antiquarian history is that traditionally employed by conservatives. It is laudable insofar as a great people use it to preserve for their future generations those cultural conditions of growth that allowed for their rise

---

60 Ibid., pp. 432–433.

61 Ibid., p. 438.

62 Ibid., pp. 447–449.

63 Nietzsche, "On the Uses and Disadvantages of History for Life" in *Untimely Meditations*, p. 67.

to greatness.[64] It affords one that rooted ancestral affirmation of one's own existence that encourages a meaningful life, rather than one wherein everything is uprooted from a heritage and seems accidental.[65] The danger is that, when a living heritage becomes a hardened tradition that chokes further growth, antiquarian history can mummify life rather than conserving it.[66] This unreflective adherence to tradition sees all greatness as lying in the past, and views history as a constant battle to slow the decline from this "golden age."[67]

The opposite danger is presented by critical history. If Nietzsche had lived longer, he would certainly have associated its abuse with Marxists who furthered the Hegelian tradition that he already explicitly criticizes for its conception of a "world process" that aims at a universal end of history.[68] Used properly, historical criticism limits forgetfulness to a bare minimum and "takes the knife to [the] roots" of a people by intensifying the causal analysis of events to the point that it deconstructs everything inherited that it takes to be oppressively unjust, such as "a privilege, a caste, a dynasty," and thereby liberates people for future development.[69] What the critical historians fail to realize is that this destruction of a heritage always actually means an attempt to implant a new habit in a people so that it becomes "second nature," and that every first nature was once actually a victorious second nature of this kind.[70] They are deluded by the Hegelian faith that world history is dialectically converging on a unification of the spirit of all peoples in a self-conscious and self-correcting abstract conceptual knowledge that, in retrospect, frames "every success

---

64   Ibid., p. 73.
65   Ibid., p. 74.
66   Ibid., p. 75.
67   Ibid., p. 72.
68   Ibid., p. 104.
69   Ibid., p. 76.
70   Ibid., p. 77.

[as] a rational necessity" and "every event [as] a victory of the logical or the 'idea' [in a purely abstract sense]."[71]

It is inherent to *life* or nature that we will forever remain "unconscious" of certain aspects of it that could literally be called *incomprehensible*; evolutionary growth through striving for the "great and the impossible" is grounded in the persistence of such unconsciousness.[72] The Hegelian (and Marxist) delusion that we will reach a point where "there are no longer any living mythologies" because art and religion have been subsumed by a scientific History or a historical Science fuels attempts to obliterate the bounded world horizon of a culture *without the will to replace it with a new, and perhaps broader, horizon of life.*[73] Nietzsche levels this charge against "a history which, lacking the direction of an inner drive to construct, does nothing but destroy."[74] In a passage that holds up as an indictment of our contemporary critical theorists and proponents of so-called "postmodern" deconstruction, many of whom claim to be his heirs, Nietzsche warns:

> When the past speaks it always speaks as an oracle: only if you are an architect of the future and know the present will you understand it. ...only he who constructs the future has a right to judge the past. ...When the historical sense reigns *without restraint*, and all its consequences are realized, it uproots the future because it destroys illusions and robs the things that exist of the atmosphere in which alone they can live. ...If the historical drive does not also contain a drive to construct, if the purpose of destroying and clearing is not to allow a future already alive in anticipation to raise its house on the ground thus liberated, if justice alone prevails, then the instinct for creation will be enfeebled and discouraged. ...only if history can endure to be transformed into a work of art will it perhaps be able to preserve instincts or even evoke them.[75]

---

71   Ibid., p. 105.

72   Ibid., p. 112.

73   Ibid., pp. 104–105.

74   Ibid., p. 96.

75   Ibid., pp. 94–96.

Unlike antiquarian history, with which it is often confused, monumental history is actually concerned with *the future* — but with a future that has a real potential for growth on account of its being rooted deeply enough in a native soil and its being protected by a world-historical horizon sufficiently bounded by a living mythology. For this reason, Nietzsche accords *monumental* history priority over both the antiquarian and the critical modes of historical consciousness.[76] They ought only to augment it. Whereas antiquarian historians are conservatives who, at best, only know how to *preserve* life by nourishing its roots, those who make and use monumental history are revolutionaries.[77] Monumental history weaves events together with a view to a meaningful whole after having simplified these events into symbols with elemental power, with disparate events in different epochs being accorded an analogical symbolic significance.[78] So-called "historians" whose research amasses detailed facts have their proper place in serving the genuine historian who is a masterful artist capable of crafting such a narrative of the past with a view to inspiring vigorous action in the present, action that is above all directed towards a certain vision of the future.[79] Remarking on his own early professional life as a Classical philologist, Nietzsche claims that the real purpose of "Classical" studies is to act counter to one's time, and "for the benefit of a time to come" on the basis of the knowledge acquired.[80]

Although he is writing nearly half a century after Nietzsche's untimely meditation on History, Heidegger concurs with him that we have amassed more historiographical knowledge than during any other era, but we are also more historically impoverished than the people of any past epoch in our civilization.[81] An account of happenings in the lore of a people may be esteemed "incorrect" from the scientific standpoint of historiography,

---

76   Ibid., p. 72.

77   Ibid., p. 75.

78   Ibid., pp. 91–93.

79   Ibid., p. 94.

80   Ibid., p. 60.

81   Heidegger, *Logic as the Question Concerning the Essence of Language*, p. 95.

but lore always expresses the historical *happening* of a people more essentially than History books of scientific ambition that may offer extremely
detailed causal accounts of events but, for all that, fail to be in the least
historical, and do not at all reflect what really *happened*.[82] What Heidegger
means by "happening" and "happened" here is that lore is always about
the *becoming* of a people and their *coming to be* — like the "happenings" of
the 1960s American counterculture, or those of 1930s Germany. History
books aspiring to scientificity will never grasp what really became of us
in those epochs, and what is still on the way from the future that those
generations were remembering.

It is in this sense that we ought to understand the central claim of
Heidegger's *magnum opus*, namely that *time is the horizon of being*, because "the understanding of being itself is taken *from time*,"[83] or to put it
more elaborately: "[T]he most essential, deepest, and broadest concept of
our understanding, activity, and thinking, the concept of being, is created
from a certain idea of time."[84] The entire unpublished second half of *Being
and Time* was supposed to undertake a deconstruction of the ontologies
of the fundamental thinkers of our tradition with a view to their understanding of time because:

> The concept of temporality itself not only determines the idea of historical be-
> ing, but, in general, the idea of what being, nonbeing, and becoming mean.
> Time is the leading realm within which we understand being. Insofar as the
> time-concept changes in history, the concept of being and our fundamental
> position on beings will alter as well.[85]

Primordial temporality is the horizon of our being-in-the-world, and
that from out of which entities within-the-world are disclosed. In other
words, Dasein's transcendence of the world through its temporality is
the condition for the possibility of its spatiality. However, the faculty of

---

82   Ibid., pp. 78–79.

83   Ibid., p. 102.

84   Ibid., p. 109.

85   Ibid., p. 112.

Understanding — which is always already interpreting everything — not only interprets entities within-the-world as objects present-at-hand "within time," but it also consequently objectifies its primordial temporality as a "world time" wherein things occur sequentially. In Heidegger's view, a particular entity "within time" that is key for this conceptual development is the Sun. Its movement and the alternation of day and night become the basis for counted time. Ultimately, the technology of the clock takes over this function, and firmly establishes a conception of time as a series of nows.[86] The problem arises when *Dasein* forgets that the making-present (at hand) of primordial temporality is the basis of its interpretation of "world time" and of entities "within time." *Dasein* then counts itself in as just another entity occurring *in* time. One makes the mistake of thinking that one can be "at a given place at a certain time," a misconception implicitly grounded in an acceptance of the Cartesian view of the way that space and time are bounded together in a mathematical grid. If time were really a series of nows, its infinite regress would force us to think of it as without beginning or end. Moreover, it should also be just as easy to reverse time so that the succession of instants becomes a regression. Yet, Heidegger notes, one rightly speaks of time as "passing away," and its evident irreversibility evinces a time that is both always prior to any given instant and that is futurally-oriented.

By losing a living connection with our lore, we are *alien*ated from what we are becoming and from the things to come. If we learn to see "history no longer as an object, but as a happening, as our, the *Volk*'s being," then we will recognize "that which has been as [the] future of our own being," because "[t]hat which essences from earlier on determines itself from our future."[87] This is to say the same thing as Heidegger does in what may be the single most revolutionary statement in *Being and Time*: "But if [destiny] constitutes the primordial historicality of Dasein, then history has its essential importance neither in what is past nor in the "today"

---

86   Heidegger, *Being and Time*, pp. 469, 474.

87   Heidegger, *Logic as the Question Concerning the Essence of Language*, pp. 96–97.

and its 'connection' with what is past, but in that authentic historizing of existence which arises from Dasein's *future*."[88] In this historical happening that grounds our existence: "Our beenness and our future do not have the character of two periods, one of which is already vacant and the other that first has to be occupied, but that which essences from earlier on is *as future of our own being*."[89] Realizing that "we must experience ourselves as those who determine themselves from the future" involves "a transformation of our whole being in its relationship with the power of time."[90]

Nietzsche was already calling us to this revolution when he demanded that, rather than remaining "pupils of declining antiquity," our understanding of the past should be oriented towards a higher goal in the distant *future*, so that once we have redeveloped "the spirit of Alexandrian-Roman culture" we can "as a reward be permitted to set ourselves the even mightier task of striving to get beyond this Alexandrian world and boldly to seek our models in... *an essentially unhistorical culture and one which is nonetheless, or rather on that account, an inexpressibly richer and more vital culture.*"[91] This is to do consciously, and while remaining rooted in a living lore, what critical historians do despite themselves in an unconscious and uprooted manner: "It is an attempt to give oneself, as it were, *a posteriori*, a past in which one would like to originate in opposition to that in which one did originate."[92] In addition to the unhistorical "art and power of *forgetting* and of enclosing oneself within a bounded *horizon*," the dominance of life over the historical also demands a *suprahistorical* turning of the eye away from inchoate becoming, and towards the enduring symbolic power of religious art.[93]

---

88   Heidegger, *Being and Time*, p. 438.

89   Heidegger, *Logic as the Question Concerning the Essence of Language*, p. 98.

90   Ibid., p. 100.

91   Nietzsche, "On the Uses and Disadvantages of History for Life" in *Untimely Meditations*, p. 103.

92   Ibid., p. 76.

93   Ibid., p. 120.

The futural projection of a foundational heritage for one's existence is grounded in the recognition that our being is *in itself* abyssal and entirely lacking in any foundational nature that would drive the putative process of world history towards some point that renders individual personalities and concrete historical peoples mere means to an end.[94] Rather, a single "republic of genius" wherein one "giant calls to another across the desert intervals of time" extends throughout history, above "the excited chattering dwarfs who creep beneath them," so that "[i]t is the task of history to be mediator between them and thus again and again to inspire and lend the strength for the production of the great man. No, the goal of humanity cannot lie in its end but only in its highest exemplars."[95] Nietzsche repeatedly states that the rebellion of, even, only a hundred such men, banding together as the youthful vanguard of a single generation, could reverse our cultural decline and bring about a new Renaissance.[96] This civilizational revitalization ought not to be insular and narrowly focused on some revival of Greek or Roman culture, or the cultivation of a uniquely German culture. Nietzsche argues that what made the Greeks so extraordinary in the first place was the fact that "their 'culture' was, rather, for a long time a chaos of foreign, Semitic, Babylonian, Lydian, Egyptian forms and ideas, and their religion truly a battle of all the gods of the East," and yet, in the end "Hellenic culture was no mere aggregate" because:

> The Greeks gradually learned *to organize the chaos* by following the Delphic teaching and thinking back to themselves, that is, to their real needs, and letting their pseudo-needs die out. Thus they again took possession of themselves; they did not long remain the overburdened heirs and epigones of the entire Orient; after hard struggle with themselves and through protracted application of that oracle, they even became the happiest enrichers and augmenters of the treasure they had inherited and the first-born and models of all future cultured nations... and... achieved victory over all other cultures.[97]

---

94   Ibid., pp. 107–108.

95   Ibid., p. 111.

96   Ibid., pp. 95, 121.

97   Ibid., pp. 122–123.

What is so revolutionary about the transformative power of modern technological science is that it utterly uproots, deconstructs, colonizes, and assimilates the worlds of all other traditional cultures. Even within our own civilization, with its Hellenic origins, the effects of Technoscience on cultural heritage are widely taken to be destructive. Yet, as I argue, the essence of Technology, which grounds theoretical science, is not something ahistorical or culturally "neutral." In his writings on technology, and in the very late *Der Spiegel* interview that he consented to have published only posthumously, and that reads like a last will and testament, Heidegger intuits that the essence of Technology is something superhuman. Every culture is technological insofar as it is predicated on tool use rather than pure instinct. However, Heidegger recognizes that the essence of Technology, in other words its utmost defining potential, has been developed only in our own civilization — in an arc that begins with the rationalistic interpretation of form and its relationship to matter in Platonism, and ends with Descartes' framing of the (totally objectified) "reality" of the whole world as a legitimate question. Such a question can only be asked by a being that has taken the place of the Platonic demiurge and is no longer merely human. It can only be posed by the engineer of Man.

This metamorphosis is superhuman, gigantic, or *titanic* in aspiration. Far from requiring us to abandon scientific research and development, this gigantism is the very essence of Technology. We ought rather to become self-conscious of the specters of Prometheus and Atlas as the hitherto occulted aesthetic ideas of anticipatory projection and world building. This is not a purely intellectual or speculative realization. If Bergson is right that, although intellect has been developed at the expense of animal instincts that we now see as "paranormal," these abilities can return to us — dialectically, as it were — at a higher level commensurate with our technical development so long as we we cultivate our intuition, then Prometheus and Atlas have another significance as well. Bergson saw the universe as a machine for making gods, and called us to become self-conscious with respect to the creative force of our biological *and psychical* evolution into a future race of supermen.

On September 23, 1966, Heidegger granted an interview with *Der Spiegel* only on the condition that it would not be published within his lifetime. Under the title "Only a god can save us now," it was printed on May 31, 1976 — five days after his death. This final interview is in some sense Heidegger's "last will and testament." The *Der Spiegel* interviewer cites a 1935 lecture course, later published as *Introduction to Metaphysics*, where Heidegger defines "the inner truth and greatness of the [National Socialist] movement" as "the encounter between technology on the planetary level and modern man." Heidegger contrasts this essence of Nazism as he sees it with "What today is bandied about as the philosophy of National Socialism." Heidegger affirms that, although the leadership of the Third Reich was "far too poorly equipped for thought," the National Socialist movement in Germany did represent the most profound reckoning hitherto with "the situation of man in the world of planetary technology," and was at least a conscious attempt to "achieve a satisfactory relationship to the essence of technology."[98] By contrast, Heidegger sees "democracy," both under the guise of Communism and of "Americanism," as forms of "the planet-wide movement of modern technology." He explains that the reason why both of these political systems fail to be anything other than conduits for the further alienation and instrumentalization of man is that "behind them all, according to my view, stands the conception that technology in its essence is something that man holds within his own hands." Whereas in fact, "this is not possible. Technology in its essence is something that man does not master by his own power." When the interviewer brings up "the case of the Sorcerer's Apprentice" as an example of how man never completely masters his tools, Heidegger corrects his misunderstanding with the following, hyperbolic statement: "[M]odern technology is no 'tool' and has nothing at all to do with tools."

---

98   Martin Heidegger, "Nur noch ein Gott kann uns retten" ("Now Only a God Can Save Us") in *Der Spiegel*, 31 May 1976, pp. 193–219.

This movement that is planetary in scope diabolically uproots man and renders him homeless in any and every land in which modern technology essentially takes root. Where seemingly universal and timeless truths predominate, where everything is taken in the same way by everyone, where a common design levels the differences between all peoples and draws them into a single framework, it is there that *alethea* — or a people's capacity to wrest truths *to live by* from its world — would seem to be most endangered. Heidegger's central, but entirely tacit, concern in his techno-scientific writings is that the essence of technology endangers all historical peoples and the whole inter-national world order. The concrete existential situation that limited the hermeneutic circle for people born with a given language and within a particular historical community has been blown out by the leveling and universalizing force of Enframing (*das Gestell*), which forges, for the first time, a world horizon common to all of humanity.

Yet this standpoint, which grounds philosophy in the fulfillment of its historical mission, only encompasses others through its violent, world-colonizing power. It is a misunderstanding to think that philosophy is somehow "neutral," or that the philosopher can avoid being what Plato understood her to be from the beginning — an imperiled warrior and a vigilant guardian that stands even over the people's gods: "The opinion is frequently held that philosophy, as the highest science, must be devoid of standpoint. One has wanted to raise this to a principle. However, there must be a standpoint; one cannot stand without a standpoint. It is not about freedom from a standpoint but about the fact that a standpoint is gained by fighting."[99]

Heidegger claims to know that "everything essential and of great magnitude has arisen only out of the fact that man had a home and was rooted in tradition." The question, then, is whether in the face of "a world movement... that either is bringing about an absolutely technical state or has done so already," there can be a counter-current by means of which

---

99   Heidegger, *Logic as the Question Concerning the Essence of Language*, p. 69.

we may craft a new abode for habitation — a new homeland. The "mystery of the planetary domination of the un-thought essence of technology" is that "man is posed, enjoined and challenged by a power that becomes manifest in the essence of technology — a power that man himself does not control."[100] This is a challenge posed by something beyond the merely human, the specter of an occulted titanic agency that is the motor driving the developmental trajectory of *techne* through the histories of those people who trace their heritage back to the Greeks.

Heidegger recognizes that modern technology in the broadest sense of limitless technical organization and instrumentalization is the culmination of a developmental trajectory that uniquely arises from out of Greek philosophy as it disintegrates into the disparate empirical sciences of modern Europe, which are in turn functionally reintegrated by cybernetics. Philosophy, in its traditional academic sense, "is at an end," and can no longer offer a response to this development. Now that "the manner of thinking of traditional metaphysics has reached its term" and "the role of philosophy in the past has been taken over by the sciences," a thinking that is at the same time "poetizing" is the only dimension from out of which the technological can be essentially "not set aside but sublated [*aufgehoben*], though not through man alone." Heidegger did not see a "great" enough poetic thinker equal to this endeavor in his time; it remained a future task:

> But the greatest need of thought consists in this, that today, so far as I can see, there is still no thinker speaking who is "great" enough to bring thought immediately and in clearly defined form before the heart of the matter [seine Sache] and thereby [set it] on its way. For us today, the greatness of what is to be thought is [all] too great...
>
> Philosophy will not be able to bring about a direct change of the present state of the world. This is true not only of philosophy but of all merely human meditations and endeavors... Only a god can save us now... I think the only possibility of salvation left to us is to prepare readiness, through thinking and poetry, for the appearance of the god or for the absence of the god during the

---

100 Heidegger, "Nur noch ein Gott kann uns retten."

decline: so that we do not, simply put, die meaningless deaths, but that when we decline, we decline in the face of the absent god.

...It is not simply a matter of just waiting until something occurs to man within 300 years, but rather to think forward without prophetic claims into the coming time in terms of the fundamental thrust of our present age that has hardly been thought through at all. Thinking is not inactivity, but is itself by its very nature an engagement that stands in dialogue with the epochal moment of the world.[101]

Heidegger explains what it was about German National Socialism that allowed it to at least attempt a sociopolitical reckoning with the essence of Technology: the unique relationship of modern German thinkers and poets with the Hellenic heritage that is foundational to our civilization as a whole. From the late nineteenth into the early twentieth century, Germany was both the most technologically advanced modern nation-state and the nation whose thinkers and artists were most intimately in dialogue with our Greek progenitors. Goethe, Hölderlin, Schelling, Schiller, Nietzsche, Klimt, and so many other Germans were engaged in the deepest excavation and renovation of Hellenic culture since the Italian Renaissance. An answer to the world-colonizing danger of technological development cannot come from some colonized culture lacking in an authentic generative relationship with the wellspring of *techne*: "I am convinced that only in the same place where the modern technological world originated can we also prepare a conversion (*Umkehr*) of it. It cannot happen by adopting Zen Buddhism or other Eastern experiences of the world. The help of the European tradition and a new appropriation of that tradition are needed for a change in thinking. Thinking will only be transformed by a thinking that has the same origin and destiny."[102]

Heidegger claims that in order to effect this conversion (*Umkehr*), Art must once again become capable of breaking through the abstraction of space and making a place on Earth for the sacred—an abode of meaning

---

101 Ibid.

102 Ibid.

that can serve as the foundational context for the projects of a people.[103] The question is, "Where does art stand? What place does it have?" The *Der Spiegel* interviewer notes that Heidegger demands "something from art" that he "no longer demand[s] from thought." Although Heidegger denies that he demands anything from art, there is certainly something to this observation.

The planetary dominion of Technology reveals the groundless praxical dimension of our existence. As noted above, for Heidegger, there is no simple return or retrieval. Once worlds are gone, they are gone.[104] More great paintings and great architecture are not what Heidegger has in mind as the response of *poesis* to the *techne* that has arisen on its basis. He admits that Hegel may essentially have been right that art is dead, at least as conceived in terms of these traditional art forms.[105] In the age of all-encompassing enframing — "the age of the World Picture" — the earth that the artwork allowed to be earthy has been hollowed out by everything being made useful for everyone. No traditional art form can fill this void of Nothingness, and no existing historical people can escape its event horizon. Nevertheless, Heidegger has in the back of his mind some possible response of *techne* as *poesis* to *techne* as *scientia*.

There is one particularly cryptic, yet very significant passage in "The Origin of the Work of Art" where Heidegger suggest that, although painting, sculpture, architecture, and so on are all modes of poetry in the deepest sense, these existing forms of art may not exhaust the bringing-forth of *poesis*.[106] What we do know, not only from Heidegger's later essays, such as "Building Dwelling Thinking," but above all from the *Der Spiegel* interview examined above, is that whatever this occulted and most original *poesis* is that is capable of transcendentally re-grounding techno-scientific development, it affords a return of the divinities. To my knowledge, what

---

103   Ibid.

104   Heidegger, *Basic Writings*, p. 166.

105   Ibid., p. 205.

106   Ibid., p. 199.

no one has yet considered is how the divinities may return to us through this deepest and darkest potential of art, especially if—as we have seen in the *Der Spiegel* interview—Heidegger insists that this homecoming of the vanquished gods will not come about through an evasion of techno-scientific development, but only by means of an apocalyptic encounter with its essence.

Indeed, in "The Question Concerning Technology," Heidegger himself flirts with the suggestion that scientific *thinkers* could cultivate a self-conscious and artfully affirmative relationship to technology as that which has rightly revealed the groundlessness of our existence. He diabolically[107] considers the possibility that only our most desperate abandonment to the frenzy of ubiquitous technology may be able to awaken us to what we really *are*.[108] Heidegger describes this "turning" with the metaphors of a flashing glance (*Einblick*) of "insight into that which is," insight into an event (*Ereignis*) that flashes-forth (*blitzen*) like a bolt of lightning, which it seems possible to miss. Heidegger asks, "Will we see the lightning-flash of Being in the essence of technology?"[109] The destining of Enframing is not a "blind" or "completely ordained fate."[110] We could choose, at this moment, to accept the responsibility of being the sentinels of the abyssal, and guardians over all unconcealment from out of concealment. Heidegger refers to this as a possibility that may be on offer "someday…in the future."[111] That "future" is now upon us. We are on the threshold of the most promising and perilous scientific discovery, the validation of paranormal phenomena as empirical evidence for the irreducibly irrational element of Nature that Heidegger refers to as "that which cannot be gotten around."[112] The fiery *vajra* of the *Ereignis* is not something graciously granted by Zeus and his jealous companions. It must be stolen from the Olympians and

---

107 In the Greek sense of *diabolein*, "to throw through," as in a generative paradox.

108 Heidegger, *Basic Writings*, p. 337.

109 Heidegger, *The Question Concerning Technology and Other Essays*, p. 49.

110 Ibid., p. 47.

111 Heidegger, *Basic Writings*, p. 338.

112 Heidegger, *The Question Concerning Technology and Other Essays*, p. 177.

brought down to Earth. The divinities to return *in* and *through* the essence of technology are the fraternal Titans: Prometheus and Atlas. They are the prehistoric gods *and the gods of the new age*, drawing together what Nietzsche called the "unhistorical" and "suprahistorical." In fact, my conception of Prometheus and Atlas as the aesthetic ideas or spectral archetypes of technological science are somewhat similar — in form, not content — to the archetypes of Apollo and Dionysus as Nietzsche employs them in his early work, *The Birth of Tragedy*.[113]

As Heidegger recognizes, for the Classical Greeks and for those dwelling in the Medieval age, man is looked upon by Being and apprehends what is present on its own basis as *hypokeimenon* or *subiectum*. Only for the man of *Der Neuzeit* does that which is come into being through his looking for it to be true according to some preconceived adequacy condition — such as *ego cogito (ergo) sum*.[114] In other words, we do not even let things be without already being sure we can adequately grasp them in the quasi-mathematical terms of rational thought. The "paranormal," or super Natural, never has a chance in the face of this normalizing process. Representing is *coagitatio*, a making stand over against an object (*das Gegen-ständige*).[115] The only way beyond modern subjectivity is to creatively reflect on its own incalculable specter of the "gigantic," or Titanic. There is a paradoxical gigantism about modern technology that is different from the "greatness" of any previous age. It has to do with the annihilation of great distances by the airplane, or the bringing-near of "remote worlds in their everydayness" by flicking on the radio. The Titanic is tremendous and yet insidious; it erases itself in annihilating human scales of space and time. It assumes "disguises," so that the gigantic is, for example, also implicated in the exceedingly small scale of modern particle physics,

113 Friedrich Nietzsche, *The Birth of Tragedy* in *Basic Writings of Nietzsche* (New York: The Modern Library, 2000).

114 Heidegger, *The Question Concerning Technology and Other Essays*, p. 149.

115 Maurice Merleau-Ponty, *The Visible and the Invisible* (Evanston: Northwestern University Press), p. 150.

which is only opened up by gargantuan machinery — such as cyclotrons and super-colliders.

In the phenomenon of the Titanic, all merely quantitative exaggerating and excelling transforms into something qualitative — an invisible shadow of a specter cast onto the subjected world. In "The Age of the World Picture," Heidegger claims that, "[b]y means of this shadow the modern world extends itself out into a space withdrawn from representation… This shadow… points to something else, which it is denied to us of today to know."[116] What we have, above all, been denied knowledge of is the "paranormal," or the Supernature that, by definition, has been *occulted*. Only in light of what this shows us about the abyss of the irrational in Nature can we see how agencies beyond the control of merely human machinations spectrally project the framework of all techno-scientific endeavors. These *daemonic* agencies are Prometheus and Atlas. Our relationship to them can be transformed through aesthetic intuition.

In Bergson's view, intuition is developed, above all, by artists who sympathetically break down the barrier that the artificial projection of space has placed between them and their models or subject matter in such a way as to grasp and express the vital force of the latter.[117] We are like the artists of the moments of our own lives; even an artist cannot foresee the final form that his portrait will take.[118] In living processes, just as in the creation of works of art by a true genius, there is the same incommensurability between what comes before and what follows.[119] Addressing the inhabitants of the benighted planet Earth, Bergson writes, "Theirs the responsibility, then, for deciding if they want merely to live, or intend to make just the extra effort required for fulfilling, even on their refractory planet, the essential function of the universe, which is a machine for the making of

---

116   Heidegger, *The Question Concerning Technology and Other Essays*, p. 136.

117   Henri Bergson, *Creative Evolution*, p. 177.

118   Ibid., p. 7.

119   Ibid., p. 29.

gods."[120] While Bergson at times speaks of man being the "term" or "end" of evolution, it quickly becomes clear that he does not mean the human being as it exists at present, but rather *the human potential.*[121]

The matter of fact that is humankind at present is an outcome of evolutionary contingencies that may have taken a different course, and in the course that they have in fact taken, certain other humanoid possibilities of being have been siphoned off along the way, perhaps having been developed elsewhere.[122] For example, a different humanoid evolution may have privileged intuitive knowing over intellectual knowledge.[123] One can imagine a human-like civilization developed on the basis of an exquisite instinct. The conscious existence that is the end of evolution is not that of human beings, but that of the "gods" or "supermen" of which terrestrial humans at their present stage of evolution are only a partial and incomplete realization.[124] Our version of humanity can complete its evolutionary realization of the Superman only by correcting its particular imbalance, so that the psychical power of intuition is retrieved and developed to a level commensurate with our hypertrophied intellect.[125] We have not entirely lost our intuitive abilities; they flash forth at moments when intellect is insufficient in the face of some vital interest that is at stake.[126] Bergson writes, "On our personality, on our liberty, on the place we occupy in the whole of nature, on our origin and perhaps also on our destiny, it throws a light feeble and vacillating, but which none the less pierces the darkness of the night in which the intellect leaves us." Moreover, there is no way to retrieve and then further develop our intuition by means of using our intellect. We may pass from intuition to intellect, but not the other

---

120 Henri Bergson, *Two Sources of Morality and Religion* (Notre Dame: University of Notre Dame Press, 2010), p. 317.

121 Bergson, *Creative Evolution*, pp. 265–266.

122 Ibid.

123 Ibid., p. 267.

124 Ibid., p. 266.

125 Ibid., p. 267.

126 Ibid., p. 267–268.

way around.[127] The philosophical practice by means of which intellect may be reabsorbed in intuition is not a means of merely facilitating speculation; it aims primarily at increasing our power to live.[128] We can *embody* Prometheus and Atlas.

There is a transformation coming in comparison to which all previous revolutions have been but fleeting portents. It will demand not only the radical metamorphosis of the scientific enterprise through which it comes about, but also the restructuring of every facet of human society. In fact, these are not two separate upheavals, or at least they ought not to be, for the coming scientific revolution is at once also a sociopolitical revolution that demands the self-conscious restructuring of our civilization around the spectral forces that have hitherto driven the worldwide development of technological science in an occulted manner — namely Prometheus and Atlas. Only a civilization that at the highest level or, if you prefer, at its foundation, single-mindedly embraces the titanic world-building spirit of scientific exploration and discovery will be able to endure such a catastrophically dangerous realization of the human potential.

---

127   Ibid., p. 268.
128   Ibid., p. 270.

CHAPTER VIII

THE POSTMODERN PROMETHEUS

Prometheus is the titan who was punished by Zeus for gifting *techne* to mortals so they would no longer need to cower before his capricious will. It is not an accident that this god who gifts mortals with the power to keep the fire alive throughout the cold darkness is bound to the Caucasus. With their leisurely coordination of routine activities, primitive tribes in parts of the world that do not experience dramatic seasonal shifts are spared from having to experience time as something that *passes*, something that can be *saved*, or in terms of events that can be *awaited* — they cannot conceive of what it would mean to *be* in a fight against time.[1]

Derived from the Greek words *pro* and *mantháno*, his name means "forethought" in the sense of pre-vision (prophecy, pre-cognition) and making provision, say, for the winter season. Prometheus is "he who knows in advance."[2] The termination *-eus* is characteristic of proper names, and the stem *methe* is related to *máthos* — the root of such words as "mathematics" and "polymath."[3] This clearly connects it to Heidegger's Greek etymology of *mathesis* or *ta mathemata*.[4] It is the always-already-learnable-in-advance essence of modern science, whereby Nature is seized in terms of the *projection* of mathematical spatio-temporality. The technical

---

1   Paul Feyerabend, *Against Method*, p. 189.

2   Carl Kerényi, *Prometheus: Archetypal Image of Human Existence* (Princeton, New Jersey: Princeton University Press, 1991), p. 36.

3   Ibid.

4   Heidegger, *The Question Concerning Technology and Other Essays*, pp. 118–119.

device that radically transforms things and places into objects and spaces allows for the anticipatory determination of beings through axioms.

For Heidegger, what makes modern science fundamentally mathematical is that it strips away from all things and places any essence whatsoever that is unique to them. Ironically, this new and allegedly *factual* science is more abstractly conceptual than its predecessor. Galileo's idea of a body left to itself, which becomes the basis for the Newtonian laws of motion, is just that — an ideal construct. Never is any such absolutely isolated body found in nature, nor can one be created under any practicable experimental conditions.[5] Yet it is only this kind of conceptualization that allows bodies to be reconceived as masses, places as positions, and motion as the action of a force (another mass) on a thing so as to divert it (redefine its position) from the straight line it would *ideally* follow were it *left to itself*: "All determinations of bodies have one basic blueprint, according to which the natural process is nothing but the space-time determination of the motion of points of mass... [a] fundamental design... [that] circumscribes its realm as everywhere uniform."[6] Heidegger explains how this template that is laid over the world is axiomatic in that it anticipates how all things are experienced and always predetermines their kind of being. *Axiomata* such as Newton's laws of motion are statements that express this anticipatory determination of beings.[7]

This also abolishes lived distances. In "The Thing," Heidegger claims that Technology's "frantic abolition of all distances brings no nearness; for nearness does not consist in shortness of distance. What is least remote from us in point of distance, by virtue of its picture on film or its sound on the radio, can remain far from us."[8] He adds, "What is incalculably far from us in point of distance can be near to us. Short distance is not in itself nearness. Nor is great distance remoteness."[9] Heidegger goes on to claim

5   Heidegger, *Basic Writings*, pp. 288–289.

6   Ibid., p. 291.

7   Ibid.

8   Heidegger, *Poetry, Language, Thought*, p. 163.

9   Ibid.

that the "merging of everything into" what he describes as "uniform distancelessness" is more "unearthly" than the "bursting apart" caused by the atomic bomb.[10] Its detonation cannot be more terrifying and unsettling than "the annihilation of the thing" already accomplished.[11] Elsewhere, Heidegger describes this as "...the profundity of the world shock that we [should] experience every hour..." we hear radio or watch *tele*-vision [*fernseher*, or "far-seer"].[12]

The reference to the atomic bomb is very significant in light of the etymological history of *theoria* that Heidegger traces in "Science and Reflection."[13] The word "theory" stems from the Greek verb *theorein*, which is associated with the noun *theoria*; these words involve a conflation of two more basic ones, *thea* and *horao* — which, taken together, mean "to look attentively on the outward appearance wherein what presences becomes visible and, through such sight — seeing — to linger with it." Heidegger claims that the old high German word *wara*, which yields *wahr*, *wahren*, and *Wahrheit* (Truth), goes back to the same Indo-European stem as the Greek *horao, ora, wora*, so that theory — in its original sense — becomes "the *beholding that watches over truth*." Heidegger traces the Roman translation of the Greek *theorein* into *contemplari*, and of *theoria* by *contemplatio. Contemplari* means "to partition something off into a separate sector and enclose it therein." It is derived from *templum*, which was originally the sector carved out of the heavens and the earth "marked out by the path of the sun," and he explains that "within this region diviners make their observations in order to determine the future from the flight, cries, and eating habits of birds." *Templum* is the Latin equivalent of the Greek *temenos*, which means to cut or divide, to partition off, and it is in this sense that *atmeton, a-tomon*, the atom, is the uncuttable.

---

10   Heidegger, *The Question Concerning Technology and Other Essays*, p. 164.

11   Heidegger, *Poetry, Language, Thought*, p. 164.

12   Heidegger, *The Question Concerning Technology and Other Essays*, pp. 157, 48.

13   Ibid., pp. 163–165.

Therefore, the technology of the atomic bomb is the epitome of the mathematical essence of modern science — it shows that, in the realm of *res extensa*, nothing is indivisible and resistant to further analysis. Even the *atom* can now be taken apart. In "The Age of the World Picture," Heidegger writes, "Within the complex of machinery that is necessary to physics in order to carry out the smashing of the atom lies hidden the whole of physics up to now."[14] The splitting of the atom is a symbol for the triumph of the practical over the metaphysical, the existential over the ideal — the titanic will over heavenly fate. It is as if to say *there is no pre-given fundamental building block* (which is what Democritus wanted the atom to be); rather, *what is fundamental in building is the defiant hand of man*. The atomic flash is the thunderbolt of Zeus stolen by Prometheus.

It is Prometheus who allows us to understand the daemonic observers without which anticipation and calculation could not take place in the sciences. Examples of these partial observers are Laplace's "demon," who could potentially calculate the future course of events based on precise knowledge of the totality of a present state of affairs; Maxwell's "demon," capable of distinguishing between slow and rapid molecules in a mixture; and the postulated "observers" of Einstein's theory of relativity, or Heisenberg's observers of indeterminate quantum phenomena.[15] A partial observer "captures what no one is there to see..." such that qualia would not shine without them.[16] They are "points of view [projected] in[to] things themselves,"[17] "forces" of a perceptive and experiential, rather than active, nature.[18] They are "golem" installed in the system of reference.[19] These Frankensteinian "golem" are conjured up by the Prometheus per-

---

14   Ibid., p. 124.

15   Gilles Deleuze, *What is Philosophy?* (New York: Columbia University Press, 1994), p. 129.

16   Ibid.

17   Ibid., p. 132.

18   Ibid., p. 130.

19   Ibid.

sona, forged in the fire stolen from Zeus, and built into Nature for the benefit of mankind.

Prometheus is a dramatic persona, and his status as the aesthetic idea of theorization may be bound up with the birth of tragedy. In *Against Method*, Feyerabend puts forward a realistic interpretation of the archaic style of Greek art and the heroic poetry that it depicts with a view to uncovering its implicit ontology. He suggests that every formal feature of the art could express the tacit assumptions of the cultural cosmology. A number of features of the archaic style, which persist irrespective of the humorous or tragic mood that the artist is trying to convey, suggest to him that the Greeks of this period actually felt themselves to be something like puppets guided by external forces, and that they experienced and treated others accordingly.[20]

The first and most important of these features is the eye that does not look anywhere so that the would-be "person" to whom it belongs does not seem to be adaptively engaged in situations experienced *subjectively*; that is, from out of an inner life.[21] The second of these features is that figural gestures are portrayed in an explanatory manner; the heroes, however agile, do not appear to move by their own will, but are set into stereotyped positions as if from the outside.[22] The third feature is that different beings are not modified in their basic typology with respect to their interactions with one another so that, for example, a dead body looks just as alive as a living body and is simply horizontally oriented into the position of death, or how a kid that is being devoured in the mouth of a lion still looks peaceful because that is how young goats typically are.[23] Fourthly, and perhaps most strikingly, Feyerabend takes the fact that this art does not feature foreshortening and perspective very seriously. He asks why we ought to assume that this is "just on account of lack of technique," as if the

20   Paul Feyerabend, *Against Method*, pp. 175–176.

21   Ibid., p. 175.

22   Ibid.

23   Ibid., p. 180.

capacities of practice were not bound up with those of perception. Even now, only those with a professional training in photography, film, and painting see the world in terms of *aspects* rather than typical *things* — a fact that is related to how badly most people draw.[24]

The ontological interpretation of these characteristics of the late geometric and early archaic style seems to be borne out by an analysis of the formal structure and ideology of the earliest Greek epics, the works attributed to Homer.[25] For example, about 90% of epics such as the *Iliad* consist of formulaic phrases that are repeated in those life situations — combat, seafaring, romance, and so forth — for which they have been appropriately prefabricated; this is a tradition that, in Greece, reaches back to Mycenaean court poetry and is paralleled in the archaic courts of the East.[26] Of course, such a style of composition that intertwines variable elements with constant ones that can be easily memorized is well suited to an oral culture in which even the poets (it would be mistaken to call them "literary figures") are illiterate and must compose without the aid of writing.[27]

This is how we wind up with descriptions of characters that are inappropriate to the situations in which they are given, such as Aphrodite being described as the "sweetly laughing" one in a scene where she is complaining tearfully (*Iliad*, 5.375), or when we hear of the "swift-footed Achilles," even though he is seated in conversation with Priam and quite decidedly has no intention of going anywhere (*Iliad*, 24.559).[28] As in the case of the artwork, the situational transformations are external, and there is no reflection whatsoever of an inner life or a dynamical nature that changes accordingly.[29] There is no underlying substance that gives beings an inner unity that persists through contortions of the body and soul, so

24   Ibid.
25   Ibid., p. 177.
26   Ibid.
27   Ibid., p. 178.
28   Ibid., p. 180.
29   Ibid.

the identity of the being in question is preserved by precluding such meta-morphoses.[30] Parts are not held together by any underlying substance, one that is invisible and can only be inferred from appearances; they are related to one another as aggregates in an assemblage, not as organic constituents of a whole that subsumes them. Likewise, men do not think; they are *visited* by emotions, passions, and striking ideas.[31]

Feyerabend notes that in archaic Greek, there is not even a single word that could be used to describe the living human body as a unified entity over and above a collection of jointed-together limbs. The body qua *demas* is the articulated structure or shape of limbs, whereas the *soma* is a corpse.[32] The puppet whose pieces are linked up together and whose limbs and trunk are set in motion does not have a soul either, since "Homer" only ever refers to emotions as either spatially and bio-physically situated in a character, or as passions that break into the figure from outside and, quite literally, move him. We have no reason to believe that mental events "such as sudden remembering, sudden acts of recognition, sudden increase of vital energy, during battle, during a strenuous escape, sudden fits of anger" were not actually felt in this way, namely as the palpable interventions of gods and demons.[33]

Feyerabend takes such a relationship to the gods to also account for the religious eclecticism of archaic man. If the mind has yet to grasp any underlying or substantial unity, including its own, then in the course of inter-tribal encounters, one's gods can easily be reconciled with other gods who may be imported into one's pantheon together with their myths in a purely additive fashion — with no attempt at a genuine synthesis, and consequently with no concern for the removal of what, to an even proto-rational mind, would appear to be contradictions.[34] In the *Iliad*, there is no

---

30   Ibid., p. 181.

31   Ibid., p. 186.

32   Ibid., p. 181.

33   Ibid., p. 182.

34   Ibid., p. 184.

expression equivalent to "god-fearing."[35] Such a relationship to the divine, namely a *religion of fear*, is established in Greece only together with the tyrannical unification around *and under* Zeus that we find as the classical Olympian pantheon takes shape.[36]

Parallel to this development is another that will ultimately undermine it. For archaic man, knowledge was purely cumulative. The wise man was one whose wealth of experience had afforded him a knowledge of *a great many wonders* or *amazing things* like eclipses, earthquakes, the strange tribal habits of people encountered on coastal explorations, and seemingly paradoxical natural phenomena, such as the rising and falling of the Nile river, with each of these phenomena being "explained" in its own way without the use of any universal principles.[37] Even Thales for the most part contents himself with *enumerating* "interesting observations" in this way, and becomes famous for accurate predictions made, not through a grasp of any enduring principles or the projective application of Laws of Nature, but on the basis of long experience of a great many things.[38] Feyerabend takes Anaximander to have been the first systematic thinker.[39]

The archaic words for knowledge were *sophia, eidenai,* and *suniemi* — which mean, respectively: masterful crafts experience or proficiency in an art; familiarity with something gained on the basis of having seen or inspected it; and hearing something in a way that means at once obeying it.[40] None of these is anything like ontological or epistemological *knowledge* as we understand it, or the kind of ethical knowing that presupposes them. Knowledge was synonymous with *polymathos*, and the supreme knower was the *polymath*: "The wider their experience, the greater the number of adventures, of things seen, heard, read, the greater their

---

35   Ibid.
36   Ibid.
37   Ibid., p. 185.
38   Ibid.
39   Ibid.
40   Ibid., p. 186.

knowledge."[41] Thus, the fundamental turn takes place when a Pre-Socratic thinker such as Heraclitus utters the judgment: "Learning of many things [*polymathy*] does not teach understanding/intelligence."[42] Parmenides also cautions people not to trust "custom born of manifold experience..." as a source of true knowledge.[43]

The kind of statements that Heraclitus makes when he says, for instance, "[Y]ou could not find the limits of the soul though you are traveling every way, so deep is its *logos*" are ones that cannot be additively amalgamated to the archaic worldview and the body of knowledge amassed within its basic structure.[44] The discovery of the "I" that persists through disparate mental states, and is expressed through various behaviors, in other words of a single *subject*, and the discovery of substances behind appearances, inevitably leads to radical departures from the ethical orientation of archaic man as well — such as the discovery that "honor may be lacking despite the presence of all its outer manifestations."[45] Within the context of the archaic worldview, such insights cannot at first be expressed without a terrible abuse of language so that, speaking in riddles and seeming paradoxes as they do, the Pre-Socratic philosophers who are on the way to a new language sound like "raving maniacs" both to those who come before them and long after them, but it remains the case that "[m]adness turns into sanity provided it is sufficiently rich and sufficiently regular to function as the basis of a new world-view."[46]

Feyerabend identifies the long speech of Achilles beginning at 9.308 in the *Iliad* as the first instance of this apparently "irrational" abuse of a language whose limits are being transgressed, in this case by a disillusioning discovery that all of the outer marks of honor may be in evidence without its truly being present — a situation that ought not to be possible in the

41   Ibid., pp. 184, 198.

42   Ibid., p. 184.

43   Ibid., p. 198.

44   Ibid., pp. 203–204.

45   Ibid., p. 203.

46   Ibid., pp. 194, 205–206.

context of the thoroughly custom-bound discourse concerning honor in the archaic period of Greek culture.[47] Achilles expresses his rebellious frustration by making impossible demands and by asking questions that cannot be answered.[48] Decisive events affect the logic that concepts, shapes, percepts, and styles obey, and in this case, Achilles' assertion of a difference between real honor and its social manifestations in terms of a language that makes it impossible to draw such a distinction is provoked by suffering an injustice so great that it unleashes an overwhelming and boundless *rage* that breaks him out of the worldview reinforced by his language.[49] Most significantly, it is a rage directed in part against the gods who have the awarding or recognition of honor in their hands, but who do not seem to Achilles to "give a damn about the aspirations of humans," and this in turn "devalues the social manifestations of honour, makes them secondary."[50] It is not merely incidental that Prometheus prophecies that if the soul of Achilles is allowed to be reborn as a god, this is the god who will overthrow Zeus. Once Zeus discovers this, he makes sure not to father Achilles as he would have would up doing, and the titanic spirit is born as a hero instead.

Thus, in parallel to the rise of the tyrannically unified Olympian pantheon of Zeus from out of eclectic archaic religiosity, a novel conception of knowledge as the discovery of unifying principles or ideals beyond mere appearances arises in tension with the religion of fearfully ignorant obedience. It is, in my view, not an accident that the new art form of tragedy arose at the culmination of the archaic period in Greek culture, as a rebellion against the language of Homeric epic poetry, and that the first known tragedian is Aeschylus — the author of the *Promethea* trilogy. As I noted above in reference to Heidegger, the word "theory" stems from the Greek verb *theorein*, the noun belonging to which is *theoria*, or "theory."

---

47   Ibid., p. 204.

48   Ibid., pp. 204, 206.

49   Ibid., pp. 207–208.

50   Ibid., p. 208.

The root *thea* is also the basis of the Greek word *theatron*, or "place" (*tron*) of "viewing," from which we have derived the word "theater."

Feyerabend cites research which suggests that the perception of perspective, both physical or geometrical perspective *and the psychological perspective that is a precondition to theorization*, was born in the late archaic and early Classical epoch in the context of the structure of Greek theater where, beginning with the productions of Aeschylus, viewers in the first rows would contemplate the drama of human action from unnaturally fixed points of view.[51] First of all, Greek drama is different from the art forms of traditional peoples before the Greeks or those after them that have not been influenced by the Greek legacy in Western civilization, insofar as it provides a unique psychological perspective on the dramas of life from the standpoint of a pure observer. Most dramatic forms in other traditional cultures, almost inevitably tied up with religious practice, involve the active participation of the tribe. Then there is the fact that, whereas in the flux of ordinary life we try to position ourselves adequately with respect to the focus of our attention, in the theater, individuals had to spend long periods of time sitting at extreme angles with respect to the performance — so that, for example, they mostly see the sides or the backs of the performers' heads. These, sometimes extreme, perspectives would shift from one performance to the other, depending on where they were sitting in the Greek amphitheater.

There is, however, something even more striking about the catalysis of perspectival perception *and the perspectival thought that is a precondition to theorization*, which has to do with how and why Aeschylus epitomizes this transformation in Greek art. One of the earliest extant Greek tragedies is Aeschylus' *The Persians*, which takes place in Susa, Iran, and is written sympathetically from the *perspective* of the Persian Emperor, Xerxes, whose naval defeat at Salamis is widely taken to be a punishment for his hubris. Greek tragedies were usually followed by satyr plays, as a sort of comic relief, and the one following performances of *The Persians*

---

51   Ibid., p. 187.

was *Prometheus, the Fire Lighter* — a lost work of Aeschylus concerning the crime by means of which Prometheus sought to empower and liberate humans, a supreme act of hubris from the point of view of Zeus.

The divinity of the Persians was, above all, symbolized by the light of an undying *fire*,[52] and his name and attributes bear a striking affinity to those of Prometheus. To this day, such fires burn in old temples in Iran. Ahura Mazda, the divinity to whom the hymns of Zarathustra are devoted, is quite literally the "Titan of Wisdom."[53] The *Ahuras*, or *Asuras* in the sister-tongue of Persian, Sanskrit, are the "titans," and Zarathustra was the first to ethically invert the status of the titans and the gods, or *daevas*, so that, following him, we have derived the word "devil" from *div* (the Middle Persian form of the Avestan and Sanskrit word *daeva*). Furthermore, Ahura Mazda — or, more faithfully to the hymns of Zarathustra, Mazdai Ahura — is described as the artisan of life and his chief attribute is "the progressive mentality" (*spenta maynu* or, in Middle Persian *spand manesh*),[54] which is an almost literal equivalent of the Greek *pro-mantháno* — "forethought" or "forward-thinking" — from which Prometheus gets his name. Mazdai Ahura, or "the Wise One among the Titans" to whom Zarathustra addresses most of his hymns, is the supreme titan that stands opposed to the gods whom the Persian sage typically epitomizes as promulgators of "the Lie" (*Dorough*).[55] Those who follow the gods are referred to as "the liars" (*droughvand*), foremost among them being the "mumbling priests" (*karapan*) and plundering princes.[56] The chief characteristic of the Lie and its followers is *angra maynu* or, in Middle Persian, *Ahriman* — "the constricted (or constrained) mentality."[57]

---

52   Piloo Nanavutty, *The Gathas of Zarathustra: Hymns in Praise of Wisdom* (Ahmedabad: Mapin Publishing, 1999), pp. 38–40.

53   Ali A. Jafarey, *The Gathas, Our Guide* (Cypress, California: Ushta Publications, 1989), p. 88.

54   Ibid., p. 89.

55   Ibid., p. 85.

56   Ibid., pp. 85, 87.

57   Ibid., pp. 69–70.

As Feyerabend notes, and as many others have observed, the archaic Greeks were in the habit of religious syncretism. Since the religions of the foreign people with whom they had the most contact were also polytheistic, and in many cases featured iterations of similar archetypes as those manifest in the Greek pantheon, they would analogize their own gods to those in the pantheon of the Egyptians or Phoenicians. This is the same practice that the Romans later followed with respect to the Greek pantheon, so that Aphrodite became Venus, Poseidon was recognized to be Neptune, and so forth.

In the Persians, the Greeks were faced not only with the first overwhelmingly superior world-conquering military force that they ever encountered, but also with a religious worldview that was radically unlike their own and those of other polytheistic peoples around them. On behalf of the "Titan of Wisdom," Zarathustra taught that all the gods are false, and despite an initial policy of extreme tolerance under the cosmopolitan Cyrus and Darius, Xerxes — who is the protagonist of Aeschylus' *The Persians* — pursued a policy of the destruction of temples dedicated to the deceptive and tyrannical gods who would keep mankind in ignorant slavery. This is why he burned the original Acropolis to the ground. What is most significant in this respect is that the leading lights among the Greeks did not simply react against this titanic crusade in the name of the Wisdom Lord, but many of them actually began to profoundly reconsider their own culture in light of it, and some even praised the Persians for their superior ways and identified with them. This is why *The Persians* is written from the perspective of Xerxes, and why its author, who penned the *Prometheus* trilogy in honor of the Wisdom Lord, chose to complement it with the satyr play *Prometheus, the Fire Lighter*.

The Hungarian mythologist Carl Kerényi has written a penetrating study of Prometheus as an "archetypal image of human existence."[58] As we shall see, the "human" here refers not to any extant or fixed nature of Man, but to the *human potential* — to the fact that Humanity is uniquely per-

---

58   Kerényi, *Prometheus: Archetypal Image of Human Existence*.

fectible and self-transcending. Kerényi proposes to interpret Greek myth in such a way that it excavates the foundation of the Greek world, which remains the foundation of our own existence. In his view, many scholars before him have taken an overly literary view of myth. If Greek myths were literary, they would deal with more purely human themes. They are, rather, existentially foundational.[59]

Among the Greeks, for whom there was no god so inflated in conception as to be the "Creator of the World," the act of world-founding was the prerogative of poets who ventured to compose *theogonies* or genealogical accounts of the genesis of gods.[60] The Greeks did not enjoy a literary type of artistic freedom concerning the subject matter of mythology; they were bound by unwritten laws with regard to the elaboration of this sacred material.[61] The view that Classical scholarship takes of myth has been distorted by its origins in the study of literature.[62]

The mythos of a people is a primeval reality on which they unconsciously pattern their social organization, and which they embody in their ritual and moral actions.[63] This implicate order is structured in terms of *archetypal* images, whose iterations in the phenomena of the mundane world are *ectypal*.[64] Although he is careful to assert his autonomy from both Jungians and existentialists, Kerényi is basically interested in a kind of existential phenomenology of these mythic archetypes and their ectypal expressions.[65]

Among these mythic archetypes interpreted existentially, that of Prometheus is unique insofar as it is the archetype of human existence as such. The fact that Prometheus is *both* the prototype of Man *and* the original Rebel against God who becomes Lord of the Earth says some-

---

59   Ibid., pp. xi–xii.
60   Ibid., p. 33.
61   Ibid., p. xxi.
62   Ibid., p. xvi.
63   Ibid., p. xviii.
64   Ibid., pp. xviii–xix.
65   Ibid., pp. xix–xx.

thing profound about the Greek conception of human existence.[66] It is in Prometheus above all that we see why Nietzsche is not a revisionist, and how the earliest poetic thinkers among the Greeks did indeed herald his existentialist view of life.[67] Yet Johann Wolfgang von Goethe preceded Nietzsche in the rediscovery of this proto-existential view of human life. At that point in his development as an artist and scientific thinker when he felt as lonely as a god among men, condemned to an abyss of solitude wherein he was left to establish the foundation for his own existence, Goethe rediscovered the archetype of Prometheus: "I liked in thought to base my whole existence upon it. The conception soon assumed a distinct form, the old mythological image of Prometheus... who, apart from the gods, peopled a world from his own workshop."[68] One has to be so alone that one needs to create a world in order to have someone to talk to, in order to maintain the will to live. As Kerényi points out, Goethe's Prometheus not only anticipates Nietzsche's existentialist view of life — it exceeds it.[69] Nietzsche's latent biologistic materialism prevents him from taking the divinities against which Prometheus rebels seriously enough to understand the gravity of that rebellion, or to fathom the supernatural character of the self-creation of a world from out of the abyss. The Faustian Goethe is still enough of an occultist to do so.

In the sixth *Nemean Ode*, Pindar expresses the predominant Classical Greek view of an eternal and absolute separation between gods and men:

> There is one
> race of men, one race of gods; both have breath
> of life from a single mother. But sundered power
> holds us divided, so that one side is nothing, while on the
> other the brazen sky is established
> a sure citadel forever.[70]

66 Ibid., p. 17.
67 Ibid.
68 Ibid., p. 13.
69 Ibid., p. 17.
70 Ibid., p. 22.

Who then are the Titans, if they are neither gods nor men? Unfortunately, though unsurprisingly given its subject matter, the epic *Titanomachia* about the War of the Titans against the host of the Heavenly Father did not survive the holocaust that Classical literature suffered at the hands of Judeo-Christianity.[71] Hesiod tells us that they are *próteroi theoí,* or "the earlier gods," and he bestows them with the epithet *chthónioi,* or "subterranean," presumably on account of their being condemned to the abyssal depths of Tartaros that lie underground, beneath the Earth.[72] The Titans are the sons of Heaven who become subterranean as a consequence of the punishment they suffer for waging war against Zeus and his Olympians.[73]

It is, however, Zeus who plays the role of the usurper here. As Kerényi sees it, the Titans are *próteroi theoí* in the sense of "those who were gods even earlier" than the Olympians led by Zeus, but not in a sequential manner that would allow for another order of divinities to have preceded them as well.[74] Titans are those who always already were and are the divinities — the primordial ones, fathered only by *Chronos,* or Time. Still, they lie in the terrifying darkness of the underworld (*érebos*), under the *ground* of Being, waiting to violently (*atasthalíe*) break forth with that hubris (*hybristes*) and exuberant vitality (*enorée hypéroplos*) on account of which the fearful and jealous Olympian usurpers bound them.[75] They are earlier than human Being, and earlier than the gods that have enslaved Man. Since Man is actually a creature of the Titans, wrought by Prometheus in his own image, the defeat that the Titans suffered at the hands of the Olympians, who go on to mockingly humiliate their creation, provokes unlimited and violent insolence (*hybristes* and *atasthalíe*).

Who among them could be more indignant than Prometheus himself, without whose unparalleled cunning Zeus could not have out-schemed and overthrown the Titans, only to see his creation, and then he him-

---

71   Ibid., p. 24.

72   Ibid., p. 25.

73   Ibid., p. 26.

74   Ibid.

75   Ibid., p. 27.

self, humiliated by Zeus? In the figure of Prometheus, we see a Greek intimation of the truth that Man was destined, by the genuine Creator or Artisan in whose image he was fashioned, to be nothing less than the immortal gods. We were supposed to be a race of new gods. Instead, some young and jealous upstart among the gods decided that we ought to be a slave race kept in subservience to the elements, to disease, and mortal frailty — above all, that we ought to be kept in the darkness of ignorance.

Listen to what Hesiod tells us in his *Works and Days*: "For the gods keep hidden from men the means of life. Else you would easily do work enough in a day to supply you for a full year even without working; soon would you put away your rudder over the smoke, and the fields worked by ox and sturdy mule would run to waste. But Zeus in the anger of his heart hid it…"[76] Prometheus would not have such treachery from the tyrant who beguiled him with promises of a new world only to misuse his cunning.[77] So, in defiance of Zeus, he gifts Man with the fiery key to the light of knowledge of all the arts and crafts (*techne*). For this, Zeus makes provision to punish him in such a way as to afford him something as close to mortal agony as possible for an immortal: although he cannot die of the wounds inflicted on him by the Eagle that feasts on his liver while he is chained to the monolithic pillar of rock with a shaft driven through him, the liver is made to grow back every day so that it can be devoured anew.[78] Why the liver? The Greeks and other ancient peoples in the time that the archaic mythos of Prometheus arose used this organ in *hepatoscopy*, a practice akin to the tea leaf reading of more contemporary seers. Soothsayers would foretell the future by reading the picture of the night's sky in the dark liver.[79] This relates to the Titan's defining foresight. The liver was also regarded as the seat of the passions.[80]

---

76   Ibid., p. 48.
77   Ibid., p. 93.
78   Ibid., p. 38.
79   Ibid., p. 39.
80   Ibid.

Who, then, are the Titans? They are an archetypal projection of all that Man was meant to be, an image of a more-than-human existence that would not be lived in cowering subservience to alien gods — deities that represent Man's alienation from his own divine heritage and destiny. According to one of the numerous Greek genealogies, Prometheus is the son of a union between Uranos, or "Heaven," and Gaia, or "Mother Earth."[81] That we were created in his image means that we have within us a pathway to the godly abode. The Titans *qua* "fallen gods" are a mythic projection of the fallenness of our existence. This is not a fallen state of "original sin"; it is an "eternal injury" suffered unjustly.[82] It should provoke a rebellion, or rekindle one, aimed at our becoming what we really are. From the perspective of the Heavenly Father, *or of those who, on Earth and Olympus, submit themselves to His capricious will,* such an insurrection appears to be driven by "mad presumption and exceeding pride."[83] The "bottomless pit" to which the Titans are condemned[84] is the abyssal underground of an existence whose ground we must lay down or bear up for ourselves. Kerényi writes, "The darkness of Prometheus signifies precisely the deficiency of one who needs fire in order to achieve a more perfect form of being. In obtaining this higher form of being for man, Prometheus shows himself to be man's double, an eternal image of man's basically imperfect form of being."[85]

The greatest creation of Prometheus qua arch-Craftsman is the genesis of Man. The archaic Greek tradition is clear — it is Prometheus, not Zeus, who created thinking beings on the Earth. The first men seem to have been of a different constitution than human beings at present. They were made in the image of Prometheus, in other words they were titanic or gigantic. As we shall see more clearly in the next chapter, Plato, among other Greeks, sometimes refers to these beings as *daemons*, and the *heros* of old

---

81   Ibid., pp. 34–35.
82   Ibid., p. 31.
83   Ibid., p. 37.
84   Ibid., p. 34.
85   Ibid., p. 78.

are hybrids born of *eros* between them and hominid women. Empedocles also equates the Titans with the *daemons* when he says that these divine spirits guilty of bloodying the Earth in primeval times are damned to wander the Earth for thrice ten thousand years—the standard term of punishment for the Titans.[86] Certain early Greek writers, for example the sixth century BC Orphic theologian Onomakritos, identified the Titans with the *Kabeiroi*.[87]

These were the "first men," the original inhabitants of the Earth before the present race of mortals, beings who lived in a great city on a remote island and were taken to be responsible for committing a primordial crime on account of which they were cast into subterranean imprisonment.[88] They were associated with the ocean, were referred to as *Karkinoi* or "Crab-like" people to the extent of sometimes being depicted with crab pincers for hands—suggesting the tongs used by blacksmiths.[89] The word *Titan* is of uncertain origin and meaning. The Greeks made up diverse etymologies for it. Two related words are *títax* and *titéne*, or "king" and "queen."[90] This would make sense if the first rulers of the Earth were the daemonic giants born of the hybridizing of gods and mortals. Mysterious secrecy surrounds these beings in the Greek tradition. Pausanias says that it was not permitted to reveal who the Kabeiroi really were.[91] Many of the names of the Titans are also listed as names of the Kabeiroi.

The most important of all of these is Prometheus, who was the most revered among the Kabeiroi as a divinity older than Hephaistos, and fulfilling what later became his divine function; he practiced the art of the blacksmith and was depicted with a hammer.[92] Initiates of sanctuaries devoted to the Kabeiroi, where there were smelting furnaces, wore iron rings

86   Ibid., p. 76.

87   Ibid., p. 57.

88   Ibid., pp. 57, 61, 81.

89   Ibid., p. 82.

90   Ibid., p. 28.

91   Ibid., p. 61.

92   Ibid., pp. 58–59.

in imitation of Prometheus.[93] An ancient Nordic law states that a man is not responsible for what is said in a forge, amidst the virile rhythm of the blacksmith's work.[94] Like Hephaistos in later myths, the early myths of the Kabeiroi have Prometheus as a lover pursuing Athena.[95] In fact, according to these myths, it is Prometheus who split the head of Zeus — with his axe or hammer — so that Athena could be delivered from this proverbial womb.[96] In Greek mythology, the mind of Zeus is described as *pykinos*, or "close-knit," meaning that it cannot be breached and nothing escapes it.[97] This mesh is often equated with the knots of Fate, of which only Zeus has omniscient awareness in a mind that is the mirror of an already completed Being. Thus it is highly significant that Prometheus alone — the god of all crafts that complete uncompleted Being — does manage to break into this mind, so that a goddess of Wisdom *and of War* could be born from out of it. A Roman sarcophagus relief in Montfaucon depicts Prometheus, with a basket of clay beside him, forming Man — who receives his soul, in the image of a butterfly, from Minerva.[98] The butterfly is a symbol of metamorphosis or transfiguration.

One aspect of the Prometheus tragedies of Aeschylus that is unique in Greek mythology is that it not only shows how the order of Zeus arises (in other words, that it has a conditioned genesis), it also suggests that, just as the age of Titans was surpassed by that of the Olympians, the latter could in the future be surpassed by the founding of a new age and a new world order that begins with the overthrow of the Heavenly Father.[99] While Aeschylus' lost third tragedy, *Prometheus Lyomenos*, is said to have eliminated this threat through the reconciliation of Prometheus with Zeus, the very idea that such a possibility could have played itself out has

---

93 Ibid., p. 73.

94 Ibid., p. 74.

95 Ibid., p. 59.

96 Ibid.

97 Ibid., p. 47.

98 Ibid., p. 17.

99 Ibid., p. 83.

been elaborated by others who developed the Prometheus mythos in a more radical direction than the conservative Aeschylus. Still, the kernel is already there in Aeschylus—the germ of the infectious idea that the order of Zeus, while appearing to be that established by an omnipotent being with an omniscient mind, is something so intolerably inhumane and ignoble that any noble soul with a conscience ought to rebel against it—no matter the consequences.[100]

Prometheus is the first and greatest Rebel. The rallying cry, "Give me liberty, or give me death!" really belongs to him, although in the mouth of this immortal it is, "Give me liberty, or something even worse than death!" Prometheus knows that he will be punished terribly for his rebellion, but he goes ahead with it anyway. He thereby sets the standard for an authentic existence chosen in the face—not of death—but of a living hell from which death would be a welcome release.[101] What a contrast to the happy Olympians who are content to be the pawns of Zeus!

Prometheus Bound begins with *Kratos*, or "Force" personified, dragging Prometheus off to be bound, with *Bia*, or "Violence," silently bearing witness. Kratos describes the new order of the world under Zeus and his Olympians thusly: "No one is free but Zeus."[102] We are confronted with the reign of an absolute tyrant who is the only one above the unrelenting Law, the *Nomos*, through which he enslaves others. The oppression is appalling. Through the mouth of Hephaistos, Aeschylus describes the torment of Prometheus as *théama dysthéaton*—a "sight that can scarcely be borne" and that "eyes should not look upon."[103] Yet Prometheus wants it to be seen. Instead of calling upon God to bear witness to this injustice, since God is here the very source of injustice, Prometheus calls upon the elements of Nature to testify to his ordeal:

---

100 Ibid., p. 88.
101 Ibid., pp. 99, 116.
102 Ibid., p. 84.
103 Ibid., p. 85.

O air of heaven and swift-winged winds,
O running river waters,
O never-numbered laughter of sea waves,
Earth, mother of all, Eye of the sun, all-seeing,
on you I call.
Behold what I, a god, endure from gods.
See… I summon you as witness.[104]

In the last scene, when he is struck down by Zeus' thunderbolt and plunges into Tartaros, Prometheus cries out, "Oh holy Mother Earth, O air and sun, / behold me. I am *wronged*."[105] Prometheus seems to particularly bemoan the humiliating disgrace of his punishment; he repeatedly describes it as shameful:

See in what shameful tortures I must struggle
through countless years of time.

This shame, these bonds, are put upon me
by the new ruler of the gods.[106]

He has been dishonored — because he honored lowly mortals, against the wishes of Zeus.

As Aeschylus relates through the mouthpiece of Hephaistos at the outset of *Prometheus Bound*, the chief crime of Prometheus is that he "gave to mortals honor in excess of justice."[107] Later Prometheus puts this into his own words:

Look at me then, in chains, a god who failed,
the enemy of Zeus, whom all gods hate,
all that go in and out of Zeus' hall.
The reason is that I loved men too well.[108]

---

104 Ibid., p. 86.
105 Ibid., p. 87.
106 Ibid., p. 86.
107 Ibid., p. 87.
108 Ibid.

The *péra díkes*, or "in excess of justice," that is referred to in the first of these two quotes is a key to the Titanic mentality in general. Of course, the so-called "justice" referred to here is simply the *nomos* of Zeus. The crime of Prometheus is that he put a very insidious idea in the human mind, one that over time would make at least some people simply incapable of submission to arbitrary force, the idea that Justice is not the will of the strongest — even if the strongest in question is God Himself.[109] Prometheus conceived an ideal order of Justice; his rebellion is based on the creative imagination of a world other than the real one, as symbolized by his prophetic vision of a future wherein Zeus is overthrown. His devious foreknowledge of things to come exceeds even that of Zeus.[110] He harbors this secret as the source of his only hope.[111] So far as we can tell, the Greek conception of *utopia* begins in the archaic Prometheus mythos. This is fitting since the titan responsible for *techne* would then be the godfather of science fiction.

Utopia can only be born out of a moment of total disenchantment and contempt for petty comforts that help one to live in an altogether unacceptable world: "To speak is pain, but silence too is pain, / and everywhere is wretchedness."[112] This moment of insight into the all-pervasive suffering of life is akin to the insight of the Buddha — not only when he arrives at the conclusion that "life *is* suffering," but also when, in somewhat more Promethean terms, his famous Fire Sermon compares the entire experience of the self that is situated in the phenomenal world to a raging inferno:

> Monks, all is burning. And what, monks, is the all that is burning? The eye is burning, forms are burning, eye-consciousness is burning, eye-contact is burning, and whatever feeling arises with eye-contact as condition — whether pleasant or painful or neither-painful-nor-pleasant — that too is burning. Burning with what? Burning with the fire of lust, with the fire of hatred, with the fire of

---

109 Ibid., p. 89.

110 Ibid., pp. 91–92.

111 Ibid., pp. 96–97.

112 Ibid., p. 90.

delusion; burning with birth, aging, and death; with sorrow, lamentation, pain, dejection, and despair, I say.[113]

A more concise and poetic rendition of this view is among the most strik-ing sayings of the Buddha compiled into the *Dhammapada*: "How can there be laughter, how can there be pleasure, when the whole world is burning?"[114] It is such a view that leads Siddhartha to condemn playing music, singing, and dancing as vain pleasures unbecoming for a seeker.[115] The response of the creative spirit of Prometheus is almost diametri-cally opposite to the stoicism of Siddhartha: not to transcend suffering by "snuffing out" the passions — for *nirvana* literally means to "snuff" or "blow out" — but to fight fire with fire by kindling an immeasurably pas-sionate revolt against "reality." *Man deserves better than this...* that incen-diary forethought is the gift of the light-bearer, the first artist.

The radical utopian aspect of Prometheus, which aspires to remake the Earth as a paradise, comes to the fore in the drama *Prometheus Unbound* by Percy Bysshe Shelley. There are two key innovations in Percy Shelley's rendition of the Prometheus mythos, both of which I would like to affirm and adopt. The first is that Shelley radicalizes the revolutionary potential of the rebellion of Prometheus against the heavenly tyranny of Zeus. As in the case of Aeschylus and Goethe, Prometheus is betrayed by Zeus after helping him to become the Sovereign, only to show his true colors as a far more tyrannous ruler than Chronos or Saturn. Shelley also follows Aeschylus and Goethe in having Prometheus harbor a precognitive fore-sight of the demise of Jupiter at the hands of a son more powerful than him. Mercury (Hermes) keeps trying to coerce Prometheus to confess the secret, but in Shelley's version, Prometheus never capitulates. In the traditional mythos, Prometheus finally reveals to Jove that his marriage to Thetis will yield the heir that usurps his throne, so that Thetis can be

113   Bhikkhu Bodhi, *In the Buddha's Words: An Anthology of Discourses from the Pali Canon* (Boston: Wisdom Publications, 2005), p. 346.

114   Juan Mascaró [Translator], *The Dhammapada* (New York: Penguin Books, 1973), p. 56.

115   Bodhi, *In the Buddha's Words*, pp. 175, 245.

married to Peleus instead — thus the soul that would have unseated the heavenly tyrant if it were born as a god is in fact born as the hero Achilles. Shelley has Prometheus endure in his torture until this marriage that spells Jove's doom comes to pass, at which point the heavenly tyrant who lives off the blood sacrifices of mankind is overthrown, and humanity is liberated in a new world order more benevolent than that of both Jupiter and Saturn before him.

The moral here is uncompromisingly progressive, and at least tacitly anti-Christian. In his drama, Shelley often uses the Latin equivalents of the Greek names of divinities: Saturn instead of Chronos, Jupiter or Jove instead of Zeus, and Mercury instead of Hermes. The one significant case where he does not do so is that of Prometheus himself, because the Latin equivalent of Prometheus would be Lucifer: the light-bearer. Shelley's Prometheus bears all the marks of Lucifer. He rebels against Jove, or Jehovah, as against a heavenly tyrant who has compelled not only subservient worship from mankind, but also what Prometheus takes to be the despicably servile obedience of the other gods or angels in Heaven. Like the archetypal Serpent at the Tree of Knowledge, by teaching mortals all the arts and sciences, he defies the other gods and their chief who want to keep human beings ignorant. Among these crafts, Shelley explicitly names metallurgy, mining, rhetoric, science, poetry, sculpture, medicine, astronomy, and navigation of the oceans.[116] Shelley refers to the will and power to remake the world by means of such crafts as "Promethean":

> And our singing shall build
> In the void's loose field
> A world for the Spirit of Wisdom to wield;
> We will take our plan
> From the new world of man,
> And our work shall be called the Promethean.[117]

---

116   Percy Bysshe Shelley, *Prometheus Unbound* (Black Box Press, 2007), p. 52.

117   Ibid., p. 78.

At its core lies the basically anti-Christian idea that Man ought to become the fulfillment of his own highest hopes, rather than await their fulfillment by a divine power that manipulates our hopes and fears to keep us submissive. There is an implication that during the reign of Saturn, we lived in blissful ignorance, and then during the reign of Jupiter under enforced ignorance. The will of this *unbound* Prometheus is neither to bargain his way towards helping the heavenly tyrant to maintain the enforced ignorance, nor to overthrow him so that we can return to blissful ignorance, but to push Man forwards towards enlightenment and liberation through the perfection of the Wisdom and Knowledge that he has, already, irrevocably attained.[118]

Percy Shelley's adaptation of the Prometheus mythos also heralds the turn it takes towards science fiction in Mary's novel. Although his drama stays within broad conventions of the romantic literature of his epoch, it is informed by a modern scientific grasp of the cosmos. The dimensions of the tragedy have been dramatically expanded in space and time. Shelley talks about cosmic kingdoms ruled over by star gods in the vastness of space beyond the constellations visible to us. He also sheds light on abyssal depths of the ocean, which conceal the ruins of an antediluvian civilization whose population "was mortal but not human."[119] Two luminous craft emerge from out of a forest and plunge into the sea to reveal ruins of this civilization — its architecture and engineering, its conveyances, and monuments — which lie alongside the remains of gigantic prehistoric beasts, some winged and others sea-creatures with shining scales.[120]

Shelley describes the "interlunar" aerial "chariots" that enter the ocean in terms that cross the border from the literary conventions of fairy lore to those characteristic of the airships and flying saucers of science fiction. Moreover, Shelley's heading to Scene 3.2 leaves no doubt that the ruined

---

118   Ibid., p. 94.
119   Ibid., p. 83.
120   Ibid., pp. 80–83.

civilization strewn in the abyssal depths of the ocean is Atlantis.[121] At one point, he describes Zeus' destruction of the Atlanteans by means of earthquakes and a worldwide deluge. In light of what we learned from Kerényi concerning the meaning of the *titanic* and Prometheus as the father of the "first men," the "mortal but not human" race that perished in this flood together with their considerable knowledge might be seen as the first children of Prometheus, and Zeus' destruction of them as a punishment of the rebel who tried to craft, in the form of this antediluvian civilization, a hearth for the heavenly light on Earth. Shelley raises Prometheus' mother, Earth, to unprecedented heights in this drama.[122] The aim of the Promethean revolt is to liberate the Earth from heavenly oppression by turning it into a self-sufficient paradise very different from Eden with its ignorant bliss, an earthly utopia wrought by the human race through the Promethean gift of crafts employing wisdom and knowledge — including, very significantly, "arts, though unimagined, yet to be."[123] With such *techne* we will "build a new earth and sea, And a heaven where yet heaven could never be."[124]

The analogizing of Prometheus to Lucifer that we see to some extent in Percy Shelley's work is further elaborated in his wife Mary Shelley's novel *Frankenstein, or the Modern Prometheus*. The metaphor that the creature most often uses to draw an analogy between his extraordinary condition and that of some other being is the metaphor of Lucifer in John Milton's *Paradise Lost*. Here is the first instance in which Frankenstein's monster compares himself to the fallen angel: "Remember, that I am thy creature; I ought to be thy Adam, but I am rather the fallen angel, whom thou drivest from joy for no misdeed."[125] These analogies are explained by the fact that the creature claims to have early on come into possession of

121 Ibid., p. 61.

122 Ibid., pp. 12–18.

123 Ibid., p. 64.

124 Ibid., p. 79.

125 Mary Shelley, *Frankenstein, or The Modern Prometheus* (New York: Penguin Books, 2003), p. 103.

several books on the basis of which he improved his language skills, and that among these was *Paradise Lost*.[126] In fact, he tells us that it was the one book among the three that "excited different and far deeper emotions."[127] He narrates how he was struck by the similarity between his own state of affairs and that depicted in this great work.[128]

The creature tells us that these feelings were further confirmed by having discovered Doctor Frankenstein's experimental journal in the pocket of the coat that he ran off with from the laboratory. This journal, which casually intermingled "accounts of domestic occurrences" with a detailed report of the process of the creature's genesis, drives home that he is the infernal creation of a demiurge.[129] Like Satan, he vows "eternal hatred and vengeance" in recompense for the cruelty of his creator, but he sees himself as even more accursed than Satan, since the rebel angel at least "had his companions, fellow-devils, to admire and encourage him."[130] The Satanic or Titanic righteous indignation turned to insatiable wrath continually resurfaces as the driving force of the creature's misdeeds.[131] He wants his Creator to fashion an Eve to be his companion and assuage the burning passion that drives him through the icy mountains.[132] After he watches Frankenstein destroy this future mate, the creature says, "Evil thenceforth become my good... the fallen angel becomes a malignant devil. Yet even that enemy of God and man had friends and associates in his desolation; I am alone."[133] The monster's intellect matches his superhuman strength and agility; he is so brilliantly crafty that sometimes it seems "as if [he is] possessed of magic powers."[134] Frankenstein's cautionary descriptions of

126   Ibid., p. 130.
127   Ibid., p. 132.
128   Ibid.
129   Ibid., pp. 132–133.
130   Ibid., p. 133.
131   Ibid., p. 148.
132   Ibid., pp. 134, 145–146.
133   Ibid., pp. 222–223.
134   Ibid., p. 195.

the creature's dialectical eloquence call to mind a comparison to silver-tongued Lucifer.[135] Indeed, Frankenstein compares himself to Lucifer as well:

> When younger... I believed myself destined for some great enterprise... When I reflected on the work I had completed, no less a one than the creation of a sensitive and rational animal, I could not rank myself with the herd of common projectors. But this thought, which supported me in the commencement of my career, now serves only to plunge me lower in the dust. All my speculations and hopes are as nothing; and, like the archangel who aspired to omnipotence, I am chained in an eternal hell... a high destiny seemed to bear me on, until I fell, never, never again to rise.[136]

The novel explores the terribly complex moral dilemma of creating "a thinking and reasoning animal."[137] Shelley reaches back to the most archaic Greek strata of the Prometheus mythos, wherein the Titan is the artisan who fathered a race of *daemons* or giants. Frankenstein decides that, in his "creation of a human being," he should work on a gigantic scale, so that the minuteness of the organic mechanisms that he has to manipulate should not pose so great a difficulty as they would with a body of ordinary size; the creature is to be "about eight feet in height, and proportionately large."[138] This gigantic stature is first illumined by a flash of lightning amidst a tempest in the Swiss alps.[139] The creature is consistently referred to as a "daemon" and described as "demoniacal."[140] This being is just as often explicitly contrasted with the "human" and "humanity."[141] The creature moves with an elusive agility comparable to bolts of lightning; shooting at him is like firing on a ghost; consequently, others may take the thing to be a conjured hallucination — as the townspeople do when their

---

135   Ibid., p. 212.
136   Ibid., p. 214.
137   Ibid., p. 170.
138   Ibid., p. 54.
139   Ibid., p. 77.
140   Ibid., pp. 27, 59, 77, 167, 171, 202.
141   Ibid., pp. 77–78.

massive manhunt comes to naught.[142] He moves with "more than mortal speed" so that his "ghastly and distorted shape" is barely discernable in the moonlight.[143] When someone does catch sight of the creature, his countenance is so "unearthly" that it is "scarring" to the beholder.[144] The peasants that encounter him in "the wilds of Tartary and Russia" react to him as to a "horrid apparition" rather than to a purely physical being.[145]

At times, Frankenstein views this monster as a projection of something inhuman within his own psyche: "I considered the being whom I had cast among mankind, and endowed with the will and power to effect purposes of horror, such as the deed which he had now done, nearly in the light of my own vampire, my own spirit let loose from the grave, and forced to destroy all that was dear to me."[146] We also see this after his destruction of the second creature, intended to be the mate of the first, when Frankenstein feels as if he no longer belongs to a race of human beings like himself, and wanders the secluded island "like a restless specter, separated from all it loved, and miserable in the separation."[147] He seems to have been under a daemonic inspiration during the creation of the titanic being, perhaps the possession of the daemonic soul seeking for him to grant it embodiment: "I remembered, shuddering, the mad enthusiasm that hurried me on to the creation of my hideous enemy, and I called to mind the night in which he first lived."[148]

At one point Frankenstein even speaks of the creature as "the monstrous Image" whose existence he has endured.[149] While at times he depicts the creature — and himself — in these spectrally superhuman terms, at others he portrays it as an animal: "Besides, the strange nature of the

---

142 Ibid., p. 200.
143 Ibid., p. 206.
144 Ibid., p. 221.
145 Ibid., p. 207.
146 Ibid., p. 78.
147 Ibid., p. 174.
148 Ibid., p. 188.
149 Ibid., p. 187.

animal would elude all pursuit... Who could arrest a creature capable of scaling the overhanging sides of Mont Salêve?"[150] Still, it is a super-human animal who "bounded over the crevices in the ice" with "super-human speed," and whose "stature... seemed to exceed that of a man."[151] Sometimes it seems that the stature of the creature is a metaphor for the gigantism of the creator's project. Frankenstein is not averse to undertakings of titanic scale, "[n]or could I consider the magnitude and complexity of my plan as any argument of its impracticability."[152]

Like Prometheus bound or Lucifer looking heavenwards from the pit of Hell, Frankenstein does his work in extreme, even inhuman, solitude. He is haunted by the sense that he has committed some tremendous crime, and he relates this to his reclusiveness — as if he would see his own guilt reflected in the eyes of those who would be his fellow men if he had not opened a chasm between them and himself.[153] Frankenstein establishes his laboratory in a secret cell at the top of the house in which he resides, separated from all of its other apartments by a gallery and a staircase, and therein he becomes insensitive to the passing of the seasons, the ordinary passions, and the companionship of even those he once took to be his closest friends.[154] If it were not for his superhuman singularity of purpose, he would succumb wholly to his increasing disintegration as a human being.[155] The deserted rocky outcrop of an island, amidst rough waters in the northern highlands of Scotland, is an even more reclusive location for his second attempt to craft a superhuman being to be the mate of his first creature.[156]

Frankenstein's solitude is a mirror of that which characterizes the places most fit as a habitation for the daemonic race that he designs. The

---

150   Ibid., p. 79.
151   Ibid., p. 101.
152   Ibid., p. 54.
153   Ibid., pp. 57, 167, 175.
154   Ibid., pp. 55–56.
155   Ibid., p. 57.
156   Ibid., p. 168.

novel features repeated references to South America in connection to the superhuman being created by Frankenstein. In the first of these the good doctor exclaims: "I would have made a pilgrimage to the highest peak of the Andes, could I, when there, have precipitated him to their base."[157] Later on, the creature promises Frankenstein that if he consents to craft a mate for him, "...neither you nor any other human being shall ever see us again: I will go to the vast wilds of South America... I swear to you, by the earth which I inhabit, and by you that made me, that with the companion you bestow I will quit the neighborhood of man, and dwell, as it may chance, in the most savage places."[158] Frankenstein thinks to himself that, "Even if they were to leave Europe, and inhabit the deserts of the new world, yet one of the first results of those sympathies for which the dae-mon thirsted would be children, and a race of devils would be propagated upon the earth, who might make the very existence of the species of man a condition precarious and full of terror."[159] It is in fear of this genesis of an entire race of daemonic beings that the good doctor tears apart his second creature to the horror of the first, whose moonlit face watches Frankenstein through the window of his laboratory.

Shelley seems to suggest a parallel between the unnaturalness of this creative endeavor, of man seeking to craft a being in his own image, and an arch-taboo of almost every human society: incest. Frankenstein refers to Elizabeth as "my more than sister" and as "the beautiful and adored companion of *all* my occupations and *my pleasures*."[160] If we are to take this statement literally, then the two have long been sexually intimate. He says that from the moment he was presented with her, as an adoptive sister or "cousin," in his childhood until her death, she belonged to him alone. Frankenstein's mother joins their hands together on her deathbed, telling them that her highest hope is their future union.[161] Her father asks

---

157   Ibid., p. 95.

158   Ibid., pp. 148–149.

159   Ibid., p. 171.

160   Ibid., p. 37, my emphasis.

161   Ibid., p. 44.

him whether his affection toward her is only that of a brother toward his sister, and whether there is any other woman that he loves; Frankenstein replies that he does not only love her as a sister but also wants her to be his wife.[162] Elizabeth has such a pure love for Victor that she is willing to give him up, as a future husband, if he feels toward her only the affection that a brother feels for his sister and he wants to marry some other woman that he sexually desires.[163] Frankenstein reassures her, this time directly, that she is more than his sister, and that he wants to marry no other. The implicit connection between his creative endeavor and incestuous intercourse also seems to be suggested by this passage: "I had an insurmountable aversion to the idea of engaging myself in my loathsome task in my father's house, while in habits of familiar intercourse with those I loved."[164] Instead of joining Elizabeth in their marriage bed on the first night of their honeymoon, Frankenstein paces about, vigilantly armed against the monster of incest with a pistol and dagger that, together with the look in his eye, helps to fill his new bride with a sense of foreboding.[165]

Frankenstein associates the mountains not only with his own gigantic creature, but with a superhuman race of beings in general: "…the mighty Alps, whose white and shining pyramids and domes towered above all, as belonging to another earth, the habitations of another race of beings."[166] Later recollecting the happy villagers along the Rhine river, Frankenstein remarks, "Oh, surely the spirit that inhabits and guards this place has a soul more in harmony with man than those who pile the glacier, or retire to the inaccessible peaks of the mountains of our own country."[167] The daemonic being makes his home where men can barely survive, so that he may be sheltered from the multitude who would seek out and destroy

---

162   Ibid., p. 156.
163   Ibid., p. 192.
164   Ibid., p. 157.
165   Ibid., pp. 196, 198.
166   Ibid., p. 97.
167   Ibid., p. 161.

him if they openly knew of his superhuman existence.[168] After the death of Frankenstein, the creature resolves to continue his trek to the North Pole where, amidst the iciest clime of the Earth, he will set up a funeral pyre in which to immolate himself so that the "light of that conflagration" consumes all the evidence that would allow anyone to emulate Frankenstein in his "unhallowed" creative arts; the fire will be a beacon that reminds man of the fatality of the Promethean quest.[169]

One aspect of the novel that the subsequent film adaptations have often ignored is the fact that, although the novel is set at the zenith of the Age of Reason, Frankenstein is not your ordinary materialistic scientist. He is an occultist and an alchemist. Frankenstein refuses to share with Walton, or with anyone else for that matter, "the particulars of his creature's formation."[170] Once, when Walton presses him, only to find that "on this point he was impenetrable," Frankenstein chastises him in a particularly revealing manner: "Are you mad, my friend? ...or whither does your senseless curiosity lead you? Would you also create for yourself and the world a demoniacal enemy?"[171] Yet it is clear enough from other clues that Shelley leaves us that the process cannot have been one in conformity with the orthodox mechanistic theories that were becoming predominant at just the historical period when the novel is set.

Frankenstein first describes his tale to Walton as one that is "supernatural," not in the sense of supra-natural, but insofar as it exposes the excessively irrational Supernature that cannot be encompassed or controlled in its becoming — wonders, marvels, prodigies — quite literally, the incomprehensible in Nature:

> Prepare to hear of occurrences which are usually deemed marvelous. Were we among the tamer scenes of nature, I might fear to encounter your unbelief, perhaps your ridicule; but many things will appear possible in these wild and mys-

168 Ibid., p. 103.
169 Ibid., pp. 224–225.
170 Ibid., p. 213.
171 Ibid.

terious regions, which would provoke the laughter of those unacquainted with the ever-varied powers of nature; — nor can I doubt but that my tale conveys in its series internal evidence of the truth of the events of which it is composed.[172]

From early on in his youth, Frankenstein saw the world as "a secret which [he] desired to divine"; he had an insatiable curiosity to discover "the hidden laws of nature" and the pursuit of these discoveries filled him with a sense of "rapture."[173]

This is not the only time that he speaks of scientific discovery in ecstatically religious terms. In another passage of this kind, Frankenstein makes an interesting equivocation between metaphysics and the physical in its highest sense — calling to mind Schelling's view of the "supernatural" as natural, but as the most deeply hidden irrational element of Nature: "It was the secrets of heaven and earth that I desired to learn; and whether it was the outward substance of things, or the inner spirit of nature and the mysterious soul of man that occupied me, still my enquiries were directed to the metaphysical, or in its highest sense, the physical secrets of the world."[174] That by "metaphysical" here he does not mean academic "metaphysics" but the understanding of occult power is made clear within short order, when Frankenstein goes on to volunteer the fact that he spent years procuring and studying the complete works of Cornelius Agrippa, Paracelsus, and Albertus Magnus.[175]

Modern natural philosophy, in other words neo-Cartesian materialism, always left him "discontented and unsatisfied."[176] He specifically attributes this to its failure to understand anything except in terms of efficient causality, which is in effect to under-stand nothing at all. It is formative and final causes that explain the world. By contrast, this is what he says concerning the three great Western alchemists mentioned above:

---

172 Ibid., p. 31.
173 Ibid., p. 38.
174 Ibid., p. 39.
175 Ibid., p. 41.
176 Ibid.

"But here were books, and here were men who had penetrated deeper and knew more... I became their disciple."[177] He acknowledges that some would — albeit erroneously — see this discipleship as an atavism in the rationalistic eighteenth century, a throwback to the occultism of natural philosophy during the Renaissance. His pursuit is one and the same as that of the occult natural philosophers of that epoch, who drew no distinction between science and spirituality, and who were consequently persecuted and martyred by the Catholic Church:

> Under the guidance of my new preceptors, I entered with the greatest diligence into the search of the philosopher's stone and the elixir of life; but the latter soon obtained my undivided attention. Wealth was an inferior object; but what glory would attend the discovery, if I could banish disease from the human frame and render man invulnerable to any but a violent death! Nor were these my only visions. The raising of ghosts or devils was a promise liberally accorded by my favorite authors, the fulfillment of which I most eagerly sought...[178]

Doctor Frankenstein is also a Renaissance man in that he understands that if one is to be a "scientist" rather than a "petty experimentalist," one has to pursue a wide range of interdisciplinary studies.[179] This citizen of the world — who we can well imagine in Ptolemaic Alexandria or Medici Italy — considers it a mere diversion from his work to study Persian, Arabic, and Sanskrit, just to be able to appreciate their marvelous (and then largely untranslated) literatures.[180] Walton's descriptions of the mad scientist leave us with no doubt that the man radiates genius and is not only a nobleman by birth, but a spiritual aristocrat: "Sometimes I have endeavored to discover what quality it is which he possesses, that elevates him so immeasurably above any other person I ever knew. I believe it to be an intuitive discernment; a quick but never-failing power of judg-

---

177 Ibid.
178 Ibid., p. 42.
179 Ibid., p. 50.
180 Ibid., p. 70.

ment; a penetration into the causes of things, unequalled for clearness and precision…"[181]

When young Frankenstein finally begins to formally study natural science at the University of Ingolstadt, the response of one of his eighteenth-century professors to the subject matter of his hitherto self-directed studies is no different than it would be today: "Have you… really spent your time in studying such nonsense?"[182] We must remember that, as Frankenstein tells us in the very first line of his narrative, he was born and raised in Geneva, a progressive center of high culture, in order to appreciate the irony when Professor Krempe goes on to add, "In what desert land have you lived, where no one was kind enough to inform you that these fancies which you have so greedily imbibed are a thousand years old and as musty as they are ancient? I little expected, in this enlightened and scientific age, to find a disciple of Albertus Magnus and Paracelsus."[183] As he begins a new, orthodox course of scientific study, Frankenstein goes so far as to say that he has "contempt for the uses of modern natural philosophy." He observes that, "It was very different, when the masters of science sought immortality and power… but now the scene was changed. The ambition of the enquirer seemed to limit itself to the annihilation of those visions on which my interest in science was chiefly founded."[184] Still, "the soul of Frankenstein" remains determined to "pioneer a new way, explore unknown powers, and unfold to the world the deepest mysteries of creation."[185]

It is clear to Frankenstein that he is a man with a destiny — a fatality that pursues him and that will not allow him to succumb to death until it has been fulfilled.[186] Like Prometheus, he has been driven to a longing for death as a release from a life that is worse than death, and since the mad

---

181   Ibid., p. 30.
182   Ibid., p. 47.
183   Ibid.
184   Ibid., p. 48.
185   Ibid., p. 49.
186   Ibid., pp. 185–186.

scientist knows that no mortal death is capable of delivering him from his destiny, this longing takes an increasingly apocalyptic form: "I often sat for hours motionless and speechless, wishing for some mighty revolution that might bury me and my destroyer in its ruins."[187] After he has witnessed the strangled body of Elizabeth, he adds, "Could I behold this, and live? Alas! Life is obstinate, and clings closest where it is most hated."[188] The creature does not primarily aim at physically killing Frankenstein. What he wants above all is to torture the creator's soul and bring it to the point of despair. Only then will he have permission to die: "I will work at your destruction, nor finish until I desolate your heart, so that you shall curse the hour of your birth."[189] Frankenstein is horrified by his own resilience as compared to lovers who suffer tragedies and go, sometimes in the space of a couple of days, from being in the prime of their life to rotting in the grave: "Of what materials was I made, that I could thus resist so many shocks, which, like the turning of the wheel, continually renewed the torture?"[190] His life becomes so traumatic that he loses his sense of reality and lives waiting to wake up from a nightmare: "The whole series of my life appeared to me as a dream; I sometimes doubted if indeed it were all true, for it never presented itself to my mind with the force of reality."[191]

Walton's preface establishes him as an explorer whose life is dedicated to scientific discovery. He is not just concerned with opening a much shorter passage from Europe to the Pacific through the North Pole, but he hopes to find the magnetic north pole and to thereby improve the consistency of celestial observations. We are told that he has studied diverse sciences, from mathematics to medicine and "those branches of physical science from which a naval adventure might derive the greatest practical advantage."[192] In this man, we see the qualities of a Galileo and a

---

187   Ibid., p. 186.
188   Ibid., p. 199.
189   Ibid., p. 148.
190   Ibid., p. 181.
191   Ibid., p. 182.
192   Ibid., pp. 15–17.

Columbus combined. He is like those early scientific experimenters who risked their own lives in order to do battle with and bend the elements of Nature that constrain human enterprise: "One man's life or death were but a small price to pay for the acquirement of the knowledge which I sought for the dominion I should acquire and transmit over the elemental foes of our race."[193]

When Frankenstein hears Walton speak in these terms, he cannot stop himself from bursting out with this reply: "Unhappy man! Do you share my madness? Have you drunk also of the intoxicating draught? Hear me — let me reveal my tale, and you will dash the cup from your lips!"[194] Later, Frankenstein evokes the image of the Serpent at the Tree of Knowledge when he adds, "You seek for knowledge and wisdom, as I once did; and I ardently hope that the gratification of your wishes may not be a serpent sting to you, as mine has been."[195] As Walton's ship is enclosed by ice and fog and his crew threatens a mutiny, the danger of exploration and discovery that pervades his own enterprise becomes an ever-closer analog to that of Frankenstein, who is on board to bear witness to the parallel.[196]

Although at first Frankenstein attempts to dissuade Walton from his pursuit and entreats him to take a lesson from his own misadventure, it is Frankenstein who ultimately makes the passionate appeals to Walton's crew so as to put down the threat of mutiny and dissolve their insistence on abandoning their mission to cross the northern pole.[197] This appeal epitomizes the Promethean spirit of his rousing speeches:

> What do you mean? What do you demand of your captain? Are you then so easily turned from your design? Did you not call this a glorious expedition? And wherefore was it glorious? Not because the way was smooth and placid as a southern sea, but because it was full of dangers and terror; because, at every new incident, your fortitude was to be called forth, and your courage exhib-

---

193 Ibid., p. 29.
194 Ibid.
195 Ibid., p. 31.
196 Ibid., p. 215.
197 Ibid., pp. 216–217.

ited; because danger and death surrounded it, and these you were to brave and overcome.[198]

At the close of his life Frankenstein even explicitly countermands his earlier despairing renunciation of the Promethean spirit, acknowledging that where he failed as a madly-inspired discoverer, Walton and others like him may succeed: "Farewell, Walton! Seek happiness in tranquility, and avoid ambition, even if it be only the apparently innocent one of distinguishing yourself in science and discoveries. Yet why do I say this? I have myself been blasted in these hopes, yet another may succeed."[199]

---

198   Ibid., p. 217.
199   Ibid., p. 220.

CHAPTER IX

ATLAS OF THE NEW ATLANTIS

Atlas figures prominently in Aeschylus' *Prometheus Bound* as the only person who has suffered as much injustice at the hands of Zeus as his brother Prometheus.[1] In his *Theogony*, Hesiod describes the punishment of Prometheus' brother in these terms: "And Atlas through hard constraint upholds the wide heaven with unwearying head and arms, standing at the borders of the earth..." To return to the mythologist Carl Kerényi for a moment, he observes that, "Atlas is not by accident a brother of Prometheus. His cast of mind is indicated in the Odyssey (I 52); he is *oloóphron*, 'baleful,' an epithet which sums up all the crafty and dangerous characteristics which Hesiod attributes to Prometheus."[2] His punishment at the Western edge of the Greek world should be taken together with that of Prometheus at its Eastern edge, to suggest that these fraternal Titans measure the Earth inhabited by the Hellenes.[3] There are archaic vase paintings that depict Prometheus chained to the pillar, with the blood spilled by his eagle turning into the flames of his stolen fire, and just across from him stands Atlas, bearing up the heavens with a Serpent behind him.[4] This vase theme may well be Friedrich Nietzsche's source for the image of the Eagle and the Serpent in *Thus Spoke Zarathustra*, or perhaps we are just

---

1   Aeschylus, *Prometheus Bound* (New York: Oxford University Press, 1975), p. 49.

2   Ibid., p. 38.

3   Ibid.

4   Carl Kerényi, *Prometheus: Archetypal Image of Human Existence*, p. 38.

seeing the unconscious ectypal expression of archetypes that are intuited to be twins — as in the architecture of New York City's Rockefeller Center.

Since the labor of Atlas allows chronological time to begin, and since the theft of Prometheus and his willingness to rebel despite the prospect of punishment inspires the enterprise of human industriousness, these two archetypal figures of hardship and suffering frame the fundamental conditions of our temporal existence.[5] As far back as Homeric Greece, Atlas was known as one who has fathomed the depths of the entire ocean, and yet who holds the celestial sphere aloft. Derived from the ancient Greek root *tienai* — meaning "to suffer," "to endure," or "to bear," the name of this bearer of the heavens was taken up by map-makers as the designation for world-encompassing schematization.

All modern science, grounded as it is on mathematical physics, is based on this astronomical model. The mechanics of the celestial sphere, which is as radically different from living processes as one can imagine, is paradigmatic for modern science.[6] Since "the main object of science is to forecast and measure," the paradigm of all scientific calculation is set by celestial mechanics.[7] It only makes sense that one capable of grasping the astral sphere would be able to encompass the Earth. The *atlas* has also been adopted in other sciences, such as topology, where it is "a collection of top-dimensional subspaces, called charts... which comprise the entirety of a manifold, such that intersecting charts... are compatible in a certain way,"[8] and also in anatomy, where an *atlas* refers to "a detailed visual conspectus of something of great and multi-faceted complexity, with its elements splayed so as to be presented in as discrete a manner as possible whilst retaining a realistic view of the whole."[9]

If the atomic bomb exploding at the Trinity test site is an epitomizing image of the Promethean archetype, then we are tempted to take the first

---

5   Ibid.

6   Henri Bergson, *Creative Evolution*, p. 335.

7   Henri Bergson, *Time and Free Will*, pp. 230, 115.

8   Wikipedia: en.wiktionary.org/wiki/atlas

9   Ibid.

photograph of the Earth captured by a space-based satellite as the same for the aesthetic idea of Atlas. Yet this metaphor does not go far enough. In "The Age of the World Picture", Heidegger insists that the word "picture" (*Bild*) as he employs it does not mean a copy or mere imitation of something, but a structured image (*Gebild*). The word *Bilden* means to set up a preformed model (*Vor-bild*) and set-forth a pre-established rule (*Vorschrift*).[10] He points us to the expression "We get the picture," so as to suggest our active setting-upon beings to frame them as scenery in a staging of life. Man has, as it were, "come on the scene." The novelty of the motion picture and the activity of its director seem to be the key metaphor here. Heidegger writes:

> ...world picture, when understood essentially, does not mean a picture of the world but the world conceived and grasped as picture. What is, in its entirety, is now taken in such a way that it first is in being and only is in being to the extent that it is set up by man, who represents and sets forth. Wherever we have the world picture, an essential decision takes place regarding what is, in its entirety... There begins that way of being human which mans the realm of human capability as a domain given over to measuring and executing, for the purpose of gaining mastery over that which is as a whole.[11]

Meanwhile, in an "Atlas of the World," *history*—including *natural history*—is counted on as a rigorous historiographical schematization of the past as "fact." Both are thereby objectified and "set in place" (*gestellt*).[12] Remember that the German term *gestellt* derives from the verb *stellen*—which means to set in place, to set upon, as in challenging-forth. In other words, truth as representation is *not* mere correspondence; but a *taking* to be true, a *setting-upon and securing*. What is essentially distinctive about modern science is the projection of a fixed ground plan in respect to some realm of beings in Nature or History. The word Heidegger uses for "ground plan" in the original German is *Grundriss*. The verb *reis-*

---

10 Heidegger, *The Question Concerning Technology and Other Essays*, p. 180.

11 Ibid., pp. 130, 132.

12 Ibid., pp. 126–127.

sen can mean "to tear," "to sketch," or "to design," while the noun form *Riss* means either "tear," "gap," or "outline."[13] All modern scientific research involves not just making a sketch of beings, or projecting an outline onto them, but tearing open what is given and building a design into it. In other words, Atlas literally holds up our world. He builds it. Each and every phenomenon taken as an object of scientific theory must be refined, or rather re-defined, in such a way as to conform to the ground plan or *atlas* that has rendered objects of its kind predictively calculable in advance. The ground plan is already latently designed into the diverse apparatus and machinery of experimentation so that Nature is controlled in advance and constrained to show itself in a particular way.

In his book *World in the Balance*, Robert Crease inadvertently provides us with an excellent case study of the world-colonizing power of Atlas as the agent of Enframing (*das Gestell*). In Crease's view, the story of measurement in many ways epitomizes the various other manifestations of globalization, and perhaps also establishes the framework for them. It is, he claims, just as startling a development as if the entire world quite suddenly came to speak a single language.[14] Crease acknowledges a debt to Heidegger at several points in his text, and the following remarks in particular are relevant to a Heideggerian reading of *World in the Balance*:

> Oddly enough, the plunder, ravagement, and exploitation that accompanied British imperialism strongly aided the metric cause in the long run. That nation's horrendous treatment of cultures in Asia, Africa, and elsewhere in the nineteenth century did much to destabilize indigenous cultures, disrupt habit and infrastructures, and wipe out local measuring systems, opening up the possibility of international consolidation around the metric system in the twentieth.[15]

---

13   Ibid., p. 118.

14   Robert Crease, *World in the Balance* (New York: W. W. Norton & Company, 2011), p. 33.

15   Ibid., p. 143.

The phrase "oddly enough" is quite out of place here. Heidegger would have seen nothing odd about it at all, and there are two reasons why he would object to Crease's treatment of the Chinese and West African cases of colonial European uprooting of local measurement practices. Firstly, he would not see them simply as an *accidental* "downside" of an otherwise positive globalizing development that fosters the unity of mankind. Rather, he would have viewed the destruction of the Akan world and the violent assault on the Chinese one as absolutely integral to the rise of the Enframing mentality characteristic of the modern age of Western civilization. Secondly, he would have rejected any attempt to analogize these two cases of local worlds being encompassed by the global network of Enframing. To his mind, the case of China would be essentially different from that of West Africa. Whereas the advent of Enframing could only have destructive consequences for the native West African world, it would have de-constructive consequences for the Chinese one that would unleash the essence of Eastern spirituality as a dimension from out of which reflection on Enframing is possible.

To say that the African Gold Coast practice of weight measurement was inefficient would be a gross understatement. All attempts to correlate specific designs to arithmetical weight values have failed.[16] There is no quasi-scientific system of measurement whatsoever underlying the iconography of these weights. No one has been able to determine any correlation even to a natural standard such as seeds or berries.[17] Moreover, since buyers would bring their own weights *and scales* to the market, the gold dust would have to be measured on both the scales of the seller and that of the buyer.[18] The implicit trust that comes with an established *system* of measurement was entirely lacking. Furthermore, Akan women — who were often employed in the capacity of vegetable vendors — were not allowed to handle weights, and were extremely suspicious of the weighing

---

16   Ibid., p. 57.
17   Ibid., p. 56.
18   Ibid., p. 66.

practices of buyers. They would criticize their weights and scales, and force them to weigh and reweigh without being able to even touch the weights themselves. Since adulterated gold dust was often used, a great deal of time would also be squandered on using shells to separate genuine gold dust from an adulterating agent, such as finely ground bronze. A purchase worth a few pennies would usually require just as protracted a process of negotiation and debate as one worth several ounces of gold.[19]

One might suspect that these inconveniences were endured on account of the fact that some deep mystical or metaphysical symbolism was encoded in the designs of the Akan weights. This is not the case.[20] No European or African scholar has been able to make a serious case that there is any cosmological conception whatsoever underlying these crafts products.[21] The designs are whimsical. Heidegger, reading Crease's own account of the Akan measurement practices, would certainly have disagreed with Crease's summation that it represents "one of the most original, innovative, and social measuring systems ever devised on the planet."[22] He would have seen it as barbarism plain and simple, a time- and energy-consuming inconvenience suggestive of a lack of striving toward any higher intellectual or aesthetic achievement. The scholars that Crease cites refer to the Akan measurement practices as having a dramatic element, but surely a culture content to waste so much time and energy over buying some vegetables at the bazaar is one unlikely to ever develop a real dramatic art. There is in all likelihood a deep, tacit connection between the metric system and the *Götterdämmerung*.

Finally, although the Akan weights and gold measures appear to have affinities with certain objects of modern art, it would be an egregious anachronism to think that the Akan would have been capable of seeing them in this way. Even the European colonialists of the nineteenth cen-

---

19   Ibid., pp. 66–67.
20   Ibid., p. 62.
21   Ibid., pp. 60, 62.
22   Ibid., p. 68.

tury would not have been able to view them as fine art objects.[23] Modern art, particularly sculptures with a quasi-African gestalt, come at the end of an Atlantic civilizational trajectory of aesthetics that begins with Classical Greek sculpture and that, consequently, presupposes — in its infancy — a stage of culture that the Akan never attained in their entire history. This is underlined by Crease's observation of how modern artists, such as Marcel Duchamp, were influenced by Henri Poincaré's position of "conventionalism" with respect to the sciences, the view that "geometries, and indeed all scientific laws…" are "mere conveniences — mental projections or frameworks — rather than actual descriptions of nature."[24]

Not only is this an understanding that could never have been arrived at by the West African natives, it is one that even escaped the Chinese civilization, whose isolation promoted an introverted and complacent adherence to traditional cosmological views. Unlike the Akan measuring practices, those of the Chinese were bound up with court rituals of religious significance *and metaphysical conceptions of the cosmos* — so much so that a change in the metrosophical system would be something akin to a significant onto-theological reformation.[25] Crease illustrates this through the story of Xun Xu, a court official from a politically well-connected family involved in the overthrow of the Wei dynasty and its replacement by the Jin dynasty. In the third century AD, Xun tried to seize the opportunity afforded by this political upheaval to introduce a small modification into the Chinese measurement system.[26] After being recruited by an elder cousin to reform the new dynasty's musicological practices, instead of carrying out the usual scholarly reexamination of inherited ceremonies with a view to validating their technical accuracy, Xun dug up an old cache of bronze pitch regulators called *lüs*, and he compared their sounds to the ones that were being used at court, concluding that those instruments were out of

---

23   Ibid., p. 64.

24   Ibid., pp. 170–171.

25   Ibid., p. 44.

26   Ibid., p. 46.

tune with those of older orchestras, which had properly embodied cosmic harmony.[27]

Xun's metrological reformations were very limited in their impact even during his own time period and within the cloistered environment of the court; they did not outlast the demise of the political faction with which he was associated.[28] On account of China's extreme isolation from other significant civilizations, the connection between musicology, metrology, court politics, and traditional religious views of cosmic order persisted for over a thousand years.[29] However, despite their isolation, unlike the Akan, the Chinese not only had a metaphysical understanding of the cosmos bound up with their measurement practices, they also had a deeper intuition of the nature of reality *beyond* this metaphysical system and the ritualistic culture in which it became encrusted.

The assault of Enframing by means of European colonialism served to shatter this ossified structure and free the soul of the Orient for an encounter with Occidental metaphysics as expressed in modern technological science. This brings us to the darker side of Atlas, his status as the world sovereign, which is emblematic of the fact that techno-scientific development is a world-colonizing force. This aspect of Atlas first manifests in the writings of Plato. Interestingly, the theme of the necessarily world-colonizing force of a civilization seeking forbidden godlike knowledge continues to feature prominently in iterations of the folklore concerning the realm of Atlas as it is taken up by two other philosophers — Francis Bacon and Rudolf Steiner.

In the opening passages of *Timaeus*, Plato offers us a recap of the social organization and educational policies of the ideal state of *The Republic*.[30] Here, Plato makes it clear that the discussion between Timaeus, Socrates, Critias, and Hermocrates in this dialogue is taking place only a day after

---

27 Ibid., p. 47.
28 Ibid., p. 51.
29 Ibid., pp. 51, 53.
30 Plato, *Timaeus* 17c–19c.

their conversation concerning the nature of Justice in the soul and in the city-state. Socrates wants to, as it were, see this ideal city in action — especially to see it brilliantly and honorably defending itself through the course of some great struggle or conflict that would test its mettle.[31]

Critias then volunteers to tell a *true* story that he heard in his youth from his grandfather, whose father had heard it from Solon — the venerable, sagacious lawmaker of Athens, who brought it back from a journey to Egypt. A few things must be noted about the attributions here. First, Solon was the most revered Athenian, and to attribute anything to him falsely would have been considered a very wicked deed. So Plato is establishing as infallible a pedigree for this story as one could, especially since he claims that had Solon completed his aborted epic poem, it would have surpassed the works of Homer and Hesiod.[32] Critias emphasizes the fact that, as a boy, with the unique absorptive memory of a fascinated child, he not only heard the story repeatedly but that, in his youth, he even studied Solon's actual manuscript, which was a family heirloom.[33] At least three times, Plato repeats the claim that this story is not a "legend" or a "fiction"; it is a "strange" but "true" story grounded in "actual fact" and "the world of reality."[34] By contrast, he describes *The Republic* as fiction. Critias claims to have been thinking of this story the whole time that Socrates was outlining his vision of the ideal state on the previous day. Plato's remarks on geological changes that have taken place, such as the erosion of topsoil and the deforestation of the Acropolis, by way of comparing the geography of antediluvian Athens to the city of his time, is one element that lends his account a realistic tenor.[35]

Solon is said to have received this story while on a journey to Egypt, to a city at the Nile Delta called Sais, which shared its patron goddess — namely Athena, or as they called her, "Neith" — in common with

---

31   Ibid., 19c.

32   Plato, *Critias*, 21c-d.

33   Ibid., 113b.

34   Plato, *Timaeus* 20d-e; 26c; 26e.

35   Plato, *Critias* 111c–112a.

Athens. In other words, this is the "sister city" of Athens in Egypt. Note that the Greeks, and then even the Romans, viewed the ancient Egyptians as an older and wiser race than themselves throughout all of Classical antiquity, and saw Egypt as a more accomplished — albeit declining — civilization with primordial origins. It is not an accident that, when a single cosmopolitan capital of Western civilization emerged in the Classical age, it was neither the Greek city of Athens nor the Italian city of Rome, but Alexandria in Egypt.

The priests of the Egyptian temples were the preservers of the most ancient knowledge of their civilization, and they tell Solon that the Greeks are really only children compared to the Egyptians. Even the history of Athens is better preserved among these Egyptian priests of her sister city than among the Greeks. The priests explain to Solon that the reason for this is that apocalyptic natural catastrophes befall the world over great epochs of time — alternating in cycles of destruction by deluge and annihilation through fire. During these events, the stars appear to fall from the sky. At one point, he describes it as "a declination of the bodies moving in the heavens" and at another time as a calamity wherein "the stream from heaven [that], like a pestilence, comes pouring down."[36] Each time, only the most geographically isolated and uncultured specimens of mankind survive, and each time they work their way back up out of devastation, poverty, famine, and so forth to reestablish a lettered culture, their cities suffer from the same fate once more.[37] Due to certain unique geographical features, Egypt is relatively immune to these cyclical catastrophes, and consequently has preserved records of the epoch before the last worldwide deluge.[38] Plato repeatedly tells us the date of that catastrophe was "nine thousand years" before his time.[39]

---

36   Plato, *Timaeus* 22d; 23a.

37   Plato, *Timaeus* 23a-b; *Critias* 109e.

38   Plato, *Timaeus* 21e–23b.

39   Plato, *Timaeus* 23e; *Critias* 111a-b.

Ostensibly, the Egyptian priests give Solon this story to bring back to Athens so that his own people can know how valiant their ancestors were, and Critias is also telling the story to Socrates with the aim of comparing the citizens of his ideal state to the nearly identical ones of antediluvian Athens. Their guardians include both men and women, reflecting the attributes of Athena herself as a warrior goddess of wisdom, and they are separated off from the rest of the citizens, living an austere and communal life of virtue.[40] However, we soon see that at least what we have of this story — which begins in the early part of *Timaeus*, and then continues in *Critias* only to break off very ominously — centers rather around the aggressor against Athens, an antediluvian world empire by the name of "Atlantis." This account, in these two dialogues of Plato, is the first mention of Atlantis that has survived from ancient times to come down to us.

Plato's Atlantis is an island empire beyond the "pillars of Hercules" — what we call today the Straits of Gibraltar. The central island is described as "larger than Libya and Asia combined."[41] In Plato's time, "Asia" was a reference to the greater Persian Empire (in other words it did not go further than Afghanistan in the East, southern Russia in the North, and the Persian Gulf and northern India in the South). If one combines this with "Libya," or central North Africa, we are talking about a landmass the size of the continental United States. In addition to the plain where its central city was located, it was famed for a ring of tall mountains that descended precipitously into the ocean.[42]

By combining every technology and luxury known in his own time in a single place and in an unsurpassed manner, Plato portrays Atlantis as a highly advanced civilization that reached the zenith of its power some 12,000 years before our time. Its hydraulic rings, cyclopean walls, and bustling harbors were titanic works of engineering, and it was engaged in the industries of mining precious metals and quarrying stone for its

---

40   Plato, *Critias* 110c-d.

41   Plato, *Timaeus* 25a.

42   Plato, *Critias* 118b.

megalithic buildings. The Atlanteans employed complex agricultural techniques, had an especially well-developed ocean-going navy lodged at harbors that employed subterranean canals for triremes, enjoyed luxuries such as indoor plumbing for seasonal cold and hot baths, and developed many natural fragrances t into perfumes.[43]

Ultimately, they became so wealthy and powerful that they turned outwards and, completely unprovoked, launched a naval invasion into the Mediterranean that subjugated all of Europe and Asia. Only Athens was able to rebel and, like David against Goliath, little Athens repelled the Atlantean forces and even liberated others in the Mediterranean. The war between Atlantis and Athens is described as "the Great War" between those within the Mediterranean and those who came from outside it. The war ends, not in victory for either side, but in the decision of the gods to decimate mankind in an earthquake and worldwide deluge.[44]

In a fragment from *Cratylus*,[45] Plato has Socrates — in dialogue with Hermogenes — lay out a division of humanoid beings into three types. Between gods and mortals, there is a middle type of humanoid being born of unions between mortal men and goddesses or mortal women and gods. These hybrids are known as *daemons* or *heros* in Greek, in ther words demigods — those born of *eros* between gods and mortals. They were also called *gigantes*, which is the source of our word "giants." So the "giant" whose tomb Gyges finds in *The Republic*, with its magic ring and the many other wondrous objects that he does not describe in detail, is one of these hybrid people. They were not only of impressive physical stature and beauty, but were both bolder and wiser than mere humans. Plato says that even wise humans with mortal bodies have *daemonic* souls and, with reference to Hesiod, he claims that in an age of remote antiquity there was "a golden race of men," by which he means not that they were literally made of the metal gold, but that they were "godlike" men. The rule of

---

43   Ibid., 114e–117e.

44   Plato, *Timaeus* 24e–25d; *Critias* 121b.

45   Plato, *Cratylus* 397e–398d.

these *daemons* gave way to the rise of an iron race. This is a reference to the "Golden Age" and "Iron Age."

These passages link up to Plato's three classes of gold, silver, and non-precious metal souls in *The Republic*. The account of Atlantis in *Timaeus* and *Critias*, which picks up where the *The Republic* left off, completes this picture of the classes of souls identified with metals being correlated to world ages also identified with those metals. If we read the Atlantis account carefully, we see that the Atlantean age represents a stage between the age of the golden men and our own age of corruption in which the lowest of the three classes of souls is dominant. The age of Atlantis is, as it were, the "Silver Age." We can see this by looking at how the Atlantean age arises from out of the Golden Age, when mortals were "the children and disciples of the gods."[46] In the Golden Age, gods and goddesses divided the Earth among themselves in an orderly fashion, and each, in her or his own territory, fashioned mortals from out of the Earth, and "when they had settled them, fell to feeding [them], their bestial flocks there, as herdsmen do their cattle."[47] One of these settlements was a huge island in the world ocean beyond the Strait of Gibraltar ("the pillars of Hercules"). It belonged to Poseidon (Neptune), and he filled it with hybrids that were the offspring of his sexual union with the human daughter of one of the first "earthborn men of that region." Poseidon undertook a massive project of terraforming engineering on this island "with his own hand — a light enough task for a god." He established his sons as the rulers of this island and other, smaller surrounding ones. Foremost among these rulers was his eldest son, *Atlas*, after whom the main island was named *Atlantis*, and the ocean surrounding it took on the designation of *Atlantic*.[48]

Initially, these godlike men prospered without seeking wealth and honor for their own sake, and amassed them only as a derivative of their virtuous lives. However, over time, increasing interbreeding with mortals

---

46 Plato, *Timaeus* 24d.

47 Plato, *Timaeus* 24c-d; *Critias* 109b,d.

48 Plato, *Critias* 113c–114b.

decreased the divine element in these Atlanteans — who were hybrids to begin with — and as the demigods became more and more human, and as certain humans were imbued with traces of the divine, their ambition increased proportionately. Corruption set in as a consequence of this intermixture. The superhuman Atlantean civilization reached an unprecedented height of material prosperity and prowess, but it also became irreverent towards the gods and bent on the domination of all other human populations on the Earth. As a result of this, Zeus decided to call an assembly of the gods to pass judgment on the Atlanteans with a view to disciplining them to get back in line. This is where the text of *Critias* breaks off.[49]

We may infer that the corruption of the Atlanteans and their attempt to conquer all of the other human communities established and ruled by the gods in the Golden Age marks the beginning of the Silver Age of an Earth ruled by Atlantean demigods, and the destruction of Atlantis marks the passage from the Silver Age to our own Dark Age of total forgetfulness (*lethe*). This frames the myth of the metals and the three classes of souls in a historical context. Especially when viewed in light of the comments in *Cratylus* that even in the age of "men of iron," the wisest men are still "men of gold," it suggests that the hierarchical organization of society laid out in *The Republic* is not inherently just — in a timeless manner — but is what justice would look like in an age of terminal spiritual decline towards oblivion. Although Plato exoterically claims that it is perverse to think that the gods quarrel among themselves, the conflict between the heavenly Zeus and the submarine Poseidon (Neptune) — with his Trident that eventually became identified with that of Satan — is notorious in Greek mythology, as can be seen in Homer's *Odyssey*. The Atlanteans were the people of Poseidon, and Zeus decides to destroy them. He also destroys the "virtuous Athenians" along with them. Are those the actions of a just god? Was the Atlantean rebellion justified? Where do Plato's sympathies really lie?

---

49   Ibid., 120e–121c.

Like the myth of Prometheus, the legendary civilization of King Atlas survived into the modern era as a symbol of the god-like powers human beings could attain through technological science. This began with the very first myth of the scientific society, *The New Atlantis*. Sir Francis Bacon's new "Atlantis" is actually in the Pacific Ocean, since the sailors who wind up taking refuge on the secret island set sail from Peru towards China and Japan.[50] In accordance with their "laws of secrecy," the inhabitants of the island have remained veiled from the rest of the habitable world while developing an extensive knowledge of it.[51] Though isolated by choice, the New Atlantis is also cosmopolitan in composition. The ancestors of its citizens hail from diverse ethnic backgrounds and geographical locales such as the Mediterranean, Persia, and India.[52] The refugees lost at sea suspect that this ability of the new Atlanteans to remain hidden from the rest of the Earth while amassing a world-encompassing knowledge is a manifestation of supernatural power, as if this were "a land of magicians, that sent forth spirits of the air into all parts, to bring them news and intelligence of other countries."[53]

In an attempt to disabuse the visitors of this notion, the governor explains that the civilization of this island has survived from a time in remote antiquity when there was a far superior capacity for seafaring (than in Bacon's time, at the height of oceanic colonization, above all by the Spanish and Portuguese), a time before the Great Flood, when the island of Bensalem (the "New Atlantis") had extensive commerce with Plato's ancient Atlantis which, interestingly, he locates in North America.[54] Since the destruction of the old Atlantis, a secret society on the remote Pacific island has sent out "Merchants of Light" to every other nation.[55] The mis-

---

50   Francis Bacon, *New Atlantis and the Great Instauration* (Wheeling, Illinois: Harlan Davidson, Inc., 1989), p. 37.

51   Ibid., p. 46.

52   Ibid., p. 49.

53   Ibid., p. 51.

54   Ibid., pp. 51–53.

55   Ibid., pp. 59, 81.

sion of these "Mystery-men" who "disguise themselves under the names of other nations" is to procure for the New Atlantis "knowledge of the affairs and state of those countries to which they were bound, and especially of the sciences, arts, manufactures, and inventions of all the world; and withal to bring unto us books, instruments, and patterns in every kind."[56]

These international men of mystery seeking illumination empower the New Atlantis to, as it were, build atlases of everything in the entire world, or, rather, it turns the island into a living atlas of the world. The leader of the scientific secret society that is the island's true governing power, and also something of a priestly caste, explains his titanic spiritual mission in these terms: "The End of our Foundation is the knowledge of Causes, and secret motions of things; and the enlarging of the bounds of Human Empire, to the effecting of all things possible."[57] Scientists of the Foundation analyze the scientific books and technological patents of every invention from other countries, not only toward the end of amassing extant knowledge or replicating the inventions, but with a view to sharpening questions that lead to new discoveries, and to improve upon existing inventions, adapting and synthesizing them to spark innovations impossible in any other nation without such global resources to draw upon.[58]

This does not go without recognition. Instead of statues of gods or kings, the island features a cosmopolitan pantheon of monumental statues of every inventor from all the peoples of the world.[59] The Foundation does not, however, share its scientific discoveries and technological breakthroughs with others outside the island, and it secrets some of these away even from the citizens of the New Atlantis, based on an evaluation of their social impact and whether certain people are psychologically prepared to employ them in a positive fashion.[60] Scientific research and development

---

56   Ibid., pp. 59, 81.
57   Ibid., p. 71.
58   Ibid., p. 81.
59   Ibid., p. 82.
60   Ibid., p. 83.

is organized in a hierarchical and compartmentalized manner, and it is presumably the "Interpreters of Nature" who "raise the former discoveries by experiments into greater observations, axioms, and aphorisms" that would be involved in making decisions on such matters, rather than the technicians who carry out various experiments.[61]

Sir Bacon's account of what the Foundation of the New Atlantis has built by drawing on the scientific knowledge and technical expertise of every culture over the course of thousands of years presents us with one of the most visionary science-fictional narratives for centuries to come. That it was written in the early seventeenth century boggles the mind. The refugees lost at sea are, albeit politely, penned into a certain port city of the island and not allowed to wander far, and for good reason, since the superhuman physical structures on the island might give them a terrible shock.

There are numerous towers, up to half-mile in height, from which astronomical and atmospheric observations are made; the entire island is surveyed from these skyscrapers, and they are also used for preservative refrigeration.[62] There are subterranean caves that have been hollowed out, in some cases to a depth of three miles, beneath the great hills and mountains.[63] In addition to being used as mines, the unique barometric pressure, temperature, and mineralogical composition of the air in these caves makes them ideal for curing certain diseases, and also for chemical experiments that yield "new artificial metals, by compositions and materials which we use, and lay there for many years."[64] The island features wind and hydro power plants installed in streams and steep waterfalls, as well as desalination plants, and artificial wells and fountains for medicinal purposes.[65] A network of tubes and pipes conveys sounds in strange lines that crisscross the island; in other words, the New Atlantis has a

---

61   Ibid., pp. 81–82.
62   Ibid., pp. 72.
63   Ibid., p. 71.
64   Ibid., p. 72.
65   Ibid., p. 73.

telephone system.[66] The skies of the island are streaked by airships, and it also harbors a fleet of submarines.[67] Not everything that flies in the air or travels underwater is manned. In addition to manufacturing androids, the Foundation produces robots of birds, fish, and other animals.[68] These mechanical marvels are produced by industrial plants, which also churn out powerful engines and complex clockworks.[69]

What lies inside various buildings is even more striking than what one could survey outdoors. In certain laboratories, metals are vitrified and minerals, crystals, and magnets of extraordinary kinds are produced.[70] There are chambers where various atmospheric phenomena are artificially replicated with a view to the generation and modification of certain forms of life.[71] Special gardens allow for the cultivation of the most exotic diversity of plants, and flowers are grown out of season and with unnatural colors, smells, and tastes; some of these are for medicinal use.[72] A bestiary containing all sorts of rare animals, including pools with sea creatures, is used for experiments with a view toward the human application of "continuing life in them, though divers parts, which you account vital, be perished and taken forth; resuscitating of some that seem dead in appearance; and the like."[73] More radically, they are subjected to experiments that dramatically alter their phenotypic expression (their height, shape, etc.) and that hybridize certain species with others in order to create new ones that are still capable of reproduction.[74] The best of every cuisine in the world is replicated, especially in order to promote health.[75] Water is

---

66   Ibid., p. 79.
67   Ibid., p. 80.
68   Ibid., p. 80.
69   Ibid., p. 80.
70   Ibid., p. 78.
71   Ibid., p. 73.
72   Ibid., p. 74.
73   Ibid., pp. 74, 75.
74   Ibid., p. 75.
75   Ibid., p. 79.

purified and even modified at the molecular level, rendering it so fine in composition that it can pass right through one's hand.[76]

Optical laboratories contain microscopes for the analysis of bodily fluids; they produce glasses as an aid to sight and manufacture powerful telescopes, as well as devices more sophisticated than prisms that can isolate any part of the light spectrum in an uncolored and transparent medium; and they possess other exotic light sources, such as laser beams and phosphorescent materials.[77] Sonic laboratories can produce a range of sound hitherto unknown, allowing for ethereally graceful music with seemingly impossible tones, but also used for modifying the sound of anyone's voice in any way.[78] The optical and sonic capabilities are brought together with others in "houses of deceits of the senses," where all manner of "false apparitions, impostures, and illusions" are perfected, with the potential for making "miracles" and "magically" distorting people's sense of space and time, but this knowledge is allegedly used foremost to avoid falling prey to deceptions.[79]

Rudolf Steiner's Atlantis features all of the main tropes of Atlantean folklore since Plato. It is a great island continent positioned in the world's oceans in such a way that, after its destruction through a cataclysm involving a great flood, what survivors there were made their way to the Americas, Europe, and Egypt.[80] They were the great civilizers who spread their culture, for better or worse, to all the other comparatively primitive peoples in the world.[81] His Atlanteans also have high technology, such as hovercrafts, intricate waterworks, exotic power sources, and the ability to manipulate morphogenesis. However, whereas Sir Bacon elaborates on the mechanical knowledge and the splendorous material accomplish-

---

76   Ibid., pp. 75–76.

77   Ibid., p. 78.

78   Ibid., p. 79.

79   Ibid., pp. 78, 80.

80   Rudolf Steiner, *Atlantis: The Fate of a Lost Land and Its Secret Knowledge* (Forest Row, East Sussex: Sophia Books, 2001), p. 40.

81   Ibid., p. 63.

ments of Plato's Atlantis, Steiner focuses on the psychic powers of its semi-divine population, and reiterates Plato's claim that they were destroyed through a profane use of godlike abilities in the service of all-too-human hubris and perversion.

As in the case of Plato's narrative, the population of Atlantis is not quite human. They are, in varying degrees, spiritual beings descended onto the Earth from a heavenly plane. Every night, during their sleep, instead of entering into a dream state, these beings would return to the spirit world and be able to communicate with others in that realm.[82] In fact, most of their labor took place on this plane, and they would return to their bodies to rest. In the earlier phases of their history, the corporeality of the more accomplished among them had not even concretized to the extent that it would leave skeletal remains.[83] Their leaders were gods who would communicate with these accomplished souls in sacred places of which the general population was unaware.[84] The divine-human hybrids that received these communications would then govern society according to principles and methods that they would never have been able to explain to those governed by means of them.[85] Education was also essentially grounded on the psychical charisma of the educator, rather than on objective assimilation or analysis of information.[86]

This education consisted largely of presenting the mind of the youth with vivid images of a variety of situations from the accumulated experience of the people.[87] They thought in images rather than in concepts.[88] Their abilities were rooted in a tremendous memory capacity that we have long lost, and in related intuitive capacities that we once shared with the

---

82   Ibid., p. 89.

83   Ibid., pp. 34–35, 39.

84   Ibid., p. 44.

85   Ibid., pp. 45, 46.

86   Ibid., p. 28.

87   Ibid., p. 28.

88   Ibid., p. 17.

animals, and which we can still observe in them today.[89] An Atlantean would act decisively by comparing a present situation with other, similar ones in the past, so greater reverence and authority was reserved for those with the greatest store of life experience — not those who could reason best or innovate based on abstract speculation.[90]

Their memory was mediated more by an exquisite instinct than by deliberation. They had other animal psychical capacities as well, such as clairvoyance, telepathy, and psychokinesis, but at a higher level of efficacy commensurate with the technical orientation towards the world that is afforded by the human form of life.[91] Most of their technology was based on the channeling of the vital force of organisms by these extrasensory or psychokinetic means.[92] Consequently, even if we were in possession of pieces of Atlantean technology, we would not be able to make it function by purely mechanical means. For example, according to Steiner, the germinal force in seeds was released psychokinetically to power the hovercraft that the Atlanteans kept in their sheds together with huge stocks of seeds (i.e., fuel).[93] Such a psychical-organic basis for the generation of motive power, lighting, and other applications ought to have made for a society with a more harmonious relationship with its ecological environment.

However, the technical mastery of psychical abilities came with its own catastrophic dangers. Since the Atlanteans were the first people to develop the use of language, and since their communications with one another were predominately telepathic, words had a power that they no longer do.[94] While they could be used to heal, these words of power could also be used for harming people at a distance and with impunity — especially people with less developed psychical faculties. Although the beginning of the rise of rational thought somewhat restrained the extent to which

---

89   Ibid., p. 19.
90   Ibid., p. 18.
91   Ibid., pp. 19, 34.
92   Ibid., p. 19.
93   Ibid., pp. 20, 38.
94   Ibid., p. 25.

one's lustful and wrathful passions would be immediately externalized by extrasensory and psychokinetic means, this also allowed for the unbridled proliferation of internalized desires, the concealment of increasingly perverse inclinations, and the festering of vengeful thoughts.[95] The rise of conceptual thought also fostered a new, untamed spirit of innovation, which was terribly destabilizing for a culture rendered so static on account of its reliance on memory and instinct.[96] Since the power of memory and the respect for those with a greater store of experience endured in the transitional phase, some of these now individualized egos abused reincarnation and created cults of personality around themselves so as to establish a monumental tyranny over what remained largely a group ego.[97] Steiner believes that Atlantean refugees who settled in Egypt and India impressed this to a degree on the pharaoh- and guru-worshiping caste systems there.

Psychical abilities that ought to have been closely guarded — by spiritual initiates with strong moral fiber, and practiced in the purification of base impulses from their souls — fell into the hands of people who used them for practical purposes and personal gain.[98] Even some of the initiates succumbed to temptation and used these holy powers for profane purposes. The human form was eventually perverted by these means as giants, dwarves, and grotesque chimera were wrought through a combination of psychical and organic techniques.[99] The inner lives of many Atlanteans were invaded so that their perception of the world was hellishly distorted by phantasmagoric hallucinations.[100] Finally, repeated abuses of psychokinetic power to control the weather even compromised the integrity of the aether, and let loose terribly destructive storms.[101] In sum, Steiner's

---

95   Ibid., pp. 31, 63.
96   Ibid., pp. 18, 32.
97   Ibid., pp. 26–27, 29, 60–61.
98   Ibid., pp. 39, 63.
99   Ibid., p. 64.
100 Ibid., p. 65.
101 Ibid., p. 38.

Atlantis ultimately symbolizes the dawn of a *radical* secularism — one that does not deny the spiritual, but renders all its vital forces profanely serviceable to man. This was latent in the psychological archetype of Atlantis from its beginnings in Greece. It also lies at the basis of that other fount of Atlantic civilization, namely the Hebraic mythology of Israel.

The idea that there was a war amongst the gods over an attempt to seed a godlike terrestrial civilization is not solely an ancient Greek idea. It is found in many different cultures, and plays an especially prominent role in Judeo-Christianity and Islam — with the exception that the other gods besides the chief god, Jehovah, are referred to as "angels" of the Lord, and those who rise in rebellion against him as "fallen angels." The first opposition to the Lord comes in the form of the Serpent in the Garden of Eden, who tempted Adam and Eve to leave a state of ignorance and blindness, and to gain wisdom from the Tree of Knowledge so that they might become like divine beings. It is very clearly stated in *Genesis* 3 that the gods (*elohim*) expelled humans from the Garden so that they would not also eat of the Tree of Life and become, not only wise, but as immortal as the gods. The motivation for this was vengeance upon mankind for having rejected its status of enforced ignorance, and a covetous jealousy that sought to keep humans in a position of servitude despite the knowledge they gained as a result of defying the gods' attempt to keep them blind. Then, shortly thereafter, we have the extraordinary passages on Noah's Flood from *Genesis* 5:21–27 and 6:1–17. Something seems to be missing here. In only a few lines, the Bible tells us that the Lord suddenly decided to wipe out the entirety of Creation? What are these evil acts that supposedly consumed humanity, and that constitute a defiance of divine laws? Should not more have been said about them, *especially given the fact that it is said that they began to take place after gods came down and interbred with humans?* Well, as it turns out, more was said, but it was excised from the Bible, as were many other parts of it over time.

The text is known as the *Book of Enoch*,[102] which is why the aforementioned passages from *Genesis* relate how Enoch "walked with god." What
that means is made clear in the *Book of Enoch*, where this prophet was
taken up and away into the heavens in one of the chariots of the Lord, and
was shown apocalyptic scenes of the future judgment of the world. The
account of the *Book of Enoch* very closely parallels Plato's story of Atlantis.
It details the rise of a hybrid civilization of demigods on the Earth, except that in this case, instead of slowly being corrupted over time, it is
made clear that the gods who bred with mortal women were an army
of angels who rebelled against the Lord and attempted to enlighten humans by teaching them all kinds of Promethean arts and sciences. This
especially improved the lot of women, whose innate psychical superiority
to men was cultivated to turn them into powerful sorceresses, and who
were taught both methods of birth control and of abortion, so that they
could take pleasure in sex as they wished and with whom they wished. It
is probably with a view to this antediluvian liberation of women that the
Bible specifically targets *female* practice of the occult arts in that famous
injunction in *Exodus* 22:17 that was cited by those in Europe and America
who burned witches at the stake for centuries: "Thou shalt not suffer a
sorceress to live." (*Exodus* 22:17)

There was a war between the hybrid human civilization that the rebel
angels spawned and the army of the Lord, and these Giants lost. Their
civilization was wiped out in a worldwide deluge, and the fallen angels
themselves were bound to remain incarcerated beneath the Earth. Later in
European history, Milton developed this theme of war between God and
the rebel leader Lucifer in *Paradise Lost*. One mention of the war amongst
the gods in the Bible itself occurs in *Revelation* 12: 7–9:

> And there was war in heaven: Michael and his angels fought against the dragon;
> and the dragon fought and his angels, And prevailed not; neither was their place
> found any more in heaven. And the great dragon was cast out, that old serpent,

---

102 Richard Laurence [Translator], *The Book of Enoch the Prophet* (San Diego: Wizard's
Bookshelf, 1995).

called the Devil and Satan, which deceiveth the whole world: he was cast out into the earth, and his angels were cast out with him.

Once humanity built itself back up again after the Flood, what seemed to be a *cosmopolitan* civilization — an urban culture with a single world language — undertook a project to build something like a tower, by means of which they would have been able to ascend to the heavens. The Lord was once again afraid and jealous of their progress, and decided to destroy this unified human civilization, scatter its survivors, and set them against each other. Here are the passages on the Tower of Babel from *Genesis* 11:1–9:

> Everyone on earth had the same language and the same words... And they said, "Come, let us build us a city, and a tower with its top in the sky, to make a name for ourselves; else we shall be scattered all over the world." The Lord came down to look at the city and tower that man had built, and the Lord said, "If, as one people with one language for all, this is how they have begun to act, then nothing that they may propose to do will be out of their reach. Let us, then, go down and confound their speech there, so that they shall not understand one another's speech." Thus the Lord scattered them from there over the face of the whole earth; and they stopped building the city. That is why it was called Babel, because there the Lord confounded the speech of the whole earth; and from there the Lord scattered them over the face of the whole earth.

It is not incidental that both Bacon and Plato's iterations of "Atlantis" as the archetype of the technoscientific society are deeply bound up with colonialism, and that Steiner's story of an antediluvian Atlantis frames the supposed "cradles" of the high civilizations of antiquity across the world as colonies seeded by the titanic survivors of a single cosmopolitan empire. The idea that colonialism and cosmopolitanism are somehow at odds with one another is bizarre and ahistorical. It is often forgotten that the British, French, Spanish, and other members of the European international system did not invent colonialism, nor should their early modern, highly centralized, monarchist, and quasi-nationalist form of colonialism be taken as representative. Classical Greece, enduring into Hellenistic Rome, was the colonialist civilization *par excellence* — a maritime empire that had spread colonies throughout the entire Mediterranean basin. The Roman adoption of Greek culture was not a late development in Classical antiquity. Already in the time of Pythagoras, at the dawn of philosophy, there was as much or more of Greece in Italy than on the mainland. The first *cosmopolis* known to recorded history is Alexandria, a Greek colony founded by Alexander the Great in a conquered Egypt.

There, at the height of Classical civilization, a level of scientific understanding of the cosmos and of the human place within it was attained that would not be equaled again until the seventeenth century.[103] At this great center of learning, scientists from as far afield as Spain and Persia came together to discover scientific truths that would subsequently be long forgotten, such as the fact that the Earth revolved around the Sun, and they also drew up remarkable mechanical patents, including one for a steam engine. It is *this* city, and not Athens or Rome, that was the capital of our *cosmopolitan* Classical civilization — until it was betrayed by Judeo-Christian fanatics, and then overrun by barbarian hordes. Here, a woman led the entire Platonic Academy until she was skinned alive on the orders of a Catholic bishop, and the world's greatest library and laboratory, that she fought so hard to protect, was burned to the ground by a Catholic mob. What little the murderers of Hypatia left intact was effaced several centuries later by Arab Muslim invaders. This might as well be seen as a second destruction of Atlantis, because that is the archetype of the kind of society that Alexandrian Egypt was evolving towards.

In *Against Method*, Feyerabend discusses the rise of a "pragmatic philosophy" in this Greek milieu, and he emphasizes how few people are capable of this. To live one's life in a way that is philosophically *pragmatic* without qualification is to encounter other ways of viewing the world in the manner that a professional traveler or journeyer experiences exotic cultures.[104] One has to have not only the openness of attitude and modes of thought conducive to experiencing them — at least to some extent — from

---

103 Justin Pollard & Howard Reid, *Alexandria: Birthplace of the Modern Mind* (New York: Viking, 2006).

104 Paul Feyerabend, *Against Method*, p. 217.

within, but also the willingness to allow one's own beliefs, judgments, tastes, and the practices that these express and reaffirm to be transformed in the process.[105]

Modern rationalists are as incapable of this as adherents of religious revelation. Feyerabend notes that no religion has ever proposed itself as just something worth trying out.[106] Religions recognize that traditions are constituted by the historically conditioned practices of different human communities, but they assert a domain lying beyond this cultural-historical construction that is essentially impervious to it. The structure of this domain becomes a context for improving and condemning merely constructed cultural practices. Believers brand one who has become intimately familiar with the religion, but still rejects it, as an inhuman monster or a hopeless idiot. Reason is, in Feyerabend's view, merely a secularized version of this transcendence of the will of God, since the basic structures of Reason are ahistorical in their perfection, even if they unfold themselves progressively in the course of history for the sake of finite and fallible beings.[107] For the rationalist, to be rational is to be human, and so one who does not accept the standards of rationality is as inhuman as the religious apostate who refuses to "see the light." Both the adherent of Rationality and that of Divine Law are promulgating *idealism* in a sense that contrasts with the aforementioned *pragmatism*. Both act like missionaries trying to "befuddle the natives" and "remove all inconsistencies" through "rules and standards" taken to be "universal, independent of mood, context, [and] historical circumstances."[108]

This reference to missionaries and natives develops a theme from the late Ludwig Wittgenstein, who had a decisive impact on Feyerabend when the latter attended his lectures at the Kraft Circle from 1949 until 1952.[109] Subsequently, Wittgenstein had agreed to take Feyerabend on as his stu-

---

105 Ibid., pp. 217–218.
106 Ibid., p. 218.
107 Ibid.
108 Ibid., p. 230.
109 Ibid., p. 254.

dent at Cambridge, but he died just before Feyerabend arrived.[110] After Wittgenstein's death, Elizabeth Anscombe — who had come to Vienna to study German for her translations of Wittgenstein — introduced Feyerabend to the manuscripts of Wittgenstein's unpublished writings, and Feyerabend engaged in months-long discussions with her concerning them. Feyerabend volunteers that "[t]hey had a profound influence upon me though it is not at all easy to specify particulars."[111] One particular idea that he does specify is one central to his entire work: that the "conservation principles" that sustain the identity of even apparently well-defined physical objects are linguistically constructed, and contingent on differences between various cultures and developmental stages of a given culture.[112] In the mid-1950s, Feyerabend rewrote Wittgenstein's *Philosophical Investigations* in the form of a systematic treatise, part of which was translated by Anscombe and published in *Philosophical Review*.[113]

Wittgenstein's reference to the missionaries and natives comes in a parenthetical remark at the end of a passage in *On Certainty* that develops key elements of the critique of his own early logical formalism that Wittgenstein puts forward in *Philosophical Investigations*. In the preface to *Philosophical Investigations*, Wittgenstein writes that he has been "forced to recognize grave mistakes" in what he wrote in the *Tractatus Logico-Philosophicus*. According to the *Tractatus*, there is one essential function of language — namely, the description of reality by means of reference. In the *Investigations*, Wittgenstein notes that there are many other functions of language, such as joking, acting, questioning, thanking, swearing, commanding, speculating, evaluating, and storytelling.[114] To think that words always function as the names of things, or that they always refer to objects (which is in fact only one type of language use), leads to the

---

110 Ibid., p. 260.

111 Ibid., p. 259.

112 Ibid., p. 260.

113 Ibid., p. 261.

114 Ludwig Wittgenstein, *Philosophical Investigations: The German Text, with a Revised English Translation* (Oxford: Blackwell Publishing, 2001), p. 23.

abstract reification of nouns like "time," "being," "nothing," and "number," as if we could meaningfully inquire into what these "things" are — as if we, as knowing subjects, could determine to what objects they actually refer. This causes these unusual "objects" to assume the pretensions of an occult significance. We are bewitched by words on account of our paying attention only to their surface grammar or apparent place in the structure of a sentence, rather than to their depth grammar or usage in everyday life.[115] Generality is a matter of degree, and "logical" words are not any more "sublime" or significant than other words.[116] The *Investigations* call the reductionist foundationalism of the *Tractatus* into question. Wittgenstein admits that he was mistaken to believe that there are basic terms from which all others are defined, or that there are any absolutely simple entities of which all others are composed. While it may be said that logic characterizes the basic structure of what is possible within a language (even what it is possible to think), this is a vacuous observation, since there are different ways of stipulating the meaning of terms such as "basic," "structure," and "possible."[117] On this view, what is taken to be "basic" and how one construes a "structure" is never a matter of objective fact; it depends on the aims and motivations of those doing the defining.

All that is universally basic to language, and can never be eliminated, is its *indeterminacy*. Such indeterminacy or vagueness of linguistic terms, and the open texture of language in which they function, does not in practice detract from their utility.[118] The meaning of the same word will differ based on the variety of ways in which it is used.[119] The various ways in which we use words can be thought of in terms of the analogy of *language games*.[120] Wittgenstein insists that, like all other games, language games

---

115   Ibid, p. 664.
116   Ibid., p. 114.
117   Ibid., pp. 89–106.
118   Ibid., pp. 69, 71.
119   Ibid., p. 43.
120   Ibid., p. 108.

only develop their significance within the context of the collective cultural *activities* of a particular society.[121]

For a child to learn language is not at all the same type of phenomenon as for an already linguistically adept British adult to travel in a foreign country and try to learn its language by means of guessing at whether certain words that the non-English speaking locals try to teach him refer to the same object-concepts as certain words in his native language do.[122] It is Wittgenstein's contention that a child first acquires the capacity for any conceptual thought at all only as she is taught language in the context of the shared cultural practices of her society. The problem, from an ethical perspective, is that while the standards of certain cultures may overlap, people brought up in very different cultures may be unable to find any rationally objective standard of ethical conduct to arbitrate in their relations with one another. Indeed, in *On Certainty*, Wittgenstein claims that where there are really two (or more) fundamentally different worldviews, there will be a "combat" that can only end with the destruction of all but one party, or with an irrational persuasion (*Überredung*, literally to "out talk" / "over speak" or verbally dazzle) that converts (*bekehren*, literally "turns") one of the combatants:

> Where two principles really do meet which cannot be reconciled with one another, then each man declares the other a fool and a heretic. I said I would 'combat' the other man, — but wouldn't I give him *reasons*? Certainly; but how far do they go? At the end of reasons comes persuasion. [*Überredung*]. (Think what happens when missionaries convert [*bekehren*] natives.)[123]

Wittgenstein does not see all empirical propositions as holding the same status.[124] "Not all corrections of our views are on the same level."[125] The sense of certain propositions hinges on certain others already being pre-

---

121   Ibid., p. 23.

122   Ibid., p. 32.

123   Ludwig Wittgenstein, *On Certainty* (New York: Harper & Row, 1972), pp. 611–12.

124   Ibid., pp. 213, 167, 308, 401.

125   Ibid., p. 300.

sumed. These "hinge propositions" are more fundamental than others: "That is to say, the *questions* that we raise and our *doubts* depend on the fact that some propositions are exempt from doubt, are as it were like hinges on which those turn."[126] Wittgenstein also uses a river's flow, the sand on its banks and bed, and the more solid bedrock of the river as an analogy for different types of empirical propositions.[127] The analogy is intended to suggest that these different types of empirical propositions admit of significantly different degrees of susceptibility to change over time, even if no sharp distinction can be drawn between them (even if the bedrock can be eroded by the water currents). None of them have the timeless certainty of *a priori* logical truths. The beliefs according to which we act are not based upon logical tautologies. Rather, our actions are grounded on empirical propositions, some of which are analogous to the riverbed and act as tacit background assumptions that lend more derivative propositions the context that allows them to be meaningful — as the hidden riverbed shapes the visible flow of the water.[128] Wittgenstein claims that "[w]hat has to be accepted, the given, is — so one could say — *forms of life*."[129] He elaborates on this claim in the following passage from *On Certainty*:

> "But is there then no objective truth?...
> "An empirical proposition can be *tested*" (we say) But how? and through what? What *counts* as its test? — "But is this an adequate test? And, if so, must it not be recognizable as such in logic?" — As if giving grounds did not come to an end sometime. But the end is not an ungrounded presupposition: it is an ungrounded way of acting.[130]

The beliefs according to which we act are not based upon such logical tautologies as A = B, B = C, therefore A = C or 2 + 2 = 4 = 1 + 3. None of

126   Ibid., p. 341.

127   Ibid., p. 96–99.

128   Ibid., p. 151, 309.

129   Wittgenstein, *Philosophical Investigations*, II: xi, p. 192.

130   Wittgenstein, *On Certainty*, pp. 108–110.

them have the timeless certainty of *a priori* logical truths; they can only be affirmed in deed. In other words, by saying that we cannot get outside of the "form" within the context of which we *always already* experience "life," Wittgenstein only means that we cannot do so until and unless we *in practical fact* take up some other form of life.

Nearly halfway through *Against Method*, Feyerabend begins to speak in Wittgensteinian terms. He refers to Copernicanism and the Aristotelian worldview that it replaced as different "forms of life" constituted by conceptual principles and grammatical rules that construct one set of facts as opposed to another.[131] He argues that the "observations, concepts, general principles, and grammatical rules which, taken together, constitute a 'form of life'" can and should be changed in order to "create new facts," and thereby increase the empirical content of scientific research.[132] Concepts do not have a purely logical content. They conjure images and are bound up with emotions in such a way that a change in conceptual systems can violate social constraints that are taken to be foundational to a certain form of life.[133]

Every truth is only "objective" according to the judgment of one or another culture.[134] It is a question of whether one takes an observer-position or a participant-position. For the narrow-minded advocate of any culture, certain things are "objectively" true facts or right practices insofar as he is a participant in that culture and refuses to take the views of it that external observers (from different cultures) would take.[135] Put in these terms, the philosophically consistent pragmatist is one who is always trying to be both an observer and a participant *at the same time* so as to gain a vantage point upon his own beliefs and the form of life that is their context, as well as to not become mired in any other culture from whose practices and modes of thought he approvingly draws some ele-

---

131 Feyerabend, *Against Method*, pp. 123–124.

132 Ibid., p. 123.

133 Ibid., p. 124.

134 Ibid., p. 221.

135 Ibid., p. 222.

ments, and even allows these to transform certain of his basic beliefs and behaviors. Consistent with his analogy between this pure pragmatist and a world-traveler, Feyerabend makes the following observation concerning colonialists with which I wholeheartedly agree: "The colonial official who proclaims new laws and a new order in the name of the king has a much better grasp of the situation than the rationalist who recites the mere letter of the law without any reference to the circumstances of its application and who regards this fatal incompleteness as proof of the 'objectivity' of the laws recited."[136]

Feyerabend goes on to offer another metaphor relevant to the provisional attitude toward knowledge taken by the pragmatist qua world-traveler qua colonial explorer: "The wanderer uses the map to find his way but he also corrects it as he proceeds, removing old idealizations and introducing new ones. Using the map no matter what will soon get him into trouble. But it is better to have maps than to proceed without them."[137] The one who draws up and handles these maps of the world pragmatically, who interchanges these atlases depending on which one the present exploratory expedition calls for, is *not a naïve missionary*, but the world-colonizing brother of Prometheus. In fact, this association of new scientific discoveries with the discovery of new lands by explorers such as Columbus and Magellan is a motif reiterated throughout *Against Method* — the idea that there is a deep relationship between the discovery of the geographical continent of America, for example, and the faith that there are also "new continents of knowledge" to be discovered.[138] It is this "America of Knowledge," as Feyerabend calls it, that becomes Francis Bacon's theme in *The New Atlantis*.

The fundamental insight of the pragmatic philosophy — insofar as there is anything "fundamental" about it — is the insight that Reason and Practice are not two orders of experience, with the seemingly irrational

---

136 Ibid.

137 Ibid., p. 223.

138 Ibid., p. 233.

chaos of the latter being subject to evaluative ordering in accordance with the stable formal structures of the former. Rather, whatever counts for "reason" or "rationality" at one or another time is a practice among other practices, and its abstraction from other practices whose accidental properties are not cleaned up in the same way, and with respect to which it assumes the position of an arbiter, is itself a pragmatic move — even if this is forgotten and covered over, again *for practical purposes*.[139]

There are no *objective* standards of epistemic or moral evaluation to decide the relative worth of different traditions, and this includes that one tradition — or aspect of a tradition — called "rationality."[140] The projections of participants in a given tradition only appear or sound "objective" because they lack self-reflexive awareness of their tradition as *a* tradition. The subjectivity of a tradition is recognized only when participants in various traditions stand in the intensity of a conflict of judgment between traditions, and at this point, those who fail to revise their view of their own tradition as objective "are just pig-headed..."[141] Historical moments when such an interaction of traditions takes place are opportunities for the individuals or groups participating in them to adopt the aforementioned pragmatic philosophy of provisional and practical "truths."[142] The *relativism* that follows from embracing this subjective turn was, in Feyerabend's view, first defended by the Greek thinker Protagoras with his maxim, "Man is the measure of all things."[143] Such an understanding is a truly *civilized* view of things.[144]

Only those "guided" by a pragmatic philosophy are capable of engaging in an "open exchange" with others — so open that we are willing to immerse ourselves in each other's worldviews and be deeply transformed by the exchange as it takes place, as opposed to a "guided exchange" wherein

---

139 Ibid., p. 224.
140 Ibid., p. 225.
141 Ibid., p. 226.
142 Ibid.
143 Ibid.
144 Ibid.

the participants must first be properly conditioned into the right view of things so that the outcome of their interaction is foreclosed in advance on all essential points.[145] Open exchange transcends sheer relativism through the fusion and transfusion of traditions that it affords, but not in a way that allows those participating in it to establish an *objective* — in other words, ahistorical and inherent — superiority over other traditions; the transcendence of the trans-traditional pragmatic philosophy depends through and through on unforeseeable and concrete historical, psychological, and material conditions.[146] A "free society" is one constituted through open exchanges, and one that protects the conditions of possibility for these free-spirited interactions, which are endangered by objectivists of all kinds.[147] In the context of such a free society, "we can build world-views on the basis of a personal choice and thus unite, for ourselves and for our friends, what was once separated by a series of historical accidents."[148] We can build in the sovereign, free spirit of Atlas.

Discovery as an *activity* presupposes the cultivation of a definite *type* of aesthetic/cultural context that first makes *inquiring individuals* possible. The homeland of philosophy is the Greece of Utopia, which runs the risk of dystopia. Beginning with Plato, in dialogues such as *The Republic*, *Timaeus*, and *Critias*, there is a Greek vision of utopia, and it is *this* unhistorical homeland of philosophy that appropriates other peoples and is at the same time re-imagined by them. *Eu-topos* — the word has a very significant double meaning: "no place" and "better place." The *topos* is also the root of topography, and is therefore bound up with the crafting of atlases. To be utopians is to be the people of permanent revolution, to imagine that the world can be a better place and that society can be shaped in a way that it has never been before.[149] It is to will backwards against time from out of the future — to will change "now here," as in the title of

---

145   Ibid., p. 227.
146   Ibid., p. 228.
147   Ibid., p. 229.
148   Ibid., p. 250.
149   Deleuze, *What is Philosophy?*, pp. 108, 110.

Samuel Butler's utopian text, *Erehwon*.[150] In this sense at least, "Atlantis" is *our* future past.

What we think of as "the scientific outlook" is really a mythic work of art. It is a *techne* that is a *poesis*, but it is unlike any other total art-works that define the worlds of traditional cultures. In *Against Method*, Feyerabend recounts how in an early article entitled "Nature as a Work of Art" he argued that "the world of modern science (and not only the description of this world) is an artwork constructed by generations of artisan/scientists" — a view with which I totally agree.[151] *Against Method* ends with this reflection: "The arts, as I see them today, are not a domain separated from abstract thought, but complementary to it and needed to fully realize its potential. Examining this function of the arts and trying to establish a mode of research that unites their power with that of science and religion seems to be a fascinating enterprise and one to which I might devote a year (or two, or three...)."[152]

There is no "Science" without *the scientist* — a very definite individual whose existence presupposes a certain type of cultural-historical situation similar to the one in which the Greeks found themselves at the time of Pythagoras. What was reborn in our Renaissance was a titanic aspiration for what either never occurred to the seekers of *nirvana*, or was rejected by them as foolish hubris: *the tragic will to risk deadly dystopia in order to build an earthly utopia.* This leitmotif of science fiction is the core of our Promethean way of life. Whether remains of Atlantis are ever found in the depths of the Atlantic between Europe and America, or whether it turns out to be a distant recollection of the cradle of Greek culture in Crete and Santorini, the tragic *folk*lore of Atlantis already binds together the European and American peoples. From deep within our philosophical heritage, this memory of the future is destining us towards a realization of the Cosmopolis.

---

150   Ibid., pp. 100, 112.

151   Feyerabend, *Against Method*, p. 270.

152   Ibid., p. 267.

The civilization of Atlas is neither culturally-geographically "Western," nor an ideological product of "Western philosophy," as if there were something philosophically Eastern, exotically Oriental, that could stand opposed to it. As Gilles Deleuze argues in *What Is Philosophy?*, the Greeks had to first become philosophers before barbarians who aspired to become philosophers had to become "Greeks."[153] Philosophy is not Greek in the sense that the Athenians at one point falsely viewed themselves as autochthonous — as the native sons of a given land. Rather, the first philosophers were refugees, exiles, travelers, and strangers.[154] Plato and Aristotle are not the beginning, but the culmination. These queer bastards of the Pre-Socratic era did not come from Athens — they came *to* Athens, together with traveling merchants and artisans, from the fringes of the Oriental empires.[155] It seems that their attempt to see through clashing religious worldviews and diverse cultural traditions not only brought them to posit *phusis* — the Way of Nature in itself — but also, immediately and inescapably, a political context for the possibility of this dangerously unorthodox contemplation.[156] The estranged outcast inquirers after Nature also needed their own homeland and their own people, but it would be a homeland of experimentation, not of tradition, because "to think is to experiment," and so it would be a coming homeland, since "experimentation is always that which is in the process of coming about — the new, remarkable, and interesting that replace the appearance of truth and are more demanding than it is."[157]

Most importantly, the imperial Persian invasion of mainland Greece uprooted even the Athenian Autochthon. A people who were already developing a free marketplace culture and a public space culture, based on their situation at the crossroads of key trade routes in the Mediterranean Sea, were uprooted from their own land to the extent that they were

153 Deleuze, *What is Philosophy?*, p. 96.

154 Ibid., p. 109.

155 Ibid., pp. 87, 109.

156 Ibid., p. 100.

157 Ibid., p. 111.

forced to reterritorialize themselves on the open sea. Water became their earth. They became the first colonialists in recorded history. The homeland of philosophy has its inception in the Delian League that was formed to defeat the Persians, and did so chiefly in the naval Battle of Salamis.[158] Within two centuries of the Persian invasion, the Greeks had colonized not only the entire Persian Empire, including its easternmost reaches in northern India, but also the high civilization of ancient Egypt, where the Ptolomies established a city that became the world's first cosmopolitan melting pot: Alexandria. Deleuze sees the modern techno-worldwide development of global capitalism as a renaissance of the sea-faring international marketplace of the Greeks. The North Atlantic Treaty Organization (NATO) can be seen as a fractal repetition of the Delian League. When Deleuze suggests that this world market can even extend "into the galaxy" after reaching the ends of the Earth, he probably has the Federation of *Star Trek* or the Rebel Alliance of *Star Wars* in mind.[159] Both are visions of "Greeks… strangely deformed in this mirror of the future."[160] Both are Atlantean.

No Greek or Roman commoner could have imagined that a descendant of the Celtic barbarians would someday most definitively appropriate the persona of Ulysses.[161] There nonetheless came a time when the worst of these northern barbarians wanted to identify themselves with the Greeks. With reference to Hölderlin's vision of the retrieval of the Greek "society of friends," Deleuze points out that this also meant that the Greeks were reterritorialized on the Germans; that in becoming Greek, the Germans of the Romantic period and of the nineteenth century (Goethe, Schiller, Schelling, Hölderlin, Nietzsche, etc.)—who have *thus far* established the most intimate relationship to the Greeks[162]—radically transformed "becoming-Greek" into something different than what the Greeks actu-

158 Ibid., p. 88.
159 Ibid., p. 97.
160 Ibid., p. 110.
161 Ibid., p. 109.
162 Ibid., pp. 101–102.

ally were as a matter of petrified historical fact.[163] The Atlantic Alliance is both Greek and the larval form of the first world government. It should not be understood as a narrow geographic reference to the "Atlantic," but in terms of Atlas — the world sovereign of Atlantis. So-called "Western" civilization should be redefined as Atlantic civilization or, more colloquially, as a new Atlantis.

Every culture that has hitherto adopted and adapted the metaphysical heritage of the Greeks has been on its way to becoming the Atlantean "people to come." Atlantis — the Greece of Utopia that risks dystopia — operates on the spectral level of the essence of Technology to determine the structure of Atlantic history as it has concretely manifested — the history of global capitalism and colonialism, but also of Soviet Communism.[164] Perhaps the most catastrophically misguided foreign policy decision in history was the humiliation of Russia after the collapse of the Soviet Union. Instead of attempting to expand NATO through Eastern Europe up to the borders of Russia, while watching the people of Dostoevsky and Tolstoy reduced to socioeconomic conditions comparable to those of a Third World country, we ought to have invited the Russians into NATO first and offered them a "Marshall Plan" for economic recovery. Perhaps it is not too late to find a way to right the wrong that fostered the formation of the Shanghai Cooperation Organization. After all, at every moment in the development of Atlantic history, the present historical state of affairs is being nourished by an unhistorical or *untimely* "event" that is on its way — the arrival of "a new people and a new earth."[165]

The maritime colonial alliance forged at Delos became a new kind of empire — one that could potentially conquer the whole world through its oceans, but without subjugating it under a vertically-oriented transcendental order.[166] Deleuze notes that in *The Crisis of European Sciences*,

---

163 Ibid., p. 113.

164 Deleuze, *What is Philosophy?*, pp. 95, 98–99.

165 Ibid., pp. 96, 99, 101, 111.

166 Ibid., p. 88.

Edmund Husserl discusses the fact that all peoples, even the most tribally diverse and socially stratified, tend to identify themselves with a greater identity — for example the "India" that Aryans and Dravidians, Brahmins and Chandalas, all claim as their own. However, no people prior to the Europeans saw the whole world as potentially "European," as in the process of increasing Europeanization — which means something other than the whole world becoming India or China.[167] Their national identities are still insular and dominated by tradition. By contrast, to become ever more "European," or more Greek, is to increasingly approximate the paragon of *humanitas*.[168] "European" is not a national identity — this is why it was ultimately able to subsume the nation-states of Europe in a new sovereign order. The Greeks established the first imperial milieu of immanence, which conquers chiefly by seducing others to become party to its polity and to creatively transform it.[169]

Deleuze speaks of "European man whose privilege it is to constantly 'Europeanize,' as the Greeks 'Greekized,' that is to say to go beyond the limits of other cultures that are preserved as psychosocial types" — which implies that Hellenization is occurring through ideas or archetypes that are not merely psychological types of one particular society[170] — namely, those of Prometheus and Atlas. There is no reason why this process should stop at the continental borders of Europe or North America. Various European peoples who trace their common heritage to Hellas were savages far more foreign to the Greeks than, for example, the Japanese are to the modern West. It is in fact in modern Japan that we meet with the most striking example of Atlas as the world-conquering sovereign of a Promethean civilization. As in the case of Francis Bacon's futuristic elaboration of Plato's folklore, this "Atlantis" is an island in the Pacific Ocean.

---

167   Ibid., pp. 97–98.

168   Ibid., p. 97: "The European can, therefore, regard himself, as the Greek did, as not one psychosocial type among others but Man par excellence, and with much more expansive force and missionary zeal than the Greek."

169   Ibid., p. 87.

170   Ibid., p. 149.

CHAPTER X

KILL A BUDDHA
ON THE WAY

Despite his claim that the cultural crisis brought on by worldwide tech-nological advancement could not be solved by a wholesale adoption of Eastern traditions such as Zen Buddhism, Heidegger engaged in many conversations with Chinese and Japanese scholars throughout his philo-sophical career.[1] His first, and perhaps most significant, encounter with the East took place as early as 1919, eight years before the publication of *Being and Time*. After having attended Heidegger's 1918 lectures, one of his Japanese students, Tomonobu Imamichi, introduced Heidegger to the concept of "being in the world." In *The Book of Tea* (1906), Tomonobu's teacher, Okakura Kakuzo, had used these words to describe an aspect of Zhuangzi's spiritual vision. *The Book of Tea* uses the tea ceremony to ex-plore the *wabi-sabi* aesthetic experience cultivated in Japanese Zen arts and crafts. The early German translation of *The Book of Tea* uses the words *das-in-der-Welt-sein*, which, via Imamichi, found their way into the heart and soul of Heidegger's 1927 *magnum opus*.[2] Interestingly, Heidegger's philosophical career not only begins under Japanese influence, it also ends with it. One of the essays in his last work, *On the Way to Language*, is "A Dialogue on Language" between "a Japanese and an inquirer" who

---

1   Reinhard May, *Heidegger's Hidden Sources: East-Asian Influences on his Work* (Routledge, 1996); Graham Parkes [Editor], *Heidegger and Asian Thought* (Honolulu: University of Hawaii Press, 1992).

2   Reinhard May, *Heidegger's Hidden Sources: East-Asian Influences on his Work* (New York: Routledge, 1996); Imamichi Tomonobu, *Betrachtungen über das Eine* (Tokyo: Tokyo University, 1968).

remain significantly *unnamed*.[3] *The Way* of the title that Heidegger chose to broadly encompass *all* of his final essays appears to be a reference to the *Tao*.

In his 1935 lecture course, entitled *Introduction to Metaphysics*, which is the definitive work of his middle period and where Heidegger makes significant references to Heraclitus, Heidegger illuminates the Greek idea of Nature (up through Aristotle) in very Taoist terms. He translates *phusis* as "the sway" of beings emerging from out of nothingness to flourish as themselves.[4] That this is a reference to "the way" is fairly clear from Heidegger's emphasis of that idea in his unfinished project to undertake a new German translation of the *Tao Te Ching* in collaboration with the Chinese scholar, Paul Shih-yi Hsiao.[5] Heidegger asked Shih-yi Hsiao to write out two lines of Chapter 15 of the *Tao Te Ching* in decorative calligraphy for him, perhaps with the intention of installing it somewhere in his Black Forest cabin. The literal translation of these two lines is, "Who is able to settle the turbid so that it gradually becomes clear? Who is able to stimulate the peaceful so that it gradually comes alive?"

With Hsiao's assistance, Heidegger arrived at his own very original German rendering of these lines: *Wer kann still sein und aus der Stille durch sie auf den Weg bringen (be-wegen) etwas so, daß es zum Erscheinen kommt? Wer vermag es, stillend etwas so ins Sein zu bringen?* (Who can be still and out of the stillness, through it, bring [move] something along The Way so that it becomes manifest? Who is able, through stillness, to bring something into being?)[6] Hsiao eventually withdrew from his collaboration with Heidegger on account of his repeatedly engaging in this kind of creative departure from the text, something he was notorious for also doing in his "translations" of Pre-Socratic Greeks such as Heraclitus. But what is most significant here is that Heidegger inserts the term *den*

3   Parkes, *Heidegger and Asian Thought*, pp. 79, 213–216.

4   Martin Heidegger, *Introduction to Metaphysics* (New Haven: Yale University Press, 2000), pp. 13–19.

5   Parkes, *Heidegger and Asian Thought*, pp. 93–100.

6   Ibid., pp. 100, 103.

Weg or *be-wegen* (The Way, Under*way*) as a reference to the *Tao* that goes unnamed in the original Chinese verse.

In his "Introduction to Heideggerian Existentialism," Leo Strauss makes much of Heidegger's "Eastern" response to the crisis of world-enframing technology in the absence of a genuine global society. Strauss observes that modern technology is forcing the material conditions of a World Society upon us, without a common world culture as its basis. It is the unification of mankind on the basis of the lowest common denominator. This leads to "lonely crowds" suffering from a pervasive sense of alienation and anomie. Furthermore, Strauss recognizes that no genuine culture in the world has ever arisen without a religious basis, or without addressing man's need for something noble and great beyond himself. So the world society, being wrought largely as a consequence of apparently valueless technological forces, is ironically one in need, not merely of a universal ethics, but of one world religion. The world religion must emerge out of the deepest reflection on the crisis of cultural relativism, and on the essence of the technological forces bringing it about:

> [Heidegger] called it the "night of the world." It means indeed, as Marx had predicted, the victory of an ever more completely urbanized, ever more completely technological West over the whole planet — complete leveling and uniformity… unity of the human race on the lowest level, complete emptiness of life… How can there be hope? Fundamentally, because there is something in man which cannot be satisfied by the world society: the desire for the genuine, for the noble, for the great. The desire has expressed itself in man's ideals, but all previous ideals have proved to be related to societies which were not world societies. The old ideals will not enable man to overcome the power, to weaken the power, of technology. We may also say: a world society can be human only if there is a world culture, a culture genuinely uniting all men. But there never has been a high culture without a religious basis: the world society can be human only if all men are genuinely united by a world religion.[7]

7   Leo Strauss, "Introduction to Heideggerian Existentialism" in *The Rebirth of Classical Political Rationalism* (Chicago: University of Chicago Press, 1989), p. 42.

Explicating Heidegger, Strauss explains that in order for it to be possible to *overcome* technology, which is not at all the same as rejecting it, there must be a sphere of thought or contemplation beyond the rationalism developed by the Greeks and forwarded in Western science and technology. This must be an understanding of the world from behind or beneath the will to mathematize all beings with a view to instrumental manipulation of them on demand (*bestand*). It must understand the difference between Being and beings, and that Being is *no-thing* that can be mastered. The *to be* which is always as present at hand is taken by Rationalism as the standard of being — that which really *is*, is *always* present, available, accessible. Instead, Strauss thinks that "a more adequate understanding of being is intimated by the assertion that *to be* means to be elusive or to be a mystery."[8] Strauss claims that "this is the Eastern understanding of Being," and he adds that, "We can hope beyond technological world society, we can hope for a genuine world society, only if we become capable of learning from the East… Heidegger is the only man who has an inkling of the dimensions of the problem of a world society."[9]

In Strauss' view, there is a primordial epoch of Western philosophy before the division between "West" and "East," and it is on the basis of descending once again into its own primordial possibility that Western thought can encounter Eastern spirituality. The great voice of the Greek beginning before the rise of Rationalism is Heraclitus, arguably the Western thinker who Heidegger revered above all others. Strauss is right that Heidegger must have been aware of the affinity between Heraclitus and the early Taoists, and that his pursuit of Pre-Socratic wisdom and his willingness to learn from the East were deeply convergent tracks. There are indeed some striking parallels between the *Fragments* of Heraclitus on the one hand, and the writings attributed to Lao Tzu and Zhuangzi on the other. The so-called "Fragments" of Heraclitus are the remaining bits and pieces of a lost text simply entitled *On Nature*, and overall, the paral-

---

8   Ibid, p. 43.
9   Ibid.

lels between Heraclitus and the early Taoists concern the "dis-covery," or unconcealing disclosure, of Nature as such.

If we descend into the primordial beginnings of Atlantic civilization, we will find that not only are there parallels with the deepest insights of Eastern spirituality, but some of these core insights into the ungraspable are more clearly apprehended by Pre-Socratic Greek sages such as Heraclitus than by their Asian counterparts. Traditional tribal cultures conflate the "ways" of their particular ancestral customs with the "ways" of the seasons as manifested in the growth of trees or the habits of animals, and they anthropomorphically imbue the courses of the stars with constellations of meaning that serve as prototypes for these customs. Both Heraclitus and the early Taoists recognize that Nature is uncreated, and without anything like human intentionality or concern.[10] Another aspect of the parallel between Heraclitus and early Taoism is the idea of *process* in Nature, which cannot be grasped by formal concepts. Both Heraclitus and the early Taoists understand that the primordial process cannot be fixed by concepts because it takes place beyond all definitional opposites, which are not simply complementary but generatively interdependent.[11] The Taoist *Taijitu* symbol for this unity of *Yin* and *Yang* is famous. Fixed names referring to beings undergoing constant change are not only inadequate; they occlude our insight into the dynamic reality of Nature.

However, the parallels to Heraclitus also betray a fundamental divergence from Taoism, and shed some light on why it was the Pre-Socratic Greeks and not the Chinese Taoists who planted the seeds of the natural and political sciences. On the face of it, certain fragments of Heraclitus may seem to be saying the same thing as Lao Tzu and Zhuangzi are saying about the limits of what can be said.[12] There are also fragments wherein

---

10   Compare chapters 5 and 32 of the *Tao Te Ching* to *Fragments* Diels 30 / Kahn XXXVII, Diels 90 / Kahn XL, and Diels102 / Kahn LXVIII.

11   Compare chapter 2 of the *Tao Te Ching* to *Fragments* Diels 8 / Kahn LXXV, Diels 51 / Kahn LXXVIII, Diels 103 / Kahn XCIX, Diels 60 / Kahn CIII, Diels 88 / Kahn XCIII, Diels 67 / Kahn CXXIII, D.64 / CXIX, D.65 / CXX, and D.10 / CXXIV.

12   Compare chapter 8 of *Zhuangzi* to *Fragments* D.1 / I, D. 34 / II, D.52, XCIV, and D.70; LVIII.

Heraclitus condemns scholastic book learning as contrived and out of touch with reality.[13] Yet there are numerous fragments where it becomes clear that Heraclitus' acknowledgement that there is a terminus to rational comprehension and expression, and his condemnation of scholasticism, does not stop him from advocating empirical inquiry into beings in Nature. He is emphatic that genuine knowledge of things unknown is possible if it is tried and tested by direct experience.[14] In striking contrast with the early Taoists, the operations of Nature are his explicit concern.[15] He does have expectations, above all that knowledge will increase by increments, and he acknowledges that it would be frustrating to always be starting from scratch.[16] Heraclitus makes specific observations of natural phenomena.[17] On their basis, he puts forth definite, falsifiable physical theories.[18] His hygienic prescriptions are also informed by a proto-scientific mentality.[19]

The radical empiricism of Heraclitus is not materialist, as was the case with some of the Pre-Socratic physicists. Heraclitus has nothing but contempt for religious dogma and ritual.[20] Yet he is interested in understanding the psyche in non-materialist terms that are also clearly non-religious.[21] Heraclitus speaks of the gods in similarly secular terms as he does of psychic phenomena; they are another race of beings in Nature, perhaps more intelligent and more beautiful than mankind, but not an object of blindly servile reverence.[22] The emphasis on empiricism in

---

13 *Fragments* D.129 / XXV, D.81 / XXVI.

14 *Fragments* D. 17 / IV, D. 55 / XIV, D.101a / XV, D. 35 / IX, D. 123 / X, D. 47 / XI, D. A23 / XII.

15 *Fragments* D.84b / LIII.

16 *Fragments* D.84b / LIII.

17 *Fragments* D.61 / LXX, D.9 / LXXI, D.13 / LXXII, D.A19 / XCV.

18 *Fragments* D.100 / XLII, D.100 / XLIIIA.

19 *Fragments* D.96 / LXXXVIII.

20 *Fragments* D.5 / CXVII.

21 *Fragments* D.113 / XXXI, D.27 / LXXXIV, D.115 / CI, D.98 / CXI, D.7 / CXII, D.A15 / CXIII, D.45 / XXXV, D.92 / XXXIV.

22 *Fragments*, D.82–3 / LVI, D.79 / LVII.

Heraclitus also translates into a radical divergence from Taoism on so-cial and political matters, a divergence that betrays how the early Taoists are not being consistent with their own dis-covery of Nature. Heraclitus recognizes that, in the realm of finite beings, the cold indifference of the cosmos translates into ceaseless conflict.[23] It is in the fragments of *On Nature* that we find the Pre-Socratic pedigree of the Hobbesian *state of nature*, or the Darwinian *evolutionary struggle*. Heraclitus recognizes that something like the *Tao* underlies this conflict. Yet he also understands that this hidden harmony is totally lacking in moral implications and can-not be used as any grounds for pacifism.[24] Fragments counseling against falling prey to violent emotions make it clear that Heraclitus is no blood-lusting warmonger. His views on the necessity of war stem from a concern with the protection of citizens from suffering harm at the whim of those bent on violently conquering the *polis* from without or delivering it over to tyranny from within. The *polis* is ever vulnerable in the face of the up-surge of violence — as an expression of the destructive force at work in the cosmos — and its law must be zealously fought for as a guarantor against chaos.[25] All of this could not be further from the anarchistic, egalitarian pacifism of the Taoist sociopolitical ethic.

The sociopolitical divergence of Heraclitus from the early Taoists is rooted, above all, in their respective views of "human nature." Heraclitus does not believe that there is any "human nature" at all.[26] Without any nat-ural guidepost for moral order, we each cultivate our own-most character, and thereby carve out our own fortune. It is for us to aspire to a greater destiny by choosing the life and (most probably *violent*) death of heroes.[27] Heraclitus upholds the supreme worth of the superior individual.[28] He is a spiritual aristocrat who has nothing but contempt for the leveling of

---

23   *Fragments* D.80 / LXXXII, XVIII.107, D.A22 / LXXXI.
24   *Fragments* D.54 / LXXX, D.53 / LXXXIII, D.43 / CIV.
25   *Fragments* D.44 / LXV.
26   *Fragments* D.78 / LV.
27   *Fragments* D.25 / XCVI.
28   *Fragments* D.49 / LXIII.

personal character that is the hallmark of egalitarian democracy.[29] We see this above all in his ferocious condemnation of his fellow Ephesians for ostracizing Hermodorus, an ally of the Persians whose highly cultivated personal character Heraclitus esteems.[30]

There are passages in *Zhuangzi* that the Western reader is liable to misunderstand as advocating something like an ethic of authenticity that gives priority to the personal experience of individuals. Yet if we look more closely at these passages, we cannot fail to notice that the "inherent nature" which is supposed to be allowed to "follow its course freely" is not a reference to the individuated character of each, but a "nature endowed by heaven" or "the light of heaven within" everyman.[31] Zhuangzi is totally unambiguous in his identification of the true "self" with the nature of human beings as predetermined by cosmic order; the little "self" of individual character must be forgotten, since it obstructs this true self that all people share in common.[32]

The sage is only able to so readily transform others and bring about harmony amongst them because they already have latent within themselves the "true ideas" that he puts forth.[33] His bringing "things which disagree to an agreement" is not a constructive process of consensus-building that requires creative adaptation on the part of various interested parties. It is an expression of his acting in accord with a dialectical process inherent to the cosmos.[34] This teleological process leads to the *perfection of mankind*, an ideal of completion that cannot be maintained other than on the basis of ascribing a fixed *species-character* to man.[35] In fact, one can

---

29   *Fragments* D.104 / LIX.
30   *Fragments* D.121 / LXIV.
31   *Zhuangzi* 8; 29.
32   *Zhuangzi* 13; 10.
33   *Zhuangzi* 25.
34   *Zhuangzi* 2; 12.
35   *Zhuangzi* 21; 12.

allegedly do this best by doing nothing at all. Non-action (*wuwei*) is the highest ideal of Taoism.[36]

At times, Zhuangzi pays a lot of attention to qualitative differences amongst things, recognizing that "the uses of implements [tools] are different" and "the natures of creatures are different."[37] Unfortunately, despite a few comments that suggest that our insight into the *Tao* is occluded so long as we remain attached to things and think and speak in terms of them, Zhuangzi ultimately lumps the human being together with tools and creatures as a — rather insignificant — *thing* amongst *things* that is as defined by an inherent nature of its own as they are.[38] The pre-civilized anarchism of the sagacious Taoist statesman is a swine-herder's ethic; it presumes that men are largely like sheep. The early Taoists postulate a fantastically romanticized *state of nature*. This departs as much from their *own* discovery of the "heartlessness" of Nature (which they share with Heraclitus) as it does from the more sober assessments of Hobbes or even Darwin.

Unlike Rousseau — who at least recognized that his "noble savage" was basically pre-human — the early Taoists believe that it is both possible and wise to revert to this idyllic state. As we saw above, the individual need not be sacrificed to the general will of the majority. Taoist "democracy" (read *anarchy*) is legitimated only by spontaneous and unanimous consensus. In stark contrast to the pacified, stateless high-tech utopias advocated by Leftists within the context of our Atlantic civilization, the kind of 'world peace' that early Taoists advocate is regressively *pre-civilized* rather than progressively *cosmopolitan*; it is predicated on maintaining an idealized conception of the most pitifully rural peasant life. We see this in Chapter 80 of the *Tao Te Ching*, where Lao Tzu claims that it would be an ideal state of affairs if people lived out the entirety of their lives in small states as near to each other as little villages, so that they could hear the dogs and

---

36   *Zhuangzi* 11; 12; 18; 17.

37   *Zhuangzi* 17; 2.

38   *Zhuangzi* 17; 19.

chickens of the next village over, without ever visiting people of another state.[39] The people of any state would be content with whatever traditional customs they each had, and they would abandon technologies and regress to the most primitive techniques, such as the use of knots for counting. What a striking contrast to the ethos of modern Japan.

Within the historical current of Asian spirituality that would incorporate many elements of the early Taoism reviewed above into the type of Buddhism that became the state religion of Japan, the romantically naturalistic idea of an "inherent nature" in harmony with the *Tao* was transformed through its encounter with the Buddhist insight into the inherent emptiness of all phenomena, including the "self." This took place in a social context that also forced Taoist pacifism to turn into its opposite: world-conquering Japanese militarism. This inversion is not a perverse accident of history, but a predictable outcome of real-world political pressures and the weight of time-honored tradition acting on the dangerous political naïveté uncovered above in Lao Tzu and Zhuangzi.

When Bodhidharma brought Buddhism from India to China in the seventh century CE, he was given shelter by a Shao-Lin monastery originally established by Taoists.[40] Unlike Indian Buddhists, who led a mendicant life, the monks there engaged in all manner of crafts and work that reflected the down-to-earth Taoist spirit. Bodhidharma, maverick that he was, embraced this ethic, and taught his students to get their hands dirty while grappling with the Dharma. Gardening, cooking, and cleaning latrines could be helpful in steadying the mind and humbling the ego. Bodhidharma and his followers also took to heart the Taoist emphasis on spontaneous, direct experience of the ineffable, and antipathy to critical scholarship or intellectual debate. Complex, theory-laden forms of meditation that characterized monastic life in India were replaced with *zazen*, and the interpretive study of canonical sutras was deemphasized in favor of the *koan*. The punch line of the most famous of these reads, "If you

---

39   *Tao Te Ching*, Chapter 80.

40   Heinrich Dumoulin, *Zen Buddhism: A History, Volume 1: India and China* (New York: MacMillan Publishing Company, 1988), p. 92.

meet the Buddha, kill him!"[41] Finally, the naturalistic Taoist aesthetic of the "uncarved block" brought Buddhism back to the rejection of artistic imagery and ornate architectural design that early orthodox Buddhism had preached, but that had been abandoned by Indian Buddhists under the cultural influence of the Greek colonial regime established by Alexander the Great.

This new *Chan* Buddhism spread eastwards, throughout China, but was never able to unseat Confucian orthodoxy on a mass scale, or even to supplant the Taoist religion of the dissenting minority which had so deeply influenced it.[42] It is only once *Chan* reached the relatively isolated island of Japan that, within a geographically-bounded arena, it gained ground over the folk religion of the natives and defined the spiritual life of an emergent nation. Then came the inevitable question of *Chan's* relevance to political administration, and to the preservation of a state through warfare.

Buddhism was a thoroughly apolitical religion. According to Gotama Buddha, the will to power is rooted in perceptual and cognitive distortions: "Whatever suffering such a person, overpowered by greed, hatred, and delusion, his thoughts controlled by them, inflicts under false pretexts upon another — by killing, imprisonment, confiscation of property, false accusations, or expulsion — being prompted in this by the thought, 'I have power and I want power,' all this is unwholesome too."[43] In Siddhartha Gotama's view, political injustice and violence on a social scale is a projection or reflection of the spiritual discord within each of us. Meaningful and lasting sociopolitical change can only be brought about on an individual level, through the inner transformation of those who constitute a given society.[44] Although wars and revolutions appear to have various historical causes that differ from place to place and in one era or another, all of these are ultimately reducible to the greed and hatred within any one

---

41   Ibid., p. 11.

42   Ibid., pp. 266–267.

43   Bodhi, *In the Buddha's Words: An Anthology of Discourses from the Pali Canon*, pp. 36–37.

44   Ibid., pp. 23–24.

of those participating in the conflict; the Buddha takes these underlying causes of conflict to be basic and unchanging.[45] As Gotama explains to one of his chief disciples:

> Thus, Ananda, in dependence upon feeling there is craving; in dependence upon craving there is pursuit; in dependence upon pursuit there is gain; in dependence upon gain there is decision-making; in dependence upon decision-making there is desire and lust; in dependence upon desire and lust there is attachment; in dependence upon attachment there is possessiveness; in dependence upon possessiveness there is defensiveness; and because of defensiveness, various evil unwholesome things originate — the taking up of clubs and weapons, conflicts, quarrels, and disputes, insults, slander, and falsehood.[46]

To view sociopolitical decision-making as inextricable from a chain of psychological delusion that begins in craving and ends with the violent and oppressive indulgence of the lust for power seems to preclude the possibility that sovereign power can be used to secure a greater measure of social justice.

To be fair, although Siddhartha thinks that the lust for power endemic to political leadership is a massive delusion that is not characteristic of a person seeking enlightenment, there are better and worse sovereigns, and Gotama is not above giving political advice geared toward the establishment of a state that is more conducive to the flourishing of the Dharma. In the *Mahaparinirvana Sutra*, there is a record of how King Ajatasattu, the ruler of Magadha, sent his prime minister to ask Siddhartha whether he had a chance in his bid to conquer the neighboring Vajjian tribal confederacy.[47] Gotama's response essentially asserts that only societies in decline can be successfully conquered, and he elaborates on the conditions necessary in a society to avoid decline, conditions which he thinks that the Vajjian society meets. In other words, while a short-term military

---

45   Ibid., p. 23.
46   Ibid., p. 36.
47   Ibid., p. 113.

campaign against them might be successful, their social fabric is strong enough to resist occupation by the Magadhans.[48]

The ideal monarch or ruler (of a republican tribal confederacy) should not busy himself with conquering others. Rather, the "wheel-turning monarch" (*raja chakkravartti*) who becomes a protector of the Dharma rules his realm in accordance with the best ethical standards possible in the political sphere (*dhammiko dhammaraja*) with a view toward leading the world by example, and eventually unifying it under a reign of universal justice and prosperity.[49] One key example of the conduct of such a ruler is that when faced with an increase of crime, he does not enact more draconian punishments, but rather more earnestly strives to improve the economic conditions of the majority of his subjects. Gotama sees poverty and oppressive hunger and need as the preeminent source of violent and immoral behavior such as theft and killing.[50] The righteous ruler will decrease crime by increasing the socioeconomic welfare of his subjects so as to eliminate poverty, the breeding ground of criminality.[51] Everyone should have the opportunity to earn an honest livelihood through hard work in a trade that is not immoral.[52] Coupled with this "righteous wealth righteously gained" by hard workers is the duty of the wealthy to be generous to the less fortunate, which is, practically speaking, also in their interests insofar as it provides them increased security through a decrease in crime.[53] The benevolent ruler is concerned even with the welfare of animals within his realm.[54]

Such a view of benevolent kingship, of all political problems as socioeconomic ones, and of conquest as attendant only to cultural decline, is essentially as politically naïve as the failure to grasp the nature of sovereign

---

48   Ibid., pp. 113–114.
49   Ibid., p. 108.
50   Ibid., p. 111.
51   Ibid., p. 114.
52   Ibid.
53   Ibid., p. 111.
54   Ibid., p. 114.

power on the part of Lao Tzu and Zhuangzi. To give just one salient coun-
terexample: the cultural cradle and heartland of Mahayana Buddhism was
the Eastern Persian Empire and Northern India (the lands stretching from
contemporary Tajikistan, Uzbekistan, and Afghanistan through Pakistan
and further south), and its arts and literature were flourishing until the
area was subjected to the "idol smashing" (*bot-* or *bodh-shekan*) Islamic
conquest. The colossal Buddhas of Bamiyan, for example, were among
many others badly mutilated by early Muslim conquistadors, before
they were finally pulverized to dust by the Taliban in 2001. The relatively
pacifistic culture of the predominately Buddhist population of this area no
doubt facilitated the destruction of its artistically and socioeconomically
vibrant world by militant conquerors whose will has prevailed there to
this day.

It is true that, in the centuries before this catastrophe that uprooted
Buddhism in the land of its birth, King Ashoka reigned very compas-
sionately in accordance with the ideal of the "wheel-turning monarch."
However, we cannot lose sight of the fact that his status as a successful
Indian king was gained through the same merciless warfare that caused
Ashoka such bitter remorse that he embraced the Dharma in repent-
ance — *after* his throne was secure. Gotama Buddha's sociopolitical advice
provides as little concrete guidance to a serious statesman faced with grim
facts on the ground as the idyllic anarchism of Lao Tzu and Zhuangzi. By
contrast with Heraclitus, who shares so much of their metaphysics, they
are blissfully oblivious to the social challenges of holding a state together
from within, and to securing it against invaders from without. Unlike
Aristotle, who set up a political science think-tank to study and improve
constitutions, or Plato, whose scathing critique of the traditional values
of his society was matched with numerous inquiries into the nature of a
just society (not only in the utopian *Republic*, but also in the more realist
Statesman and the *Laws*), neither the early Buddhists nor the Taoists had
any positive political vision. Thus, the *Chan* hybrid that arrived in Japan
was totally lacking in the kind of serious political thought and inquiry

into social justice that we see in Greek philosophy, and so this vacuum was filled with the knightly ethic of Japanese feudalism. The latter was in turn imbued with a compelling metaphysical authority.

The stopgap against this for the early Taoists was the idea of an idyllic "inherent nature" of all things and creatures, including human beings. This was deconstructed in *Chan* by the Buddhist metaphysical understanding of how all beings lack any inherent existence. In Gotama's exposition of the Dharma, one of the deepest and most difficult insights leading to the perfection of wisdom (*prajnaparamitta*) is the understanding that the self is an illusory phenomenon conditioned by the appropriation of things constituted by the five aggregates of form — feeling, perception, volitional formations, and consciousness — as well as the identification with any number of them.[55] Gotama encapsulates this delusion in the following terms: "This is mine, this I am, this is my self" (*etam mama, eso 'ham asmi, eso me attâ*).[56] In this formulation, the "This is mine" signifies the craving (*tanha*) that motivates this delusion, while the "This is my self" and "This I am" respectively represent two different types of identification, a clinging to rationalizing views (*ditthi*) that theoretically identify the self with some aggregate — whether a material body or an immaterial soul, or some combination thereof — and a more deep-seated egotistical conceit (*mana*) that persists even when one has intellectually dispelled the wrong views of a personal identity (*sakkayaditthi*).[57] The full understanding of non-self (*annata, anatman*) is considered the final stage in the perfection of wisdom, since even those who crave only the realm of forms and have been liberated from karmic rebirth in the realm of the senses continue to suffer from egotistical conceit pertaining to what they still, at least subconsciously, see as *their* spiritual attainment, despite intellectually knowing that the six sense bases (*phassana*) are as empty as the five aggregates (*skhandas*) that condition consciousness, and so their seeming identity

---

55   Ibid., pp. 307–308.
56   Ibid., p. 308.
57   Ibid.

as a conscious self is illusory.[58] On account of this persisting, imperious sense of the "I" as a reality, they are reborn in the subtler form or formless realms rather than attaining *nirvana*.[59]

The understanding of non-self is also central to the Buddha's teaching of "dependent origination." Siddhartha accords such an importance to dependent origination that he even suggests that a true understanding of it is tantamount to a comprehension of the whole of the Dharma.[60] The insight into dependent origination is the foremost accomplishment of a Buddha.[61] Basically, it is an account of how experienced phenomena can arise, and how actions can have consequences, even though no thing — including the self — has any essential being or inherent nature.[62] The twelve chain-link account of dependent origination, which is the most common form for its exposition, stretches across three lifetimes.[63] Its initial phases, such as ignorance, volitional formations, and consciousness, are meant to address the factors from out of which one's present life was formed, whereas the six sense bases — contact, feeling, craving, and clinging — are pertinent to how one's future life is woven from out of one's present intentions and actions, culminating in rebirth, aging, and death.

Dependent origination is referred to as a "teaching by the middle" (*majjhena tathagato dhammam deseti*), or the Middle Way, because it does not err in one of two directions.[64] One of these is the view of annihilationism (*ucchedavada*) or nonexistence (*vibhavaditthi*).[65] As Siddhartha puts it: "Now some are troubled, ashamed, and disgusted by this very same existence and they rejoice in nonexistence, saying, 'In as much as this self, good sirs, is annihilated and destroyed with the breakup of the body and

---

58   Ibid., pp. 309, 310–311.
59   Ibid., pp. 380–381.
60   Ibid., p. 312.
61   Ibid., p. 313.
62   Ibid., p. 314.
63   Ibid., p. 314.
64   Ibid., p. 315.
65   Ibid., p. 189.

does not exist after death, this is peaceful, this is excellent, this is just so!' Thus, monks, do some overreach."[66] Ironically, the nihilistic wish for it to be true that there is total annihilation upon bodily death is often bound up with a desperate and even depraved clinging to the same, seemingly meaningless, and consequently loathsome, existence.[67] As we saw in the second chapter, the Marquis de Sade epitomizes such vacillation. On the opposite extreme, there are people who cling to existence believing that it can be eternal; such a wrong view usually involves identifying themselves with an imperishable self and believing that there is an all-powerful God that created this soul and can see to its everlasting welfare. This is known as the view of eternalism (*sassatavada*), or simply as the view of existence (*bhavaditthi*) — in other words, absolute existence or Being as such.[68] Unlike the former view, which presumably would be immediately dispelled upon bodily death, this delusion is one that gods can also suffer from: "Devas and human beings delight in existence, are delighted with existence, rejoice in existence. When the Dhamma is taught to them for the cessation of existence, their minds do not enter into it, acquire confidence in it, settle upon it, or resolve upon it. Thus, monks, do some hold back."[69] Siddhartha thinks that disenchantment and dispassion is the proper attitude towards a world that is coming to be, a world of Becoming, rather than one identifiable with Being or reducible to Nothingness.[70]

Interestingly, the godly and human delusion of eternal existence can often facilitate the mental focus required to attain profoundly blissful meditative states (by focusing the mind single-pointedly on an idea such as "God," or divine union with the inner core of one's "true self"), and one who experiences such states in turn runs the risk of misinterpreting them to be a validation of an ultimately transcendent and eternal divine

---

66 Ibid., p. 215.
67 Ibid., p. 190.
68 Ibid., p. 189.
69 Ibid., p. 215.
70 Ibid., p. 216.

reality that could become a secure dwelling for an imperishable self.[71] Recognizing the thoroughly conditioned nature of all phenomena and their fundamentally inter-dependent genesis dispels the illusion that any being has an essence eternally complete in itself, one that is not always already deferred to those from which it differs as it comes into its own for a time and then disintegrates. Nevertheless, in such a view, beings do have a relative stability and autonomy that allows for responsible agency.[72]

The deconstructed inherent nature of Taoism was not replaced by the Buddhist morality of compassion, because in *Chan*, the Buddhist moral code had in turn been deconstructed by the Taoist rejection of morality in favor of spontaneous natural virtue (something akin to the uncultivated ethic of Rousseau's "noble savage"). Consequently, certain Taoist precepts took on a different meaning than they had within a worldview of inherent natures essentially predisposed towards harmony. Once the Taoist idea of an inherent human nature is deconstructed by the doctrine of non-self, what determines the unchanging character of the steadfast man who dispassionately adapts to the necessities of his present circumstances? The views of the *volk*, or common folk. Remember how early Taoists presumed that a sage could somehow bring peace and balance to a law-breaking, disruptive person by becoming of one mind with him and indulging him. This presumes a naïve faith in an inherent human nature. That faith was rightly deconstructed by an encounter with the Buddhist metaphysics of abyssal nothingness. Thus, a Taoist teaching originally aimed at critiquing Confucian orthodoxy ended up as a vehicle for the negation of individuality in a submissive will to loyally defend the values of *the people*.

This encapsulates my speculation on the psychological dynamics at work in the development of Japanese *Zen*. The concrete political conditions that provoked it began as early as the wars between the Medieval shogunates. Militant adherents of Japan's native Shinto religion initially viewed Buddhism as a foreign threat to be rooted out, and so Zen masters

---

71   Ibid., p. 190.

72   Ibid., pp. 315–316.

secured protection for their monasteries by offering meditation training tailored at enhancing their concentration and willpower to the warriors who were in the service of the local feudal lord.[73] These psychophysical disciplines eventually coalesced into *bushido*, the subject of a new genre of Zen literature. The Indian Buddhist metaphor of the Bodhisattva Manjushri's sword that cuts through illusion received a literal reinterpretation in Bushido treatises, such as *The Unfettered Mind* by Rinzai Zen master Takuan Soho (1573–1645) and *The Book of Five Rings* by the samurai warrior Miyamoto Musashi (1584–1645).[74] By the end of the Tokugawa era (1868), not only had Buddhism become the state religion of Japan, the Zen Buddhist "priesthood" had become an extension of the feudal government and an indispensable provider of training to the law-enforcing Samurai class.

So it should be no surprise that, in the 1930s and '40s, the two major schools of Japanese Zen, the Soto and the Rinzai, competed with each other in offering material support to the Japanese war effort. This was not limited to monastic activities such as copying out *sutras* (some written out in blood) with special dedications to the war effort, praying for "continuing victory in the holy war," and renaming Kanzeon (Chinese *Kuan Yin*, Indian *Avalokiteshvara*), the Bodhisattva of Compassion, the "Kanzeon Shogun."[75] It also included raising funds for the production of five fighter planes (two dedicated by the Soto, three by the Rinzai).[76] In *Zen at War*, a landmark study that dynamites the idea that "there has never been a Buddhist war," Brian Victoria demonstrates that the most revered Zen masters of the late nineteenth and early twentieth century were ferocious warmongers who wholeheartedly supported the aggressive imperial expansion that culminated in the atrocities committed by Japanese soldiers

---

73   Heinrich Dumoulin, *Zen Buddhism: A History, Volume 2: Japan* (New York: MacMillan Publishing Company, 1990), p. 43.

74   Miyamoto Musashi, *The Book of Five Rings* (Kodansha International, 2002).

75   Brian Victoria, *Zen at War* (New York: Weatherhill, 1997), p. 142.

76   Ibid., pp. 142–143.

during the Second World War.[77] What Victoria, as a committed Buddhist, fails to realize, is that this is no "perversion" of Buddhism; its metaphysical basis was prepared over the course of centuries as Taoist and Buddhist "sages" neglected to take the question of sociopolitical justice seriously. When the Chinese city of Nanking fell to the advancing Japanese occupiers, they proceeded to kill more civilians than later died in Hiroshima and Nagasaki combined, and subjected hundreds of thousands more to rape, torture, and mutilation. Amidst the carnage, lieutenants relished providing their troops with instructive demonstrations in how to properly sever heads in accordance with the established etiquette of the Zen *art* of swordsmanship. At the very same time, in 1937, D. T. Suzuki was finishing *Zen and Japanese Culture*, a book popular with Western disciples of Zen, in which he writes:

> ...the art of swordsmanship distinguishes between the sword that kills and the sword that gives life. The one that is used by a technician cannot go any further than killing... The case is altogether different with the one who is compelled to lift the sword. For it is really not he but the sword itself that does the killing. He had no desire to harm anybody, but the enemy appears and makes himself a victim. It is as though the sword automatically performs its function of justice, which is the function of mercy... the swordsman turns into an artist of the first grade, engaged in producing a work of genuine originality.[78]

Although the thinkers of the Kyoto School of Philosophy were in favor of the war and have been collectively referred to as the "philosophers of nothingness," some of them had a more constructive vision of how the Buddhist understanding of the void could complement the techno-scientific thinking of the West in order to bring about a new global civilization. Key figures among them, such as Nishida Kitaro, were students of Heidegger as early as the 1920s, and like Heidegger, they saw the World War as the means to bring about a global culture that would ground techno-scientific development in a spirituality transcending insular and traditional values.

---

77 Ibid., *Zen At War*.

78 D. T. Suzuki, *Zen and Japanese Culture* (Princeton University Press, 1959).

Remember that the Indian caste system that Nietzsche so admired, and that was based on regimented and hierarchically stratified class divisions, was a function of the Aryan conquest of the native Dravidian population of India. This origin is reflected in the Sanskrit name for the "caste" of the caste system, *varna*, which literally means "color," that it may once have been a color-coding system. The four classes were: the *Brahmins* — the Vedic priests or scholars (including those who engaged in various proto-scientific practices); the *Kshatriyas* — the caste of knightly warriors, including feudal lords who were chief amongst them; the *Vaishyas* — the business class, including both farmers and various types of merchants; and the *Shudras* — menial laborers, usually involved in undignified or hard labor. Finally, there were also "outcaste untouchables" who were relegated to an inhumanly low status.[79] "Prince" Siddhartha Gotama belonged to the *Kshatriya* class. The Buddha was a light-skinned, blue-eyed Aryan whose father was a feudal lord, and who was expected to become a knight. In his late writings, Nishida Kitaro explains how "Indian culture," from which Japan inherited Buddhism (including the symbol of the swastika that is ubiquitous in Japanese temples), and which shares the Aryan, or "Indo-European," ethnic roots of European culture, "has evolved as an opposite pole to modern European culture... [and] may thereby be able to contribute to a global modern culture from its own vantage point."[80] What is the "global modern culture" that Nishida envisions, and in what way can it be conceived of as an Aryan world order?

He certainly views it as having a religious basis, and he thinks that the World War during which he is writing is a means of achieving it: "And does not the spirit of modern times seek a religion of infinite compassion rather than that of the Lord of ten thousand hosts? It demands reflection in the spirit of Buddhist compassion. This is the spirit which says that the present world war must be for the sake of negating world wars, for the

---

79 Bodhi, *In the Buddha's Words*, p. 112.

80 Nishida Kitaro, *Last Writings: Nothingness and the Religious Worldview* (Honolulu: University of Hawaii Press, 1993), p. 94.

sake of eternal peace."[81] In every true religion, the divine is an absolute love that embraces its opposite, to the extent of even becoming Satan, and this is the meaning of the concept of *upaya*, or shrewdly bringing to bear "skillful means" in Mahayana Buddhism so that "the miracles" of "this world may be said to be... the Buddha's expedient means."[82] This all-embracing character of the divine, as that which encompasses what one would take to be its opposite, "is the basic reason why we are beings who can be compassionate to others and who can experience the compassion of others. Compassion always signifies that opposites are one in the dynamic reciprocity of their own contradictory identity."[83]

A God who is the Lord (*Dominus*) in the sense of an ultimately transcendent substance cannot be a truly creative God.[84] Creation *ex nihilo* would be both arbitrary and superfluous; it must be out of love that God or Buddha creatively manifests the world from out of its own self-negation.[85] Nishida believes that the school of *Prajnaparamita* thought in Mahayana Buddhism, established by Nagarjuna, has a deeper and more adequate understanding of this than pantheistic Western thinkers of dialectical synthesis, such as the Hegelians, who remain within the realm of reason even in their negative theologies.[86] Nishida nevertheless refers to his ontology of the absolute's self-expression and transformation as "Trinitarian," and compares it to Neo-Platonic thought.[87]

However, Neo-Platonism, and all pagan Western thought, falls short insofar as it fails to see Satan, or "absolute evil," as an aspect of God.[88] He adds, "The absolute God must include absolute negation within himself, and must be the God who descends into ultimate evil. The highest form

---

81 Ibid., p. 103.
82 Ibid., p. 100.
83 Ibid., p. 107.
84 Ibid., p. 71.
85 Ibid., pp. 70–71.
86 Ibid., p. 70.
87 Ibid., p. 74.
88 Ibid.

must be one that transforms the lowest matter into itself. Absolute *agape* must reach even to the absolutely evil man. This is again the paradox of God: God is hidden even within the heart of the absolutely evil man. A God who merely judges the good and the bad is not truly absolute."[89] In passages such as these, we see that *Shunyata* (in Sanskrit, *Mu* in Japanese) is not the Nothing of Descartes at all. Quite to the contrary of serving as an entirely distinct polar opposite of a Perfect Being that would exonerate the latter from being the source of any imperfection, this Nothingness is an inner dynamic tension within Being — as expressed in the spectral incompleteness and interdependent interpenetration of all beings. Dependent origination is the Buddhist ontology of the spectral, or rather the spectral deconstruction of ontological thinking.

The battle between God and Nothingness in the heart of man, the "dynamic equilibrium" between "is" and "is not," may be paradoxical, but it is also the existential "ground" of the volitional person.[90] "Radical evil" lies ineradicably at the root of our freedom.[91] We are always already "both satanic and divine."[92] Nishida claims that the Buddha — or any other conception of divinity — outside of one's own existential potentiality is not the true Buddha:

> Only in this existential experience of religious remorse does the self encounter what Rudolf Otto calls the numinous. Subjectively speaking, the encounter is a deep reflection upon the existential depths of the self itself; and as the Buddhists say, it means to see our essential nature, to see the true self. In Buddhism, this seeing means, not to see Buddha objectively outside, but to see into the bottomless depths of one's own soul. If we see God externally, it is merely magic. ... Illusion is the fountainhead of all evil. Illusion arises when we conceive of the objectified self as the true self. The source of illusion is in seeing the self in terms of object logic. It is for this reason that Mahayana Buddhism says that we are saved through enlightenment. But this enlightenment is generally misunder-

---

89   Ibid., p. 75.
90   Ibid.
91   Ibid., p. 76.
92   Ibid.

stood. For it does not mean to see anything objectively... It is rather an ultimate seeing of the bottomless nothingness of the self that is simultaneously a seeing of the fountainhead of sin and evil.[93]

In this Zen injunction to kill any conception of a Buddha outside one-self, Nishida does not deny the cycle of birth and death, or *samsara*, as an empirical or phenomenological fact. He simply insists that the truly religious consciousness is one that has recognized the identity of *samsara* and *nirvana*. On his terms, and according to the sages of the esoteric Buddhist tradition, *nirvana* does not mean to attain some state distinct from and after *samsara*, but to recognize that in every moment of the cycle of reincarnation, the perfection beyond the impurity of *karma* is already present.[94] This does not mean that the self "transcends its own historical actuality — it does not transcend its own karma — but rather that it realizes the bottomless bottom of its own karma."[95]

This relatively late Mahayanist view is anathema to the teaching of Siddhartha Gotama and the early Indian Buddhism founded upon it. According to the Buddha Dharma, just as there are physical, biological, and psychological laws operative in the cosmos, there is also an ethical law. The law of *karma* is a lawful relationship between one's actions, in-cluding verbal and unspoken mental acts that express one's volition (*cet-ana*), and both the realm within which one is reborn as well as the condi-tions of life that one experiences within this realm.[96] The ethical quality of one's volition is supposed to resonate with the qualitative character of a certain realm of existence, and to tune into this realm, as it were, as a consequence of being on the same wavelength.[97] Within these more gen-eral parameters, what one experiences within a given realm of existence is conditioned by one's actions both within the present life and in past

---

93   Ibid., pp. 77, 79–81.
94   Ibid., pp. 87–88.
95   Ibid., p. 90.
96   Bodhi, *In the Buddha's Words*, pp. 145–146.
97   Ibid., p. 148.

lives.[98] The fundamental presupposition here is that even if an action or intention does not appear to bear fruit (*phala*) presently, it reverberates in ways that one may remain unconscious of until it finally yields some tangible results (*vipaka*) — possibly later in one's present life, but perhaps not until a future life.[99]

While psychological research in the wake of the spectral revolution in Science might validate certain classes of phenomena associated with Buddhism as genuine natural phenomena, it is likely to reveal significant Buddhist misunderstandings of these very same phenomena, and to profoundly challenge Buddhist codes of ethics. This is the case with the reincarnation research of the late Dr. Ian Stevenson, which was introduced in Chapter 2. What would disturb Buddhists most about Stevenson's apparent validation of one of the central tenants of their religion is that the ethical idea of *karma* is untenable in light of his scientific research into the reality of reincarnation as a natural phenomenon. What Stevenson found is that a person's strong psychic impression of localized bodily injury at the time of a violent death or terrible accident could affect fetal development of the body that will be subsequently inhabited by that person, producing a birthmark or birth defect corresponding to the site of injury, and even the shape or type of injury.[100] In other words, there are many cases of the following type: an innocent person is attacked and has his arm hacked off by a murderer, and while the victim is reborn with that arm badly deformed, the murderer not only gets away scot free in his present incarnation, he also does not suffer any apparent ill effects in his subsequent incarnation.

Nirvana is the goal of the path, the aim of the Buddha Dharma. Yet, it is the most obscure element of Gotama's teachings and, unlike karma, meditation, and the moral disciplines, it is one of the ideas most unique to his understanding of the Dharma as compared to the various pre-Buddhist forms of Sanatana Dharma (a.k.a., Hinduism). It is referred to at times as

---

98   Ibid., p. 145.

99   Ibid., p. 146.

100 Ian Stevenson, *Reincarnation and Biology*, 2 Volumes.

an element or a state, a state of supreme bliss, and yet it is supposed to be beyond any conditioned state, whether painful or even pleasurable.[101] At times, Siddhartha discusses *nirvana* as if it were attainable amidst the present life, and at other times it seems like a total annihilation that a perfectly enlightened person can pass into upon the disintegration of what will be his final body.[102] This raises the question: what is the difference between this annihilation and the so-called "annihilationism" that is one of the wrong views most destructive to an ethical life? Is the Buddha Dharma, in its original form, essentially a grand doctrine of suicide? Does it opt out of actual suicide because it will not do any good, since the underlying tendencies of the psyche are still active and will reorganize around a new physical aggregate, so that suicide can only be truly successful by unbinding the threads of this psyche — by disintegrating the soul?

Nirvana means "snuffing out" or "blowing out," as in putting out a flame or fire.[103] Orthodox Buddhists of the Theravada tradition most directly descended from the teachings of Gotama suggest that the answer to the perplexing question as to who attains *nirvana* and where he attains it, namely as to whether a Buddha or arahant *exists in nirvana* after death or is annihilated and passes into nothingness, can be simply answered by saying that the perfectly enlightened person simply "goes out," or is "put out."[104] He was a flame burning with the fire of life, but this fire of ceaseless suffering has been put out. *Phew!* Can there be a more pessimistic and nihilistic view of life? At least the man who actually commits suicide affirms a life that would be worth living in comparison to his own, which he judges intolerable only as compared to some ideal. He would also be affirming a sense of history wherein the future can be meaningfully different from any past epoch, an understanding of time that warrants a historical struggle — even if not one that he can personally bear to participate in

101   Bodhi, *In the Buddha's Words*, p. 320.

102   Ibid., p. 318.

103   Ibid., p. 320.

104   Ibid., p. 319.

here and now. It is above all in Japan where early Buddhist nihilism gave way to the world-historical ethos of the fiery forge.

Nishida draws a distinction between physical, biological, and historical life. The teleological irreversibility of time in the course of organic development is key to his distinction between the first two. Whereas the world of biological life forms remains partially spatial and material, in the human world, time negates space and the spatialized chronological "time" relevant to inorganic physics.[105] As Nishida puts it, "We can even say that there is no death for a merely biological being. For death entails that a self enter into eternal nothingness. It is because a self enters into eternal nothingness that it is historically irrepeatable, unique, and individual."[106] Only in the face of this "eternal death" *qua* nothingness is genuine individuation possible, and only the real individual becomes agitated by the religious question.[107] A being who carries out its moral duty for duty's sake, in other words out of adherence to what Kant frames as the categorical imperative, would have no individuality; religion can have no meaning for such an abstract subject without any concrete will.[108] Groundless nothingness (*Shunyata*) is the unstable and ghostly horizon of one's finite existence, and existential awareness of this ultimate and inescapable negation of one's self is not a merely noetic reflection.[109]

Nishida approvingly attributes to Fyodor Dostoevsky the "standpoint of freedom" which holds that "[t]here is nothing at all that determines the self at the very ground of the self."[110] From the vantage point of his own time, Nishida sees the spirit of Dostoevsky as the closest point of contact between Japanese spirituality and the West. He admonishes the Japanese for having remained too insular, and says that the spiritual sense for the ordinary and everyday that Japan shares with Dostoevsky has hitherto

---

105   Ibid., p. 57.
106   Ibid., p. 77.
107   Ibid., p. 67, 77.
108   Ibid., p. 72.
109   Ibid., p. 67.
110   Ibid., p. 110.

been too superficial. "At this juncture," he says, "it must come to possess an acute Dostoievskian spirit in an eschatological sense, as the Japanese spirit participating in world history." Nishida hopes that "in this way," the hybridized Japanese civilization "can become a point of departure for a new global culture."[111] Nishida sees the way that the Yahweh "folk religion of the Jewish race" evolved into a world religion, and one that served as the basis for a Medieval European culture that he clearly admires, as a model for a potential globalizing evolution of Japanese tradition.[112] The "scientific" secularization characteristic of modern Western civilization, wherein "old worlds lose their specific traditions," is a necessary phase in the formation of "a global humanity."[113] It is, in a dialectical sense, a negatively determinative moment in "the world's transformation."[114] However, it must be recognized that "science is also a form of culture," and that "the world of science may also be said to be religious."[115] The failure to recognize this has been chiefly responsible for the fact that "such a thing as the decline and fall of the West has been proclaimed."[116]

Dostoevsky diagnosed the causes of this decline perspicaciously in *Notes from Underground* (1864), which is widely considered the first existentialist novel.[117] It is a response to the situation of the Cartesian ego, which, as I explained in Chapter 3, is sadistically enmeshed in murderous machinery over which he takes himself to have no control. The underground man is crippled by his hyperconsciousness. He is unlike the common man of action insofar as he can trace all effects back to ever-receding causes such that, for example, he is incapable of mistaking vengeance for justice, since the would-be target of a retributive act is not *ultimately* responsible for it. He is also unlike people who are cruel only out of stupid-

---

111   Ibid., p. 112.
112   Ibid., pp. 116–117.
113   Ibid., p. 117.
114   Ibid.
115   Ibid., p. 118.
116   Ibid., p. 119.
117   Fyodor Dostoevsky, *Notes from Underground* (New York: E. P. Dutton & Co., 1991).

ity, because he cannot even stop at the egoistic passions that they take to be primary causes. Under a more intensely rational scrutiny, comprehending these passions also dissolves them as any solid basis for action. The underground man challenges the claim that other materialistic rationalists make, to the effect that a person cannot but act in such a way as is to his advantage. Dostoevsky asks us to suppose that we were able to arrive at a formulation of the Laws of Nature, including biological and psychological laws, so precise that we could calculate, in every case, what a man will do by knowing what is at that moment to his advantage — not as an individual, but *as an organism* that microcosmically expresses the survivalist egoism of Nature. A man who became aware of this calculation would spitefully do something else, anything else, just to prove that he was not "a piano key" or an "organ pedal" whose thoughts and passions could, in principle, be encompassed by a formula, tabulated, and predicted according to statistical probability. Dostoevsky equates the sum total of any comprehensive formula for the Laws of Nature, of the kind that physicists today are still searching for under the rubric of a *theory of everything*, with "an endlessly recurring zero," because it nullifies meaningful action.

The underground man would act *contrary* to his advantage. He would humiliatingly sacrifice himself to others, be beaten and brutalized, become impoverished through impossible generosity, and in every other way fail and suffer in life just so as to demonstrate that life "is not simply extracting square roots." On the one hand, he knows that "two times two makes four"; in other words, the Laws of Nature cannot be changed, and so "there is nothing left for you to do or to understand." On the other hand, he has a painful awareness that "Consciousness… is infinitely superior to two times two makes four." The underground man decides that "if you stick to consciousness, even though you attain the same result, you can at least flog yourself at times, and that will, at any rate, liven you up. It may be reactionary, but corporal punishment is still better than nothing." If "natural science and mathematics" were able to prove to him that *even this* reaction were predictable in accordance with some "mathematical formula," he "would purposely go mad in order to be rid of reason," and moreover, he would try to hurl the whole of the world into an abyss of "chaos and darkness and curses." This is what the underground man is referring to when he admits, "The long and the short of it is, gentlemen, that it is better to do nothing! Better conscious inertia! And so hurrah for underground! …But after all, even now I am lying! I am lying because I know myself as surely as two times two makes four, that it is not at all underground that is better, but something different, quite different, for which I long but which I cannot find! Damn underground!" Nishida is in search of what the underground man could not find as a cure to the mechanistic materialism dominating science under the Cartesian paradigm, but what he believed that Dostoevsky himself *did* find — albeit in an overly Judeo-Christian form that would benefit from a deconstructive encounter with the abyssal void of Zen.

Consciousness always consists of both an extending out over oneself as one's world, and a determination of oneself by that world, so that "subjectivity" and "objectivity" are abstractions of a creative world-forming process that one can intuit in the abyssal or groundless inner depths of the self prior to its interpretation as an ego.[118] Nishida thinks "discovery in the scientific domain exemplifies the same point," namely, "seeing *by becoming things* and hearing *by becoming things*."[119] Nishida goes so far as to proclaim the ontological priority of the religious form of life over both scientific practice and social mores: "Both science and morality have their basis in the religious form of life."[120] Nishida later repeats this point with respect to scientific practice: "Active intuition is fundamental even for science. Science itself is grounded in the fact that we see *by becoming things* and hear *by becoming things*. Active intuition refers to that standpoint which Dogen characterizes as achieving enlightenment 'by all things advancing.'"[121] According to Nishida, the religious form of life is

---

118   Nishida, *Last Writings*, p. 84.

119   Ibid, p. 90.

120   Ibid, p. 91.

121   Ibid, p. 102.

more fundamental than scientific cognition and the knowledge gained by means of it; the quest for scientific knowledge is a mode of the essentially religious character of our existence:

> I hold that even scientific cognition is grounded in this structure of spiritual-ity. Scientific knowledge cannot be grounded in the standpoint of the merely abstract conscious self. As I have said in another place, it rather derives from the standpoint of the embodied self's own self-awareness. And therefore, as a fundamental fact of human life, the religious form of life is not the exclusive possession of special individuals. The religious mind is present in everyone. One who does not notice this cannot be a philosopher.[122]

Nishida proclaims that "[a] new cultural direction has now to be sought. A new mankind must be born… a new global culture."[123] Although Nishida admits that "the new age must primarily be scientific," he sees a radicaliza-tion of the immanent view of divinity in Dostoyevsky and Russian mysti-cism in general through an encounter with Japanese Buddhism as playing a key role in defining "the religion of the future."[124] Yet the Buddhism that contributes to the formation of the religion of the new age, the religion of the global culture, must transcend the racial character of the Japanese: "From the perspective of present-day global history, it will perhaps be Buddhism that contributes to the formation of the new historical age. But if it too is only the conventional Buddhism of bygone days, it will merely be a relic of the past. The universal religions, insofar as they are already crystallized, have distinctive features corresponding to the times and places of the races that formed them."[125] It is inevitable that our ethos reflects a national character, but "the nation does not save our souls."[126] A

---

122 Ibid, p. 85.
123 Ibid, p. 120.
124 Ibid, pp. 121–122.
125 Ibid, p. 121.
126 Ibid, p. 122.

true nation or civilization must be based on a world religion, and not the other way around.[127]

As it turns out, it would not be through a synthesis with Russian mysticism that Japanese culture would hybridize in a cosmopolitan direction and contribute to the rise of a world religion. That would instead come through a traumatic encounter with the other pole of the West during the epoch of the Cold War, namely, the United States of America. The American conquest of Japan epitomizes the world-colonizing power of Atlantic civilization to restructure the psyche of traditional peoples around the aesthetic ideas of Prometheus and Atlas — the arch-divinities of the religiosity that Nishida intuited to be intrinsic to scientific practice.

During the Second World War, the Japanese were prepared to resist defeat until the bitter end. They were spurred on by Zen masters such as Daiun Sogaku Harada (the main source of Philip Kapleau's popular *Three Pillars of Zen*), who prepared the masses for a possible American ground invasion by teaching that Zen discipline demanded that the entire Japanese nation be prepared to die rather than allow the Emperor to be defeated.[128] What they were not prepared for was the atomic bomb. In a study of postwar Japanese popular culture, one is immediately confronted with a thinly-veiled psychological obsession with atomic radiation and its power to cause mutations.

At first, this manifests itself fairly crudely, in the *Gojira* mythos. The word *Gojira* is a fusion of the Japanese words for "gorilla" and "whale." Godzilla is a mutant born out of a sea-based nuclear test, and makes his first appearance in an attack on a fishing boat — clearly a reference to the United States *Operation Castle Bravo* thermonuclear test on islands near Japan, which accidentally irradiated the Japanese fishing boat *Daigo Fukuyu Maru*.[129] The *Castle Bravo* bomb had the highest yield of any ever exploded by the US. Godzilla's destruction of Tokyo in the original 1954

---

127 Ibid, p. 120–122.

128 Victoria, *Zen at War*, pp. 102, 135, 167.

129 Takashi Murakami, *Little Boy* (New Haven: Yale University Press, 2005), pp. 20, 126.

film is clearly an allegory for the destruction wrought on Japanese cities by the American atomic bombings. The monster is hardly visible in many scenes of destruction, signaled only by radioactive flashes of his fire-breath. Conventional weapons marshaled by the Defense Forces are no use against this unexpected destructive force, so an inventor's dangerous device is brought to bear.

By the 1980s, with the arrival of a new postwar generation, this crude physical embodiment of the transformational force of the atomic bomb began to be set aside like a child's transitional object. With the arrival of the *Akira* (1982) manga of Katsuhiro Otomo, and its anime adaptation (1988), we see a recognition that the Japanese psyche is the real subject (I wouldn't say "victim") of the mutation brought about under the promethium sky of Hiroshima.[130] *Akira* takes place in the futuristic, dystopian metropolis of Neo-Tokyo, which is built after a Third World War that is sparked by the destruction of the Tokyo of today by what appears to be an atomic explosion.[131] That "atomic" explosion is the striking, opening scene of the *Akira* anime. However, we come to learn that the explosion was not actually triggered by a nuclear device. Instead, it was an uncontrollable burst of psychic energy released by Akira, a boy who is the most powerful member of a group of ESPers. The Espers are test subjects of a secret government scientific research program aimed at understanding and developing ESP and PK abilities.

In other words, *Akira* is grounded upon an image that perfectly captures what I attempt to convey in Chapter 8, where I present the splitting of the atom as a symbol for the Promethean theft of the deadly lightning of Zeus, the thunderbolt that roughly translates into the Buddhist *vajra*. Considering that a radioactive element that is very similar to the tritium used in nuclear weapons has been named *promethium*, I cannot have been the first person to make this connection. In the manga and anime versions of the story, apocalyptic cults worship the Esper boy Akira as a god, and

---

130 Katsuhiro Otomo, *Akira* (Long Beach, California: Geneon, 2001).

131 Murakami, *Little Boy*, pp. 48–51, 107–112.

the directors of the classified government program wonder whether they are dabbling with a power that mankind is not meant to master. As I suggest in Chapter 8, the splitting of the *atom* — which, in the original Greek is, by definition, "the uncuttable" — represents the triumph of the power of technological *praxis* over metaphysical schemas that try to construct the world out of ideally indestructible building blocks. Models of the ultimate nature of reality that are based, in one way or another, on such mathematically predictable objects — even if they are "hidden variables" in Quantum Theory — are models with no place for irrational psychic phenomena, such as the ESP and PK that feature so prominently in *Akira*.

Through the lens of the interpersonal struggle amongst a group of very well developed characters, *Akira* explores the social and political consequences of humanity's arrival at a scientific knowledge of these latent psychic abilities. The consequences are potentially catastrophic, but they also promise an evolutionary leap if we are ready for it — a mutation of mankind into a superhuman condition. The atomic bomb can be seen as a symbol for a Science that gets a handle on the irrational in Nature without rendering it entirely predictable, a Science liberated and empowered by the Promethean realization that *techne* is more fundamental than *theoria*. Just because you cannot rationalize how something could exist does not mean that it does not exist, or that it must remain a forbidden object of mystical reverence. Even if a phenomenon resists being fit into an airtight building-block schema, one can still develop a fine *working* knowledge of it.

In fact, a working knowledge of such abilities featured in Siddhartha Gotama's teachings concerning the mind-expanding effects of various types of meditative practices at even the earliest stages. The more subtle states of mind attendant to more advanced types of meditation are so ethereal that there may be a danger of self-delusion with regard to what stage of the path to wisdom one has really attained. A good litmus test for the trainee is to see whether he or she has developed miraculous abilities or superpowers (*siddhis*) that are supposed to arise fairly early on in the practice of meditation, including adoption of the moral disciplines. Unless one has developed such magical powers, which are comparable to the "miraculous" feats of Moses or Jesus, one is nowhere near the higher *jhanas* or dwelling in the four bases beyond them.

In Gotama's view, these powers are not miraculous, and they do not necessarily involve divine intervention, even though the gods in general have these abilities to a greater degree than earthlings do. Rather, these are mental powers attendant to an increasing refinement and disciplining of the mind.[132] While the aspirant should not seek these parlor tricks for their own sake, become fixated on them, or become intoxicated by wielding them, the abilities themselves (or lack thereof) do provide the trainee with a very concrete benchmark for his or her spiritual progress. These abilities include telepathy (reading and knowing other minds intimately), clairvoyance (seeing anything anywhere at a distance), clairaudience (the same type of extrasensory perception, except with hearing), precognition, telekinesis or psychokinesis (including extreme forms of this such as walking through walls), bi-location (bodily presence in more than one place simultaneously), and levitating to the point of being able to fly through the air.

Mahapurusha, or "Superman," is an epithet used in early Buddhist literature to refer to Siddhartha, among others, who had attained *siddhis*.[133] The advanced aspirant is also supposed to be able to have total recall of his or her past lives, as well as be able to know the past lives of other people and to see their karma at work even precognitively.[134] Yet the practice of orthodox moral disciplines of *right action* that are essential to the Eightfold Path — such as pacifism, perfect honesty, and abstaining from sex and alcohol — were taken by Siddhartha and early Indian Buddhists to be a necessary and enduring prerequisite to the attainment of such abilities.[135]

---

132 Bodhi, *In the Buddha's Words*, pp. 273–275.

133 Ibid., p. 274.

134 Ibid., pp. 275–275.

135 Ibid., p. 120.

The ways in which the Zen mentality moved beyond both the Taoism and Buddhism that shaped it played a part in preparing the Japanese for the ruthlessly pragmatic insight that this, like the "law of karma" as a whole, is an unjustified moralistic prejudice. Zen was a necessary condition for such an insight, but without Hiroshima, it remained an insufficient one.

Nuclear imagery also plays a prominent role in the most celebrated *and most controversial* work of Japanese animation, Hideaki Anno's *Neon Genesis Evangelion* series (1995–1996), that canonically culminates in the cinematic masterpiece *End of Evangelion* (1997).[136] Like the explosion of psychic energy in *Akira*, First and "Second Impact" are primarily *spectral* events that superficially manifest a similarity to nuclear detonations. Extensive use is made of tactical nuclear weapons referred to as "N-2 mines." Like Godzilla, the genetically engineered EVAs cannot be fought by a military with conventional weapons and tactics. With their towering stature and prehistoric appearance, they are a clear evolution of *daikaiju* such as Godzilla, except that now their genesis is a result of deliberate design rather than reckless accident, and there is a human pilot ensconced in their heads, endowing the would-be mindless beasts with exceptional intelligence.

This is terribly significant from a psychological perspective. We can read it as a sign that the Japanese psyche has identified with, and taken control of, a transformational force that was at first so monstrously horrifying that it had to be externalized and fought from without. Moreover, the EVA pilots are a reaction against the Zen ideal of *kamikazes* rendered faceless through their absolute devotion to duty. *Evangelion* is structured around their complex inner struggles to come to terms with the personal traumas of their lives, to define themselves as individuals, and develop meaningful interpersonal relationships. The atomic bomb dropped on Hiroshima was code named "Little Boy," and it is not an accident that these prodigies, each freakishly unique, are all precociously underage;[137]

136   Hideaki Anno, *End of Evangelion* (GAINAX, 2002).

137   Murakami, *Little Boy*, pp. 88, 112–113, 127–132.

they represent the emerging postwar generation's rebellion against the traditional Asian values that crystallized in wartime Japanese Zen.

Yet it is not a simple rejection of this native spiritual tradition. Rather, the *End of Evangelion* deals at great length with the philosophical idea of how *Shunyata* need not be viewed as the negation of personal identity. All beings may indeed be *inherently* empty of any permanent essence, but what Shinji Ikari learns in the course of his rejection of "Instrumentality" is that this ontological nothingness should not be viewed as an escape from oneself or a refuge from the evanescent — but *real* — joy, and inevitable pain, of interpersonal relationships built on trust. In a world where Nothingness is ultimate rather than God, and where any really existing gods are acknowledged to be technological artifacts, we are even more compelled — perhaps *condemned* — to freely define our own character and build a life together with the others without whom we would all find ourselves maddeningly alone.

This can be a sickening realization, as it is for Asuka, as she lies under Shinji in the final scene of *End of Evangelion*. Ikari is torn between loving her and strangling her to death as he succumbs to shudders of profound sorrow and ineffable pleasure. This is the same realization that causes Nietzsche's Zarathustra to fall ill when he realizes that the Superman cannot exist alone and must "go under"; it is the existential "nausea" referred to by Sartre, and what Sartre meant by depicting an inescapable "hell [that] is *other people*" in *No Exit*. The kind of existential humanism that we see in *Evangelion* is as mutually exclusive to belief in God as it is incompatible with the traditional Buddhist idea of *nirvana*. Nothing can guarantee us an abode of safety beyond the creatively destructive play of Nature, which wells up even from within our own angst-ridden psyches, and thereby inescapably individuates them. Technology is apocalyptically dangerous insofar as we believe — as the SEELE cabal, which features in this series, did — that it could instrumentalize human *being* in such a way as to take the place of this absent God, and thereby deliver His promised paradise of perpetual peace.

Evangelion creatively appropriates Abrahamic mythology and turns it against itself, responding to the cancer of "revelation" from out of the essence of Asian spirituality — an essence that has in turn been distilled in the crucible of a Promethean-Atlantic self-critique that takes the virginity of Taoism and sheds the husks of Buddhist dogma. Gendo Ikari's reply to the Western SEELE cabalists who are trying to use him as a tool is a critique of both the nihilistic Zen Japanese equation of life and death, and the Abrahamic glorification of death as a path to an unearthly, static paradise. Gendo knows that his attempt to clandestinely use NERV against the cabalists, to battle the angels and hold back the apocalypse, will inevitably fail. He fights anyway, because each and every day that humanity's independence is defended is another day for individuals to decide their own destiny by meaningfully crafting their own lives. There could not be a more compelling expression of the tragic Greek spirit. NERV evinces a crafty Promethean technological prowess as it outschemes SEELE's "divine plan" to use it as a pawn, while Gendo is an emanation of King Atlas: the world-bearing sovereign in a godless world — or rather, a world where God and his servile gods are plotting the demise of mankind. In *Neon Genesis Evangelion*, we see the Atlantic mentality seamlessly coupled with the Promethean ethos. The underwater structure at Yonaguni is a distraction to those yearning to find a "Japanese Atlantis." It is Tokyo-3, with NERV at its center, that instantiates the aesthetic idea of embattled Atlantis.

Together with our Japanese allies, we must struggle against those nationalistic traditionalists who stand in the way of the transformation of real-world Tokyo into the New Atlantis envisioned by the generation of *Neon Genesis Evangelion*. We also cannot allow economizing technocrats to cobble Japan together with a dozen other neighboring countries into a Chinese-dominated Asia-Pacific Commonwealth. What shared cultural values could such an organization possibly reflect? Personal character effaced in favor of filial piety and clan interest? The dynamic creativity and spontaneity of individual genius sacrificed to disciplined collective planning?

For 60 years now, the Japanese people have been boldly moving beyond these "Asian" values. It would be the height of irresponsibility to allow a regress. The horrific suffering that culminated in the atomic bombings of Hiroshima and Nagasaki cannot have been in vain. The spectral significance of the promethium sky over Japan in those days of devastation cannot be forgotten. It was not just physically destructive, but also psychologically de-constructive. The Japanese psyche was torn apart and restructured around the aesthetic ideas of Prometheus and Atlas. We must see to it that the metamorphosis then set into motion is irreversible. It is not a question of sustaining the American military occupation of Japan, but of understanding the gravity with which the Japanese cultural vanguard has been captured by the spiritual orbit of Atlantic civilization. Moreover, at least insofar as this vanguard is concerned, the Japanese role in Atlantic civilization is by no means subordinate. It is in Japan where, unburdened by the Judeo-Christian heritage, visionary artists have best crystallized transformative images of the coming metamorphosis of the merely human being into a more diabolically daring and dynamic super-human race, destined to liberate a capriciously ruled cosmos and conquer the inner space of latent psychic powers.

CHAPTER XI

BEING BOUND
FOR FREEDOM

Prometheus and Atlas, as the aesthetic ideas of Technoscience, afford us a radically empiricist understanding of what were once taken to be "miraculous" occurrences that bedazzled people into submitting to the will of a Heavenly Lord who used them to fallaciously claim to be omnipotent and omniscient; to claim, in effect, that resistance is futile. Through their titanic rebellion, Prometheus and Atlas put the lie to His threats. Zeus, or Jehovah, has been cut down to size as the petty dictator that he is.

The radical empiricism that William James advocated with respect to the study of psychic phenomena establishes him as the first parapsychologist in the modern sense. One of the great philosophers of religion in our time, James led the American branch of the Society for Psychical Research (SPR), and was convinced that study of the paranormal would lead to the next great scientific revolution, ushering in a radical empiricism unconditioned by mechanistic metaphysics. He also saw the paranormal as confirming his pluralistic ontology, including its most important ethical implication: that since Nature is incomplete, forever open to addition and revision, we co-constitute it through our personal intentions and creative acts. This also means that there are real tragedies in life which could have been averted if only we had done otherwise, rather than the farce that every tragedy becomes when it is seen as an actualization of one of the predetermined possibilities always already surveyed by an all-knowing God.

James interpreted religion in light of his radical empiricism and his pluralistic ontology, arriving at the conclusion that many of the miraculous occurrences recounted in scripture are on a continuum with more contemporary cases of mediumistic trances, telepathic communications, psychokinetic demonstrations, and other such manifestations that he studied during his years as a pioneering parapsychologist at the SPR. I draw a comparison between one particular case of telepathy that James wrote about and the mediumistic "revelation" of the *Qur'an* to the "prophet" Muhammad. I then go on to discuss James' view that a truly radical empiricism cannot avoid admitting the possibility that superhuman beings in the cosmos may be the sources of such communications, but that from the standpoint of pluralistic ontology, they are finite and fallible beings such as ourselves — whatever else they may mumble through our mouths to their own benefit, and however much their superior powers might impress us.

In his chapter on "Religion" in *Pragmatism*, William James frames the question of choosing between the alternatives of the monistic and pluralistic worldviews as "the final question of philosophy," and "the deepest and most pregnant question that our minds can frame."[1] Remaining neutral with respect to these two alternatives, and keeping this momentous question open indefinitely, is not an option. There is, rather, an urgent "pragmatistic need... of frankly adopting either."[2] James recognizes that the conflict between pluralism and monism really hinges on whether or not there are genuine possibilities in life.[3] Both Rationalism and religious faith in an omniscient and omnipotent God assert that everything "good" (read: what should happen) certainly does happen, and anything "evil" (read: what should not happen) never really does happen.

James takes the thought of G. W. F. Hegel to be the greatest expression of this view. Hegel does not disregard the destructive change that things undergo on account of an inability to assert themselves as fixed and independent of what is in their environment. Rather, the Hegelian dialec-

---

1   William James, *Pragmatism and the Meaning of Truth* (Cambridge, Massachusetts: Harvard University Press, 1978), pp. 140–141.

2   Ibid., p. 141.

3   Ibid., p. 135.

tic subsumes this transformation through friction and opposition into a merely *apparent* temporal process taking place within an eternally completed Whole to which "there is no imaginable…outlying alternative."[4] Everything was, is, and will be as it is supposed to be — no matter what: "Whatever the details of experience may prove to be, *after the fact of them* the absolute will adopt them… *That*, whatever it may be, will have been in point of fact the sort of world which the absolute was pleased to offer to itself as a spectacle."[5]

Meanwhile, those who subscribe to the pluralistic empiricist variety of religion believe it is possible that things will not turn out as they should; whether or not they do is, at least partly, up to us. Any genuine possibility requires certain concrete conditions for its actualization, some of which may not in fact be in place. James explains this in terms of the example of "a concretely possible chicken," the actualization of whose self-consistent idea needs not only an actual egg, but the absence of a threat to this egg from any number of sources. He suggests applying the same notion to the idea of the salvation of the world.[6] This is not a possibility in the face of which one can be legitimately or believably neutral. James proposes that there is a middle way between a pessimism that denies outright the possibility of the world's salvation, and an optimism that takes it to be inevitable. He calls this middle way the doctrine or attitude of *meliorism*, according to which the salvation of the world is a genuine possibility, one whose probability increases or decreases depending on how many of the concrete conditions for the actualization of this possibility materialize. According to James, "It is clear that pragmatism must incline towards meliorism."[7] He opposes "pluralistic pragmatism" to Rationalism in such

---

4   William James, *A Pluralistic Universe* (Lincoln: University of Nebraska Press, 1996), pp. 89–90; 102–103.

5   Ibid., p. 126.

6   Ibid., p. 136.

7   James, *Pragmatism and the Meaning of Truth*, p. 137.

a way that "pluralistic" adjectivally describes "pragmatism," rather than indicating a species of the genus pragmatism-in-general.[8]

James elaborates the melioristic view by presenting an idea that he later develops at length in *A Pluralistic Universe*. It is the view that there are causal gaps in the universe, moments of opportunity, which are only filled in by our chosen actions. Beings such as ourselves contribute integrally to the growth of the universe. Each of us makes things happen that never would have happened but for our creative act to make it so. James refers to our sphere of action as "the workshop of being" — a wonderfully Promethean image. We co-constitute existence, which, consequently, is finite and relativistic. "New being comes in local spots and patches" — in other words, "piecemeal," and these concentrations of existence are not necessarily harmoniously integrated with what already exists.[9] Again, the discontinuities, or "gaps," are what allow for our actions to make a fundamental difference. In other words, one can expect events that defy so-called "Laws of Nature" (which are really no more than approximate generalizations), and moreover, in this view, some of those events will manifest the way in which we, conscious beings, occasionally play a role in constituting "physical reality."[10]

James repeatedly refers to this fundamentally pluralistic universe as "irrational" when viewed from the traditional perspective.[11] Although, in a polemically provocative spirit, James occasionally embraces the label of "irrationalist", his more serious response to this charge of irrationality is that it is based on a false ideal of rationality and reasons. *Living reason* is not that of abstractions such as logic, necessity, and categories. The only *real reason* something should come into being in the course of human events is that "someone wishes it to be here."[12] To expect that the universe should somehow "make sense" in itself, as if isolated from human actions

---

8   Ibid., p. 125.

9   Ibid., pp. 138–139.

10   Ibid., pp. 60–61.

11   Ibid., pp. 138–139.

12   Ibid., p. 138.

that shape *our* world of meaning, is a false expectation — and so horror in the face of an illogical or insane universe is misplaced. The abyssal lack of an inherent and immutable order can be seen as the free space for *us* to *make* the world meaningful in one way or another.

In his chapter on "Hegel and His Method" in *A Pluralistic Universe*, James offers a different critique of Rationalism. There he suggests that there are four dimensions of rationality, with the intellectual being only one of them. Things can also be rational or irrational in an aesthetic, moral, or practical sense. The "world of mechanical materialism" may be the most rational world *intellectually*, but it makes nonsense out of aesthetic, moral, and practical experience. The monistic worldview is irrational even intellectually, since it contradicts its own demand that the whole be perfect, whereas the parts of this whole are imperfect. A truly rational view is one that is most rational *on balance* in all four dimensions of human experience.[13] James thinks that his pluralism passes this test.

In the pluralistic view, one can imagine that, while the salvation of the universe (i.e., attaining the best possible outcome for those concerned) may be possible, it is a very risky affair to participate in such a universe — because success or failure is partly up to us, and there is a lot to lose.[14] Perhaps it is even more risky, psychologically, than if one were to dismiss the possibility of "salvation" altogether, in which case one has nothing to lose. It demands much more trust of others, because all we really have in the end are each other, and even if there are gods, they are also finite others with limited power.[15]

This bounded finitude of Being redeems human creativity as a genuine phenomenon, an ability to introduce novelties into a world that is not completed in an eternity beyond time.[16] It allows us to be bound for unforeseeable discoveries, headed for an undiscovered country that no one

---

13   James, *A Pluralistic Universe*, pp. 112–113; 123.

14   James, *Pragmatism and the Meaning of Truth*, p. 139.

15   Ibid., p. 139.

16   Ibid., p. 59.

has mapped out before us. There may be gods, but nothing all-powerful capable of guaranteeing any particular outcome in advance.[17] James takes the radically *humanist* view that "[t]he world stands really malleable, waiting to receive its *final* touches at *our* hands."[18] James believes that, if given the choice between this and nothingness, most people would choose to participate in this humanistic "universe with only a fighting chance of safety."[19]

There are, however, religious people of another type who are "reduced to their last sick extremity," and do not have the strength of character or the moral courage to accept this risk. They need to psychologically secure themselves against the possibility of accidents and against the possibility of failure; in a word, against the possibility of real possibilities. James writes, with strikingly decisive force: "Nirvana means safety from this everlasting round of adventures... The hindoo and the Buddhist, for this is essentially their attitude, are simply afraid, afraid of more experience, afraid of life."[20] As the *Dhammapada* puts it, release from *samsara* in the attainment of *nirvana* is accomplished only by "he for whom things future or past or present are nothing, who has nothing and desires nothing."[21] Despite its denial of the One True God, the Dharma remains a monistic doctrine wherein nothing is at stake and suffering is to be escaped — not channeled as a wellspring of tragic art. Being is bounded in the destructive or de-structuring ontology of dependent origination, but not in a way that allows us to be bound *for* freedom. Nirvana is a freedom *from*, not a freedom *for* creative evolution — not an affirmation of potentially infinite creativity through a recognition of existential finitude.

James explicitly sets his attempt to interpret religion "pragmatically" against the Transcendentalism of Kant. As we saw in Chapter 4, Kant's *Religion within the Limits of Reason Alone* epitomizes the fearful

---

17   Ibid., p. 135.

18   Ibid., p. 123, my emphasis.

19   Ibid., p. 140.

20   James, *Pragmatism and the Meaning of Truth*, p. 140.

21   Bhikkhu Bodhi, *In the Buddha's Words*, p. 421.

refusal to reckon with the paranormal substrate of religious experience.[22] Transcendental Idealists, like Kant, merely offer an *ideal* interpretation of the *same* world of facts acknowledged by materialist scientists (in Kant's own time, people such as Julien Offray de La Mettrie). In this view, "ideal entities" cannot ever interfere causally in the course of events in the "phenomenal" realm. Ideal things in themselves (what Kant called *noumena*) are *a priori* parallel to perceived phenomena, as they appear according to a closed nexus of efficient causality that is pre-consciously determined by the cognitive apparatus of the perceiver.[23] No individual act is free or creative by contrast with other natural happenings. The will can only lie behind everything, and no thing in particular. James calls this a refined, universalistic supernaturalism that turns theology into a study of the (subjective) meanings of (objective) material facts.

In opposition to this, James affirms the causal efficacy of the will and the intrusion of irregular events *within* the world of phenomena, in other words the "crass... miracles" of the "older theology."[24] James' basic objection is that rationalistic philosophies of religion do not realize that the "world interpreted religiously is not the materialistic world over again" — rather "it must have, over and above the altered expression, *a natural constitution* different at some point from that which a materialistic world would have. It must be such that different events can be expected in it..."[25] James insists that religion does make claims about the *facts* of the world, and that it should be empirically evaluated on this basis.[26]

James acknowledges that, interpreted pragmatically, religion is "largely based" upon events of "revelation," and he suggests that certain scriptures may have been "composed automatically," in other words by means of the kind of *automatic writing* prevalent among late nineteenth-century trance

---

22   William James, *Writings: 1902–1910* (New York: The Library of America, 1987), pp. 402; 464.

23   Ibid., p. 389.

24   Ibid., p. 464.

25   Ibid., pp. 462–463.

26   Ibid., p. 467.

mediums that he studied in the course of his quarter-century of empirical research into psychic phenomena.[27] Most relevant among these is the case of Albert Le Baron, whose experiences were studied by William James and other members of the *Society for Psychical Research* in 1896.[28] The particularities of Le Baron's experiences are very similar to those involved in the "revelation" of the *Qur'an* to the "prophet" Muhammad in a state of mediumistic trance. (*Qur'an* 5:101–103; 10:15–17; 11:13–14; 75:19–20)

Le Baron experienced episodes of "psychic automatism"; in other words, the involuntary movement of his mouth and hands to utter or write out messages that seemed to come from some source other than himself, or at least, other than his conscious mind. As in the case of Muhammad, his initially skeptical and distrustful attitude toward these manifestations was eroded by repeated attempts of certain religiously indoctrinated and impassioned women around him to convince him that he was being addressed by a divine being.[29] Also, as in the case of the prophet of Islam, the receiver could not necessarily remember the message after it was transmitted. At one point in the *Qur'an*, there is a break in the "revelation," as if it were a "mental radio" transmission being interrupted for a word from the station, directly from Allah to Muhammad, telling him that he need not try to memorize the words as they come, because they will be rebroadcast to him if and when he again requires them. (*Qur'an*, 75:19–20) Le Baron's source of "revelation" speaks of Le Baron in the third person, just as Allah speaks of Muhammad through his mouth. (*Qur'an*, 80:1–16; 81:22) While the messages did at times contain information of which Le Baron was not consciously aware, and could not have obtained by sensory means, he recognized that the prolific deific rhetorical flourishes were often as devoid of meaningful content as they were poetically expressed.

---

27   Ibid., pp. 14; 402.

28   William James, *Essays in Psychical Research* (Cambridge, Massachusetts: Harvard University Press, 1986), pp. 143–165.

29   Martin Lings, *Muhammad: His Life Based on the Earliest Sources* (Rochester, Vermont: Inner Traditions, 2006), pp. 44–46.

The source of the "revelations" attempted to convince Le Baron that he was a prophet, and it commanded him to undertake long journeys, of the kind that Muhammad also undertook during the course of his own career, to various locations where significant events were promised to take place or further revelations were to be forthcoming. These began with a command to travel to the village of Stowe, Vermont (unheard of at that time by Le Baron) and ended with absurdities, such as the demand that he seek out the Emperor of China. One is reminded of the emissaries that Muhammad sent to deliver ultimatums to the Emperor of Persia. Le Baron's mediumistic "control" also provoked feelings of abject submission in him, as if he were being asked to surrender himself as something lower than dirt, and to empty himself out and become a "pure" vessel for divine commands. The parallels to the Muhammadan spirit go without saying.

Fortunately, unlike Muhammad, Albert Le Baron was an intellectual given to reading Kant's *Critique of Pure Reason* in his spare time, and so he eventually concluded that he might well be subject to telepathic manipulation "from some... awfully naughty source," which ought to be evaluated scientifically so that its operative psychological laws could be discovered.[30] For this, he turned to the Society for Psychical Research. Le Baron rightly suspected that the faculty at work here is likely the same as that responsible for successful controlled experiments at the SPR on the extrasensory transference of thoughts and symbolic images, the protocols of which William James helped to design, and the results of which he reports on in his 1895 paper on "Telepathy."[31] James explicitly draws this connection when, in this paper, he claims that the Society's tests on the renowned medium, Mrs. Piper, were among the most impressively verified displays of telepathic ability — *so* impressive that James describes himself "as convinced of the reality of the phenomenon in her as he can be convinced of anything in the world."[32]

---

30   James, *Essays in Psychical Research*, pp. 161, 163.

31   Ibid., pp. 120–121.

32   Ibid., p. 125.

In *Pragmatism*, James considers that the sources of such "revelations" as those conferred to Le Baron — or Muhammad — may be superhuman beings, but these are finite and fallible entities within our pluralistic universe; we stand in a similar relation to them as the non-human animals that we interact with stand in relation to us:

> I firmly disbelieve, myself, that our human experience is the highest form of experience extant in the universe. I believe rather that we stand in much the same relation to the whole of the universe as our canine and feline pets do to the whole of human life. They inhabit our drawing-rooms and libraries. They take part in scenes of whose significance they have no inkling... But, just as many of the dog's and cat's ideals coincide with our ideals, and the dogs and cats have daily living proof of the fact, so we may well believe, on the proof that religious experience affords, that higher powers exist and are at work to save the world on ideal lines similar to our own.[33]

Of course, just as not all people who interact with animals are pet owners — some are unethical scientists — and just as even some pet owners leave much to be desired in their treatment of their animals, James' view here leaves open the possibility that some of the superhuman beings in the universe are, from the perspective of our own interests, either terrifyingly indifferent or malevolently threatening influences on earthly affairs.

Yet at other times, James loses sight of the fact that religion, as it is historically manifest, is not some evanescent "mystical" psychological state, utterly without intrinsic content and lasting for "a half hour or an hour at most." James refers to the authors of the Bible as "great-souled persons" grappling with "inner experiences,"[34] as if they were on a level with solitary, contemplative mystics like Teresa of Avila, whereas in fact there would be almost nothing remarkable left of the accounts of the lives and missions of men like Moses, Ezekiel, and Paul if one were to remove the many paranormal occurrences that were the channel for the acceptance of their "revelations" by stubborn masses. These miracles are, moreover,

---

33   James, *Pragmatism and the Meaning of Truth*, p. 143.

34   James, *Writings: 1902–1910*, p. 14.

not intended simply to *inspire* "faith." They are, often, intended to terrify people into obedience. The Lord in the Whirlwind (*II Kings* 2:11) repeatedly gives instructions for massacres and acts of genocide to be carried out, even intervening on certain occasions to decide the outcome of a military conflict.

Let us begin at the beginning, not with Moses, but with the founder of the Abrahamic tradition, Abraham, and the closely related story of his nephew, Lot. After leaving Mesopotamia for Canaan, the land that would become Israel, Abraham and his nephew Lot agree to spread out. (*Genesis* 13) Lot settles in Sodom, which was on the plain of Jordan, together with its twin city of Gomorrah. Both men have encounters with the Lord that further illuminate the very finite, human character of the Abrahamic "God." Three men appear outside Abraham's tent, and the Lord is clearly one of them: "The Lord appeared to him by the terebinths of Mamre; he was sitting at the entrance of the tent as the day grew hot. Looking up, he saw three men standing near him. As soon as he saw them, he ran from the entrance of the tent to greet them and, bowing to the ground, he said, 'My lords, if it please you, do not go on past your servant.'" (*Genesis* 18:1–5) As Abraham and his wife Sarah hurry to cater to these guests, one of them tells Sarah that, despite being an old and "withered" woman far past menopause, when he returns in the following year she will have had a child by her 100-year-old husband. While she conceals any outward expression of how ridiculous she finds this, the man is able to read her mind and confronts her for faithless skepticism with the rebuke, "Is anything too wondrous for the Lord?" (*Genesis* 18:9–15)

The three men then take Abraham up to a hill wherein they can overlook the plain of Sodom and Gomorrah, where Abraham's nephew, Lot, has settled. Since he has now been chosen as an insider, the Lord decides to reveal to him the divine plan for the imminent destruction of these cities whose inhabitants are supposed to have become so sinful that the outcry against them has reached the Lord. The transition from this scene, where the three men are with Abraham, to the next one, wherein the two *elohim* — the "angels," or literally *messengers* of the Lord — enter the town of Sodom to retrieve Lot is key. The text of *Genesis* 18–19 reads, "The [three men] set out from there and looked down toward Sodom, Abraham walking with them to see them off.... The men went on from there to Sodom, while Abraham remained standing before the Lord. ... The two angels arrived in Sodom in the evening, as Lot was sitting in the gate of Sodom." In other words, the Lord is definitely one of the three men who visit Abraham and Sarah at their encampment. While he remains behind with Abraham, he sends his two lieutenants into Sodom to evacuate Abraham's nephew and his family before he subjects Sodom and Gomorrah to an aerial attack. The details in the description of this fiery assault from the sky witnessed by Abraham as Lot and his family head for the hills are noteworthy:

> As dawn broke, the angels urged Lot on, saying, "Up, take your wife and your two remaining daughters, lest you be swept away because of the iniquity of the city. Still he delayed. So the men seized his hand, and the hands of his wife and two daughters — in the Lord's mercy on him — and brought him out and left him outside the city. When they had brought them outside, one said, "Flee for your life! Do not look behind you, nor stop anywhere in the Plain; flee to the hills, lest you be swept away." But Lot said to them, "Oh no, my lord! You have been so gracious to your servant, and have already shown me so much kindness in order to save my life; but I cannot flee to the hills, lest the disaster overtake me and I die. Look, that town there is near enough to flee to; it is such a little place! Let me flee there — it is such a little place — and let my life be saved." He replied, "Very well, I will grant you this favor too, and I will not annihilate the town of which you have spoken. Hurry, flee to there, for I cannot do anything until you arrive there." Hence the town came to be called Zoar ["a little place"]. As the sun rose upon the earth and Lot entered Zoar, the Lord rained upon Sodom and Gomorrah sulfurous fire from the Lord out of heaven. He annihilated those cities and the entire Plain, and all the inhabitants of the cities and the vegetation of the ground. Lot's wife looked back, and she thereupon turned into a pillar of salt. Next morning, Abraham hurried to the place where he had stood before the Lord, and, looking down toward Sodom and Gomorrah and all the land of the Plain, he saw the smoke of the land rising like the smoke of a kiln. Thus it was that, when God destroyed the cities of the Plain and annihilated the cities where

Lot dwelt, God was mindful of Abraham and removed Lot from the midst of the upheaval. Lot went up from Zoar and settled in the hill country with his two daughters, for he was afraid to dwell in Zoar; and he and his two daughters lived in a cave. (*Genesis* 19:15–30)

This cannot but evoke, in the mind of a modern reader, the image of a mushroom cloud and the poisonous radioactive fallout following a nuclear strike. Although one of the gods promises Lot that the little town nearby Sodom and Gomorrah will be spared, he is still afraid to dwell there on account of its proximity to the recently-destroyed cities. What *natural* catastrophe could prompt such a fear *after* it had destroyed the two cities? While Lot and his daughters make it to a cave where they are safe from the proverbial "fallout" in the days after the strike, Lot's wife, who turned back, undergoes a strange transformation that the chronicler grasps at a metaphor in order to express — perhaps it is a deadly metamorphosis akin to that suffered by victims of radiation poisoning.

Just as the three men eat and drink the meal prepared by Sarah, the two of them that continue on to Sodom also eat a feast and have their dirty feet washed. They are carnal enough to be lusted after by the men of Sodom, although they have the seemingly magical power to blind this mob with a flash of light once the mob attempts to storm Lot's house. (*Genesis* 19:11) Interestingly, Lot's sons-in-law find the warnings from the men ridiculous, and think that Lot is joking when he asks them to leave with him before the city is destroyed by the Lord. (*Genesis* 19:12–14) This means that, despite their telepathic and psychokinetic abilities, there was nothing so evidently "divine" about these men that they would be believed without question. The *elohim* who act as "angels" or *messengers* of the Lord in the Old Testament, for the most part, do not have wings. This is a much later artistic convention.

Finally, as in the case of the place of slaves in the covenant of Abraham, we have to ask about the ethics of the destruction of Sodom and Gomorrah. Before the two of the three "men" arrive at Sodom, Abraham negotiates with their leader, who stays behind, namely the Lord, over how many righteous people would have to be in this supposedly wicked city in order for the Lord to spare it for their sake. Abraham gets the Lord to keep lowering the number. (*Genesis* 18: 22–32) However, in the end, we know that only Lot and his family are forcibly evacuated by the Lord's two agents, and not even his whole family, but only his daughters. His sons stay behind and his wife turns back. This means that the Lord considers Lot the only righteous man in Sodom. But how virtuous is a man who offers up his two virgin daughters to be raped by a mob of lecherous men gathered around his house? (*Genesis* 19:6–8) After the destruction of Sodom, the same man has sex with his two daughters. We are told that they get him so drunk that, on two nights in a row, he does not realize that he is having sex first with his older daughter, and then his younger one. (*Genesis* 19:31–35) This is an old man. If he were that drunk, he would not have been able to go through with the act, leading to him fathering children by both of these girls. Is it then not much more likely that Lot is spared because he is the nephew of Abraham, rather than on account of his own virtue?

This, however, only begs the question of Abraham's own virtue or lack thereof. No episode in the narrative of *Genesis* is more relevant to this question than the famous (or infamous) offering up of Isaac as a sacrificial animal. The story is told in *Genesis* 22, which begins with these lines:

> Some time afterward, God put Abraham to the test. He said to him, "Abraham," and he answered, "Here I am." And He said, "Take your son, your favored one, Isaac, whom you love, and go to the land of Moriah, and offer him there as a burnt offering on one of the heights that I will point out to you." Once Abraham arrives at Mount Moriah and begins to ascend with the firestone and knife, having left his servants behind with their mules, Isaac, who is carrying the logs on which, unbeknownst to himself, his father plans to sacrifice him, the boy hauntingly asks: "Father! ... Here are the firestone and the wood; but where is the sheep for the burnt offering?" And Abraham said, "God will see to the sheep for His burnt offering, my son." (*Genesis* 22: 7–8)

The narrative reaches its culmination with Abraham's evident willingness to murder his bound son on the command of the Lord, and the Lord's approval of this sign of Abraham's absolute obedience, as expressed through one of His angels:

> They arrived at the place of which God had told him. Abraham built an altar there; he laid out the wood; he bound his son Isaac; he laid him on the altar, on top of the wood. And Abraham picked up the knife to slay his son. Then an angel of the Lord called to him from heaven: "Abraham! Abraham!" And he answered, "Here I am." And he said, "Do not raise your hand against the boy, or do anything to him. For now I know that you fear God, since you have not withheld your son, your favored one, from Me... Because you have done this and have not withheld your son, your favored one, I will bestow My blessing upon you and make your descendants as numerous as the stars of heaven and the sands on the seashore; and your descendants shall seize the gates of their foes. All the nations of the earth shall bless themselves by your descendants, because you have obeyed My command." (Genesis 22:9–12, 15–18)

All of this is as much as to say that the conquest of the world by the Abrahamic peoples, the Judeo-Christians and the Muslims, with the support of a Lord who appears now for the first of many times to come as a heavenly or celestial warlord, is founded on the willingness of Abraham to unquestioningly bind his own son for slaughter in obedience to a voice from the sky.

Now let us turn to Moses, the first of the three greatest prophets of the Abrahamic tradition. In Moses' first encounter with *elohim*, he is spoken to from amidst a luminous object that settled within a thicket, an object whose white light is so striking that Moses is astonished that it does not burn the thicket as would a fire (which is the only thing within his sphere of knowledge that is capable of producing such a light). (*Exodus* 3:2) As we have seen, the *elohim* of the Old Testament are simply visiting strangers who have unusual abilities, like being able to render an old woman such as Abraham's wife Sarah fertile (*Genesis* 18:1,2), set Jacob's hip bone out of joint simply by touching it (*Genesis* 32:24–25), or strike down the Sodomite mob amassed at Lot's house by projecting a blinding flash of light, sometime shortly before the twin cities of Sodom and Gomorrah are subjected to aerial bombardment by the *elohim*. (*Genesis* 19) It is with a contest in the use of such unusual abilities that the foundational narrative of the religion of Moses, Jesus, and Muhammad begins. Moses and his associate Aron are in Pharaoh's court, demanding freedom for their people, and a battle in the display of psychic abilities ensues between them and Pharaoh's practitioners of alchemy (*al-kemiya*, "the art/craft [i.e., *techne*] from Khemit"; *Khemit* being the indigenous name of Ancient Egypt). They both throw down their rods, or "magic wands," and have them turn into serpents. (*Exodus* 7:8–13) It becomes clear that both sides are adept in wielding the "serpent power," and so the Lord eventually resorts to plagues and the overnight slaughter of innocent Egyptian newborns in order to intimidate Pharaoh into freeing the Jews.

When the Lord hears the cry of his people, the Israelites, and decides the time has come to free them from slavery in Egypt, He himself "hardens Pharaoh's heart" and those of his courtiers into the unbelievably obstinate stubbornness we see as Pharaoh fails to draw a lesson from the plagues administered and cleansed through Moses. The Hebrew Lord claims to have done this in order that it might provide an excuse to show "His signs" to mock and strike fear into the hearts of the Egyptians. (*Exodus* 10:1–2) We are then told that, even though most of the common Egyptian people take kindly to Moses and the Israelites, the Lord punishes them terribly for the (divinely predetermined) recalcitrance of Pharaoh and his royal court. Their innocent firstborn children are mercilessly slaughtered as Egyptian mothers and fathers are left crying out in terror like never before into the darkness of the desert night. (*Exodus* 11:3–7)

Apparently, familiar with the malevolent use of psychic ability, and regretful of having been intimidated by such parlor tricks, Pharaoh repents of this decision to free the Jewish servants and sends his army into the Sinai desert in pursuit, as they are on their way to the "promised land." Throughout their years-long exodus in the Sinai, the Israelites are led by a purposively-guided aerial object that appears as "a pillar ['*am-*

mud, column] of cloud" by day and as "a pillar [or column] of fire" by night. (*Exodus* 13:21,22) The column is low-flying enough for them to observe its cylindrical structure, which has a steel-grey "cloud"-like hue during the day and glows with a fiery light after sunset. We are told that the Lord, in all his glory, is inside (aboard?) the pillar of fire and cloud (*Exodus* 16:10; 14:24). The "tent of the meeting" — the center-point of the Israelites' pitched camp during the exodus — is set up and removed, based on where the cylindrical object comes to a halt and hovers at a stationary position (*Exodus* 40:33–38), or where it occasionally even touches down (*Numbers* 9:17).

There is one particular night when the object does not emit its usual fiery glow. The Egyptian army has come up to the rear of the Israelites, who are effectively cornered at the Red Sea, with no place to run unless they can somehow cross it. "The cloud" then takes a position between the Egyptians and the Israelites and remains there throughout the night, as if to block the Egyptians from attacking the Israelites and — by effectively "turning off its light" — it prevents the Egyptians from even *seeing* the Israelite camp as they might have, had the object been hovering above them in its usually luminous nocturnal mode that allowed the Israelites to march at night. (*Exodus* 14:19,20; 13:21) The following morning, the Israelites awake to see the object hovering over the Red Sea, and directly beneath it is a channel cut into the Sea with the water neatly parted into walls on either side. (*Exodus* 14:24; 14:22; 15:8)

Even more surprisingly, when the Israelites cross the channel — probably expecting to be wading knee deep in mud — they find that the seabed is dry and firm underfoot. (*Exodus* 14:22) Once the Egyptian army enters the channel in pursuit of the Israelites, Moses is told (telepathically?) by the Lord to raise his hand over the sea (as if he were about to command it by his own "magical" powers), whereupon two very striking events take place. First, the Egyptians appear as if they are suddenly struggling greatly. Their horses look like they require the strain of a gallop just to move at all, and their chariots are crushed under an invisible weight that rips their wheels off. (*Exodus* 14:24,25) Then the walls of water on either side of the Egyptians give way, collapsing the channel through the Red Sea, *but only in the area behind the Israelites who are still advancing through the artificial channel.* (*Exodus* 14:26–29)

All of the phenomenological descriptions of the channel are consistent with the projection of some kind of anti-gravitational beam from out of the cylindrical object hovering over the Sea. Such a beam might have pressed down so hard on the seabed after having cleared the water aside into walls that it compressed all the moisture out of the mud into a dry crossing path. The beam could then have been phased out at its center to allow the Israelites to cross, and then filled in again to crush the Egyptians by artificially increasing their weight, before the beam was removed altogether in that portion of the channel in order to drown Pharaoh's army.

Our narrative culminates, and its sociopolitical significance becomes clear, once the Israelites arrive at Mount Sinai. The cylindrical object comes down upon the mountain in an illuminated state, causing great tremors and raising up smoke or dust. (*Exodus* 19:16–18) This cannot be a description of volcanic activity, because the pillar comes down and sits at the top of the mountain (which would have been blown open by a volcanic eruption). (*Exodus* 19:20) The Israelites are warned in advance not to come too close to the mountain when "the cloud" lands on it (*Exodus* 19:12, 21, 24), and Moses — although apparently shielded in some way from said danger — would return to the people with a peculiar glow about him after prolonged proximal exposure. (*Exodus* 34:29–35) Finally, Moses actually enters "the cloud" (*Exodus* 24:15–18), and comes out having received stone tablets that the Lord has engraved with commandments (*Exodus* 24:12) that are to provide the foundation for, not only the political state of the Jews, but the entire Abrahamic tradition of revealed religion.

Of course, Moses broke the first set of tablets in a rage upon finding that his people had reverted to boisterous pagan rites during his long stay inside the object on the mountain. After pleading with the Lord not to destroy the entire Israelite camp as a punishment, and in order to assuage the Lord's anger with a lesser punishment, Moses rounds up his faithful men and has them massacre hundreds of their own brothers, sisters, mothers, fathers, and children, all for some singing and dancing around the idol of a golden calf. (*Exodus* 32) In evident approval of the massacre, the Lord then descends again in "the cloud" to meet with Moses and engrave a second set of tablets. (*Exodus* 34:5) Specific orders are also given for the construction and style of furnishing for a Tabernacle to house the stone tablets engraved with the Law, and once constructed, the Tent of the Meeting would be filled with light from the pillar at night, and *elohim* would even come down into the structure to receive sacrifices and give commands in person, face to face or "mouth to mouth." (*Exodus* 40:34, 38; *Numbers* 11:25; *Numbers* 12:4–8) At one point, angered with the Israelites, the Lord strikes out from the Tabernacle and sets fire to parts of the Israelite camp. (*Numbers* 11:1)

Moses was not the only one of the Israelites who was permitted to be inside the Tabernacle while the *elohim* were visiting it. Joshua was also allowed to do so as a young man. (*Exodus* 33:11) So it is unsurprising that after the death of Moses, the Lord appoints him to be the next leader of the Israelites (*Joshua* 1:5), the general who will actually conquer the land that Moses merely promised them. Success in this conquest is contingent on strict obedience to the law that was revealed to Moses. (*Joshua* 1: 6–8) The Lord commands Joshua to leave the livestock and other possessions of the Israelites (including their women) on the near side of the Jordan River, and to send an army of "fighting men" across it to conquer the land. (*Joshua* 1:14) When Joshua conveys this directive to his men, they swear to obey his commands just as they had obeyed those of Moses, so long as he is "strong and resolute," and they also threaten to put to death anyone who disobeys the orders of Joshua — which would include anyone who might conscientiously dissent with respect to the plan to invade and conquer Canaan. (*Joshua* 1:16–18)

The seizure of the fortified city of Jericho is to be the beachhead of the Israelite invasion of Canaan, and it begins when two spies enter the city on a reconnaissance mission. These find refuge in the house of a harlot named Rahab, who relates to them how the entire population is already intimidated by the Israelites on account of having heard of the "miracles" performed by the Lord on their behalf, such as the parting of the Red Sea. (*Joshua* 2:9–11) In exchange for her collaboration, including her misdirection of a search party trying to capture the spies, the spies promise Rahab that her family will be spared by the invading Israelites as long as they do not step outside of her house — which is to be marked with a crimson cord. (*Joshua* 3:13–19) Later, we learn that *only* Rahab and her household are spared in the destruction of Jericho. (*Joshua* 1:17, 22, 24–25)

On the way toward Jericho, the Israelites are told to march at a fixed distance behind the Ark of the Covenant — which is being carried by priests wearing special garments — and the Ark apparently acts as a pathfinder or guidance system to help the Israelites march along a route that they have never traveled before. (*Joshua* 3:1–4) As they are encamped along the Jordan River, Joshua tells his people to purify themselves, since the Lord is about to, once again, "perform wonders" in their midst. (*Joshua* 3:5) The first of these wonders concerns the manner in which the Israelites are to cross the Jordan River into the territory that the Lord has promised to them and intends to help them conquer. Here is what Joshua relates to his people concerning this impending act of God:

> "Come closer and listen to the words of the Lord your God… you shall know that a living God is among you, and that He will dispossess for you the Canaanites, Hittites, Hivites, Perizzites, Girgashites, Amorites, and Jebusites: the Ark of the Covenant of the Sovereign of all the earth is advancing before you into the Jordan. Now select twelve men from the tribes of Israel, one man from each tribe. When the feet of the priests bearing the Ark of the Lord, the Sovereign of all the earth, come to rest in the waters of the Jordan, the waters of the Jordan — the water coming from upstream — will be cut off and will stand in a single heap." (*Joshua* 3:9–13)

The text of this chapter goes on to explain the distinctly paranormal, not to say "supernatural," character of this event:

> Now the Jordan keeps flowing over its entire bed throughout the harvest season. But as soon as the bearers of the Ark reached the Jordan, and the feet of the priests bearing the Ark dipped into the water at its edge, the waters coming down from upstream piled up in a single heap a great way off, at Adam, the town next to Zarethan; and those flowing away downstream to the Sea of the Arabah (the Dead Sea) ran out completely. So the people crossed near Jericho. The priests who bore the Ark of the Lord's Covenant stood on dry land exactly in the middle of the Jordan, while all Israel crossed over on dry land, until the entire nation had finished crossing the Jordan... As soon as the priests who bore the Ark of the Lord's Covenant came up out of the Jordan, and the feet of the priests stepped onto the dry ground, the waters of the Jordan resumed their course, flowing over its entire bed as before. (*Joshua* 3:15–16, 4:18)

In other words, Joshua's crossing of the Jordan River is described in similar terms as the parting of the Red Sea by "the cloud," except that since it is a flowing river rather than a sea, the water is dammed up into an invisible wall only on one side of the Israelites. The Lord tells Joshua to demand that the Israelites commemorate this wonder by setting up a monument of twelve stones in the drained riverbed of the Jordan, one for each of Israel's twelve tribes. (*Joshua* 4:1–9) These stones, which are alleged to have been there underwater up to the day this narrative was put into writing, constitute a *sacred* site, or consecrated place. Ask yourself what, then, it is that makes a place consecrated to the "Sovereign of all the earth"? Or listen to the prophet Joshua when he explains that:

> "In time to come, when your children ask their fathers, 'What is the meaning of those stones?' tell your children: 'Here the Israelites crossed the Jordan on dry land.' For the Lord your God dried up the waters of the Jordan before you until you crossed, just as the Lord your God did to the Sea of Reeds, which He dried up before us until we crossed. *Thus all the peoples of the earth shall know how mighty is the hand of the Lord, and you shall fear the Lord your God always.*" (*Joshua* 4:21–24)

As "forty thousand shock troops" cross the Jordan "at the insistence of the Lord, to the steppes of Jericho for battle," we are told that on that day, the Lord exalted Joshua in the sight of all Israel, so that they revered him all his days as they had revered Moses. (*Joshua* 4:13–14) This establishes that the same Lord guiding Moses is now acting as the supreme commander of Joshua's troops as they begin the conquest of Canaan (the land that is to become Israel) with the sacking of Jericho. If there were any remaining doubt as to the fact that the plunder, rape, and wholesale slaughter of an entire civilian population that we are about to witness is taking place under the order of the Lord of the *Elohim*, the next episode in the book of Joshua makes this crystal clear. On the far side of the river crossing, *a man* claiming to be the "captain of the Lord's army" (the word "host" in this context means a military force) meets Joshua in order to brief him on coordinating with the Lord for the military task ahead. (*Joshua* 5:13,14) The very human-like appearance of this god is clear from the fact that at first, Joshua thinks that he might be an enemy soldier. (*Joshua* 5:13) Once it becomes clear who this is, Joshua prostrates himself face down on the ground in front of the god who is standing there with his sword drawn and asks, "What does my lord command his servant?" The "captain of the Lord's army" asks Joshua to remove his sandals in respect because, on account of his very presence, the ground on which they are standing is holy ground. (*Joshua* 5:14–15) All of this amounts to a deputizing of Joshua and a divine mandate for his mission.

The Lord's intervention here, however, continues in an even more direct fashion. He gives specific instructions to Joshua, again involving use of the Ark, to bring down the legendary fortifications of Jericho so that the Israelites can storm the city. This is the second of the promised "wonders." The Lord's Ark has already been used as a navigational instrument and as the source of a force capable of repelling water. Now it is used as a sonic weapon: it interacts with vibrations of sound, possibly amplifying and concentrating the sonic waves before directing them at the walls of Jericho. The Lord gives specific instructions for how this is to be accomplished: "Let all your troops march around the city and complete one circuit of the city. Do this six days, with seven priests carrying seven ram's horns preceding the Ark. On the seventh day, march around the city seven times, with the priests blowing the horns. And when a long blast is sounded on the horn — as soon as you hear that sound of the horn — all the people shall give a mighty shout. Thereupon the city wall will collapse, and the people shall advance, every man straight ahead." (*Joshua* 6:2–5) The Israelites follow these instructions, and after marching around the city the designated number of times with the Ark of the Covenant carried at their head, the army of Israel — who have been ordered to remain silent until the last circuit on the last day — shout out at once on the order of Joshua, when the ram's horns are sounded, and the walls of Jericho suddenly come crumbling down. (*Joshua* 6:20)

This allows for the army of Israel to rush in and capture the city. Here is what we are told about the conduct of the men under Joshua's command, and thus ultimately under the command of the Lord of the *elohim*:

> They exterminated everything in the city with the sword: man and woman, young and old, ox and sheep and ass. …They burned down the city and everything in it. But the silver and gold and the objects of copper and iron were deposited in the treasury of the House of the Lord. Only Rahab the harlot and her father's family were spared by Joshua… For she had hidden the messengers that Joshua sent to spy out Jericho. …The Lord was with Joshua, and his fame spread throughout the land. (*Joshua* 6:21–27)

So every civilian, including innocent children, was slaughtered in a lightning war directed by the Lord himself and accomplished with his wondrous instrument, the Ark. The only people judged worthy of survival are the family members of a prostitute who treasonously collaborated in the slaughter of her fellow citizens — again, including the women and children in her city.

We are told that the conquest of the rest of Canaan by the Israelites, who turn Canaan into the land of Israel by decimating its native population, proceeds in a comparably merciless manner. One particularly noteworthy episode in the course of this conquest takes place when the king of Jerusalem (this is Jerusalem *before* it becomes an Israelite city) assembles an alliance five kings, himself included, to meet Joshua's army and halt their advance. In the face of this massive alliance Joshua remains undismayed:

> Joshua addressed the Lord; he said in the presence of the Israelites:
> "Stand still, O sun, at Gibeon,
> O moon, in the Valley of Aijalon!"
> And the sun stood still
> And the moon halted,
> While a nation wreaked judgment on its foes —
> … Thus the sun halted in midheaven, and did not press on to set, for a whole day; for the Lord fought for Israel. Neither before nor since has there ever been such a day, when the Lord acted on words spoken by a man. (*Joshua* 10:12–14)

Once Joshua and his men capture the five kings allied against them, he has his officers place their feet on the kings' necks as a sign of victory, and then he impales the five kings on stakes throughout the evening before throwing their corpses in a cave. (*Joshua* 10: 24–27)

Ezekiel is yet another biblical prophet whose revelations are associated with repeated close encounters with unidentified flying objects and their occupants. Ezekiel has numerous distinct encounters with UFOs and the beings associated with them, and he describes these on at least ten occasions in his book, often referring back to the first encounter at the Chebar Canal in Babylonia to assert that the phenomena witnessed are the very same as those experienced there. These ten instances are *Ezekiel* 1:4–28; 3:12–15, 22–27; 8:2–4; 9:3; 10:1–21; 11:22–25; 37:27; 40:2–4; 43:1–7; and 44:1–4. By setting these complex and often confusing descriptions side by side, we can form a somewhat adequate phenomenological description of the objects and beings in question. It would be helpful to analyze the account of the sights, sounds, and sensations that Ezekiel experienced in terms of the visual appearance of the objects and associated beings, their situation in terms of the surrounding environment, their effect on their environs, and their capabilities to interact with people. There seem to be three or four types of objects described, although a couple of these might be the same object or objects viewed from different vantage points, or under varied conditions.

The first is a fiery "whirlwind" with a glowing amber light within it. This is a flying object that makes a roaring or whooshing sound. It may also cause the earth to tremble. This whirlwind can abduct a person and carry him up and away against his will, depositing him elsewhere — for example, on a mountaintop, or in a different city — in a state of shock and disorientation. The second object is a "wheelwork" consisting of four freestanding wheels that can revolve in any direction, each of which is cut through by another such wheel. In other words, each of the four wheels described consists of two rings, one set within the other, each revolving in any direction — so that the two rings revolving together often appear as if they are cutting through each other. This sounds something like a gyroscope. The wheels are described as being made of a material similar to beryl — a crystalline substance. They have markings that look like eyes inscribed all around them. These wheels are flying objects that can move in any one of the four cardinal directions at any point in their flight. This means that they can alter direction instantaneously, without veering or swerving. Although there does not appear to be any material connection between the four wheels, they seem organizationally associated into a "wheelwork" consisting of all of them, and it is possible for a man to step within this wheelwork.

Each of these wheels is associated with a being of humanoid form, except that they have four faces (that of a human, a lion, a bull, and an eagle), each facing in one of the four directions, and they have two pairs of wings, one pair extending outward to touch the wingtips of the other "cherubs," and two wings that cover their arms and hands, when these are not extending toward someone or something. When their wings move, for example during their ascent into the sky, loud sounds like the "din and clattering" of an army are heard. This sound is described as the voice of the Almighty, when he speaks.

These beings handle objects like hot coals inside the wheelwork, and flashes of lightning and fire flare up around them. Note that these winged beings, which are identified as "cherubim," are the same beings that the Lord appoints to guard the garden of the *elohim* at Eden, with similar rotating fiery swords or thunderbolts. At one point, one of them gives some of the glowing coal-like things to a man. Whenever these beings move, the wheels adjacent to them move as well, and vice versa; we are told that this is because the "spirit" of the beings is in the wheels.

Another object closely associated with these wheels is a platform that appears somewhat like sapphire. Above the platform is a fiery being whose upper parts are human in shape, but whose lower extremities fade into fire. In the upper part of the being, the fire seems contained in a man-shaped glassy form, or perhaps the fiery-appearing man is inside a glassy dome. There is a great deal of rainbow-colored light radiating around this being. One final type of object described seems to be the very same pillar of cloud from *Exodus*. This is also a flying or hovering object that, at one point, comes to rest within the court of the Temple at Jerusalem and, when it does so, it illuminates the entire area — just as the pillar of cloud did when it became a pillar of fire by night, guiding the Israelites through the Sinai desert by its light. The voice of the Lord is said to emanate from within this cloud. It is also associated with its own type of being, a man who looks like he is made of copper, and who guides Ezekiel around the Third Temple, precisely taking all of its measurements and teaching him its blueprint. I cannot help but to think of this metal man as a robot or android, especially since his sole task is precise measurement.

The phrase "the Presence of the Lord" is used with reference to one or more of these objects, and in one instance we have a description of the roaring sound and rumble as this "Presence of the Lord" lifts off from where it is standing and takes to the sky. (*Ezekiel* 3:12) At *Ezekiel* 37:27, the translators of the Jewish Publication Society's scholarly edition of the *Tanakh* have clarified that this word "Presence" literally means "dwelling place" — in other words, the Lord of the *elohim* is inside the object referred to, and seems to be using it to travel from place to place, and to interact with the prophet and others. It is clear from numerous passages that this Presence, within which the Lord is located, moves from one distinct place to another (*Ezekiel* 10:4–5, 18–20; 11:22–23; 43:1–4; 44:1–2). Passages such as these explicitly state that the Lord of Israel is a finite being that occupies one or another definite space at any given time. Moreover, setting them in the context of the other passages cited above, we see that He does so by means of a conveyance that gives off light when it flies, and that produces loud sound and vibrations when it is lifting off or landing. But what exactly is the agenda of this UFO occupant?

Ezekiel is chosen by the celestial warlord as a prophet of the tribulations that Israel will suffer on account of its defiance of the law and order that the *elohim* revealed through Abraham and Moses. One of the main concerns of the book of Ezekiel is to give an account of the transgressions for which the Israelites are being punished. Especially relevant in this regard are *Ezekiel* 6, 8, 16, and 23. These passages charge the Israelites with setting up altars to gods other than the Lord of the *elohim*, burning precious oils and scent-producing materials as incense in honor of these fetishes, shaping the gold granted by the Lord as war booty into phallic objects that feature on these altars and that they used as dildos, decorating these altars with fine fabrics and the images of various animals or gods in the shamanic shape of animals (like the golden calf during the exodus in the desert, which was a symbol of Hathor), building these shrines in various natural settings (mountaintops, large trees, springs, etc.), carrying out ritual sexual acts or orgies, emulating the peoples surrounding them by engaging in such pagan practices, and intermixing with these various aliens — in other words, abandoning their revealed law in favor of an eclectic, cosmopolitan culture.

Throughout *Ezekiel* 16, the Lord uses some very sexually charged language to compare Jerusalem to a whore on account of these syncretizing practices. Of particular interest in this chapter is the idea that the Lord found the people of Israel in a state of extraordinary vulnerability, like a naked and abandoned girl child. He claims that this girl, whom He took it upon Himself to become her guardian until she became a beautiful and self-confident woman, repaid him by playing the whore and, moreover, a "self-willed whore" who does not serve men for money, but freely takes whatever lovers she wishes for her pleasure. (*Ezekiel* 16:30–34) Since Ezekiel as a whole is especially concerned with the Babylonian exile community and the conquest of Israel by the Babylonians (*Ezekiel* 11–12), the language of this chapter can be seen to foreshadow that of the "whore of Babylon" (i.e., the goddess Ishtar) later on in the Bible. This is also the implication of the verses in *Ezekiel* 23 that compare the two great Israelite territories of Samaria and Jerusalem to two whores who lust after and breed with Assyrian and Chaldean governors and warriors from greater Babylonia. This cosmopolitanizing harlotry is compared to the early Egyptian influence on the Jews.

The Lord repeatedly describes these allegedly perverse "abominations" as acts of "rebellion," and he goes so far as to call the Israelites a uniquely "rebellious" people. He demands that Ezekiel prophesy to Israel the vengeance that he is going to exact upon them, and he reveals some of these acts of vengeance to the prophet in visions of the future. Therefore, the prophet Ezekiel is exemplary of prophecy in the sense of a warning of things to come. At *Ezekiel* 4–5 and 37, we see the Lord instructing Ezekiel in the use of sympathetic magic to help actualize these prophecies. These are essentially the same methods that, when used without the Lord's authorization, are condemned as sorcery or black magic. The episode of sorcery at *Ezekiel* 37 is especially noteworthy, since it prefigures the resurrection of the dead in Christianity. The Lord carries Ezekiel to a valley filled with dry bones, and he is told to utter incantations over them that cause them to reassemble, become covered with flesh, and which are then filled with the breath of life. The specific language of a future opening of the graves and a raising-up of the dead is first used here.

Two of Ezekiel's prophecies are of particular note insofar as they have been especially influential on subsequent Judeo-Christian expectations of a future apocalypse. These are the prophecies concerning Gog of Magog and the Third Temple at Jerusalem. We are presented with these, respectively, at *Ezekiel* 38–39 and 40–45. These prophecies are supposed to concern "the distant future" (38:8) when the Israelites, after having been scattered all over the world, are reunited in the land of Israel — at the center of the world — where they live with great wealth amassed in towns without walls or gates. On this "distant day," when the people of Israel are living in apparent security (38:14–16), there will be an invasion of Israel by a leader named Gog from an empire called Magog to the east and north of Israel — which apparently includes Persia, among other unidentifiable kingdoms. (38:5) This is the territory at the heart of the present-day Islamic world. This massive ground invasion of Israel will result in raging fires and earthquakes as part of a battle that litters Israelite territory with corpses and incinerates the cities of Magog. Following this, a Third Temple will be built in Jerusalem. Ezekiel is taken to the future and given a tour of this temple by a copper man who measures all of its proportions for him. (*Ezekiel* 40–45) Ezekiel reveals the template for the future kingdom of God on the Earth.

Several things are particularly noteworthy with respect to the prophecies of Ezekiel. Firstly, at *Ezekiel* 17, the Lord asks Ezekiel to "propound a riddle and relate an allegory to the House of Israel." The meaning of this allegory, in which a vine or tree and two eagles feature as symbols, is interpreted by the Lord Himself, and is significant insofar as it allows us to see that the author of this text is very clear on the distinction between an allegory with symbolic significance, which is set apart as such, and non-allegorical narratives which are characteristic of most of the prophecies in the book. This example is also relevant to the biblical literature in general. The authors of these books of the Bible were in many cases aware of what is allegorical or symbolic imagery, and so we are distorting the text if we read narratives that are intended to be historical, including those that set forth a precognitive history of a future yet to come, as purely allegorical or symbolic rather than factual.

Secondly, when Ezekiel prophesies, he appears to be very directly under the control of the Lord. Towards the end of *Ezekiel 3*, we are told that the Lord makes Ezekiel mute, except at times when he is to convey a specific message on behalf of the *elohim*. The prophet is, quite literally, struck dumb and unable to speak in his own voice. Remember that Muhammad was chosen by the Lord in part because he was illiterate and untrained in the poetic arts, so he supposedly could not have composed the *Qur'an* on his own. Several passages throughout the book of Ezekiel also speak of the prophet being controlled, in body and mind, as if he were a puppet. (*Ezekiel 2:1–2*) He is fed a scroll featuring the "lamentations, dirges, and woes" that he is going to speak like an old computer being fed a punch card. (*Ezekiel 2:9–10*) Overall, the impression we are given of Ezekiel is that of a ventriloquist's dummy.

Thirdly, and most importantly, Ezekiel is ethically appalled by some of the things that the Lord reveals that He intends to do to the Israelites. We see this very clearly in *Ezekiel 9*, especially 9:8–11, when, in a passage reminiscent of Abraham's (unsuccessful) negotiations with the Lord to spare the inhabitants of Sodom, the prophet Ezekiel asks the Lord in horror how or why he could treat people the way that he intends to. The specific act of vengeance that catalyzes Ezekiel's protest is the Lord's command to five armed men, accompanied by a sixth who is a scribe dressed in the manner of a Levite priest, to go through the city and murder everyone, including old men, women, and little children who do not object to the various practices of pagan idolatry that the Israelites are engaging in.

Before Ezekiel registers this complaint, we have already been told that the Lord plans to annihilate his "chosen" people by letting loose pestilence or diseases upon them, subjecting them to a famine on account of which they will turn to cannibalism, and setting numerous foreign armies against them in order to slay them by the sword and drive them into exile in disparate lands; the Lord seems very proud of the fact that he will do all this in wrathful passion, and without showing the least bit of compassion for anyone. (*Ezekiel 5:5–15*) One way that the Lord intends to spread disease seems to be by making the Israelites eat unclean bread that they have to bake using their own excrement, so he is in effect telling them to eat shit and die. (*Ezekiel* 4:12–13) Another, obviously, would be children eating their parents, and vice versa.

These passages — and many others like them — demonstrate that it is indeed far too arbitrary to take "revealed" religion to be limited to "the feelings, acts, and experiences of individual men in their solitude, so far as they apprehend themselves to stand in relation to whatever they may consider the divine."[35] William James remarks that he could "escape much controversial matter by this arbitrary definition," and indeed he does, but at the cost of maintaining his pragmatic, radically empiricist stance with respect to the subject at hand. Whether or not it is the case that "for each man to stay in his own experience, whate'er it be, and for others to tolerate him there, is surely best,"[36] that is almost the *opposite* of how it stands empirically with "revealed" religion, which is now, and always has been, a socially binding phenomenon — if not *the* social phenomenon *par excellence*. The very word "religion" itself derives from the root *religere*, meaning to link, to yoke, or to bind. Religion is what binds one most, to the sacred and to others who hold the same to be sacred or deserving of the ultimate sacrifice.

Nowhere is the political character of religion more apparent than in the case of Islam, the most current and — by its own lights — most uncontaminated and pristine "revealed" religion. In verses 6:114–116; 10:15; 10:65; 43:2; 85:21–22; 86:12–14; and 2:174–177, the *Qur'an* takes great pains to make clear that its injunctions are perfect, eternally valid, and are to be obeyed without any alteration; a perfect and complete guide to life that should be followed over the opinions of the majority of people in the world. Verse 2:85 makes it perfectly clear that you cannot pick what parts of it you believe in. At 3:6–7, it is stated that the literal verses of the *Qur'an* (such as the legal ones) are its foundation; they are separate from the alle-

---

35   Ibid., p. 36.
36   Ibid., p. 438.

gorical passages, and are not to be interpreted metaphorically or modified thereby. 5:44–45 demands either forgiveness of a crime by its victim or strict adherence to Islamic laws. 2:194 establishes the law of *talion* — eye for an eye, commensurate justice. 5:38 establishes amputation (cutting off hands) as the Islamic punishment for theft. 4:34 permits men to beat those of their wives from whom they fear disobedience. 4:16 states that men are allowed many wives and slave girls captured in battle, but a woman who sleeps with any other man than her husband is put under house arrest until death. In 2:223, we see that a woman does not have a right to refuse a man sex when he wants it, which highlights the fact that a woman's sexuality belongs to her husband. Women can only inherit half of the property that men do (4:11), and in court, the testimony of any woman is worth half that of a man, because she is supposedly feebleminded. (2:82) Finally, the *Qur'an* not only constitutes a political state, it establishes a basic economic policy. In 16:71,75, God forbids raising a slave, who is legitimately one's property, up to the level of one's social or economic equal; he favors maintaining the economic inequality of rich and poor. Religious revelation is not primarily about "the interest of the individual in his private personal destiny."[37]

The remarks above, which compare Le Baron's mediumistic trances to those episodes of psychic automatism wherein the *Qur'an* was revealed to Muhammad (over a period of 22 years), do not do justice to the intensity of *public* engagement with human affairs on the part of Muhammad's "divine" handlers. An army of angels led by Gabriel was promised to Muhammad at the Battle of Badr, where a better equipped army of Meccans outnumbered the prophet's forces by more than 3 to 1. The *hadith* recount the presence of God's soldiers on the battlefield alongside Muhammad's forces. They were invisible to the eyes of most, but not all, of those fighting. The angelic forces arrived in a noisy "cloud"-like vehicle, which deployed them from the sky down onto the battlefield.[38] The "Lord

---

37   Ibid., pp. 439–440.

38   Lings, *Muhammad*, p. 152.

of the Worlds" gives direct instructions to his battalions of troops to de-capitate opposing forces (a quick, merciful death) or strike off their fingers (so that they will be unable to hold swords). (*Qur'an* 8:12) Soldiers fight-ing with Muhammad reported seeing heads severed without any appar-ent causes, and others who actually glimpsed the Lord's soldiers at work described them being conveyed by something like horses whose hooves never touched the ground.[39] They wore distinct garments and headgear, and were led by Gabriel.

One should recall that, like the *elohim* of the Old Testament, Gabriel appears *plainly in the form of a man*. This man brought the first Qur'anic revelation to Muhammad on the night that he was alone in a cave in the hills outside Mecca. A stranger sneaks up on Muhammad in the cave, grabs hold of him repeatedly, and asks him to "recite" what has been telepathically conveyed to him each time he is let loose.[40] After twice protesting to the visitor that he is no "reciter" or poet, Muhammad — an illiterate — finally senses that the words of the first *surah* are imprinted on his mind, and he repeats them as if without any effort on his own part. Muhammad grows suddenly afraid that an evil spirit has possessed him, and he runs out of the cave. As he is scampering away down the hillside, he hears the voice of the man he encountered in the cave, again telepathi-cally, and when he looks up, he sees a large, luminescent object in the clear night sky above him — from which the "voice" seems to be emanating.[41] This object moves, as if instantaneously, to meet Muhammad's gaze at every point on the horizon as he turns his head in disbelief from one car-dinal direction to another.[42] This experience, recorded in the *hadith*, is the context for verse 81:23 in the *Qur'an*: "No, your compatriot [Muhammad, as often referred to through his own mouth in the third person] is not

39   Ibid., p. 152.
40   Ibid., pp. 44–45.
41   Ibid.
42   Ibid.

mad. He saw him [Gabriel] on the clear horizon. He does not grudge the secrets of the unseen; nor is this the utterance of an accursed devil."

The incident with the flying cloud-like (steel grey) object at Badr, which deploys the Lord's host, or Gabriel's luminescent conveyance on the night of the first revelation, are not the only verses in the *Qur'an* that are peculiarly evocative of space travel and other metaphors that sound curiously technological. Verse 32:5 reads, "He governs all, from heaven to earth. And all will ascend to Him in a single day, a day whose space is a thousand years by your reckoning." Verses 55:33–34 are even more curious: "Mankind and *jinn*, if you have power to penetrate the confines of heaven and earth, then penetrate them! But this you shall not do except with Our own authority." The *jinn* are a titanic humanoid race that lived on Earth during the First Creation, before Noah's Flood. *Jinn* is the Arabic term for the fallen "watchers" (*nephilim*) of *Genesis* [and the *Book of Enoch*]. The First Creation, during which they ruled the Earth, is explicitly referenced in this equally tantalizing passage which, to my mind at least, evokes something like genetic engineering: "It was We that ordained death among you. Nothing can hinder Us from replacing you by others like yourselves or transforming you into beings you know nothing of. You surely know of the First Creation. Why, then, do you not reflect?" (*Qur'an* 56:58–59) The ordaining of death among mortals is clearly a reference back to the decision of the *elohim* in Genesis to cut short the human lifespan to a fraction of what it was (for the *jinn*) before the Flood of Noah destroyed their godless high civilization. Finally, there is Muhammad's space-time distorting night flight to Jerusalem riding aboard *buraq*, during which he infamously imprints the Temple rock.[43]

---

43   Ibid., pp. 104–107.

CHAPTER XII

MERCURIAL HERMENEUTICS

Many of the "miraculous" occurrences recounted in the scriptures of revealed religions make much more sense if they are read as historical narratives of paranormal phenomena — sometimes directly affecting multiple persons and witnessed by massive crowds. Failure to recognize this involvement of the masses in the religious experiences constitutive of the major revealed religions is another shortcoming of William James' interpretation of Religion in *The Varieties of Religious Experience*. He concerns himself only with the personal "mystical" experiences of individuals in isolation, but that is not what wrought the Abrahamic religions. Nor can one posit that it is simply a combination of such personal experiences and a shrewd political sense that is at work here. Instead, what we have are experiences — often with multiple participants and witnesses — that are on a continuum with contemporary incidents of the paranormal, especially those usually characterized as "UFO" related phenomena. This has been missed by most researchers of "Unidentified Flying Objects" for two main reasons: first, they fail to recognize the antiquity of the worldwide phenomenon, which stretches, unbroken from modern encounters with "flying objects" and their occupants back through similar accounts from the nineteenth century, records from the Renaissance and the Middle Ages, all the way into the Classical period and the even more remote human past; and second, in seeking to establish their enterprise as a "nuts and bolts" scientific research project more respectable than that of parapsychology, Ufologists have underplayed or outright denied the extensive psychic elements of "UFO" phenomena.

This is the argument made by Jacques Vallée, whose accomplishments include working with DARPA as the single most significant contributor to designing the architecture of the Internet, and developing the first digital map of Mars for NASA. Vallée first studied Unidentified Flying Objects when he was hired by the US Air Force to assist Professor J. Allen Hynek of Northwestern University on Project Blue Book. In this capacity, Vallée witnessed the distortion or suppression of evidence for unexplained encounters with UFOs. With unique access to the data that he and Hynek had amassed, Vallée went on to write an early scientific analysis entitled *Unidentified Flying Objects: Anatomy of a Phenomenon*. It remains one of the classic scientific studies of hard evidence for the UFO phenomenon — such as multiple expert witness sightings, radar tapes confirming objects carrying impossible maneuvers suggestive of intelligence at incredible speeds, carefully analyzed photographs, and material traces at landing sites. Vallée had first encountered psychic phenomena while developing the DARPA Network. He later became directly acquainted with parapsychological research when the Stanford Research Institute (SRI) requested his presence as a consultant on the remote viewing project that had been outsourced to them by the Central Intelligence Agency and the Department of Defense. It did not take long for him to realize the deep connection between the two phenomena, UFOs and psi, or even that they are two aspects of the same phenomenon — which has been with us throughout our recorded history.

Possessed of the honesty of a true scientist, an eye for wonder, and the fearless curiosity of those rare discoverers responsible for scientific revolutions, Vallée came to realize that the UFO phenomenon was in some sense a parapsychological anomaly "beyond reason."[1] He explains, "Whenever a set of unusual circumstances is presented, it is in the nature

---

[1]   Jacques Vallée, *Passport to Magonia: On UFOs and Folklore* (Chicago: Contemporary Books), p. 154.

of the human mind to analyze it until a rational pattern is encountered at some level. But it is quite conceivable that nature should present us with circumstances so deeply organized that our observational and logical errors would entirely mask the pattern to be identified. To the [genuine] scientist there is nothing new here."[2] Non-governmental groups such as the Aerial Phenomena Research Organization (APRO) or the National Investigations Committee on Aerial Phenomena (NICAP), let alone government-funded "studies" like Project Blue Book or the Condon Report, were filtering out large percentages of raw data in a vain attempt to understand what was going on in an entirely rational, nuts-and-bolts manner.[3] In his search for patterns, Vallée discovered one far less conventional than those he had earlier suggested when he hypothesized regular UFO "waves" or "flaps" coordinated in some way with sidereal time. Examining the discarded data on a continuum with the accepted facts, and without the preconceived intellectual constraints of the prevailing scientific paradigm of materialist Rationalism, the pattern that Vallée now saw was one connecting modern UFO sightings back to the fairy faith and folklore of olden times. Vallée first set out this thesis in *Passport to Magonia*. While *Passport to Magonia* already involved an engagement with the psychical dimension of the UFO phenomenon insofar as the construction of folklore is a psychological process, in *The Invisible College*, Vallée makes his thesis about the centrality of parapsychological phenomena to close encounters explicit, and he expands his historical contextualization of close encounters from folklore to religious "revelations" and "miracles."

Vallée begins *The Invisible College* with the observation that, despite what nuts-and-bolts researchers expecting to find straightforward visitations from another planet in the context of established physical theories would like to believe, close encounters with what we contemporarily refer to as UFOs and their occupants usually involve one or more of the phe-

---

2   Ibid., p. 154.

3   Ibid., pp. 110–111.

nomena studied by parapsychologists.[4] People who observe UFOs often "hear" messages conveyed to them during the observation, and some of those who claim to be in contact with the occupants of these craft channel large quantities of information from the supposed entities in question by essentially the same means — automatic writing and so forth — as nineteenth-century mediums used with the aim of communicating with the dead.[5] Certain close encounters will involve distortions of the sense of time and space that are akin to those experienced by a person who enters a trance for some time; after seeing UFOs, such people might drive to unfamiliar distant locations, as if guided by a will other than their own, and then, once they have come to their senses, wonder why they are wherever they are. Those with a history of involvement with UFOs will sometimes also display psychokinetic abilities, such as spoon bending, levitation, or the ability to pass through solid surfaces.[6] Some people have been healed of serious ailments, including blindness and broken bones, on account of proximity to the objects or their occupants; others have been harmed — their bodies marked by geometrically shaped burns or scars, and drained of all vitality.[7]

The sudden apparitions of the craft themselves, their strange transmogrifications, and equally sudden disappearance are more akin to the materializations of "ectoplasm" during the most astonishing séances in the epoch of spiritualism than they are to any future astronautics technology that we could conceivably extrapolate from our own.[8] These "objects" move as erratically as poltergeist phenomena — changing directions nearly instantaneously, or coming to an abrupt stop at speeds measured by radar in the range of thousands of miles per hour, which defies known

4   Jacques Vallée, *The Invisible College: What a Group of Scientists Has Discovered About UFO Influences on the Human Race* (New York: E. P. Dutton & Co., 1975), pp. 17–18, 20.

5   Ibid., pp. 71, 73.

6   Ibid., pp. 137–138.

7   Ibid., pp. 150, 158.

8   Ibid., p. 6.

gravitational laws and ought to involve inertial forces that would crush any pilots onboard. The extensive radar recordings, collisions, landing traces, and certain consistent observational characteristics establish that UFOs do indeed manifest as *physical* objects — but they are also *psychic* devices.[9] They have a technological basis, but one with profound psychical effects.[10]

It is not as if one can, by anything other than arbitrary prejudice, separate the cases for which there is only "hard evidence" — as in evidence that does not contradict established physical theories — from those that involve various forms of Extrasensory Perception and Psychokinesis.[11] For example, Vallée presents a July 1959 case that has since become a matter of public record wherein six men from the Central Intelligence Agency and a representative of the office of Naval Intelligence were sent by the colonel in charge of Project Blue Book to investigate a medium who claimed to be in contact with Uranus.[12] It may not be so remarkable to anyone familiar with parapsychological studies that this medium was able to train one of the government officials to replicate her feats of automatic writing at the behest of an entity calling itself "Affa," which was getting in touch from Uranus.[13] We ought, however, to be disturbed by the fact that when the officials attending this modern-day séance requested that Affa manifest itself in the form of a UFO one afternoon, that is exactly what they got. Not only did all three official witnesses file a report stating that they observed the same flying disc in the sky after Affa told them to go to the window, their request for radar confirmation met with the response that radar returns in that particular sector had somehow been knocked out.[14] It is relevant to note that John Dee, the astrologer, chief advisor, and intelligence officer who worked for Queen Elizabeth under the code name 007

---

9   Ibid., p. 202.
10   Ibid., p. 154.
11   Ibid., p. 186.
12   Ibid., p. 72.
13   Ibid., p. 73.
14   Ibid., pp. 74, 76.

claimed to be in communication with otherworldly beings who taught him their "Enochian" language and that, in this "celestial language," which was adopted by the occultist Aleister Crowley (also a British intelligence operative) and his followers, the word *Affa* means "empty."[15] Were the medium and the military intelligence men sent to investigate her after being told that they were receiving hot air from Uranus?! No wonder saucers are mistaken for "swamp gas."[16]

What is most philosophically significant about the "phenomeno-logical" approach that Vallée recommends in *The Invisible College* is his suggestion that this phenomenon forces us to rethink the supposed distinction between the physical and psychical.[17] UFOs are, in his view, manifestations of a psychic or psychokinetic technology that functions as a control system. The mechanism is able to maintain control precisely by means of the apparent absurdity of the apparitions that it projects.[18] First of all, the lurid character of so many of these contacts prevents them from being taken seriously by the scientific establishment of the target society, and instead these experiences are allowed to sink into the deeper, dreamlike psychical substrate that defines the mythic folklore of a culture.[19] "Myths," Vallée explains, "are operated upon by symbols, and the language these symbols form constitutes a complete system. This system is meta-logical... It violates no laws because it is the substance of which laws are made."[20] The lack of serious scientific study attendant to the absurdity of the apparitions in turn ensures that there will also be no coordinated military or political response to the interventions.[21] Now essentially rendered defenseless, ordinary people in the target society are confronted with encounters that are confusing, or even paradoxical, by

---

15   Ibid., p. 85.
16   Ibid., pp. 42–43.
17   Ibid., p. 2.
18   Ibid., pp. 26–27.
19   Ibid., pp. 4, 202.
20   Ibid., p. 202.
21   Ibid., pp. 27, 202.

design.[22] The average human mind, being incapable of remaining in a state of profoundly disturbing confusion, is broken open and rendered uniquely vulnerable to suggestion by such catalysts.

Vallée draws a comparison to attendees of a really spectacular magic show who are so troubled by the extraordinary feats they have witnessed that they accept bogus explanations given by the magician, and only later realize that if they try to replicate the "trick," that the explanation does not add up.[23] Actually, the situation is somewhat worse than this, because all but the most well-funded government agencies or private corporations would never be in a position to try and replicate *this* magic trick. Prepared to seize on any explanation that makes at least a little more sense than the patent absurdity with which she has been faced, a witness who has experienced a close encounter believes it when she is told that higher beings in some such place as Uranus have chosen her for a special mission.

Those who have not been contacted in this fashion, and who have no sense of what it means to try to abide in absurdity, ridicule and ostracize the contactees to the point of isolating them from their family, friends, and the rest of society.[24] They form their own cult and, as could be expected from any traumatized and marginalized group left to fend for itself, these cultists turn increasingly inwards in their conviction that their hardship reflects their having been "chosen" for deliverance, that it is everyone else who is deluded, and that theirs is the only way.[25] Shrill prophecies emerge concerning their own triumph and the cataclysms to be suffered by those who refuse to see the light.[26] These awe-full interventions in human society take place with the kind of phased irregularity of behavioral conditioning mechanisms applied to laboratory rats, which

---

22   Ibid., pp. 116–117.

23   Ibid., pp. 59–60.

24   Ibid., p. 173.

25   Ibid., pp. 66, 70.

26   Ibid., p. 63.

are conditioned faster if they are not presented with stimuli in too regular a fashion.[27]

Vallée writes that he is tired of behaving like a lab rat pressing levers.[28] As an information scientist, he knows that there is a way to gain access to the reference level of every control system rather than being distracted by what it displays. Vallée draws an interesting analogy between the UFO control system and a thermostat:

> We have seen that the control system operates like a thermostat and other such systems. It progresses by oscillations, drawing from the antagonism of fire and ice, warm and cold, evil and good, all myths for the feeble minds of men... Few people have grasped both the physics and the beauty of it... Thermostats control temperature; gyroscopes control the direction in which a rock flies. What could a paranormal phenomenon control? *I suggest that it is human belief that is being controlled and conditioned.*[29]

He remarks that even a small child can get at a thermostat and elicit *some kind* of change in its functioning by climbing up on a chair and fiddling with it, though his rebellious curiosity is likely to meet with a spanking from his father.[30] A scientist ought to risk this.

When the men of knowledge of the Classical age failed to take up this challenge, we lost our civilization. From start to finish, the formative phase of the Christian religion is just as thoroughly conditioned by manifestations of the UFO type as the careers of the Jewish prophets who paved the way for the coming of this alleged Messiah. Mary conceives after a visitation, and probably an insemination, by Gabriel that she finds terrifying; he appears plainly in the form of a man, just as the *elohim* of old. (*Luke* 1:26–29) The relevant passages of scripture are clear that the so-called "star" that the three Magi from the Persian Empire followed to the birthplace of Jesus in Bethlehem is a moving, luminous object under

---

27   Ibid., p. 199.

28   Ibid., p. 206.

29   Ibid., p. 201.

30   Ibid., p. 196.

apparently intelligent control, and *not* an actual star or planet that crosses the heavens in a fixed manner together with other stars; it finally stops flying and comes to stand over where the newborn child is so that the shepherds there are also filled by fear at its radiant glory. (*Matthew* 2:9; *Luke* 2:9) When Jesus is baptized by John in the Jordan, "the heavens were opened," and the spirit of God descends in physical form, flying down like a dove — in other words, relatively motionless despite its wings being spread — before assuming a stationary position and hovering directly over him. (*John* 1:32; *Luke* 3:22) Regarding the metaphor of the "dove," it is worthy of note that it is directly connected to the pillar of fire and "cloud" of *Exodus* in a verse from *Isaiah* that reads, "Who are these that fly like a cloud, and like doves to their windows?" (*Isaiah* 60:8) A voice emanates from the object to declare, "This is my beloved Son, with whom I am well pleased," whereupon Jesus is lifted straight up out of the water and carried into the sky — as if by a tractor beam — to be deposited some distance away, in the desert wilderness, where he is to be tempted by the devil. (*Matthew* 3:16–4:1) This kind of abduction and dislocation by the "whirlwind" that God rides in would often happen to Elijah. (*II Kings* 2:16)

In fact, the so-called Transfiguration incident during the course of which Jesus introduces his disciples to both Elijah and Moses on a mountaintop is another instance wherein a bright, luminous object appears, and it is this object that makes the face and garments of Jesus shine brightly in its white light; it acts both as a conveyance for these apparently still-living ancient prophets and to broadcast the message, once again: "This is my beloved Son, with whom I am well pleased; listen to him." (*Matthew* 17:1–8) The same "angels," or *elohim*, that are present at the birth of Jesus, that saw to his needs during his lifetime (*Matthew* 4:11), and one of whom Mary Magdalene encounters at the open tomb on Easter Sunday (*Matthew* 28:1–7), are also present at the so-called Ascension, wherein the resurrected Jesus is carried up and away by a UFO for the last time before the promised Second Coming, and in full view of his astonished disciples, who are gazing skywards with their mouths agape. (*Acts* 1:6–11)

Nor did the interventions cease with the departure of Christ. The text of Acts 9, 22, and 26, when taken together, make it quite clear that the other men who were traveling with Paul on the road to Damascus, while he was still a chief Jewish adversary of the nascent Christian movement, experienced the same stunning light descending from the sky, brighter than the Sun. Moreover, the voice that he hears is not one readily identifiable by him, so that the interpretation that he was simply experiencing a pang of conscience translated into an auditory hallucination is unwarranted. It is only once Paul asks the voice emanating from the luminous aerial object what lordly person it is who says, "Saul, Saul, why do you persecute me?" that he receives the answer that it is Christ. Apparently, Jesus was still traveling around in his heavenly father's aerial object that he boarded at the Ascension.

Vallée comments on the extensive similarities between contemporary close encounters and the prophetic literature recounting angelic interventions in the Middle East.[31] He suggests that we ought to take a quite literal reading of accounts like that of the flying wheel of Ezekiel, and the beams of light that shine down on those elected for "revelations," as phenomenological descriptions ventured by people whose minds were struggling to grasp the technology with which they found themselves confronted.[32] No major thinker of Classical Rome took these accounts seriously or viewed the cult formed around them as a viable social force — until it seized control of the Roman Empire and, for over a thousand years, the study of Plato and his colleagues was eclipsed by enforced faith in inanities comparable to the ravings of those now receiving apocalyptic communications from a viral culture based somewhere on Uranus.[33] The best that the leading lights of the Classical academies could do when Justinian finally closed down their schools altogether was to escape to neighboring Persia, but only shortly thereafter, the Persians also appear to have been targeted

---

31 Ibid., pp. 79, 126.

32 Ibid., pp. 125, 134, 136–137.

33 Ibid., p. 126.

by what Vallée calls the control system. This is not the place to show how the so-called "Islamic Golden Age" was a restricted and slowed-down abortion, or miscarriage, of a Renaissance that could have taken place in Iran — through a synthesis of Hellenistic and Zoroastrian modes of thought — hundreds of years before it finally dawned in Europe, had it not been for the Muhammadan invaders who bound and then raped the Promethean Persian genius.

As I have already noted in my comparison of the *Qur'an* with the messages channeled by Albert Le Baron, Vallée remarks that the "revelations" received by contemporary UFO contactees seem to function in the same way as the communications of spiritualist mediums.[34] The control system may release latent abilities for poetic expression in a medium, or allow him to telepathically draw on the abilities of others close to him, but it does not volunteer anything beyond what is already available *at an unconscious level* to those involved in contact, within the context of their own epoch.[35] Far be it from Uranus to actually enrich human knowledge! The following remarks of Vallée are particularly relevant to the composition of the *Qur'an*, whose poetic manner of expression — coupled with the illiteracy of its medium, namely Muhammad — is taken for evidence of its divine origin:

> In the psychic literature there are cases where the entities which manifest themselves by guiding the hand or using the voice of a human channel seem to exhibit a level of knowledge beyond that of the medium; however, such a fact can seldom be proved. The fact that the writing appears much more beautiful than anything the person can produce in a normal state means nothing, as it is often sufficient simply to unlock the unconscious mind to release a veritable stream of artistic energy. To use it productively is another matter, as the adepts of the psychedelic movement have painfully discovered. ...Communications may be received from a variety of sources... These entities have been known to masquerade as departed souls, as great minds of antiquity, as denizens of other planets. There is no question that some of their statements can achieve dimensions of real beauty and can assume a very prophetic stance.[36]

---

34   Ibid., p. 77.

35   Ibid., pp. 30, 82, 86.

36   Ibid., p. 86.

The Judeo-Christian *Bible* and the *Qur'an* reflect the unconscious knowledge-base of the lower social strata of their time and place, just as the ramblings of genuine mediums in all likelihood unwittingly drew from the unconscious knowledge, hopes, and fears of séance attendees, rather than from departed spirits "on the other side."[37] A reader of Classical Philosophy in Alexandria at the zenith of pagan Rome, or a composer of Persian astronomical or medical treatises at Gondeshapur in the period right before the Islamic conquest, would have dismissed them as ignorant nonsense in just the way that the cosmology presented by Uri Geller is dismissed as nonsense by physicists, even though it contains tensor equations, which seem to be telepathically drawn out of the unconscious of his more scientifically eloquent promoter, Andrej Puharich, rather than from his "space brothers."[38] We are dealing with another Moses and Aron routine here.

Vallée argues that we who are scientifically-minded ignore the increasing numbers of UFO prophets like Uri Geller at our own risk as an ever greater segment of the population takes their experiences and abilities as evidence that "a higher intelligence is not only cognizant of our existence and development here on earth, but has decided to interfere with human affairs."[39] Should we continue to do so, "reality" is likely to be as violently redefined for us as it was for that generation of Roman gentlemen *and learned women* who ignored and mocked the Christians until they were forced to watch the Library of Alexandria go up in flames. When another Constantine baptizes armies under the banner of an alien god, who will be ready to speak for Earth?

Many of the "miraculous" events constitutive of "revealed" religions take place on a mass scale over extended periods of time, in the context of which it is hard to deny that a seemingly superhuman agency is bringing some form of *techne* to bear on the reconstruction of human belief

---

37   Ibid., p. 80.
38   Ibid., pp. 71–72, 82.
39   Ibid., p. 185.

systems. Fatima is one fairly recent case of this kind, which seamlessly bridges the epochs of angelic intervention and UFO visitation. Vallée's account of what happened at Fatima, Portugal, between the summer and fall of 1917 is very compelling.[40] However, a more updated interpretation of the Fatima "miracles" as close encounter experiences is provided by the American philosopher of religion, Jeffrey Kripal, in his study of the paranormal and sacred entitled *Authors of the Impossible*, which features an entire chapter on Jacques Vallée.[41] Kripal, who chairs the religious studies department at Rice University, takes Vallée's basic thesis very seriously, in which he claims that many religious "revelations" and "miracles" not only involve the kind of extraordinary human capacities studied by psychical researchers such as William James and Frederic Myers, but that these interactions with "heavenly" beings are on a historical continuum with what is now perceived as the UFO phenomenon.[42] In his capacity as a scholar of religion, Kripal thinks that Fatima may have been "the most spectacular religious event of the 20th century."[43] The following account of the Fatima manifestations synthesizes key elements in the narratives of Vallée and Kripal.

The story revolves around three little illiterate Portuguese shepherds: Jacinta, age seven; her brother Francisco, age nine; and their cousin, Lucia, age ten. Beginning on Sunday, May 13, 1917, at a desolate rocky cove in the Fatima district of Portugal, these children witnessed lightning without thunder and the apparition of a beautiful little lady, who claimed that she was "from Heaven," alight on an oak tree. Quite unlike later, Catholicized images of Our Lady of Fatima, this being wore a tight-fitting knee-high dress with a cape. Her feet did not touch the ground, and her lips did not move when she "spoke" or, rather, when the children *telepathically* "heard" her communications. She gave the two younger children some liquid sub-

---

40   Ibid., pp. 141–153.

41   Jeffrey Kripal, *Authors of the Impossible* (Chicago: University of Chicago Press, 2010), pp. 275–282.

42   Ibid., pp. 143–197.

43   Ibid., p. 275.

stance to ingest, and Lucia was offered some solid form of "communion." The Lady promised that a great miracle would take place on October 13 and told the children to return regularly until then. Each time they did so, more and more people would join them. At first, many were unconvinced that these were divine rather than diabolical manifestations. Lucia herself was afraid that she might be witnessing one of the Devil's spectacles, and she initially resisted her devout father's interpretation that the being was Our Lady. Not all of those who gathered around the tree with the children could see the being, but they saw, heard, smelled, and felt many other strange things — all of which are associated with close encounters, including orbs of light and oval-shaped "clouds" darting around the sky, and a buzzing or hissing sound similar to that of bees or cicadas, but somewhat more mechanical in tone. Even though many could not see the being inside the orb of light that would descend onto the oak tree, they did notice that it bent the upper limbs of this tree just as an object with a real mass would have. Strange odors also periodically wafted through the air.

The principal events took place on the thirteenth day of each month from May until October, with the number of people in attendance on these six occasions rising as follows: 3, 50, 4,500, 30,000, and finally 70,000. The three children received a number of grim prophecies from the apparition. These included, in 1917, the warning that if mankind did not repent, beginning with the reign of a Pope who took office in 1939, there would be another world war even more terrible than the present one. The flash of an atomic bomb also seems to be described as a harbinger of the destruction of mankind. The entity instructed the children to keep part of the prophecy secret until 1960, an interesting date given that in 1962 the Cuban Missile Crisis brought us closer to nuclear armageddon than ever before or since. Such a connection seems especially warranted in light of the fact that the children claim that the apparition viewed the conversion of Russia as key to averting this ultimate catastrophe that was heralded by the light that turns night into day.

On October 13, 1917, with anywhere from 50–70,000 people in attendance, the long awaited great "miracle" took place. By now all of the
newspapers had been covering the events, with numerous professional
journalists on site. This had brought not only believers, but also many
skeptics and atheists to the valley. After months of being stripped for de-
votional relics, the oak tree was already reduced to a stump. It had been
raining in the morning, soaking the clothes of the tens of thousands of
people already gathered there. The rain stopped suddenly and the clouds
parted to reveal a silvery disc-shaped object. After darkening the actual
Sun to the point where some people claim to have been able to make out
the stars and the Moon, this flying disc turned on its edge and began to
spin in a globe-like fashion in the place of the Sun. Certain of those gathered felt waves of intense heat; the clothes of some dried instantly, while
others remained soaked.

A white, flaky substance fell from the sky like snow. Most of it de-
materialized as people reached for it, or once it touched the ground, but
some were able to gather a bit and pull it apart into thin fibers before it
disintegrated. This substance has since come to be known as "angel hair"
or "fibralvina" in the Ufological literature, wherein certain researchers
speculate that it may be an ionization effect. The spinning disc projected
a kaleidoscopic display of monochromatic sectors of colored light from
its rather defined edge. To the awe of tens of thousands of witnesses, the
terrain was covered in geometric sectors of violet, yellow, blue, red, and
green light. People heard a buzzing sound.

Finally, to the horror of all those assembled, and many others watching
from a further distance, the disc that had taken the place of the Sun — and
that appeared to many *to be* the Sun on account of how it had managed to
dim the actual solar disc — returned to a more horizontal orientation and
began to fall from the sky with the swaying motion of a leaf. Anyone at all
familiar with UFO research will recognize this as the pattern of motion
most characteristic of disc-shaped craft that are hovering in a single area.
By this time, a number of the skeptical atheists present had fallen on their

knees together with the believers. People began to plead for mercy and confess their sins to each other en masse. Once the flying disc reached treetop level, it suddenly shot back up into the sky and disappeared into the actual Sun, the natural luminosity of which was then restored. Such an interplay between the actual Sun and a UFO taking on the appearance of a Sun-like globe — and for some time replacing, and dimming the actual Sun, while remaining in place — may account for the aforementioned incident wherein Joshua successfully commands "the Sun" to stand still so that the Israelite armies can fight on to victory in one of their key battles during the genocidal conquest of Canaan.

Francisco and Jacinta died within a few years of the Fatima encounters. While Francisco appears to have been a casualty of the 1918 flu pandemic, Jacinta, who was just barely an adolescent, seems to have died of lung cancer caused by radiation poisoning. Lucia was whisked off against her will to a private boarding school with instructions not to reveal her true identity or any of what she had witnessed from May to October of 1917, and her letters to her family were screened by the Church. Subsequently, she was shut up in a cloistered convent for the rest of her life, with any communications to the outside world being conducted through a bishop acting as a censor on behalf of the Holy Congregation for the Doctrine of the Faith (formerly known as the Holy Inquisition). Lucia felt as if she had been "buried alive in a sepulcher." In 1930, after thirteen years of official interrogations and deliberations, the Holy Roman Catholic Church recognized the Fatima manifestations as a divine miracle, and advanced its own Judeo-Christian interpretation of the Miracle of the Sun and the encounters with the Blessed Virgin. As per instruction, the sealed, secret part of the Fatima prophecy was not opened by the cardinals until 1960 — when witnesses report that they emerged from a closed-door meeting with expressions of horror on their faces, refusing to reveal the contents even to those individuals within the Church who were closest to them, but who were not present at the meeting.

Vallée argues that modern UFO sightings are on a continuum that extends back to the faith and folklore of olden times, with a bridge between these two phases in the form of widely-publicized and well-substantiated late-nineteenth century close encounters with impossibly strange airships more sophisticated than the contraptions of Jules Verne, together with their intrepid or sinister crews, at a time just barely after the most primitive dirigibles had been invented.[44] In fact, there is an intermediate phase between the airships and the UFOs that binds ethereal aerial encounters throughout history into an even tighter continuum, namely the "Ghost Rockets" that were seen flying under the most adverse weather conditions in northern Europe as early as the 1920s, before the development of the V-2 rocket by the Germans.[45] The airship sightings peaked between fall of 1896 and spring of 1897, in an area stretching from California to Iowa. In November, hundreds of residents of San Francisco saw a large, cigar-shaped craft with brilliant searchlights capable of flying against the wind. In March, at Sioux City, Iowa, an even stranger and more complex airship released an "anchor" that dragged a man several dozen feet by his clothes before dropping him back down to the ground.[46] A month later, another was seen in Iowa, this time by the most highly respected residents of Fontanelle — at least according to the *Chicago Chronicle* of April 13, 1897.[47] These airships would very often land, usually in the midst of vast farms, to make repairs and to resupply.

During these stopovers, rural farmers who certainly had no access to anything like the novels of Jules Verne would see intricate machines on a par with the best science fiction of the era — gadgets that make sense in the context of the speculations of scientifically-minded engineers of the time, but that we now know are totally fantastic.[48] Sometimes the crew would

---

44   Jacques Vallée, *Passport to Magonia: On UFOs, Folklore, and Parallel Worlds* (Chicago: Contemporary Books, 1993), p. 110.

45   Ibid., p. 162.

46   Ibid., p. 140.

47   Ibid., p. 143.

48   Ibid., pp. 141–143.

warn observers away from taking a closer look, before the airships would lift off and speed away "like a shot out of a gun."[49] Vallée cites the major mainstream city newspapers of the time that carefully chronicled these events and fostered the widespread expectation that the public announcement of the invention of this fantastic airship technology was imminent. In fact, one airship crewman explicitly claimed that this was the case, and that a stock company was being formed in view of it.[50] One frightening airship incident of 1897 is that of Alexander Hamilton, a prominent citizen of Kansas at the time, who reported observing the "hideous people" inside the "glass" carriage of the airship as they fastened a tether around one of his cattle, a two-year-old heifer, and carried it up off into the air as they departed.[51] Hamilton later discovered the head and other mutilated remains of his heifer dropped to the ground some distance away. Vallée relates this incident to contemporary high-precision mutilations of livestock, where no traces of a perpetrator are left behind.[52]

One of the first studies of this phenomenon is found in Vallée's *Messengers of Deception*.[53] The mutilated cattle with which we are here concerned have had various internal organs removed with surgical precision, often through perfectly cut holes that seem almost too small for the operation. (Most of the cases are from long before the development of laparoscopic surgery.) Their rectums are cored out and their sex organs are cleanly excised. Sometimes the hide is removed in certain places without any damage to the tissue immediately beneath it. Veterinarians and other surgeons who have been called in by baffled sheriffs to examine the remains have repeatedly testified to the fact that these mutilations cannot have been the work of predators, and that the surgical skill involved pushed the limits of even what they could have done in a proper operating

---

49   Ibid., p. 145.

50   Ibid., p. 146.

51   Ibid., p. 46.

52   Ibid., p. 47.

53   Jacques Vallée, *Messengers of Deception* (Berkeley, California: And/Or Press, 1979), pp. 181–212.

theater, let alone in the dark of night on rugged farmland. There is no evidence of human perpetrators, either. Although in many cases the ground has been wet, muddy, or covered with snow, no tracks were found in the area surrounding the carcasses. In some cases, it is clear that they were dropped from the air — often in the middle of perfectly circular clearings that had been burned into wheat fields, as if they were being put on display.

What is most disturbing is that whatever is behind the mutilations seems to have a very dark sense of humor and to be showing off. Calves dropped from the air may be wedged on the ground between very tall, massive trees, in a space that could not even be navigated by a helicopter. In some cases, the cattle have been removed from their original location and dropped off inside a locked and penned enclosure that they could never have found their way into on their own. Certain of the mutilated carcasses have precise geometrical shapes whimsically cut into their hide, and one or another organ — such as a teat — has been completely hollowed out, but the skin remains and is filled with sand. At times, the extracted organs have been neatly placed on top of the carcass, showing that there is no practical motive of resource acquisition involved. It is as if those responsible are saying: "Ta-Da!" Sometimes, absurdly crude implements will be left behind that clearly were not the instruments by means of which the mutilation was accomplished, as in, for example, a rusty old army surplus scalpel. Again, no tracks are found.

By 1975, the situation in the western United States had grown so severe that tens of high-ranking officials from Nebraska, Wyoming, and Colorado met at Fort Morgan to organize a coordinated response. In addition to addressing the concerns of enraged and frightened cattle ranchers, they were no doubt also galvanized by an emerging pattern: most of the mutilations took place in close proximity to sensitive military installations. Mutilated cattle were even dropped off within the security perimeter of North American Air Defense (NORAD) Command at Cheyenne Mountain, Colorado. Richard D. Lamm, the Governor of Colorado, finally went to confer with the executive board of the Cattlemen's Association, and made a public statement on September 4, 1975 wherein he called the incidents "one of the greatest outrages in the history of the western cattle industry," and acknowledged that "[i]t is no longer possible to blame predators for the mutilations."[54] According to a local newspaper, "the largest force of law enforcement manpower ever assembled in the history of Colorado" was deployed to apprehend the culprits.[55] It failed to identify even a single suspect, let alone take one into custody.

The FBI was called in, but refused to become involved because there was no evidence anyone or anything had actually crossed state lines, even if the mutilations were occurring in at least 15 western states. Carl Whiteside of the Colorado Bureau of Investigation stated that "trying to catch the culprits was like chasing a ghost."[56] There were occasionally strange lights seen in the sky or in the fields during the night before mutilated cattle being discovered. Sometimes there would be the blood-curdling scream of an animal being slaughtered, but these things usually happened under the cover of darkness without so much as a whisper. The few accounts of any beings sighted in association with these lights are preposterous. More than one witness has reported little dwarves in silver diving suits. On one occasion, a couple of the dwarves curiously made a fuss over some caged rabbits, and took them back aboard their luminous egg before they departed. On another occasion, a farmer who tried to clobber one of these imps in the head with a shovel was temporarily paralyzed. Some other people nearby also saw the little bugger and threw stones at it before it hobbled away.

In the *Homeric Hymn* to Hermes, the Trickster god deceitfully steals Apollo's cattle, bringing them from the divine world, where they do not sexually reproduce and are immortally fixed in number, to the human world, where they are bred with one another in stables and are butchered

---

54   Ibid., p. 193.
55   Ibid.
56   Ibid., p. 204.

by men for food.[57] Hermes, in his capacity as liar and thief, is the source of the cultural institutions for slaughtering cattle and preparing them to be eaten.[58] That Hermes does not eat the sacrificial meat establishes a connection between self-denial of appetite and the rise of *noos* (intellect).[59] It is somewhat like an animal that gets wise enough to tame its hunger and find a way to steal the bait.[60] To steal and then lie about the theft, but not in order to gain anything concrete, is a moment of dawning self-consciousness that is part of almost everyone's childhood.[61] This is the moment when the child crosses over the boundaries set by others and, by means of the lie, proliferates meanings of her own making.[62]

According to Plato, in his dialogue *Cratylus*, Hermes invented language. The passage in which he makes this claim draws a constellation of connections between interpretation, bargaining, stealing, and lying, or "telling tales": "I should imagine that he is the interpreter [*hermeneus*], or messenger, or thief, or liar, or bargainer; all that sort of thing has a great deal to do with language." Plato proposes that Hermes is a synthesis of the Greek words for "to tell" and "to contrive," and this is the origin of "the name of the God who invented language and speech," and who is "the contriver of tales or speeches."[63] This suggests that the invention of language and the will to deceive are contemporaneous.[64] Hermeneutics, the science of linguistic and literary interpretation, is the *art of Hermes* whereby meaning is made — and remade — from out of ambiguous polyvalence.[65] An old Greek proverb ays, "Hermes leads the way or leads

57   Lewis Hyde, *Trickster Makes This World* (New York: Farrar, Straus, and Giroux, 1998), pp. 60–61.

58   Ibid., p. 9.

59   Ibid., p. 59.

60   Ibid., p. 75.

61   Ibid., p. 64.

62   Ibid., p. 65.

63   Ibid., p. 75.

64   Ibid., p. 76.

65   Ibid., p. 300.

astray."[66] Travelers used to mark roads by means of which he had granted them safe passage with a cairn, each one adding another such stone to what became, over time, an altar-like pile. More than a trail marker, the cairn signified the cunning intelligence that one needed to traverse a space of heightened uncertainty.[67]

Hermes does not just seize Apollo's cattle. In exchange for giving his lyre to Apollo, he is also given the Apollonian gift of *prophecy*—but it is a different kind of prophecy than that of Apollo, the minor oracle of the Bee Maidens.[68] Of the Bee Maidens, Apollo says, "There are certain sacred sisters, three virgins lifted on swift wings... They teach their own kind of fortune telling... The sisters fly back and forth from their home, feeding on waxy honeycombs... They like to tell the truth when they have eaten honey and the spirit is on them; but if they've been deprived of that divine sweetness, they buzz about and mumble lies."[69] There is a connection between hunger and telling lies.[70] It is the self-satisfied full-belly who always tells the truth. When there is nothing to digest, the stomach acid of hunger begins to break down illusory "truths" and to recollect things conveniently "forgotten." *Anamnesis*, or un-forgetting, is not a recitation of "truth," pure and simple.[71] It is not the Solar Oracle of Apollo — shining brightly, clear, and pure. It is a shifty oracle that hides a hungry black humor, one that delights in shaping new artifices for the sake of mocking older ones or making them look into a funhouse mirror. If Hermes is *the* messenger of Zeus — archetypally synonymous with the Gabriel of the Abrahamic faiths — and if Hermes is known to also be a trickster and arch-comedian who buzzes about mumbling lies, then either there is a higher heavenly truth, but our only access to it is distorted by this untrustworthy character, or, more radically, there is no Zeus at all, and this

---

66 Ibid., p. 121.

67 Ibid., p. 6.

68 Ibid., p. 290.

69 Ibid., pp. 290–291.

70 Ibid., p. 66.

71 Ibid., p. 78.

Messenger of Deception is making it *all* up, including the authority of his own appointment as the announcer of divine revelation,[72] and "[i]f you don't believe it, try keeping Hermes away from your cattle."[73]

Jacques Vallée's research aims at identifying certain "stable, invariant features" of this "chameleonlike" phenomenon that stretches from encounters with occupants of celestial chariots and fairy aerial conveyances, to airships and UFOs.[74] The invariant features include bright moving lights in the sky that crystallize into, or are associated with, some type of "object" or "objects," serious time distortions, and other confused perceptions experienced by those who encounter these, and the disappearances of tangible things and persons — sometimes to be returned at a later time, and possibly to a different place. In the instances where beings are reported in connection with these lights, practically the only consistent elements of their behavior across the whole historical spectrum of manifestations is that their conduct, while perhaps appearing to be self-consistent at the time, is at least in retrospect recognized by intelligent people to be as absurd as the construction of their ludicrous craft, and where there is anything like verbal communication, it is deliberately and systematically misleading.[75] Vallée finds that the "secondary attributes of the sightings" vary in accordance with "the cultural environment into which they are projected."[76]

Vallée is, foremost, an information scientist, and it is in search of patterns of signification that he attempts to see what might be gained by looking afresh at the findings of his UFO research through the lens of faith and folklore. In *Passport to Magonia*, Vallée observes that the belief in Ufonauts is rising among those on the fringe of contemporary society, and he projects that it might soon take on an organized religious form of

---

72 Ibid., p. 300.

73 Ibid., p. 292.

74 Vallée, *Passport to Magonia*, p. 149.

75 Ibid., p. 161.

76 Ibid., p. 149.

its own. This passage in particular stands out, especially on account of its having been written well before the rise of the Raelians and Heaven's Gate:

> In the absence of a rational solution to the mystery, and public interest in the matter being intense, it is quite likely that in the coming years... although it is not possible to predict its exact form... We may very well be living in the early years of a new mythological movement, and it may eventually give our techno-logical age its Olympus, its fairyland, or its Walhalla, whether we regard such a development as an asset or as a blow to our culture. Because many observations of UFO phenomena appear self-consistent and at the same time irreconcilable with scientific knowledge, a logical vacuum has been created that human im-agination tries to fill... Such situations have been... observed in the past, and they have given us both the highest and the basest forms of religious, poetic, and political activity. It is entirely possible that the phenomenon we study here will give rise to similar developments, because its manifestations coincide with a renewal of interest in the human value of technology.[77]

The scientific validation of psychic phenomena and the recognition of the antiquity of the UFO phenomenon, when taken together, do not allow us to simply tolerate revealed religion as if it were "mere belief." There is no such thing as a *mere* belief—especially when it involves passionately motivated *collectives* that build mass cults. Intentions, whether they are conscious thoughts or subconscious desires, can have immediate *physical* consequences for the well-being of others. I agree with Vallée that if the scientific community continues to refuse to seriously examine paranormal phenomena, including UFOs, it is possible that future mass events might precipitously lead to the collapse of scientific authority and the descent of our civilization into a new dark age. We could see the rise of yet another destructive belief system offering the masses answers to questions that scientists have not even begun seriously asking.

As a harbinger of such a disaster, witness the case of Ted Owens, who was studied by Jeffrey Mishlove—the first person to receive a Ph.D. in parapsychology from a major American university, the University of California at Berkeley (with an interdisciplinary dissertation committee

---

77   Ibid., p. 155.

consisting of both philosophers and psychologists). Mishlove went on to become the host of the nationally syndicated program *Thinking Allowed*, which was a series of one-on-one interviews with brilliant minds doing research on the edge of various disciplines. It was probably the most effective medium that there has ever been for the communication of parapsychological ideas to the general public. While still a graduate student, Mishlove became involved with Harold Puthoff and Russell Targ of the Stanford Research Institute, whose government-funded studies of "remote viewing" or clairvoyance I reviewed in the second chapter. Targ and Puthoff had done some work testing the claims of Uri Geller, and had recently been contacted by another man with psychokinetic powers who claimed to also be in communication with UFOs. And yet the alleged abilities of Ted Owens dwarfed those of Geller, which were already difficult for skeptics to stomach, and his personal character was even less conducive to constructive participation in controlled experiments. Geller's persona as a flashy stage entertainer already posed a problem for the SRI physicists in their attempt to maintain their professional reputation and have their work taken seriously by the scientific community and their government contractors. Owens was, by contrast, outright dangerous.

The self-styled "PK Man" was a loose cannon who routinely made threats against those whom he deemed to be offensively skeptical of his claims and, by his own admission, his track record in the use of psychokinetic abilities included demonstrations that had harmed certain individuals and killed others. During his doctoral research, Mishlove had already discovered that there was an inextricable link between psi phenomena and UFOs. He had both the interest and the courage to take on the Owens case despite the considerable risk of working with such a person, which he later discovered first-hand when, having angered the PK Man, he seems to have — albeit only very briefly — been rendered physically ill by Owens' intent. In 1976, Puthoff and Targ handed over a six-inch-thick dossier on Owens that they had put together at SRI, and Mishlove continued to study the PK Man until his death in 1987. By 1979, Mishlove had already put together a book about the Owens case with D. Scott Rogo but, for reasons that will be easy to understand, he suppressed the manuscript for decades before recently rewriting it and finally publishing it as *The PK Man*.

As in the case of D. D. Home, psychic ability ran in the family of Ted Owens.[78] He first discovered his own abilities during incidents of spontaneous levitation that began during his teens.[79] When he heard about the rain dances of Native American shamans, Owens devised his own simple rituals for conjuring storms and controlling the weather. Most dramatically, numerous witnesses attest to his having been able to summon up freak lightning storms and to direct lightning bolts to strike precise locations suggested by others, and which he would indicate by the point of his finger — a psychokinetic feat that brings to mind the image of Zeus![80] The shamans of certain west African tribes in the region of Nigeria claim that their ancestors used directed lightning strikes of this kind as an instrument of war.[81] Owens seems to have used this ability to down several aircraft, including a commercial airliner that was directly in front of one he was travelling in as it came in for a landing at JFK International Airport on June 25, 1975.[82]

More than a hundred people were killed in what was then considered the single worst air disaster in US history. Lightning had never been known to destroy an airframe of the kind compromised in that incident, so the official NTSB report attributed the crash to high winds. Yet witnesses claim that the plane was struck by lightning just before it began to fly erratically and crash land.[83] Immediately prior to the lightning strike, Owens had been bragging to probably incredulous stewardesses about having downed smaller aircraft with his psychokinesis before, and he was

---

78　Jeffrey Mishlove, *The PK Man: A True Story of Mind Over Matter* (Charlottesville, Virginia: Hampton Roads Publishing Company, 2000), p. 44.

79　Ibid., pp. 45–48.

80　Ibid., pp. 53–55.

81　Ibid., pp. 263–264.

82　Ibid., p. 205.

83　Ibid., p. 206.

brandishing a copy of a magazine article with a story recounting these exploits. The mental focus on the article, combined with his character-istic child-like desire to prove himself to others who were incredulously dismissive (in this case the crew of his own plane), may have combined to informally provide him with the kind of "PK maps" that he often used in his demonstrations. These maps of a target area would be marked with bullseyes for PK strikes, as it were, and were an aid in visualization and concentration. He seems to have used one of them to trigger the eruption of the Mt. Saint Helens volcano in May of 1980.[84] Fifty-seven lives were lost in the eruption. Owens claimed that it was an accident, and that he had situated himself (and his family) with his PK map on site prior to the eruption, only for a training exercise — one that had apparently gone too far.

There were, however, numerous occasions documented when Owens did intend to do harm. He would send letters to more than one person, Mishlove, Puthoff, and Targ included, boasting that he would cause a storm, a blackout, or forest fire within a certain target area and within a certain predefined span of time, and this would then come to pass. While precognition cannot entirely be ruled out as the means for these "demonstrations," the actual circumstances of a number of them are more suggestive of psychokinesis. For example, in July 1977 he arrived in the San Francisco Bay Area with the intention of demanding that local news-papers acknowledge his having brought an end to the drought that had recently plagued California.[85] When he was roundly dismissed by journal-ists and even escorted out of the offices of certain Bay Area papers by the police, he promised to punish California with raging wildfires. This was really going out on a limb, because the fire season had already started, and it had been a relatively mild one; the US Forest Service had projected that it would be one of the mildest fire seasons in recent history. Almost imme-diately after the PK Man declared his intention to seek vengeance, terrible

---

84   Ibid., p. 217.
85   Ibid., p. 208.

wildfires began to break out, and the summer of 1977 ended up seeing the most catastrophic and costly outbreak of forest fires for a decade.[86] Owens was also known to capriciously alter the outcomes of sporting events, and even the fortunes of a team that had offended him over the course of an entire season, by hexing their players through his television screen.[87] Once he dramatically altered the course of a single game, and called in to angrily state his intention to do so, as a punishment against a team that had refused his offer to help them win. A sportscaster had derisively revealed this refusal over the air. Owens then called in and asked them to watch what he did to the team in the second half. *Sports* magazine ran a story on this particular use of his abilities. Furthermore, the storms that Owens claimed to have conjured up, and the hurricanes whose paths he claimed to have altered, sometimes evinced freakish patterns and properties uncharacteristic of acts of Nature.

What is most relevant to our concerns here is that Ted Owens claimed that his abilities were being facilitated or directed by certain "Space Intelligences" aboard UFOs, and one of his most stunning powers was the ability to manifest UFO phenomena on demand, or following a declared intention to do so within a certain area and during a specified time period. At one point, he demonstrated this ability to the satisfaction of the Mensa director of Science and Education, Dr. Max L. Fogel.[88] After promising Mishlove that he would provide a similar demonstration, some of the best-documented UFO sightings in the Bay Area ensued. The "craft" were witnessed by hundreds of onlookers and even filmed, since they appeared amidst a high-profile aerial art show.[89] The aerial artist also witnessed the UFO at close range from his plane. On occasion, these UFO demonstrations would be associated with power failures and close encounters with apparently alien creatures within the target area.[90]

---

86   Ibid., pp. 208–209.
87   Ibid., pp. 160–162.
88   Ibid., pp. 27–28.
89   Ibid., pp. 33–34.
90   Ibid., p. 28.

In fact, Owens made the absurd claim that two grasshopper-like alien creatures dubbed "Twitter" and "Tweeter" were stationed aboard a
mother ship outside the Earth's atmosphere to coordinate the deployment
of other UFOs and the targeting of his psi abilities. He vacillated between
attributing all of his psychokinetic feats to the Space Intelligences, when
this was convenient to exculpate him for monstrously unethical acts, and
the more self-aggrandizing claim that he was in control of the power and
was "chosen" by the Space Intelligences on account of it — after they had
searched for centuries to find someone with abilities sufficient to act as
their sole ambassador to the Earth. At times, Owens admitted that Twitter
and Tweeter were thought-forms assumed by the SIs for the purpose of
psychical rapport with him, whereas they really consisted of "light" or
"energy." Once, he essentially made the same admission regarding his
UFOs, comparing them to optical illusions or holograms.[91] The UFOs
manifested by Owens took all kinds of forms, ranging from multi-colored
lights that darted erratically around the sky and materialized out of what
at first appeared to be clouds, to slowly hovering, football field-sized craft
with a more discernable structure.

Interestingly, the Owens case even offers a possible answer to how it is
that UFOs could essentially be psychokinetic projections and yet register
on radar as if they were solid objects. After allegedly receiving a telepathic
message from the Space Intelligences to make phenomena appear on radar, Owens convinced a radar operator who was a friend of his to give
him a tutorial on radar operation and allow him the use of a radar facility.
He was able to produce anomalous returns on the radarscope in regular
patterns of a kind that the experienced operator had never seen before.[92]
Within 48 hours of Owens' demonstration at the radar facility, planes
began to crash in the Chesapeake Bay area within the radar monitoring
range of the installation.[93]

---

91   Ibid., p. 79.

92   Ibid., pp. 197–198.

93   Ibid., p. 199.

As Mishlove explains, parapsychology researchers have noted a "linger" or "lag" effect in their laboratory experiments on PK, wherein psychokinetic force directed toward a certain outcome or concentrated on a circumscribed space will yield an observable effect, either some time after the expressed intention, or else will continue to resonate in this field subsequent to it.[94] He suggests that, rather than simply producing a PK effect on the radar equipment itself in the manner that Random Number Generators (RNGs) were targeted at Princeton, Owens could have set up a "PK field" in the Chesapeake Bay area itself, one that lingered and caused the airplane crashes.[95] In light of the decades of testimony from air force officials from around the world concerning incidents of nearly disastrous equipment failures during aerial dogfights, or near-collisions with UFOs, one has to wonder whether the downed pilots in the Chesapeake Bay area also witnessed UFOs before meeting with disaster, and whether the locations of these "objects" would have correlated with the returns on the radar screen in front of Owens. Also relevant in this regard is the fact that homes within areas where Owens manifested UFOs were simultaneously haunted by poltergeist phenomena.[96]

A number of the planes that were affected were US Navy jets, and indeed, after failing to interest the US government in his offer to help them wage psychic warfare against the Soviet Union (a service for which he would no doubt have been well compensated), Owens began to make increasingly shrill claims that the Space Intelligences were going to target American assets until and unless Owens was recognized as their ambassador. The most disturbing example of the many incidents in which he claimed to have made good on this threat is the Space Shuttle *Challenger* disaster of January 28, 1986 — one of those terrible events that we all recall vividly in terms of where we were and what we were doing when we heard the news. I was in a kindergarten classroom where the focus of

---

94   Ibid., pp. 201–202.

95   Ibid., p. 203.

96   Ibid., p. 186.

the very carefully-worded (and, in retrospect, surprising) announcement concerned the loss of the 37-year old teacher, Christa McAuliffe, who had been on board the *Challenger* with the doomed astronauts. On July 22, 1985, Owens sent a letter to Mishlove claiming that the bugs recently suffered by NASA during a number of mission experiments were an exercise of compassionate constraint on behalf of the Space Intelligences, who were now about to let loose their full fury, and he threatened with destruction the four NASA space shuttles in existence at that time by name.[97] Owens sent similar warnings to other individuals before the *Challenger* disaster, and Mishlove received a phone call in December 1985 — just a month before the incident — specifically threatening to destroy that Shuttle.[98] We can only wonder whether *Atlantis, Discovery,* and *Columbia* would all have suffered the wrath of Twitter and Tweeter had Owens gone on to live beyond 1987.

In light of the mercurial hermeneutics of the Bible being advanced here, a comparison to the threats of Moses against Pharaoh on behalf of the capricious *elohim* ought to have suggested itself to the reader even if Owens himself had not drawn this comparison as explicitly and repeatedly as he did. On multiple occasions, Owens compared himself and the struggle of the Space Intelligences against the US government to the prophet Moses and his campaign of terror against Pharaoh and the Egyptian people.[99] Once this was couched in terms of a response to a letter written by Mishlove in which he criticized Owens' unethical use of his abilities, pointing out his relative insignificance, and the futility of his demonstrations of power in the face of a juggernaut on the scale of the US government. Owens replied, "I must assume that your *very same letter* must have been sent to Moses while he was attacking Pharaoh and the

---

97   Ibid., p. 225.

98   Ibid., p. 226.

99   Ibid., p. 7.

Egyptians. Moses' people didn't like his attitude and behavior either. And may I ask... how 'futile' was that little flea, Moses?"[100]

Like Moses and other prophets, Owens assembled a faithful core of followers around him, some of whom were quite wealthy individuals, and this allowed him to just barely eke out an existence from the late 1960s, when he quit the last in a long series of diverse occupations, until his death in 1987. Moreover, he had a training protocol — what in antiquity would have been considered an initiation rite — that allowed his followers to contact the Space Intelligences themselves. This training program, studied by Mishlove, largely adapted techniques of autohypnosis — but one must remember that (as discussed in Chapter 5) in the early days of hypnotism, or "mesmerism," the manifestation of psi abilities such as telepathy and psychokinesis were associated with deep "magnetic trances."[101] At any rate, a number of these followers were able to summon UFOs in the presence of other observers. Interestingly, many of these appeared to be star-like, and are described by those who witnessed them as guiding lights of a sort that call to mind the so-called "Star" of Bethlehem.[102] Some of them also claimed to be able to channel the same psychokinetic powers that Owens exerted on behalf of the Space Intelligences.

The account of one of these claimants is particularly disturbing in view of how it aligns with a subsequently revealed, and highly classified, incident that took place at a US military installation. This "SI contact" eventually fell out with Owens over his objection to what he considered inhumane cattle mutilations in his home state of Colorado and nearby states. Apparently, Owens held Twitter and Tweeter responsible for this. In a letter to Mishlove, this individual boasted that before this falling out, he "started having increased SIM [Space Intelligence Masters] contact in the early 1970s and became an SI operative," during the course of which he "went on a mission for SIMs into the U.S. military in 1973 and sparked

---

100 Ibid., p. 223.

101 Ibid., pp. 176–177.

102 Ibid., pp. 180–183.

a U.S. military red alert from within a nuclear weapons storage depot in October 1974..." He added that the "red alert I helped to spark resulted in a cylindrical UFO appearing at the periphery of the nuclear weapons depot..."[103] Finally, and most absurdly, the "operative" relates that at "the time of the red alert and sighting of the UFO cylinder and UFO stars, I had a vision of Tweeter and Twitter as they made interface with my brain consciousness..."[104]

This grotesque absurdity becomes quite a chilling tale when one considers two related incidents that occurred in Montana in March 1967. On the morning of March 16, UFOs visiting Echo Flight facility caused all of its nuclear-tipped Intercontinental Ballistic Missiles (ICBMs) to cease functioning. A week later, on March 24, a glowing red oval-shaped UFO was spotted hovering over the Oscar Flight Launch Control Center at Malmstrom Air Force Base. All ten ICBMs at the facility were disabled while the UFO was overhead, even though the missiles were located 5–10 miles from the control center and were each approximately one mile apart from each other. All of them had independent backup power sources that apparently did not prevent them from being put into a "no go" mode by the UFO, each within ten seconds of the others. In other words, within the span of a week, 20 American ICBMs were disabled so that they could not be launched in response to a Soviet attack.[105]

Technicians from Boeing conducted a thorough examination, and could never find any cause for the missile failures. They speculated that each of the missiles had been independently subjected to an electromagnetic pulse, which would have had to have penetrated sixty feet underground into their silos in order to do the damage that was done.[106] Could the Ted Owens trainee have subsequently caused a similar incident? Incidents such as these could have led to a panic precipitating the

103   Ibid., pp. 188–189.

104   Ibid., p. 189.

105   Leslie Kean, *UFOs: Generals, Pilots, and Government Officials Go On the Record* (New York: Harmony Books, 2010), p. 144.

106   Ibid., p. 145.

inadvertent initiation of nuclear war. It is also worthy of note that Owens claimed to be responsible for malfunctions at five different nuclear power plants between March and April of 1980, after a stated and documented intention to attack the power grid.[107] Fortunately, while these malfunctions did cause outages and merited evaluative investigations, none of them was serious enough to cause a meltdown or a release of radioactivity into their surroundings.

Mishlove is right to remind us that individuals like Ted Owens remain beyond the reach of the law, and that the last time the legal system of our civilization recognized the efficacy of psychokinesis, it was within a paradigm that considered it an expression of daemonic power so that those practicing it — for ill *or for good* — were prosecuted as "witches" and burned at the stake.[108] A world wherein psi abilities are recognized by mainstream science is one wherein we are going to have to learn how to control not only our conscious thoughts, but also our hitherto unconscious intentions towards others.[109] In my view, the Space Intelligences of "Twitter" and "Tweeter," or the "God" of Uranus going by any other name, cannot be allowed to serve as a psychological crutch and a religiously-tolerated alibi for capricious cult leaders who would tyrannize over our souls by terrorizing the whole Earth in the manner that the Mosaic or Muhammadan revelations spooked the ancient Near East into submission. We must likewise be aware of the kind of insidious infiltration that slowly but surely destroyed the humanistic Alexandrian civilization, ushering in the inquisitorial Medieval epoch of a triumphant Christianity.

A scientifically-minded awareness of the potential for nefarious psychical manipulation on the part of powerful beings in the cosmos who are purporting to be a source of "revelation" goes all the way back to William James. Despite being a central thesis of *The Varieties of Religious Experience*, James acknowledges that mystical states are not always saving

---

107 Mishlove, *The PK Man*, pp. 211–212.

108 Ibid., pp. 6–7, 266.

109 Ibid., p. 266.

experiences through which a healthy-minded person is fortified against a loss of spiritual equanimity, and a "sick soul" is afforded a resolution to psychological uneasiness or personal suffering by the strength of a "higher" part of his Self, a subliminal Self that is wider than his self-conscious ego, but also continuous with it.[110] Rather, James acknowledges that there are *"diabolical… lower mysticisms"* that "spring from the same mental level, from that great subliminal or transmarginal region of which science is beginning to admit the existence, but of which so little is really known."[111] These also feature "texts and words coming with new meanings, the same voices and visions and leadings and missions, the same controlling by extraneous powers; only this time…instead of consolations we have desolations; the meanings are dreadful; and the powers are enemies to life."[112] James claims that, even within the traditional sphere of religious belief, any paranormal occurrence might be of "diabolical" rather than "angelic" origin.[113] So, in the final analysis, a religious revelation must be judged on ethical grounds.

At the conclusion of the *Varieties* chapter on "Conversion," James writes, "If the *fruits for life* of the state of conversion are good, we ought to idealize and venerate it, even though it be a piece of natural psychology; if not, we ought to make short work with it, no matter what supernatural being may have infused it."[114] The contrast between "natural psychology" and "supernatural being" in this passage clearly suggests that the last line means that even if there *were* an empirically verifiable God, we should not obey him if he is unethical. This collapses the moral dimension of "religious experience" to radically secular (but non-materialistic) criteria of ethical evaluation. Meanwhile, the study of the *facts* of religious experience can, in principle, become the object of a science that has moved beyond the narrow paradigm of materialist reductionism. What

---

110 James, *Writings: 1902–1910*, pp. 454; 460.

111 Ibid., p. 384.

112 Ibid.

113 Ibid., p. 223.

114 Ibid., p. 219.

James loosely refers to as "supernatural" would then only be the super Natural — an aspect of Nature that is not yet understood, which is what Schelling and Bergson took it to be.

There are a few instances in *Varieties* where James makes an exception to the opposition he sets up there between impersonal science and personal religion. In one significant footnote that alludes to his own psychical research, James criticizes advocates of scientism for being unscientific in their rejection of the "mass of raw fact" that paranormal occurrences represent, and he speculates that phenomena of extrasensory perception such as "prophecy" or psychokinetic abilities such as "levitation" that are traditionally associated with religion might eventually be admitted into a new scientific paradigm that is not "impersonal," in the sense that it would allow for the personal intentions of conscious beings to play a constitutive role in nature.[115]

In his 1909 essay, "Final Impressions of a Psychical Researcher," James goes even further on this point, committing himself to the view that honest empirical study of such phenomena that have been traditionally associated with "religion" will lead to the next great scientific revolution.[116] It would be a revolution wherein scientists recognized that, for utility's sake, *we* read mathematics into space and time, covering over our uneven experiences of places and our durational sense of time.[117] The technological control of Nature to which science aspires would then no longer threaten to alienate us from the fundamental human experience in which scientific research is rooted, and the live possibilities of which it is the proper purpose of science to enrich.[118] In his 1896 "Address of the President [of the Society for Psychical Research]," James speaks of the coming revolutionary re-personalization of science, which will be provoked by the understanding of psychic phenomena, and which promises to render

---

115   Ibid., pp. 448–449.

116   Ibid., p. 799.

117   James, *Pragmatism and the Meaning of Truth*, pp. 84; 87.

118   Ibid., p. 91.

scientific research genuinely "empirical" in the sense of being faithful to human *experience* (*emperia*) unfiltered by prejudicing beliefs (whether of the traditional or *a priori* type).[119]

At another point in *Varieties*, James suggests that absent what he vaguely refers to as "religious feeling," animistic interpretations of Nature would have gradually yielded to scientific ones, and all that would have remained valid of animistic "religion" (and its associated practices of "sympathetic magic") would be the kinds of phenomena *scientifically* studied in psychical research. He claims that our materialistic science will also probably have to readmit these phenomena as well, reaching the same point of completion (in method and epistemological structure, though not necessarily in content) as the counterfactual science of a world without "religious feeling."[120] If this "religious feeling" is the consoling psychological state of cosmic safety, then, as we saw above, James himself admits that this is not *always* the only kind of "religious" feeling; its opposite, Gnostic horror in the face of an "evil" cosmos, is just as "religious." So what residue of religion is there that could forever elude the future "scientific conquests" of a psychology freed from neurological reductionism? On what grounds does James claim that "on the battle-field of human history" it will always be the case that "religion will drive irreligion to the wall"?[121]

In his essay on "The Moral Philosopher and Moral Life" in *The Will to Believe*, James draws a contrast between the *strenuous* and *easy-going* moods, and identifies their divergence as the "deepest difference, practically, in the moral life of man."[122] James' idea of the "strenuous mood" is essentially the capacity to sacrifice present comforts for a higher purpose, to take the more challenging path less traveled in passionate pursuit of all that is great — such as beautiful, noble, and awe-inspiring ideals of "justice, truth, or freedom" — while contemptuously casting aside petty "lesser

119   James, *Essays in Psychical Research*, pp. 136–137.
120   James, *Writings: 1902–1910*, p. 388.
121   William James, *The Will to Believe* (New York: Dover Publications, 1956), p. 213.
122   Ibid., p. 211.

claims," and even cruelly going to battle with those who refuse to die away by simply being ignored.[123] The strenuously-spirited person refuses the easy-going attitude that "it's all good," or, at any rate, that things are as they had to be; he is capable of indignation at things that are not as they *should* have been or as they *could* be.[124] In other words, the sense of the "tragically challenging" has to be alive in the strenuous person.[125] But is faith in a God who knows and wills all really compatible with *the tragic sense of life*? Are the Exodus narrative or the exile of Muhammad from Mecca really tragedies — in the *Greek* sense of tragedy that Nietzsche reawakened? No, absolutely not. They are supposed to have been the work of God, and not the potentially futile — and therefore *really* perilous — sacrifices of great men or gods finite enough to really suffer.

Of course, as we have seen, in later works such as *Pragmatism*, *Varieties of Religious Experience*, and *A Pluralistic Universe*, James clearly wants to reject the idea of an omniscient and omnipotent God. One of his most central concerns in "The Moral Philosopher and Moral Life" is to argue that codes of ethics "never can be *final*," because genuinely ethical behavior requires rule-breaking to accommodate the actual case, and there would be no true moral dilemmas if adequate rules to address them were readily available.[126] If, together with James, we wish to reject *both* defining ideas of religious revelation, namely that of an all-powerful omniscient Lord *and* that of the eternal infallibility of His revealed moral code, why then should we continue to talk in terms of "God" at all, rather than simply of *the sacred*, or of that context of meaning which is affirmed more unquestionably than all that it alone makes possible?

James may be right that "in a merely human world without a god, the appeal to our moral energy falls short of its maximal stimulating power."[127] However, this does *not* necessarily force us to acquiesce in the permanent

---

123   Ibid., pp. 211; 213.

124   Ibid., p. 211.

125   Ibid., p. 213.

126   Ibid., pp. 209–210.

127   Ibid., p. 212.

survival of religious faith in the One True God. Rather, it can be taken as a Nietzschean call to overcome the "merely human" and to become god-like beings ourselves, by way of cleansing our hands of the blood of a Tyrant that we have murdered with the scalpels of Gay Science.[128] For Nietzsche, the project of developing a non-mechanistic science of the future is one and the same project as cultivating a spiritual aristocracy of post-human supermen.[129]

When James claims of the strenuous mood that "a world where all the mountains are brought down and all the valleys are exalted is no congenial place for its habitation,"[130] he seems to forget that the metaphor of flattening mountains and valleys into a serene sea of abject submission is just the humiliating end-game that the God of revealed religion claims to have in store for mankind. It is neither Moses nor Muhammad, but Prometheus and Atlas who embody the spirit of James' "alpine eagle" perched on the precipice.[131] These fraternal titans remind us that in the gravest battles — such as *the revolutionary war against the One True God* — even great heroes need each other. If, in "the [Heraclitean] game of existence," it is necessary for us to postulate "a god" only "as a pretext for living hard,"[132] then finite divinities with only a fighting chance are a more suitable sacred ideal. Nothing less is demanded of us than the perseverance of an Atlas, and the daring of a Prometheus. Mankind is about to be *gift*ed with a new world — but only if *we* can bear it, and only if *we* can steal it.

---

128 Friedrich Nietzsche, *The Gay Science* (New York: Vintage Books, 1974), p. 181.

129 Ibid., pp. 173; 334–336.

130 James, *The Will to Believe*, p. 212.

131 Ibid., p. 213.

132 Ibid., pp. 213–14; 178–179.

BIBLIOGRAPHY

Aeschylus, *Prometheus Bound* (New York: Oxford University Press, 1975).

Afnan, Ruhi. *Zoroaster's Influence on Anaxagoras, the Greek Tragedians and Socrates* (New York: Philosophical Library, 1969).

Anno, Hideaki. *End of Evangelion* (Gainax, 2002).

Anno, Hideaki. *Neon Genesis Evangelion* (Gainax, 2005).

Bacon, Francis. *New Atlantis and the Great Instauration* (Wheeling, Illinois: Harlan Davidson, Inc., 1989).

Barnes, Jonathan. *Early Greek Philosophy* (New York: Penguin Books, 1987).

Barnstone, Willis and Marvin Meyer [Editors], *The Gnostic Bible: Revised and Expanded Edition* (Boston: Shambhala, 2009).

Bergson, Henri. *Creative Evolution* (Mineola, New York: Dover Publications, 1998).

Bergson, Henri. *Time and Free Will* (Mineola, New York: Dover Publications, 2001).

Bergson, Henri. *Matter and Memory* (New York: Zone Books, 2005).

Bergson, Henri. *Two Sources of Morality and Religion* (Notre Dame: University of Notre Dame Press, 2010).

Blakney, R. B. *The Way of Life: The Classic Translation of Lao Tzu's Tao Te Ching* (New York: Penguin Books, 1983).

Bodhi, Bhikkhu. *In the Buddha's Words: An Anthology of Discourses from the Pali Canon* (Boston: Wisdom Publications, 2005).

Braude, Stephen E. *The Limits of Influence: Psychokinesis and Philosophy of Science* (Lanham, Maryland: University Press of America, 1997).

Buchanan, Lyn. *The Seventh Sense* (New York: Simon & Schuster, 2003).

Churton, Tobias. *Gnostic Philosophy: From Ancient Persia to Modern Times* (Rochester, VT: Inner Traditions, 2005).

Cottingham, John [Editor]. *Descartes: Selected Philosophical Writings* (New York: Cambridge University Press, 1999).

Crease, Robert. *World in the Balance* (New York: W. W. Norton & Company, 2011).

Deleuze, Gilles. *What is Philosophy?* (New York: Columbia University Press, 1994).

Derrida, Jacques. *Specters of Marx* (New York: Routledge, 1994).

Derrida, Jacques. "Telepathy" in *Psyche: Inventions of the Other, Volume I* (Palo Alto, CA: Stanford University Press, 2007).

Descartes, René. *Meditations and Other Metaphysical Writings* (New York: Penguin Books, 1998).

Dostoevsky, Fyodor. *Notes from Underground* (New York: E. P. Dutton & Co., 1991).

Dumoulin, Heinrich. *Zen Buddhism: A History, Volume 1: India and China* (New York: MacMillan Publishing Company, 1988).

Dumoulin, Heinrich. *Zen Buddhism: A History, Volume 2: Japan* (New York: MacMillan Publishing Company, 1990).

Feyerabend, Paul. *Against Method* (New York: Verso, 2008).

Foucault, Michel. *The Archeology of Knowledge and the Discourse on Language* (New York: Pantheon, 1972).

Foucault, Michel. *Power/Knowledge: Selected Interviews and Other Writings, 1972–1977* (New York: Pantheon, 1980).

Frye, Richard. *The Heritage of Persia* (California: Mazda Publishers, 1993).

Funk, Robert W., with Roy W. Hoover and the Jesus Seminar, *The Five Gospels: The Search for the Authentic Words of Jesus* (San Francisco: Harper Collins, 1993).

Grayling, A. C. *Descartes: The Life and Times of a Genius* (New York: Walker and Company, 2005).

Griffin, Roger. *Modernism and Fascism: The Sense of a Beginning under Mussolini and Hitler* (New York: Palgrave Macmillan, 2007).

Guthrie, Kenneth Sylvan. *The Pythagorean Sourcebook and Library* (Grand Rapids, Michigan: Phanes Press, 1988).

Hansen, George P. *The Trickster and the Paranormal* (Philadelphia: Xlibris Corporation, 2001).

Heidegger, Martin. *Being and Time* (New York: Harper Collins, 1962).

Heidegger, Martin. "Nur noch ein Gott kann uns retten" ("Only a God Can Save Us"), in *Der Spiegel*, 31 May 1976.

Heidegger, Martin. *Poetry, Language, Thought* (New York: Harper Collins, 1971).

Heidegger, Martin. *Basic Writings* (New York: Harper Collins, 1977).

Heidegger, Martin. *The Question Concerning Technology and Other Essays* (New York: Harper Collins, 1977).

Heidegger, Martin. *Zollikon Seminars: Protocols, Conversations, Letters* (Evanston, Illinois: Northwestern University Press, 2001).

Heidegger, Martin. *Logic as the Question Concerning the Essence of Language* (Albany: SUNY Press, 2009).

Henry, Jane. *Parapsychology: Research on Exceptional Experiences* (New York: Routledge, 2006).

Herodotus, *The History* (Chicago: University of Chicago Press, 1987).

Höchsmann, Hyun & Yang Guorong. [Translators, Editors] *Zhuangzi* (New York: Pearson Longman, 2007).

Hyde, Lewis. *Trickster Makes This World* (New York: Farrar, Straus, and Giroux, 1998).

Insler, Stanley. "An Introduction to the Gathas of Zarathustra" (New Haven: Yale University Press, 1975).

Jafarey, Ali A. *The Gathas, Our Guide* (Cypress, California: Ushta Publications, 1989).

Jahn, Robert & Brenda J. Dunne, *Margins of Reality: The Role of Consciousness in the Physical World* (New York: Harcourt, 1987).

Jahn, Robert & Brenda J. Dunne, "Science of the Subjective." *Journal of Scientific Exploration*, Vol. 11, No. 2, 1997.

Jahn, Robert & Brenda J. Dunne, "The PEAR Proposition," *Journal of Scientific Exploration*, Vol. 19, No.2, 2005.

James, William. *The Will to Believe* (Mineola, New York: Dover Publications, 1956).

James, William. *The Writings of William James: A Comprehensive Edition* (Chicago: University of Chicago Press, 1977).

James, William. *Pragmatism and the Meaning of Truth* (Cambridge, Massachusetts: Harvard University Press, 1978).

James, William. *Essays in Psychical Research* (Cambridge, Massachusetts: Harvard University Press, 1986).

James, William. *Writings: 1902–1910* (New York: The Library of America, 1987).

James, William. *A Pluralistic Universe* (Lincoln: University of Nebraska Press, 1996).

Johnson, Gregory R. [Editor], *Kant on Swedenborg: Dreams of a Spirit-Seer and Other Writings* (Westchester, Pennsylvania: Swedenborg Foundation Publishers, 2002).

Jung, C. G. *Synchronicity: An Acausal Connecting Principle* (Princeton: Princeton University Press, 1973).

Jung, C. G. *Flying Saucers* (Princeton: Princeton University Press, 1979).

Jung, C. G. *Archetypes and the Collective Unconscious* (Princeton: Princeton University Press, 1981).

Jung, C. G. *Jung on Synchronicity and the Paranormal* (London: Routledge, 1997).

Kahn, Charles H. *The Art and Thought of Heraclitus: An Edition of the Fragments with Translation and Commentary* (New York: Cambridge University Press, 1999).

Kant, Immanuel. *Religion within the Limits of Reason Alone* (New York: Harper Torchbooks, 1960).

Kant, Immanuel. *Critique of Pure Reason* (New York: Cambridge University Press, 1998).

Kant, Immanuel. "Groundwork of the Metaphysics of Morals" in *Practical Philosophy* (New York: Cambridge University Press, 2006).

Kant, Immanuel. *Critique of the Power of Judgment* (New York: Cambridge University Press, 2006).

Kean, Leslie. *UFOs: Generals, Pilots, and Government Officials Go On the Record* (New York: Harmony Books, 2010).

Kerényi, Carl. *Prometheus: Archetypal Image of Human Existence* (Princeton, New Jersey: Princeton University Press, 1991).

Kripal, Jeffrey. *Authors of the Impossible* (Chicago: University of Chicago Press, 2010).

Krishnamurti, Jiddu. *Freedom from the Known* (San Francisco: HarperSanFrancisco, 2009).

Kuhn, Thomas. *The Structure of Scientific Revolutions* (Chicago: University of Chicago Press, 1996).

La Carriere, Jacques. *The Gnostics* (San Francisco: City Lights Books, 1989).

La Mettrie, Julien Offray de, *Machine Man and Other Writings* (New York: Cambridge University Press, 1996).

Laurence, Richard [Translator]. *The Book of Enoch the Prophet* (San Diego: Wizard's Bookshelf, 1995).

Levenda, Peter. *Unholy Alliance: A History of Nazi Involvement with the Occult* (New York, Continuum, 2002).

Lings, Martin. *Muhammad: His Life Based on the Earliest Sources* (Rochester, Vermont: Inner Traditions, 2006).

Mack, Burton. *Who Wrote the New Testament? The Making of the Christian Myth* (New York: Harper Collins, 1995).

Magee, Glenn Alexander, *Hegel and the Hermetic Tradition* (London: Cornell University Press, 2001).

Mascaró, Juan [Translator]. *The Dhammapada* (New York: Penguin Books, 1973).

May, Reinhard. *Heidegger's Hidden Sources: East-Asian Influences on his Work* (New York: Routledge, 1996).

Meyer, Marvin. *The Gnostic Gospels of Jesus: The Definitive Collection of Mystical Gospels and Secret Books about Jesus of Nazareth* (New York: Harper Collins, 2005).

Merleau-Ponty, Maurice. *The Visible and the Invisible* (Evanston, Illinois: Northwestern University Press, 1968).

Mills, M. L. *Early Greek Philosophy and the Orient* (Oxford: Clarendon Press, 1971).

Miller, A. V. and J. N. Findlay, *Hegel's Philosophy of Mind* (New York: Oxford University Press, 2003).

Mishlove, Jeffrey. *The PK Man: A True Story of Mind Over Matter* (Charlottesville, Virginia: Hampton Roads Publishing Company, 2000).

Mitchell, Stephen. *Tao Te Ching: A New English Version* (New York: Harper Perennial, 1998).

Morehouse, David. *Psychic Warrior* (New York: St. Martin's Press, 1996).

Murakami, Takashi. *Little Boy* (New Haven, Connecticut: Yale University Press, 2005).

Musashi, Miyamoto. *The Book of Five Rings* (Kodansha International, 2002).

Nanavutty, Piloo. *The Gathas of Zarathustra: Hymns in Praise of Wisdom* (Ahmedabad: Mapin Publishing, 1999).

Nietzsche, Friedrich. *The Will to Power* (New York: Vintage Books, 1968).

Nietzsche, Friedrich. *The Gay Science* (New York: Vintage Books, 1974).

Nietzsche, Friedrich. *Twilight of the Idols / The Anti-Christ* (New York: Penguin Books, 1990).

Nietzsche, Friedrich. "On the Uses and Disadvantages of History for Life" in *Untimely Meditations* (Cambridge: Cambridge University Press, 1997).

Nietzsche, Friedrich. "The Birth of Tragedy" in *Basic Writings of Nietzsche* (New York: The Modern Library, 2000).

Nietzsche, Friedrich. *The Pre-Platonic Philosophers* (Chicago: University of Chicago Press, 2001).

Nishida, Kitaro. *Last Writings on Nothingness* (Honolulu: University of Hawaii Press, 1993).

Ostrander, Sheila & Lynn Schroeder. *Psychic Discoveries Behind the Iron Curtain* (New York: Marlowe and Company, 1997).

Otomo, Katsuhiro. *Akira* (Geneon, 2001).

Pagels, Elaine. *The Gnostic Gospels* (New York: Vintage Books, 1989).

Parkes, Graham. *Heidegger and Asian Thought* (Motilal Banarsidass, 1992).

Pine, Red [Translator] *Lao Tzu's Tao Te Ching* (Port Townsend, Washington: Copper Canyon Press, 2009).

Plato. *Timaeus and Critias* (New York: Penguin Books, 1977).

Plato. *The Collected Dialogues of Plato, including The Letters.* Edited by Edith Hamilton and Huntington Cairns. (Princeton: Princeton University Press, 1999).

Pollard, Justin and Howard Reid, *Alexandria: Birthplace of the Modern Mind* (New York: Viking, 2006).

Radin, Dean. *The Conscious Universe: The Scientific Truth of Psychic Phenomena* (San Francisco: Harper Collins, 1997).

Sade, Marquis de. *Philosophy in the Boudoir* (Creation Books, 2000).

Sade, Marquis de. *Philosophy in the Boudoir* (New York: Penguin Classics, 2006).

Schwaller de Lubicz, R. A. *Symbol and the Symbolic: Ancient Egypt, Science, and the Evolution of Consciousness* (New York: Inner Traditions, 1978).

Schelling, F. W. J. *Bruno, or On the Natural and the Divine Principle of Things* (Albany: State University of New York Press, 1984).

Schelling, F. W. J. "System of Transcendental Idealism" in *German Aesthetic and Literary Criticism: Kant, Fichte, Schelling, Schopenhauer, Hegel.* Edited with Introduction by David Simpson. (New York: Cambridge University Press, 1984).

Schelling, F. W. J. "Philosophical Letters on Dogmatism and Criticism" in *The Unconditional in Human Knowledge* (Lewisburg: Bucknell University Press).

Schelling, F. W. J. *The Abyss of Freedom and the Ages of the World.* Translated with an introduction by Slavoj Žižek. (Ann Arbor: The University of Michigan Press, 1997).

Schelling, F. W. J. *Clara or, On Nature's Connection to the Spirit World* (Albany: State University of New York Press, 2002).

Schoch, Robert M. *Voices of the Rocks: A Scientist Looks at Catastrophes and Ancient Civilizations* (New York: Harmony Books, 1999).

Scott, Ridley. *Prometheus* (Twentieth Century Fox, 2012).

Sheldrake, Rupert. *Dogs That Know When Their Owners Are Coming Home and Other Unexplained Powers of Animals* (New York: Random House, 1999).

Sheldrake, Rupert. *The Sense of Being Stared At and Other Unexplained Powers of the Human Mind* (New York: Random House, 2003).

Shelley, Mary. *Frankenstein, or The Modern Prometheus* (New York: Penguin Books, 2003).

Shelley, Mary. "Note on *Prometheus Unbound*" in Percy Bysshe Shelley, *Prometheus Unbound* (Black Box Press, 2007).

Shelley, Percy Bysshe. *Prometheus Unbound* (Black Box Press, 2007).

Soho, Takuan. *The Unfettered Mind* (Kodansha International, 2003).

Stevenson, Ian. *Where Reincarnation and Biology Intersect* (London: Praeger, 1997).

Stevenson, Ian. *Reincarnation and Biology*, 2 Vols. (London: Praeger, 1997).

Steiner, Rudolf. *Atlantis: The Fate of a Lost Land and its Secret Knowledge* (Forest Row, East Sussex: Sophia Books, 2001).

Strauss, Leo. "Introduction to Heideggerian Existentialism" in *The Rebirth of Classical Political Rationalism* (Chicago: University of Chicago Press, 1989).

Suzuki, D. T. *Zen and Japanese Culture* (Princeton University Press, 1959).

Targ, Russell & Harold E. Puthoff, *Mind Reach: Scientists Look at Psychic Abilities* (Hampton Roads Publishing Company, 2005).

Tart, Charles. *Learning to Use Extrasensory Perception* (Chicago: The University of Chicago Press, 1976).

Turing, A. M. "Computing machinery and intelligence" in *Mind*, 59 (1950).

Vallée, Jacques. *The Invisible College: What a Group of Scientists Has Discovered About UFO Influences on the Human Race* (New York: E. P. Dutton & Co., 1975).

Vallée, Jacques. *Messengers of Deception* (Berkeley, California: And/Or Press, 1979).

Vallée, Jacques. *Passport to Magonia: On UFOs, Folklore, and Parallel Worlds* (Chicago: Contemporary Books, 1993).

Victoria, Brian. *Zen at War* (Rowman & Littlefield, 2006).

Verbrugghe, Gerald P. & John M. Wickersham, *Berossos and Manetho, Introduced and Translated: Native Traditions in Ancient Mesopotamia and Egypt* (Ann Arbor: University of Michigan Press, 2000).

Wessell, Leonard P. *Prometheus Bound: The Mythic Structure of Karl Marx's Scientific Thinking* (Baton Rouge: Louisiana State University Press, 1984).

Wilde, Lyn Webster. *On the Trail of the Women Warriors: The Amazons in Myth and History* (New York: St. Martin's Press, 2000).

Wilson, Colin & Rand Flem-Ath. *The Atlantis Blueprint: Unlocking the Ancient Mysteries of a Long-Lost Civilization* (New York: Random House, 2002).

Wittgenstein, Ludwig. *On Certainty* (New York: Harper & Row, 1972).

Wittgenstein, Ludwig. *Philosophical Investigations: The German text, with a Revised English translation* (Oxford: Blackwell Publishing, 2001).

INDEX

OTHER BOOKS PUBLISHED BY ARKTOS

OTHER BOOKS PUBLISHED BY ARKTOS

OTHER BOOKS PUBLISHED BY ARKTOS

OTHER BOOKS PUBLISHED BY ARKTOS

BAL GANGADHAR TILAK   *The Arctic Home in the Vedas*

DOMINIQUE VENNER   *The Shock of History*

MARKUS WILLINGER   *A Europe of Nations*
                                       Generation Identity

DAVID J. WINGFIELD (ED.)   *The Initiate: Journal of*
                                       Traditional Studies

CPSIA information can be obtained
at www.ICGtesting.com
Printed in the USA
LVOW11*0909091116
512142LV00009BA/146/P